LEGAL EDUCATION THROUGH AN INDIGENOUS LENS

This book provides a comprehensive resource for accommodating and pursuing Indigenous perspectives in legal education.

The book is divided into three sections. The first section highlights the continuing issues that Indigenous people face in law schools and universities, including the ongoing impacts of colonisation and intergenerational trauma, institutional racism and exclusion. This section also includes chapters that explore arguments for the recognition of Indigenous legal knowledge and of the impact of settler law, and the incorporation of Indigenous concepts, laws and ways of thinking about settler law across the curriculum. The second section explores how Indigenous ways of reading and thinking about settler law make a difference to how settler law is understood and interpreted. Contributors consider the power of storytelling and address the prospect of law's decolonisation. The third section of the book grapples with how traditional law school subjects can be taught through an Indigenous lens, including torts, public law, criminal law and sentencing, clinical legal education, and native title. Throughout, the book demonstrates the importance of, and offers practical advice for, teaching law in a way that includes critical Indigenous perspectives.

This book will be of enormous value to teachers, researchers, students in law, legal studies and Indigenous studies, and others with an interest in decolonising legal education.

Nicole Watson is a Mununjali and Birri Gubba woman from south-east Queensland. She is Professor of Law at the University of Technology Sydney (UTS), Australia.

Heather Douglas, whose heritage is Scottish and Irish, is Professor of Law at The University of Melbourne, Australia.

LEGAL EDUCATION THROUGH AN INDIGENOUS LENS

Decolonising the Law School

Edited by Nicole Watson and Heather Douglas

Routledge
Taylor & Francis Group
a GlassHouse Book

Designed cover image: *Redfern* by Dunghutti/Gomeroi Artist, Nioka Lowe-Brennan

First published 2025
by Routledge
4 Park Square, Milton Park, Abingdon, Oxon OX14 4RN

and by Routledge
605 Third Avenue, New York, NY 10158

Routledge is an imprint of the Taylor & Francis Group, an informa business

A GlassHouse book

British Library Cataloguing-in-Publication Data
A catalogue record for this book is available from the British Library

Library of Congress Cataloging-in-Publication Data
Names: Watson, Nicole, editor. | Douglas, Heather, editor.
Title: Legal education through an indigenous lens : decolonising the law school / edited by Nicole Watson and Heather Douglas.
Description: Abingdon, Oxon [UK] ; New York, NY : Routledge, 2025. | Includes bibliographical references and index.
Identifiers: LCCN 2024040788 (print) | LCCN 2024040789 (ebook) | ISBN 9781032753164 (hardback) | ISBN 9781032753157 (paperback) | ISBN 9781003473404 (ebook)
Subjects: LCSH: Indigenous peoples—Legal status, laws, etc. | Indigenous peoples—Education (Higher). | Law—Study and teaching.
Classification: LCC KI280 .L44 2025 (print) | LCC KI280 (ebook) | DDC 340.071/1—dc23/eng/20240905
LC record available at https://lccn.loc.gov/2024040788
LC ebook record available at https://lccn.loc.gov/2024040789

ISBN: 978-1-032-75316-4 (hbk)
ISBN: 978-1-032-75315-7 (pbk)
ISBN: 978-1-003-47340-4 (ebk)

DOI: 10.4324/9781003473404

Typeset in Sabon
by Apex CoVantage, LLC

CONTENTS

ACKNOWLEDGEMENTS

This project was brought to life through the generous support of the Australian Research Council ('ARC'). We are thankful for being beneficiaries of the ARC's Discovery Indigenous Scheme,[1] and we recognise its important role in supporting Aboriginal and Torres Strait Islander research. Heather would also like to acknowledge the support of the ARC Centre of Excellence for the Elimination of Violence Against Women (CEVAW).[2]

We express our gratitude to our colleagues who shared their experiences and hopes for Australian legal education in this book. We are also grateful to those who took time away from their loved ones to participate in a workshop at the University of Technology Sydney in July 2023, where they presented their draft chapters. The workshop ran smoothly due to the efforts of our research assistant, Ced Hassing.

We acknowledge the contributions of our colleagues who reviewed the chapters, namely, Elisa Arcioni, Allan Ardill, Louise Boon-Kuo, Melissa Castan, Kyllie Cripps, Kate Galloway, Mary Graham, Stephen Gray, Anthony Hopkins, Brad Jessup, Dylan Lino, Craig Longman, Sophie Rigney, Tamara Walsh and Irene Watson. We also acknowledge the wise counsel of our colleague Shaun McVeigh.

Completing this manuscript was a Herculean task, so we will always be grateful to Claire Bredenoord for providing exceptional research assistance. Claire studiously proof-read the chapters and wrote the abstracts. We are

1 The editors were the recipients of a Discovery Indigenous grant, and Nicole Watson holds a Discovery Australian Aboriginal and Torres Strait Islander Award (Bringing Indigenous Voices into Judicial Decision Making IN180100021).

2 CE230100004.

also grateful to Matthew Sidebotham at Workwisewords for casting his astute editorial lens over the final manuscript. We acknowledge Colin Perrin at Routledge, who got behind our proposal for *Indigenous Legal Judgments* and extended his support to this book. We thank Nioka Lowe-Brennan for granting permission for her artwork, Redfern, to appear on the cover. Nicole would like to thank her colleague, Paddy Gibson, for sharing his research on the *Tribune's* coverage of her father's activism, which is referred to in Chapter 12. Nicole would also like to thank her colleagues on the First Peoples Partnership Working Party that provides advice to the Council of Australian Law Deans, from whom she has learnt a great deal.

Nicole would like to thank her husband, Russell, for his enduring sense of humour. She also acknowledges Gertie the cat and Willi the dog, neither of whom contributed anything to this book, but she loves them anyway. Heather would like to thank her family—Paul, Zachary, Felix and Isabella—for their love, support, good humour and endless tolerance of her late nights on the computer.

CONTRIBUTORS

Narelle Bedford is Assistant Professor in the Faculty of Law, Bond University. Narelle's mum is Jackie Bedford from the Yuin people of the South Coast New South Wales, who spent most of her life living in and serving the Tharawal community.

Larissa Behrendt AO is a Euahleyai/Gamillaroi woman, Distinguished Professor of Law and the Laureate Fellow at the Jumbunna Institute for Indigenous Education and Research, University of Technology Sydney.

Karinda Burns is a Wajarri Yamaji and Yued Noongar woman and Lecturer at the Law School at the University of Western Australia where she is also Co-Lead of the Indigenisation of the Juris Doctor program.

Marcelle Burns is a Gomeroi-Kamilaroi woman and Associate Dean Indigenous, Faculty of Law, University of Technology Sydney. Her research examines the relationship between First Nations and state-centred legal systems, as well as Indigenous cultural competency in legal education.

Emma Colvin is Associate Professor in Law and Criminology at Charles Sturt University in New South Wales, Wiradyuri/Wiradjuri Country.

Eddie Cubillo is a descendant of the Larrakia, Wadjigan and Central Arrente peoples in the Northern Territory. He is currently Director of the Indigenous Law and Justice Hub at Melbourne Law School, The University of Melbourne.

Heather Douglas AM is Professor at Melbourne Law School, The University of Melbourne and Deputy Director of the ARC Centre of Excellence for the Elimination of Violence Against Women ('CEVAW').

Jaynaya Dwyer is a lecturer at the Indigenous Law and Justice Hub, Melbourne Law School.

Annette Gainsford is a Wiradyuri/Wiradjuri woman and Professor/Associate Dean Indigenous Teaching and Learning, University of Technology Sydney.

Alison Gerard is Professor of Law/Criminology at Canberra Law School, University of Canberra.

Lee Godden is Professor at Melbourne Law School, The University of Melbourne.

Kirsten Gray is a Muruwari/Yuwaalaraay lawyer and member of the policy and research team at the Jumbunna Institute for Indigenous Education and Research, University of Technology Sydney.

Paul Gray is a Wiradjuri man and Associate Professor at the Jumbunna Institute for Indigenous Education and Research, University of Technology Sydney, where he leads their child protection research hub.

Terri Libesman is Professor in the Faculty of Law, University of Technology Sydney.

Aurora Milroy is a Palyku woman and Lecturer at the Law School at The University of Western Australia where she is also Co-Lead of the Indigenisation of the Juris Doctor program.

Osca Monaghan is a Guugu Yimithirr lawyer and academic; they currently work at both the University of New South Wales and the Aboriginal Legal Service (NSW/ACT).

Jennifer Nielsen is Associate Professor in the Faculty of Business, Law, and Arts at Southern Cross University.

Suvendrini Perera was born in Lanka, and she now lives on Whadjak Noongar land. She is John Curtin Distinguished Emeritus Professor at Curtin University.

Amanda Porter is a Koori academic of Aboriginal (Yuin) and settler (Scottish and Greek) descent. She is Associate Professor of Criminology and Criminal Law in the School of Social and Political Sciences at The University of Melbourne.

Pekeri Ruska is a Goenpul woman and PhD Candidate with the TC Beirne School of Law, University of Queensland.

Kirstie Smith is a Mununjali, Yugembeh woman and lawyer and First Nations Law Lecturer at the University of Southern Queensland School of Law and Justice and Centre for Heritage and Culture.

Mary Spiers Williams descends from the First Peoples of the sandstone Country (what is known as Sydney and stretching north to Dyarrabbin; her father is Darkeñung) and first settlers. Mary is Associate Dean Indigenous Studies in the College of Arts and Social Sciences, Australian National University. Her research focuses on the impacts of state laws and colonialism on First Peoples and settlers.

Nicole Watson belongs to the Mununjali and Birri Gubba Peoples from what is now known as Queensland. She is Professor in the Faculty of Law, University of Technology Sydney.

Simon Young is Professor at the University of Southern Queensland's School of Law and Justice and Centre for Heritage and Culture, Adjunct Professor at The University of Western Australia, and External Fellow of the University of Queensland's Centre for Public, International and Comparative Law.

GLOSSARY

This list provides an overview of seminal works that have brought Indigenous perspectives into Australian legal education, and they are frequently referenced throughout this book.

The Behrendt Review

This review was commissioned by the Australian Government to evaluate and improve higher education outcomes for Aboriginal and Torres Strait Islander students in all areas of study. Key recommendations aimed to achieve parity in higher education outcomes between Indigenous and non-Indigenous Australians. These recommendations emphasised the need for systemic change, greater Indigenous representation in decision-making processes, and the incorporation of Indigenous knowledge and perspectives into curricula. Larissa Behrendt et al., *Review of Higher Education Access and Outcomes for Aboriginal and Torres Strait Islander People* (Final Report, 2012) <https://apo.org.au/sites/default/files/resource-files/2012-09/apo-nid31135.pdf>.

Bringing Them Home

The National Inquiry into the Separation of Aboriginal and Torres Strait Islander Children from their Families was established by the Commonwealth in 1995 in response to campaigns by Indigenous agencies to bring to light the policies that gave rise to the Stolen Generations. It received evidence from 535 Indigenous people in relation to their experiences of child removal. The Inquiry's report, *Bringing Them Home*, contained 54 recommendations, which were designed to support the healing of those affected by such policies. Australian Human Rights Commission, *Bringing Them Home – Report of the National Inquiry into the Separation of Aboriginal and Torres Strait Islander Children from their Families* (Australian Human Rights Commission, 1997) <https://humanrights.gov.au/our-work/projects/bringing-them-home-report-1997>.

Indigenous Cultural Competency for Legal Academics Program ('ICCLAP')

The ICCLAP surveyed capabilities and gaps in fostering the cultural competency of legal academics. Later, it developed tools to build the capacity of legal academics to engage with Indigenous Peoples in their professional and academic work. Marcelle Burns, Anita Lee Hong and Asmi Wood, *Indigenous Cultural Competency for Legal Academics Program -Final Report*, (Australian Government, 2019) <https://ltr.edu.au/resources/ID14-3906_Burns_FinalReport_2019.pdf>.

Indigenous Strategy 2017–2020

This strategy was developed by Universities Australia in response to the United Nations Declaration on the Rights of Indigenous Peoples. It sought to increase the numbers of Aboriginal and Torres Strait Islander people participating in all areas of higher education (students and staff), increase non-Indigenous peoples' engagement with Indigenous knowledges and improve the university environment for Indigenous people. Universities Australia, *Indigenous Strategy 2017–2020* (*Strategic Plan*) (Universities Australia, 2017) <https://universitiesaustralia.edu.au/publication/indigenous-strategy-2017-2020/>.

Indigenous Strategy 2022–2025

In its second Indigenous strategy, Universities Australia focused on areas that included supporting Aboriginal and Torres Strait Islander students to complete degrees, providing pathways for career advancement of Indigenous staff, improving cultural safety, taking action against racism and embedding Indigenous knowledges in teaching and research. Universities Australia, *Indigenous Strategy 2022–2025* (*Strategic Plan*) (Universities Australia, 2022) <https://universitiesaustralia.edu.au/publication/indigenous-strategy-2022-25/>.

National Best Practice Framework for Indigenous Cultural Competency in Australian Universities

Produced by Universities Australia as part of the *Indigenous Cultural Competency in Australian Universities Project*, the framework reports on the status of Indigenous representation in higher education and shows how to develop Indigenous cultural competency across Australian universities. Universities Australia, *National Best Practice Framework for Indigenous Cultural Competency in Australian Universities* (Universities Australia, 2011) <https://universitiesaustralia.edu.au/wp-content/uploads/2019/06/National-Best-Practice-Framework-for-Indigenous-Cultural-Competency-in-Australian-Universities.pdf>.

Royal Commission into Aboriginal Deaths in Custody ('RCIADIC')

In 1987 former Prime Minister Bob Hawke established a royal commission in response to concerns surrounding 99 deaths of Aboriginal and Torres Strait Islander people who had been in the custody of police officers and correctional institutions. The Commission investigated not only each death individually but also the relevant legal, social and economic factors contributing to the deceased's contact with the criminal justice system. The final report contained 339 recommendations relating broadly to improving Indigenous peoples' interactions with police and addressing socio-political issues such as self-determination, education, health and employment. *Royal Commission into Aboriginal Deaths in Custody* (Final Report, 1991) <https://www.austlii.edu.au/au/other/IndigLRes/rciadic/>.

Uluru Statement from the Heart

The Statement was developed in 2017 by the First Nations National Constitutional Convention and represents the culmination of dialogues among Indigenous peoples from across Australia. It is an 'invitation' from Aboriginal and Torres Strait Islander delegates to non-Indigenous Australians to engage in a process of substantive constitutional reform through a constitutionally enshrined voice to parliament and to produce a treaty and determine the truth through the establishment of a Makarrata Commission. Uluru Statement from the Heart (Web Page) *<https://ulurustatement.org/the-statement/view-the-statement/>*.

Universities Australia ('UA')

The peak body for the Australian university sector, which aims to advance higher education through policy development, advice and publications on behalf of its 39 members. <https://universitiesaustralia.edu.au/>.

Yoorrook Justice Commission ('Yoorrook')

In partnership with the First Peoples' Assembly of Victoria, the Victorian Government established Yoorrook to facilitate the first formal truth-telling process into historical and ongoing injustices experienced by First Peoples in

Victoria. The aims of Yoorrook include the following: to establish an official public record of the impact of colonisation on First Peoples in Victoria; develop a shared understanding among all Victorians on the impact of colonisation and on the diversity, strength and resilience of First Peoples' cultures; and make recommendations not only for healing, system reform and practical changes to laws, policy and education but also for matters to be included in future treaties. See 'About Yoorrook', *Yoorrook Justice Commission* (Web Page) <https://yoorrookjusticecommission.org.au/about/>.

1

INTRODUCTION

Decolonising the Law School

Heather Douglas and Nicole Watson

Introduction

Law schools have an aura of power and exclusivity. Some graduates go on to become parliamentarians, senior public servants, titans of industry or judges. Many law schools are also dominated by students who went to private schools, with some having intergenerational ties to the legal profession. For those who were not born into such privilege, law school can be daunting. When one of us, Nicole, reflects on her experiences as a law student in the 1990s, she visualises a grandiose building with rooms named after powerful white men. Indigenous peoples were all but invisible (and still are in many law schools). It is implicitly understood that the story of Australian law began with the arrival of the First Fleet in Eora Country.

Much has changed over the past thirty years. Strides have been taken by the Council of Australian Law Deans (CALD), which has encouraged all law schools to 'work in partnership with First Nations peoples' to build cultural competence and safety into courses.[1] It is now common for Indigenous artworks to hang on the walls of law faculties, and meetings are routinely opened with an acknowledgement of Country. There are still too few Indigenous legal scholars and law students, but they are a burgeoning community.

Despite such positive developments, the meaningful inclusion of Indigenous peoples and their legal traditions is yet to be achieved. The goal of this edited collection is to provide fresh impetus to this essential transformation of legal education. By reflecting on their own teaching practices and drawing

1 Council of Australian Law Deans, 'CALD Statement on Racism and Law Schools', *Council of Australian Law Deans* (Web Page, 31 January 2024) <https://cald.asn.au/first-nations-peoples/>.

DOI: 10.4324/9781003473404-1

upon tools from Indigenous studies and critical race theory, the authors show how to overcome obstacles to the incorporation of Indigenous perspectives in the curriculum.

Standpoint

One of the issues often raised by Indigenous scholars, including some of the contributors to this book, is the importance of one's standpoint. As stated by the Gomeroi/Kamilaroi academic Marcelle Burns in her chapter,

> our 'standpoint' is significant because it informs how we view the world and our place within it. Standpoint theory also recognises that all knowledges are historically, socially, and culturally contingent. Standpoint also sheds light on power relations and how knowledge is produced.[2]

Consequently, we share our standpoints, which seep into our work as academics and have shaped our approach to this collection:

Heather

Heather's heritage is Scottish and Irish, but she is yet to explore her heritage beyond the last three generations of her family. Heather's childhood in country Victoria and Melbourne/Naarm, living on the lands of the Wurundjeri people of the Kulin Nation people, was privileged. Formative for Heather, in the context of this collection, were performing volunteer roles at community legal centres and working as a criminal lawyer in Melbourne/Naarm and with the Aboriginal Legal Service in Alice Springs/Mparntwe on the lands of the Arrernte people. These experiences highlighted not only the injustices that the law could mete out but also its potential, and they have informed her scholarship.

Nicole

Nicole belongs to the Birri Gubba and Mununjali Peoples, whose lands lie within what is now known as the state of Queensland. Nicole was born into a family of activists during the reign of the despotic and deeply conservative Bjelke-Petersen Government. She grew up hearing stories about elders who were removed from their families as children to become domestic workers and Indigenous activists who were violently harassed by police officers.

2 Marcelle Burns, 'Relationality in Indigenous Teaching Praxis in Legal Education' in Nicole Watson and Heather Douglas (eds), *Legal Education through an Indigenous Lens: Decolonising the Law School* (Routledge, 2025) (citations omitted).

Those stories have had an indelible impact on her scholarship, which illuminates both the racism that pervades the legal system and the unconquerable resilience of Indigenous peoples.

This Collection

Just as standpoint is relevant to our scholarship, so, too, are the relationships that have nurtured this book. Heather and Nicole met in the late 1990s in Brisbane, the capital of Queensland. At the time, Heather was an academic in the Faculty of Law at Griffith University and was conducting research into the experiences of Indigenous law students. Nicole had recently completed her law studies at the University of Queensland and was interviewed for Heather's research. This was the first time Nicole was able to give voice to her experiences as one of the few Indigenous law students in her cohort. She felt empowered, and the seeds of a future academic career were planted.

Australia in the early 1990s was, in many respects, a time of great promise. In 1992, the High Court expunged the doctrine of terra nullius from Australian law in *Mabo v Queensland [No 2]*.[3] The Keating Government responded to this historic decision with a statutory recognition process, a land fund for Indigenous people who could not meet the requirements for recognition of their native title, and the promise of a social justice package.[4] In the country's law schools, however, a psychological terra nullius prevailed[5] that found resonance in Heather's research—Indigenous participants reported experiencing profound alienation and racism during their years in law school.[6] Some dropped out, and those who persevered grappled with isolation and disillusionment.[7] Over the ensuing years, a small but impactful community of academics whose work engaged with Indigenous people and the law emerged. Each one of us who has been involved in this book project is a proud member of that coalition of scholars. Some of the authors have been colleagues for decades. Others are new friends who have generously shared their time and insights with us.

Readers of this collection may, on occasion, be surprised by the tone of the writing, which often departs from the staid language of legal texts. They

3 (1992) HCA 23.

4 Bryan Keon-Cohen, 'From Euphoria to Extinguishment to Co-Existence' (2017) 23 *James Cook University Law Review* 9.

5 For an explanation of 'psychological terra nullius', see Larissa Behrendt, 'Mabo Ten Years On—A Psychological Terra Nullius Remains' (July 2002) *Impact* 1.

6 Heather Douglas, 'Indigenous Legal Education: Towards Indigenization' (2005) 6(8) *Indigenous Law Bulletin* 12.

7 Heather Douglas, 'This Is Not Just About Me': Indigenous Students' Insights About Law School Study' (1998) 20(2) *Adelaide Law Review* 315.

will also be confronted by a panoply of emotions—optimism, frustration and hurt—as the authors reflect on their experiences. The criticisms made by some of the authors in this book are not motivated by a desire to disparage our non-Indigenous colleagues or to make them feel guilty. Rather, they are made in the spirit of collegiality. Indigenous legal academics and law students do not want to languish at the margins of their respective institutions. They want to take their rightful place as members of the academy. They are also aware that all law students, irrespective of cultural background, can benefit from learning about the only legal traditions to have supported human beings to live sustainably in this place that all of us call 'home'.

This collection may be used as a standalone resource or as a companion text to *Indigenous Legal Judgments: Bringing Indigenous Voices into Judicial Decision Making*.[8] The latter is a collection of 16 judgments of Australian courts that are reimagined from Aboriginal and Torres Strait Islander perspectives. The judgments, which are accompanied by commentaries that explain the original decision, span across a range of areas, encompassing criminal law, native title, family law and others. *Indigenous Legal Judgments* shows how the stories of Indigenous people can be written into judgments, whereas this book answers questions such as the following: How can concepts such as relationality inform pedagogy? Can settler law be decolonised? How can First Nations' perspectives be integrated into the teaching of core subjects such as torts, criminal law and public law?

This introductory chapter is presented in three parts. Part One discusses the history of Indigenous Australians in legal education and their entry into the legal profession. Part Two reviews the literature about policy interventions regarding changing curriculum in Australian law schools. In this part, we also review the literature about racism in Australian universities. The final part introduces readers to the structure of this book and its consecutive chapters.

At this point, we offer a clarification regarding the use of terminology. Throughout Australia, Indigenous peoples draw upon a range of terms to identify themselves and one another. Although some prefer 'First Nations', 'First Peoples', 'Aboriginal and Torres Strait Islander' or 'Blak', others identify by their membership in particular nations.[9] We recognise that such debates are complex and outside the scope of this collection. Throughout this book, all such language is used interchangeably.

8 Nicole Watson and Heather Douglas (eds), *Indigenous Legal Judgments: Bringing Indigenous Voices into Judicial Decision Making* (Routledge, 2021).

9 See the AIATSIS map of Indigenous Australia, which 'serves as a visual reminder of the richness and diversity of Aboriginal and Torres Strait Islander Australia': 'Map of Indigenous Australia', *AIATSIS* (Web Page) <https://aiatsis.gov.au/explore/map-indigenous-australia>.

Part One: Indigenous People in the Law

Historically, Australia's law schools were the embodiment of terra nullius. Indigenous peoples' affinity with their lands and age-old legal traditions were, for the most part, erased. Inequalities in state education systems meant that Indigenous people rarely finished high school, leaving few prepared for the rigours of law school. Unsurprisingly, Indigenous people did not begin to enter legal education until the 1970s. This development coincided with the emergence of the Black Power movement and the establishment of Aboriginal Legal Services.[10]

The first such service was created by activists and their supporters in the Sydney suburb of Redfern in 1970.[11] At the time, Indigenous people in Redfern were subject to unrelenting violence from police officers. Those who lived through this era have described random arrests in establishments frequented by Aboriginal patrons, such as the Empress Hotel.[12] There was also an unofficial curfew imposed on any Aboriginal person walking the streets after 10 o'clock at night.[13]

A core group of activists that included Gary Foley, Paul Coe and Gary Williams drew upon tactics used by the American Black Panthers, such as the 'pig patrols', in which courageous observers recorded incidents of police violence.[14] They also worked with Hal Wootten, Dean of the Law Faculty at the University of New South Wales, and volunteer solicitors to establish what would become 'Australia's first free, shop-front, legal aid centre'.[15] With access to legal representation, Blak people could finally challenge baseless charges that were designed to, in the words of Paul Coe, 'keep us in our place'.[16]

It is important to recognise the contributions made by Wootten and his colleagues at the University of New South Wales in the 1970s. Garth Nettheim was among the first legal scholars to challenge the invisibility of Indigenous people in legal education. In the 1970s, Nettheim became aware

10 For discussion about the nexus between the Black Power movement and the emergence of Aboriginal Legal Services, see Tanya Mitchell and Amanda Porter, '*Walker v New South Wales* [1994] HCA 64' in Nicole Watson and Heather Douglas (eds), *Indigenous Legal Judgments: Bringing Indigenous Voices into Judicial Decision Making* (Routledge, 2021) 54, 57.

11 '50+ Years of Resistance, Resilience and Solidarity', *Aboriginal Legal Service (NSW/ACT) Ltd* (Web Page) <www.alsnswact.org.au/history>.

12 Kathy Lothian, 'Seizing the Time: Australian Aborigines and the Influence of the Black Panther Party, 1969–1972' (2005) 35(4) *Journal of Black Studies* 179, 191.

13 Kathy Lothian, 'Seizing the Time: Australian Aborigines and the Influence of the Black Panther Party, 1969–1972' (2005) 35(4) *Journal of Black Studies* 179, 191.

14 Johanna Perheentupa, *Redfern: Aboriginal Activism in the 1970s* (Aboriginal Studies Press, 2020) 36.

15 Gary Foley, 'Black Power in Redfern 1968–1972', *VU Research Repository* (Web Page, 5 October 2001) <https://vuir.vu.edu.au/27009/1/Black%20power%20in%20Redfern%201968-1972.pdf>.

16 Perheentupa (n 14) 36.

of Queensland legislation that discriminated against Aboriginal and Torres Strait Islander people, an experience so shocking that the 'hairs stood up on the back of his neck'.[17] He went on to establish Australia's first course on Indigenous people and the law at the University of New South Wales in 1979.[18]

The University of New South Wales also created a special admissions scheme for Indigenous people who aspired to study law in 1971.[19] Among those to seize this opportunity was Kuku Yalanji woman Pat O'Shane. After graduating in 1976,[20] O'Shane would go on to work for Aboriginal Legal Services in Sydney and Alice Springs, head the New South Wales Department of Aboriginal Affairs, and become the first Aboriginal magistrate in 1981.[21]

Much has been achieved over the ensuing decades. More than six hundred Indigenous people have entered the legal profession since O'Shane and her contemporaries blazed their trails.[22] Lawyers such as Yawuru man Mick Dodson have played pivotal roles in processes that brought the stories of the Stolen Generations into the public consciousness.[23] Today, Indigenous lawyers represent the most disadvantaged members of our society in the criminal courts, they secure justice for the victims of historical wage theft by state governments[24] and lead community organisations.

Although bound by the rules and professional etiquette applicable to all lawyers, the Indigenous legal profession is unique because its members continue to draw upon the perspectives and experiential knowledge of their communities. Lawyers such as our colleague, Euahleyai and Kamillaroi woman Larissa Behrendt, are fusing age-old storytelling traditions with the mediums of fiction and documentary filmmaking to highlight systemic racism in the legal system.

17 Rosyln Cook, 'Garth Nettheim: A Profile: How It All Began . . .' (2006) 6(22) *Indigenous Law Bulletin* 10.
18 Marlene LeBrun, 'Book Review—Aboriginal Legal Issues' (1992) 1(54) *Aboriginal Law Bulletin* 16.
19 Perheentupa (n 14) 41.
20 'UNSW's 70th Anniversary', *University of New South Wales* (Web Page) <https://alumni.unsw.edu.au/70th-anniversary/1970s>.
21 Nikki Henningham, 'O'Shane, Pat', *The Encyclopedia of Women & Leadership in Twentieth-Century Australia* (Web Page) <www.womenaustralia.info/leaders/biogs/WLE0771b.htm>.
22 Kate Allman and Amy Dale, 'The State of the Profession 2021' *Law Society Journal* (online, 9 August 2021) <https://lsj.com.au/articles/the-state-of-the-profession-2021/>.
23 National Inquiry into the Separation of Aboriginal and Torres Strait Islander Children from their Families, *Bringing Them Home* (Report, 1997) <https://humanrights.gov.au/our-work/projects/bringing-them-home-report-1997>.
24 'Landmark Stolen Wages Case Settles for $190 Million', *Griffith Chambers* (Web Page, 10 July 2019) <www.griffithchambers.com.au/post/2019/07/10/landmark-stolen-wages-case-settles-for-190-million>.

Some are using their skills to illuminate the hypocrisy of a legal system that is premised on noble values, such as equality before the law, but overlooks the unjust invasion that underwrote the founding of Australia. Trawlwoolway and Pinterrairer lawyer Michael Mansell has been an indefatigable advocate for the rights of Indigenous peoples for over 50 years. He was instrumental to the creation of the Aboriginal Provisional Government in 1990, which asserts a continuing Aboriginal sovereignty in ways that include the issuing of Aboriginal passports.[25] Most recently, Mansell spoke out against the proposal for the constitutional entrenchment of an Aboriginal and Torres Strait Islander Voice to the Parliament, arguing that because it would have been advisory in nature, such a body could never have delivered self-determination.[26]

Countering such arguments and leading the 'Yes' campaign for an Aboriginal and Torres Strait Islander Voice were Indigenous lawyers such as Cobble Cobble woman Megan Davis and Noel Pearson, a member of the Guugu Yimithirr community of Hopevale. On 14 October 2023, Australians voted overwhelmingly against this reform.[27] Among other efforts, this demonstrates that although great strides have been made over the past five decades, there is still a long way to go.

Likewise, there is much to be achieved before Indigenous people gain parity in the legal profession. The lack of representation among the country's barristers is bleak. There are only 20 Indigenous barristers throughout Australia.[28] This paucity is mirrored in the legal academy. We are unaware of any recent surveys of Indigenous academics in Australia's law schools, but we estimate that the size of this community is comparable to that of the Indigenous Bar. Clearly, change is necessary, and such reform must begin in Australia's law schools. In the following, we discuss the work that has been undertaken over recent decades to challenge racism in higher education, and specifically, legal education.

Part Two: Challenging Racism in Higher Education

Over the past 20 years, there has been significant policy activity in relation to both access to and outcomes for Aboriginal and Torres Strait Islander people in higher education. A 2012 review led by Larissa Behrendt

25 'About the Aboriginal Provisional Government', *Aboriginal Provisional Government* (Web Page) <http://apg.org.au/about.php>.

26 Michael Mansell, 'We Have a Voice: It's Not Listened to', *Arena* (September 2023) <https://arena.org.au/we-have-a-voice-its-not-listened-to/>.

27 'Referendum on Aboriginal and Torres Strait Islander Voice', *National Indigenous Australians Agency* (Web Page) <www.niaa.gov.au/indigenous-affairs/referendum-aboriginal-and-torres-strait-islander-voice>.

28 Michael Pelly, 'Bar Vote on Voice a "Complete Mess": Indigenous Barrister', *Australian Financial Review* (online, 11 May 2023) <www.afr.com/companies/professional-services/bar-vote-on-voice-a-complete-mess-indigenous-barrister-20230509-p5d6wn>.

('the Behrendt Review')[29] identified that Aboriginal and Torres Strait Islander people are significantly underrepresented in higher education and that this contributes to the high levels of social and economic disadvantage that they often experience. To begin with, the Behrendt Review set an aim for parity of Aboriginal and Torres Strait Islander students and staff in higher education in terms of enrolment, completion/recruitment and retention.[30] The Behrendt Review highlighted the success of approaches that ensure that universities 'grow their own' graduate research enrolment and workforce through flexible pathways and mentoring activities.[31] The Behrendt Review acknowledged that

> [t]he legitimacy and acceptance of this embedding of Aboriginal and Torres Strait Islander perspectives within Australian universities is a matter of ongoing and current debate, with divergent viewpoints being expressed among both Aboriginal and Torres Strait Islander and non-Indigenous academics, particularly regarding curriculums.[32]

The Behrendt Review noted that a paper, prepared by Ngarrindjeri scholar Daryle Rigney,[33] stated there were three categories of commitment by Australian universities to teaching Indigenous knowledges:

Category 1: Indigenous peoples are invisible, marginalised, limited, non-existent;
Category 2: Indigenous studies are a single, separate and discrete unit of work focusing on Indigenous peoples; and
Category 3: Indigenous perspectives are embedded in relevant degrees and topics, for example, science, environmental studies, law, education, medicine, psychology and art.

29 Larissa Behrendt et al., *Review of Higher Education Access and Outcomes for Aboriginal and Torres Strait Islander People* (Final Report, 2012) 9 ('the Behrendt Review') <https://www.education.gov.au/aboriginal-and-torres-strait-islander-higher-education/review-higher-education-access-and-outcomes-aboriginal-and-torres-strait-islander-people>.
30 Larissa Behrendt et al., *Review of Higher Education Access and Outcomes for Aboriginal and Torres Strait Islander People* (Final Report, 2012) 29.
31 Larissa Behrendt et al., *Review of Higher Education Access and Outcomes for Aboriginal and Torres Strait Islander People* (Final Report, 2012) 138.
32 Larissa Behrendt et al., *Review of Higher Education Access and Outcomes for Aboriginal and Torres Strait Islander People* (Final Report, 2012) 95.
33 Larissa Behrendt et al., *Review of Higher Education Access and Outcomes for Aboriginal and Torres Strait Islander People* (Final Report, 2012) 9; Daryle Rigney, 'Indigenous Higher Education Reform and Indigenous Knowledges' (Report, *Review of Higher Education Access and Outcomes for Aboriginal and Torres Strait Islander People*, Department of Education, Employment and Workplace Relations, 2011).

Prepared five years after the Behrendt Review, Universities Australia's Indigenous Strategy 2017–2020 ('the Strategy')[34] again drew attention to the low enrolment and high attrition rates of Aboriginal and Torres Strait Islander students and the few Indigenous staff in the higher education sector. The Strategy was committed to achieving similar actions to the Behrendt Review—grow the rate of Aboriginal and Torres Strait Islander students enrolled in and completing higher degrees, increase the number of Aboriginal and Torres Strait Islander people employed in universities and ensure that all students engage with Aboriginal and Torres Strait Islander cultural content as an integral part of their course of study by 2020.[35]

More specific reports focusing on law schools have followed. Many of these were produced as part of the Indigenous Cultural Competency for Legal Academics Program ('ICCLAP') led by Marcelle Burns,[36] which was recommended as part of the Behrendt Review. The ICCLAP identified a need to improve the inclusion of Indigenous cultural competency in law school curricula but recognised that this required strong leadership and ongoing commitment from law schools.[37] To this end, and similarly to previous reports, the ICCLAP recommended that priority should be given to the recruitment and retention of Indigenous legal academics to support the embedding of Indigenous cultural competency in the curriculum and that law schools should take measures to ensure the cultural safety of Indigenous academics and students.[38]

In 2020, the Council of Australian Law Deans (CALD) clearly identified in the Australian Law School Standards that the content of the law course should seek to develop 'Aboriginal and Torres Strait Islander perspectives on and intersections with the law'.[39] Furthermore, law school curricula 'should be designed with a view to fostering Indigenous cultural competency' and be able to show how this has occurred.[40] The standards also note that it is desirable

34 Universities Australia, 'Indigenous Strategy 2017–2020' (Universities, 2017) <https://universitiesaustralia.edu.au/wp-content/uploads/2019/06/Indigenous-Strategy-2019.pdf>.

35 Universities Australia, 'Indigenous Strategy 2017–2020' (Universities, 2017) 14.

36 Marcelle Burns, Anita Lee Hong and Asmi Wood, *Indigenous Cultural Competency for Legal Academics Program* (Final Report, 2019) vi, 49 <https://universitiesaustralia.edu.au/wp-content/uploads/2019/06/Indigenous-Strategy-2019.pdf>.

37 Marcelle Burns, Anita Lee Hong and Asmi Wood, *Indigenous Cultural Competency for Legal Academics Program* (Final Report, 2019) vii.

38 Marcelle Burns, Anita Lee Hong and Asmi Wood, *Indigenous Cultural Competency for Legal Academics Program* (Final Report, 2019) vi, 49 <https://universitiesaustralia.edu.au/wp-content/uploads/2019/06/Indigenous-Strategy-2019.pdf>.

39 Council of Australian Law Deans, 'Australian Law School Standards with Guidance Notes' (30 July 2020) [2.3.3] (a) <https://cald.asn.au/wp-content/uploads/2020/07/Australian-Law-School-Standards-v1.3-30-Jul-2020.pdf.>.

40 Council of Australian Law Deans, 'Australian Law School Standards with Guidance Notes' (30 July 2020) [2.3.3] 17.

that Aboriginal or Torres Strait Islander Australians teach in subjects that require Indigenous knowledge.[41] Consistent with these standards, law schools would need to give priority to the appointment and promotion of Aboriginal and Torres Strait Islander staff.[42]

The ICCLAP reviewed the critiques regarding the inclusion of Indigenous cultural competency in the curriculum. Such critiques include that it may perpetuate stereotypes of Aboriginal and Torres Strait Islander people; it may 'other' Indigenous people, leading to new forms of racism; it might re-centre whiteness as the normative standard; it could suggest that simply learning a group's history (without focusing on addressing social injustices) may be enough; or it might fail to grapple with racism and colonialism.[43] For example, Sámi scholar Rauna Koukkanen has warned of the dangers of 'mere inclusion' of Indigenous issues in the curriculum, commenting that this approach will often lead to the content being interpreted through a non-Indigenous lens and is a form of 'epistemic violence'.[44] This 'ad hoc embedding phenomenon'[45] risks appearing tokenistic and could actually serve to undercut Indigenous knowledges and increase inequalities.[46]

Despite these critiques, scholars have identified clear arguments to 'decolonise' the legal curriculum. Asmi Wood, a lawyer with ancestors from the western Torres Strait, and Nicole Watson compellingly argue that

> Firstly, it is illogical to confine legal education to a system of laws that has operated on Australian soil for a mere 230 years, while utterly ignoring laws that have been practised here for thousands of years. Secondly, Indigenous laws have intrinsic value because they are the only bodies of law that have enabled human beings to live here sustainably. Finally, Indigenous laws should be incorporated out of recognition that settler law has consistently proven to be inept in keeping Indigenous communities safe from violence.[47]

41 Council of Australian Law Deans, 'Australian Law School Standards with Guidance Notes' (30 July 2020) [2.3.3] 27.

42 Council of Australian Law Deans, 'Australian Law School Standards with Guidance Notes' (30 July 2020) [2.3.3] 28.

43 See the discussion and literature review in Burns, Lee Hong and Wood (n 36); Heron Loban, 'Decolonised Law Degrees: A Misnomer' (2022) 47(4) *Alternative Law Journal* 296, 297.

44 Rauna Kuokkanen, 'Toward a New Relation of Hospitality in the Academy' (2003) 27(1/2) *American Indian Quarterly* 267, 297. See also Marcelle Burns, 'Towards Growing Indigenous Culturally Competent Legal Professionals in Australia' (2013) 12(1) *International Education Journal: Comparative Perspectives* 230.

45 Loban (n 43) 297.

46 Kevin Lowe, Nikki Moodie and Sara Weuffen, 'Refusing Reconciliation in Indigenous Curriculum' in Bill Green, Mary Roberts and Marie Brennan (eds), *Curriculum Challenges and Opportunities in a Changing World* (Springer, 2021) 71, 79.

47 Asmi Wood and Nicole Watson, 'Mirror, Mirror on the Wall, Who Is the Fairest of Them All?' (2018) 28 *Legal Education Review* 1, 12. See also Loban (n 43).

However, although there is arguably an increasingly supportive policy setting and clear arguments for the inclusion of Aboriginal and Torres Strait Islander peoples and their knowledge in law schools, change has been slow and arduous.

Continuing Exclusion

Why is inclusion in the law school curriculum taking such a long time? Racism is one explanation for the slow pace of change, and one that we will return to, but other explanations have also been proffered. Academic laziness—with academics not being willing to divert time and attention away from their specialist academic interests—may be another reason.[48] This 'laziness' may also be connected to the massively increased pressures on academics to teach, research, contribute to both university and community service activities and engage in writing and communicating with non-academic audiences, all within the window of a 38-hour week.[49] In such gruelling conditions, 'Indigenising the curriculum' might be seen as yet another 'task' in an ever-growing list.

Added to these pressures on academics is the twofold setback of expanding class sizes and increasing pressure from students who are paying increasingly more for their degrees and therefore expect their teachers to provide greater levels of service (time, feedback, etc.). The challenges for academics to manage artificial intelligence in teaching and assessment are also real and growing.[50] Torres Strait Islander lawyer Heron Loban has highlighted similar concerns about the impacts of inadequate resourcing and the rise of managerialism in universities in relation to properly embedding Indigenous knowledge in the law school curriculum.[51]

Academic work conditions are on the national agenda. Notably, after successful wage theft claims at some of Australia's most prestigious educational institutions,[52] universities are now striking for better wages and conditions, particularly for casual sessional and contract staff.[53] Sessional and contract

48 Kuokkanen (n 44) 272.

49 Craig Whitsed and Antonia Girardi, 'Where Has the Joy of Working in Australian Universities Gone?', *The Conversation* (online, 7 June 2022) <https://theconversation.com/where-has-the-joy-of-working-in-australian-universities-gone-184251>.

50 Australian Government, *Australian Universities Accord* (Discussion Paper, February 2023) 32 <www.education.gov.au/australian-universities-accord/resources/australian-universities-accord-panel-discussion-paper>.

51 Loban (n 43) 297.

52 National Tertiary Education Union, *NTEU Wage Theft Report* (2023) <https://apo.org.au/sites/default/files/resource-files/2023-02/apo-nid321580.pdf>.

53 John Ross, 'Australian Universities Face a New Wave of Strikes', *Times Higher Education* (online, 7 April 2023) <www.timeshighereducation.com/news/australian-universities-face-new-wave-strikes>.

staff have always been an important part of the teaching support in Australian universities, with 50–80 per cent of undergraduate teaching in universities delivered by sessional staff.[54] The numbers of casual staff have continued to grow,[55] and some law courses rely almost entirely on sessional staff. Sessional staff are paid relatively poor hourly rates, they do not have the certainty of ongoing roles, and they may not know their employer's aspirations in relation to the inclusion of Indigenous content. Even if they know, their hourly rates support limited time for preparation and they receive minimal support when grappling with the Indigenous content of the subject(s) that they teach. Furthermore, sessional academics, such as full-time and permanent academic staff, often face complex pressures—many are juggling PhD study, teaching across multiple courses and managing other employment at the same time.

Some law teachers, whether sessional or not, do not feel supported to teach Indigenous issues and expect that this task will be accomplished, or supported, by their Indigenous colleagues.[56] As observed earlier, the ICCLAP recognised the importance of Indigenous academic support for curriculum development and recommended that Indigenous legal academics be recruited to support the embedding of Indigenous cultural competency in the curriculum.[57] However, this aspiration creates further issues. First, there may not be Indigenous law graduates available (or interested) to work in the university environment. Second, as Kuokkanen observes,

> relying on Indigenous scholars to educate primarily non-Indigenous students . . . poses a problem of the politics of distraction—diverting the attention of Indigenous people from their own priorities to the priorities of the dominant society.[58]

The politics of treaty and truth-telling processes, support for inquests, and other key issues are almost certainly always greater priorities for the small group of Indigenous law experts in Australia. Furthermore, the recruitment of Aboriginal staff to support the broader curriculum project also risks them being viewed by academic colleagues as a 'resource' or 'object to be used' by the 'dominant structure' (the law school).[59] In such circumstances, Indigenous academics may feel tokenised, and colonialism can be reinscribed.

54 Australian Government (n 50) 29.
55 Australian Government (n 50) 28.
56 Susan Page and Christine Asmar, 'Sources of Satisfaction and Stress among Indigenous Academic Teachers' (2009) 29(3) *Asia Pacific Journal of Education* 387.
57 Burns, Lee Hong and Wood (n 36) vii.
58 Kuokkanen (n 44) 273.
59 Marcelle Marie Gareau, 'Colonization within the University System' (2003) 27(1/2) *American Indian Quarterly* 196, 197–99.

An argument that might be made by some academics to justify their refusal to introduce more Aboriginal and Torres Strait Islander content into the curriculum appeals to the protection of their freedom of speech or academic freedom. Intrinsic to this argument is the view that academics should always be able to use their professional judgement to determine what and how 'their' subject is taught. The culture of the institution, the insulation of disciplines, the siloing of subjects and the managerial context of universities all help to protect the status quo.[60]

Academic freedom, however, is not just about the teacher; it also extends to the student. At least part of the aim of law school is to enable students to become critical thinkers.[61] In her work, Nicole Watson has said that if she could talk with her lecturer who told the administrative law class with a smile that specific land was sacred to Aboriginal people only because it once held a brewery,

> I would remind him of his responsibility to nurture all of the young minds in his class, not only those who shared his privilege. After all, equality in legal education is not a charitable gesture from the establishment, but a right that we demand.[62]

One final argument that might be used to justify the exclusion of Indigenous-authored research from the curriculum is that the research methodology is not reliable, recognised or 'rigorous'.[63] However, as Koukkanen argues,

> the privileged group whose epistemes are taken for granted in the academy feel threatened when faced with perspectives and information that challenges their earlier knowledge and ingrained views of the world.[64]

This is a concern taken up by many of the chapters in this collection.

Although these practical issues and ideological arguments may operate to some extent to slow the pace of inclusion of Indigenous content in Australian law schools, we argue that racism—both institutional and individual—lies at

60 Polly Walker, 'Colonising Research: Academia's Structural Violence Towards Indigenous Peoples' (2003) 22(3) *Social Alternatives* 37, 38.

61 Bruce McFarlane, 'Re-Framing Student Academic Freedom: A Capability Framework' (2012) 63 *Higher Education* 719, 720.

62 Nicole Watson, 'Indigenous People in Legal Education: Staring into a Mirror without Reflection' (2005) 6 *Indigenous Law Bulletin* 4, 5.

63 Walker (n 60) 38.

64 Kuokkanen (n 44) 272.

the centre of such exclusion. When we use the term 'racism', we refer to the definition provided by the Australian Human Rights Commission:

> Racism is a process by which systems and policies, actions and attitudes create inequitable opportunities and outcomes for people based on perceived [racial difference]. Racism is more than just prejudice in thought or action. Racism—whether individual or institutional—includes the power to discriminate against, oppress or limit the rights of others.[65]

Numerous studies have identified the obstacles that Aboriginal and Torres Strait Islander students face in law school, including disrespect.[66] A survey of current and former Indigenous University of New South Wales law students raised several key themes: experiences of alienation, imposter syndrome and lack of cultural safety; limited institutional understanding of the complex lives of many Indigenous students, including issues involving mental health and family/parenting responsibilities; the need for academic and non-academic support (and the interrelatedness of the two); and financial hardship and accommodation needs.[67]

The experiences of Aboriginal and Torres Strait Islander academics have been reported to be equally painful.[68] Phillip Falk describes the experience as an 'on-going struggle against colonial domination'.[69] Similarly traumatic experiences are reported by Indigenous academics in other colonised countries. Native American scholar of Esselen and Chumash descent Deborah Miranda describes the experience of working in a university setting as 'heartbreaking'.[70] In New Zealand, Māori academic Tara McAllister lists 50 reasons why there are no Māori people in the science department where she undertook postdoctoral work.[71] These reasons, which are too numerous to repeat here, include the following:

> . . . because we are tired.
> Tired of trying.
> Tired of fighting.

65 'What Is Racism?', *Australian Human Rights Commission* (Web Page) <https://humanrights.gov.au/our-work/race-discrimination/what-racism>.
66 Burns (n 44) 230.
67 Melanie Schwartz, 'Retaining Our Best: Imposter Syndrome, Cultural Safety, Complex Lives and Indigenous Student Experiences of Law School' (2018) 28(2) *Legal Education Review* 1, 5.
68 Bronwyn Fredericks, 'The Epistemology that Maintains White Race Privilege, Power and Control of Indigenous Studies and Indigenous Peoples' Participation in Universities' (2009) 5(1) *Critical Race and Whiteness Studies* 1, 5.
69 Quoted in Jean Phillips, 'Guest Editor's Introduction: Decolonising the Centre' (2003) 22(3) *Social Alternatives* 3.
70 Deborah Miranda, 'What's Wrong with a Little Fancy? Storytelling from the (Still) Ivory Tower' (2003) 27(1/2) *American Indian Quarterly* 333, 344.
71 Tara McAllister, '50 Reasons There Are No Māori in Your Science Department', *E-Tangata* (online, 28 May 2023) <https://e-tangata.co.nz/>.

> Tired of Indigenising.
> Tired of banging our heads against brick walls.
> Tired of being overlooked, underpaid, and undervalued.
> Tired of being labelled the angry Māori for doing anything other than smiling and nodding to appease the Great White Sharks.[72]

Racism lies at the core of these experiences. In her analysis of racism against Aboriginal academics in an Indigenous studies program, Indigenous scholar Bronwyn Fredericks points out that contemporary racism is 'less bloody than in earlier Australian history but it is still perpetuated by non-Indigenous people with privilege and power'.[73] Like other forms of violence, racism 'is not stagnant; it morphs, shifts, and has an intrinsic relationship to its historical context'.[74] Racism can be 'subtle', 'covert', banal and 'everyday'.[75] In their discussion of the banality of racism, George Sefa Dei and colleagues observe that racism is

> [m]ore than linguistic in nature, such social alienations are expressed through multiple sign systems and symbolic gestures like a rejected handshake, an empty seat on a bus or a smile-turned-down when you enter a room. Ultimately, they are all part of a complex interplay between meanings and socially constructed boundaries.[76]

Thus, although we tend to think about racism as working 'primarily through volume and violence',[77] in general, this is not how it is perpetrated in the university context. For many non-Indigenous people working in any given institution, the everyday incidents of racism may go unnoticed.[78] However, for victims, the effects can be highly corrosive. The place itself begins to feel unsafe.[79] To survive racism, a person may self-censor and silence themselves, limit their exposure to certain people and places that may lead to a racist

72 Tara McAllister, '50 Reasons There Are No Māori in Your Science Department', *E-Tangata* (online, 28 May 2023) <https://e-tangata.co.nz/>.
73 Fredericks (n 68) 5.
74 Samuel Mattson, 'A Report on the Banality of Racism' (Honours Thesis, Rhodes College, 2015) 7.
75 Watson (n 62) 5.
76 George Sefa Dei, Leeno Karumanchery and Nisha Karumanchery-Luik, 'The Banality of Racism: Living "within" the Traumatic' (2004) 244 *Counterpoints* 127, 131. See also Richard Brooks, 'The Banality of Racial Inequality' (2015) 124 *The Yale Law Journal* 2627.
77 Ta-Nehisi Coates, 'The Banality of Racism', *The Atlantic* (4 January 2012) <https://www.theatlantic.com/national/archive/2012/01/the-banality-of-racism/250779/>.
78 Mattson (n 74) 8. See also Tricia McGuire-Adams, 'Settler Allies Are Made, Not Self-Proclaimed: Unsettling Conversations for Non-Indigenous Researchers and Educators Involved in Indigenous Health' (2021) 80(7) *Health Education Journal* 761, 764 discussing 'everyday microaggression' and the 'normalisation of whiteness'.
79 Fredericks (n 68).

encounter[80] or leave.[81] As Nicole Watson puts it, 'All too often, the price of survival is silencing the voice inside one's psyche.'[82] When a person is expected to be comforting and protective but instead shatters this sense of security through racism, the consequences for the victim can be particularly traumatic.[83] In the final part of this chapter, we reveal how the authors of this book have experienced racism in legal education, developed strategies to introduce cultural safety into their classrooms and laid foundations for all students to learn about the extraordinary histories and wisdom of Indigenous peoples.

Part Three: The Structure of This Book

Part I: Recognising That Terra Nullius Never Left and Reimagining Law and Legal Education to Achieve Our Own Ends

This book is divided into three interlinked parts. Part I begins with three chapters written by authors who have come face-to-face with the violence of a post-*Mabo* legal system that simultaneously disavows the doctrine of terra nullius while constantly reinforcing its influence. This poses the question: Is the settler legal system even capable of reform?

Guugu Yimithirr lawyer and academic Osca Monaghan begins with poignant reflections on being an Indigenous lawyer immersed in a criminal justice system that harms Indigenous adults and children with such regularity that violence has become normalised (Chapter Two). Even on their best days, Indigenous lawyers may do 'little more than facilitate the system's operation'. Monaghan goes on to interrogate current forms of Indigenous political agitation, particularly rights and recognition-based approaches and Indigenous nation-building endeavours, and ultimately advocates for a more critical engagement with political power.

Eddie Cubillo, who is a descendant of the Larrakia, Wadjigan and Central Arrente peoples in the Northern Territory, and Jaynaya Dwyer draw upon the former's evidence to the Yoorrook Justice Commission (Chapter Three) to cast light on the racism endured by Indigenous actors within the legal system and legal education. Cubillo's experiences have included indignities such as being mistaken for being a defendant by court staff and being treated as the cleaner by students at an elite law school. The pressures on individuals are compounded by their responsibilities to their families and communities. As Cubillo and Dwyer write, 'this is not a game for us'.

Terri Libesman, Wiradjuri man Paul Gray, and Muruwari-Yuwaalaraay lawyer Kirsten Gray, speak back to the state child protection system, a

80 Sefa Dei, Karumanchery and Karumanchery-Luik (n 76) 137.
81 McAllister (n 71); Gareau (n 59) 199.
82 Watson (n 62) 4.
83 Sefa Dei, Karumanchery and Karumanchery-Luik (n 76) 139.

system that is imbued with whiteness and unyielding to meaningful reform (Chapter Four). They argue that if we are to move beyond the pervasive terra nullius within the state child protection system, the self-determination of First Nations peoples must be realised. Rather than piecemeal reforms that achieve minimal progress, First Nations peoples must be empowered to make decisions that are grounded in their expectations in relation to child rearing and long-term aspirations for their children.

The two final chapters in Part I show how existing structures within universities and professional bodies can be harnessed by Indigenous peoples to pursue their goals. Simon Young and Mununjali-Yugembeh lawyer Kirstie Smith reflect on tools that are being used in a young regional law school to pull down institutional fences and create space for the meaningful inclusion of Indigenous people and their legal traditions (Chapter Five). Building partnerships with Indigenous colleagues across the university and cultivating relationships with local communities are some of the steps that prepare law schools to become spaces in which Indigenous students feel safe, and all students can learn about legal traditions that nurtured life in this beautiful land for thousands of years. Wiradyuri/Wiradjuri legal scholar Annette Gainsford, Alison Gerard and Emma Colvin argue that when decolonising the legal curriculum, it is imperative that law schools ensure that Indigenous staff and stakeholders are culturally safe (Chapter Six). They suggest mechanisms for achieving this goal that include university-wide Indigenous graduate attributes and professional accreditation standards.

Part II: Changing Thinking through Theory

The chapters in this section explore how Indigenous approaches to knowledge, such as standpoint, relationality and storytelling, make a difference to how settler law is understood and taught. Euahleyai and Kamillaroi lawyer and scholar Larissa Behrendt discusses how the Indigenous methodology of storytelling is a powerful means of deconstructing colonial narratives while empowering Indigenous victims of the law's violence (Chapter Seven). When Indigenous voices are brought to the centre through the medium of storytelling, Indigenous agency and continuing connections to Country are powerfully illuminated.

Suvendi Perera argues that the storytelling of Bundjalung writer Ruby Langford Ginibi is an exemplar of Aboriginal women's outlaw culture (Chapter Eight).[84] Perera focuses on Ginibi's book *Haunted by the Past*,[85] which was largely concerned with Ginibi's reflections of the experiences of her son, Nobby, in the criminal justice system. Ginibi connected Nobby's

84 For an explanation of Aboriginal women's outlaw culture, see Nicole Watson, *Aboriginal Women, Law and Critical Race Theory: Storytelling from the Margins* (Springer, 2021).

85 Ruby Langford Ginibi, *Haunted by the Past* (Allen & Unwin, 1999).

incarceration to the historical and ongoing use of the law as a tool of colonisation and thus spoke back to a system that perpetuates violence. The continuing relevance of Ginibi's work is brought into stark relief in Perera's conclusion, which informs us that between 1991 and 2024, over 500 Indigenous people died in custody. Tragically, Ginibi's sentiment that the 'killing times are still with us'[86] has lost none of its currency.

When Gomeroi/Kamilaroi scholar Marcelle Burns left legal practice for the Academy, she arrived with a 'mission' to ensure that law graduates were better prepared to work with Indigenous people (Chapter Nine). She carried out that mission through a pedagogy that drew upon Indigenous concepts of relationality and reciprocity. These approaches were woven into assessments that included discussion forums and reflective journals. In their chapter, Goenpul woman Pekeri Ruska and Jennifer Nielsen critically explore how the common law struggles not only to translate the relational, spiritual and interdependent philosophy inherent in Aboriginal relationships to Country but also convey the deep responsibilities to care for Country and protect cultural integrity for future generations (Chapter Ten). To give context to their discussion, the authors share their insight into how cultural heritage legislation such as the *Aboriginal and Torres Strait Islander Heritage Protection Act 1984* (Cth) can be decolonised.

This part concludes with a chapter by Narelle Bedford, a legal scholar whose mum is Jackie Bedford from the Yuin people of the South Coast of New South Wales (Chapter Eleven). Bedford considers how to include Indigenous teaching and learning methodologies in legal education, including storytelling/yarning, deep listening and lived experience. Her chapter highlights the importance of these methodologies on the path towards legal pluralism in Australia and the decolonisation of legal education. Bedford also makes comparisons with developments in Canada, Aotearoa/New Zealand and South Africa. These comparisons serve to highlight how far behind Australia lags in recognising the continuing significance of Indigenous legal traditions.

Part III: Applying an Indigenous Lens to Law School Curricula

In this final part, the authors grapple with how critical Indigenous perspectives can be incorporated into the teaching of traditional law subjects. In her chapter, Nicole Watson argues that judgments in intentional torts cases brought by Indigenous plaintiffs against police officers tend to lack any serious engagement with the plaintiff's race (Chapter Twelve). This marginalisation of race supports a narrative in which the plaintiffs are the random victims of flawed individuals within the police force. Watson shows how an

86 Ruby Langford Ginibi, *Haunted by the Past* (Allen & Unwin, 1999) 142.

alternative reading practice that engages with the experiential knowledge of Indigenous communities reveals another narrative, one in which such violence is a structural and everyday occurrence.

Mary Spiers Williams, who is descended from the first peoples of the sandstone Country (from what is known as Sydney and stretching north to Dyarrabbin) and whose father is Darkeñung, considers how conventional approaches to teaching criminal law contribute to systemic bias against First Peoples (Chapter Thirteen). As students are taught to focus narrowly on the elements of offences, they are trained to overlook social context. Materials that First Peoples may consider to be relevant to the question of guilt, such as transgenerational trauma, are automatically diverted to sentencing, if they are considered at all. Spiers Williams proposes steps that can be taken to address systemic racism, beginning with reflective practice. She concludes that individuals should always reflect on their own standing and role in the criminal justice system.

Aurora Milroy, a Palyku legal scholar, and Karinda Burns, a Wajarri Yamaji and Yued Noongar legal scholar, advocate for the inclusion of Indigenous content and perspectives in the curriculum by emphasising the importance of working with local Indigenous knowledge holders, centring Indigenous voices, and ensuring teacher readiness to teach Indigenous content. Specifically, their chapter (Chapter Fourteen) proposes a more holistic and comprehensive approach to public law curriculum and legal education more broadly to enrich students' understanding of governance and shift the embedded narratives of Australian law curricula.

Koori academic of Aboriginal (Yuin) and settler (Scottish and Greek) descent Amanda Porter and Eddie Cubillo argue that because clinical legal education has long been presumed to be progressive, it has avoided sustained decolonial critique (Chapter Fifteen). However, clinical legal education suffers from the same flaws that befall other traditional law subjects, namely, the erasure of settler colonialism and Indigenous peoples' continuing sovereignty and agency. The authors share their approach to teaching clinical legal education that involves partnering with Aboriginal community-controlled organisations, championing the work of Indigenous scholars, and imparting the stories of grass roots campaigns. In the final chapter (Chapter Sixteen), Lee Godden draws upon her decades-long experience of teaching native title to address critical questions, beginning with what is native title? Although potentially transformative, native title is a creature of the common law and, as such, remains to be decolonised. Godden also considers where native title should be included in the curriculum, such as introductory subjects, for example, property law, or a wider range of courses, for example, environmental and energy law.

Conclusion

For much of our/their shared history, law students have been taught that prior to the arrival of the British, what is now called 'Australia' was a legal vacuum. According to such mythology, Indigenous peoples had no pre-existing rights to their lands and waters because they were so uncivilised that they did not have laws of their own. It was not until the momentous decision of *Mabo v State of Queensland [No 2]* that this racist narrative was finally dispelled. For Indigenous peoples, the *Mabo* decision was a great testament to the strength and courage of the plaintiffs, who were led by the indefatigable Eddie Koiki Mabo. But the notion that they should have legal rights and interests based on age-old connections to Country was hardly a revelation. If anything, it was a first step towards atonement for an unjust invasion. For those within Australia's law schools, however, the decision raised questions that many continue to wrestle with three decades later. These questions include whether Indigenous legal orders should be included in legal curricula and if so, how?

In this chapter, we have acknowledged the advances towards the meaningful inclusion of Indigenous peoples' legal traditions and experiential knowledge that have been made to date. We applaud interventions by the CALD and the groundbreaking work undertaken by the Behrendt Review and the ICCLAP. Nonetheless, progress has been painfully slow and impeded by ballooning workloads, the growing casualisation of the academic workforce and racism.

In the chapters that follow, the authors share insights that have been gained from working in spaces that have often felt unsafe. They also share their imagined futures for Australian legal education. In such spaces, all students will thrive from curricula that will be inclusive of both settler law and Indigenous legal orders that are rooted in the soil. As practitioners, they will draw upon not only a knowledge of legal doctrine that was cultivated during law school but also skills developed through engagement with Indigenous pedagogies, such as deep listening, that can enhance their communication with those in need of their counsel.

PART I

Recognising That Terra Nullius Never Left and Reimagining Law and Legal Education to Achieve Our Own Ends

2

INDIGENOUS LAWYERING

Colonial Legal Formations and Decolonial Manoeuvres

Osca Monaghan

Introduction

At the heart of my intellectual and political life are two related questions: how can the colonial relation be understood—to therefore dismantle it? The colonial relation is not all-encompassing, but it does operate, and is sustained, in the political, legal, economic and social realms. Each of these considerations animates my practice as both a lawyer and a scholar. In this chapter, I reflect on the tensions inherent in legal practice for an Indigenous lawyer with decolonial ambitions and consider the epistemological constraints on our liberatory thinking imposed by our legal training and the legal system. More specifically, I am concerned with the application of a decolonial lens to the law and to our political efforts so that we, as decolonial lawyers, can make clearsighted manoeuvres within our practice as lawyers, thinkers and activists. To that end, after making some observations about the tensions and contradictions inherent in legal practice for an Indigenous or decolonial lawyer, I then consider the dominant forms of Indigenous political demand to examine the realities of colonial legal formations and their implications for decolonisation. I ultimately conclude that the dominant forms of Indigenous political demand cannot properly be conceived of as decolonial. In the final section, I offer an invitation to engage in radical decolonial imagining that goes beyond these dominant forms. My central provocation in this piece concerns the extent to which our utopian imaginaries have been delimited by our internalisation of the logics of coloniality.

As a work intended to accompany my chapter 'Indigenous Judging' in *Indigenous Legal Judgments*,[1] I do not propose to re-cover the same ground

1 Osca Monaghan, 'Indigenous Judging' in Nicole Watson and Heather Douglas (eds), *Indigenous Legal Judgments: Bringing Indigenous Voices into Judicial Decision Making* (Routledge, 2021) 25.

DOI: 10.4324/9781003473404-3

contained in the first part of that chapter relating to Indigenous subjectivity. For the present purposes, it will suffice to say that I understand 'Indigenous' to be a political category that emerges only in relation to colonial power and that to be 'Indigenous' is to be in resistance to colonial power. It is a term that I do not otherwise wish to imbue with meaning, and I deploy it strategically.[2] Similarly, I do not re-tread the same terrain as the second section of that chapter concerning colonial law as a tool of colonial power. Instead, my hope for this present chapter is that it takes up and develops some of the threads offered in the final section of 'Indigenous Judging' in relation to the imperative to invest in places outside the colonial legal system as a decolonial tactic.

Following Waziyatawin Angela Wilson (Pezihutazizi Otunwe) and Michael Yellow Bird (Mandan, Hidatsa and Arikara nation), I understand decolonisation to be

> the intelligent, calculated, and active resistance to the forces of colonialism that perpetuate the subjugation and/or exploitation of our minds, bodies, and lands, and it is engaged for the ultimate purpose of overturning the colonial structure and realizing Indigenous liberation.[3]

In its pursuit, we must attend to the structural nature of settler colonialism and always consider the 'fundamental questions of jurisdiction, sovereignty, and authority'.[4] As such, decolonisation requires a refutation of the settler state and its ability 'to inaugurate law on lands acquired through colonial settlement'.[5]

On Indigenous Lawyering in Practice

A lawyer loses and gains something in the process of their legal training. Our training takes place within a very conservative environment, with limited options for critical intellectual exploration. Although law schools are often perceived as sites of liberalism and progressivism, in reality, 'the intellectual

2 Although for important conversations occurring within Critical Indigenous Studies around this question, see, e.g., Brendan Hokowhitu, 'Monster: Post-Indigenous Studies' in Aileen Moreton-Robinson (ed), *Critical Indigenous Studies: Engagements in First World Locations* (University of Arizona Press, 2016) 83; Aileen Moreton-Robinson, 'Race and Cultural Entrapment: Critical Indigenous Studies in the Twenty-First Century' in Aileen Moreton-Robinson (ed), *Critical Indigenous Studies: Engagements in First World Locations* (University of Arizona Press, 2016) 102.

3 Waziyatawin Angela Wilson and Michael Yellow Bird, *For Indigenous Eyes Only: A Decolonization Handbook* (School of American Research Press, 2005) 2.

4 Monaghan (n 1) 30.

5 Shiri Pasternak, 'Jurisdiction and Settler Colonialism: Where Do Laws Meet?' (2014) 29(2) *Canadian Journal of Australian Studies* 145, 146.

and political environments are so mildly reformist (at best) that they will feel shockingly conservative to anyone who wants to see significant change'.[6] As the end result is a professional degree, the goal of a legal education is to inculcate within students the norms and principles of the prevailing legal system—usually by presenting this system as neutral, unproblematic and incontestable.[7] We learn that, for a lawyer, contest occurs in a particular way; to be a good lawyer is to learn the appropriate forms and tools of contest and then deploy them within the appropriate forums against appropriate opponents. It is no surprise, then, that '[m]ost legal work maintains systems of maldistribution, it does not transform them'.[8] I have come to understand that to embark on a law degree is to beg entry into the master's house, seeking tutelage in the use of his tools.[9]

Against this backdrop, an Indigenous lawyer must constantly defend against internalising the logics of the systems that we work within. If we are not careful, then we can come to accept the lies, fictions and founding mythologies that have justified the establishment and maintenance of the settler state. These fictions permit the erection and maintenance of economies predicated on the exploitation of people and Country. We may never come to believe in the inherent criminality or degeneracy of our peoples, but we might find ourselves believing in—and, therefore, investing in—the systems that remove our children and that incarcerate us and them. Although many of us come to the law to defend our people against these systems, it is difficult and constant work to negotiate our space within them. Once we enter legal practice, we find ourselves immediately and continually confronted with the necessity of compromise on multiple fronts.[10]

I write from my own experience as a criminal defence lawyer working for an Aboriginal community-controlled organisation in New South Wales.

6 Dean Spade, 'For Those Considering Law School', *deanspade.net* (October 2010) 6 <www.deanspade.net/wp-content/uploads/2010/10/For-Those-Considering-Law-School.pdf>.

7 For a comprehensive discussion of the narrow scope of legal education, see Folúkẹ́ Adébísí, *Decolonisation and Legal Knowledge: Reflections on Power and Possibility* (Bristol University Press, 2023) 1–13.

8 Folúkẹ́ Adébísí, *Decolonisation and Legal Knowledge: Reflections on Power and Possibility* (Bristol University Press, 2023) 1.

9 The decision whether to attend law school is an individual one, but it is one that many, myself included, make without full awareness of the rigorously conservative training that we will receive as part of our legal education.

10 A number of Indigenous scholars have considered the epistemological challenges experienced in their encounters with settler legal education and practice; see, e.g., Alison Whittaker, 'Observing Aboriginality, Aboriginality Observing: Epistemic and Methodological Paths to an Indigenous Student Jurisprudence from Within' (2016) 5 *Ngiya: Talk the Law* 1; Nicole Watson, 'Indigenous Legal Traditions and Australian Legal Education' in Peter Cane, Lisa Ford and Mark McMillan (eds), *The Cambridge Legal History of Australia* (Cambridge University Press, 2022) 721.

From my very first day, I have witnessed unrelenting injustice and incalculable indignities inflicted on both children and adults by the criminal 'justice' system—most of whom were appearing before a criminal court primarily because of the evident consequences of structural racism, multiple traumas (intergenerational and otherwise) and poverty. All were before the court because of multiple systemic failures of care prior to that moment. The system dealt with them violently; without exception, more harm was enacted by the system than was ever prevented by it.[11] The harm and violence perpetuated by this system was, all the while, normalised and rationalised by every participant in the system (with the sometimes-exception of the person charged).[12]

While in practice, I had cause to frequently reflect on what makes a good lawyer in this context. My immediate obligation was to my client, but I was regularly reminded that my paramount obligation was to the court. According to one rendering, a good lawyer is someone who can balance these obligations while obtaining the best possible outcome for one's client. This perhaps seems like a sensible definition, but for decolonial lawyers—or, in fact, for any lawyer with a radical praxis—meeting it has required that we bracket our decolonial or radical praxes, as even the best outcome permitted by the system is still a harmful outcome. Despite sometimes feeling a certain satisfaction after a victory in court, I nonetheless was forced to reckon with the fact that even on good days—where I (maybe) truly mitigated harm—ultimately, I had done little more than facilitate the system's operation.

To give one illustration, there were many times that I appeared on release applications for both children and adults;[13] the obvious good outcome for the person making such application is for the application to be granted and for the person to be released from prison into the community. Release will usually be conditional, however, with many—often onerous and frequently inappropriate—conditions able to be imposed by the court. Release often

11 See generally Angela Yvonne Davis, *Are Prisons Obsolete?* (Seven Stories Press, 2003); Eileen Baldry, Bree Carlton and Chris Cunneen, 'Abolitionism and the Paradox of Penal Reform in Australia: Indigenous Women, Colonial Patriarchy, and Co-option' (2014) 41(3) *Social Justice* 168, especially 171–73; Eric A Stanley and Nat Smith (eds), *Captive Genders: Trans Embodiment and the Prison Industrial Complex* (AL Press, 2011); Mariame Kaba (ed), *We Do This 'til We Free Us: Abolitionist Organizing and Transforming Justice* (Haymarket Books, 2021).

12 For a powerful discussion of the impact of participation in the colonial legal system, see Eddie Cubillo and Jayana Dwyer, Evidence given by Eddie Cubillo to the Yoorrook Justice Commission, (this collection).

13 In the jurisdiction that I work in, a release (bail) application occurs when a person has been charged with at least one offence by police, and police have found that person to be an 'unacceptable risk' of certain criteria in the *Bail Act 2013* (NSW) and have refused bail. Once a person has been refused bail by police, they are taken to a court where a magistrate will apply the same law as the police did after hearing submissions from the prosecution (usually, the police) and the person's defence lawyer.

involved a serious curtailment of a person's liberty (up to, and including, house arrest) and the concomitant police surveillance occasioned by this curtailment, which many times would have significant consequences not only for that person but also for the people closest to them and their wider community. Moreover, although securing someone's release was inarguably a good thing, it exposed the person to bail conditions with which many would struggle to comply. It also did nothing to address the socioeconomic and structural factors that contributed to their initial charge, which means that they often reappeared before the same court with fresh charges and a decreased likelihood of release.

I came to the criminal law after a short stint at the academy, and I felt the need to do something that would materially assist people experiencing the full brunt of the colonial criminal system. I anticipated difficulty working as a criminal defence lawyer, but I was somewhat unprepared for the realities of practice and the daily compromises required of me. Any decolonial or radical lawyer who enters legal practice will find themselves immediately confronted with choices about what we can concede and what we cannot. As an abolitionist,[14] can I ever concede that imprisonment is an 'appropriate' penalty, as per section 5(1) of the *Crimes (Sentencing Procedure) Act 1999* (NSW)? If I refuse to concede the 'section 5 threshold' in circumstances where the black-letter principles are clear, then would I lose credibility in the eyes of the magistrate or judge—perhaps undermining my other submissions to the detriment of this client or the next? As an Indigenous lawyer, should I recite my client's history of disadvantage and trauma to the packed and open courtrooms that make up the local court to obtain a lesser penalty,[15] when I know the feelings of shame that it will produce in my client and the risk of re-traumatisation?

I had to develop my own answers to these questions and my own body of practice, but the sustainability of my tenure as a lawyer was undercut by an incompatibility between my fundamental beliefs about justice, healing and the need for decolonial action and the compromises required in daily legal work. Yes, it is essential to get people out of prisons; but prisons should not exist,[16] and the work of a criminal defence lawyer does not denaturalise

14 Perhaps at this juncture I should make the point that my abolitionist politics and my decolonial politics are deeply connected. My yearning for decolonisation is a yearning for all of us to be free from the colonial structures of domination that are antithetical to human flourishing. To be explicit, the decolonial future that I imagine is one without prisons and without police.

15 Such factors are not factors of mitigation under s 21A(3) of the *Crimes (Sentencing Procedure) Act 1999* (NSW), but evidence of disadvantage and trauma can be adduced to reduce moral culpability and to contribute to arguments relating to individualised justice; see, e.g., *Bugmy v The Queen* (2013) 249 CLR 571; *R v Fernando* (1992) 76 A Crim R 58.

16 Prison is not an appropriate response to the social problems that produce the kinds of harm that we call 'crime'. See e.g. Allegra M. Mcleod, 'Prison Abolition and Grounded Justice' (2015) 62 *UCLA Law Review* 1156.

or challenge the existence of prisons in any way. The courtroom is not an appropriate forum for responding to harm—only for reproducing it[17]—and yet it is the forum in which a defence lawyer operates. I went into the criminal law aware of these contradictions and aware that there would be a tension between what makes a person a good lawyer and what makes a good decolonial radical, but I had assumed that I would have the capacity to still engage in more radical work outside the parameters of legal practice. Unfortunately, the reality of life at an under-funded, under-resourced and under-staffed community legal centre left little time to do even the legal and service-oriented work I wanted to do, let alone anything substantively intellectual or political outside of it.

A further difficulty emerges for the Indigenous, decolonial or radical lawyer who is committed to working in social justice spaces. Most of these spaces are constrained either by their reliance on state or philanthropic funding sources or by the perceived necessity of maintaining relationships with the government and its agencies. The funding that community legal centres or other non-governmental organisations receive is conditional, whether it comes from the state (directly or through a governmental agency) or from philanthropic foundations. Lawyers working in these spaces may find it difficult to fully render their critiques, make radical statements or take radical actions, lest relationships with funders be jeopardised. The other risk for lawyers in these spaces is that they will find themselves caught in a cycle of grant-writing and grant-reporting rather than doing the service work that initially attracted them to social justice work in the first place. These are not new critiques,[18] and these are not reasons to avoid working in these spaces; our choices are necessarily circumscribed by the era of neoliberal late capitalism that we find ourselves struggling against, but they do form part of the landscape of compromises that is experienced in legal practice.[19]

The reality is that nothing I ever did—or could ever do—in a courtroom was going to be decolonial, radical or revolutionary. The danger here for Indigenous lawyers is not just that we will be ineffective at bringing about change—though we will be. The danger is that we will internalise the self-annihilating logics of the colonial legal system; the danger is that we will allow ourselves to be distracted by the slim promises of reform perpetually

17 See, e.g., Vanessa Lynn Lovelace, 'Abolish the Courthouse: Uncovering the Space of "Justice" in a Black Feminist Criminal Trial' in Viviane Saleh-Hanna, Jason Williams and Michael J Coyle (eds), *Abolish Criminology* (Routledge, 2023) 140.

18 See, e.g., INCITE! (ed), *The Revolution Will Not Be Funded: Beyond the Non-Profit Industrial Complex* (Duke University Press, 2007).

19 See also Craig Willse, *The Value of Homelessness: Managing Surplus Life in the United States* (University of Minnesota Press, 2015); Megan Ming Francis, 'The Price of Civil Rights: Black Lives, White Funding, and Movement Capture' (2019) 53(1) *Law & Society Review* 275; Julia C Morris, 'Strange Bedfellows? NGOs and the Politics of Value(s) in Offshore Asylum' in Gül İnaç and Themba Lewis (eds), *Forced Displacement and NGOs in Asia and the Pacific* (Routledge, 2022).

on offer as the system makes minute recalibrations in lieu of actual change.[20] *The danger is that we will allow the horizon of our liberation to be determined by the coloniser and that we will come to imagine the possibilities of liberation only through the prism of the modern nation state.*

Contemporary Approaches to Indigenous Justice or Liberation

In this section, I consider the current dominant forms of Indigenous political agitation in australia and in other settler colonial nation states. Specifically, I discuss, first, rights and recognition-based approaches and then, Indigenous nation-building endeavours. I consider each one's decolonial potential. As indicated in the introduction, this section is in direct conversation with the final section of my chapter 'Indigenous Judging',[21] with the hope that it usefully extends the arguments offered there.

Rights and Recognition-Based Approaches

Under the banner of rights and recognition-based approaches to Indigenous justice, I place all attempts to either have the settler state recognise Indigenous sovereignty (variously defined) or to carve out explicit rights that flow to Indigenous peoples by virtue of their Indigenous status; all are efforts that are located 'within legal and political state frameworks'.[22] Examples of this type of politics are requests for treaties, constitutional recognition, the establishment of representative bodies, the improvement of native title laws, land rights, the establishment of separate sentencing courts, and the recognition of customary law. Such claims have an important place within the history of Indigenous resistance and political agitation in this country and elsewhere. Many bold assertions of Indigenous presence, resistance and entitlement have incorporated demands in these or similar terms,[23] and it is partly through the persistent efforts of so many Indigenous people making claims of this kind that we have secured some measures of progress, which have given us an Indigenous present from which we can continue to fight for our liberation.[24]

20 For an analysis of the way that Indigenous political efforts in australia are embedded in existing settler colonial relations, see, e.g., Damien Short, *Reconciliation and Colonial Power: Indigenous Rights in Australia* (Ashgate, 2008).

21 Monaghan (n 1) 29–32.

22 Janine Gertz, 'Gugu Badhun Sovereignty, Self-Determination, and Nationhood' (PhD Thesis, James Cook University, 2022) 96.

23 See, e.g., Joe Anderson's (King Burraga) demand for recognition (1933); The Barunga Statement (1988); and the Eva Valley statement (1993), which was made directly in response to the shortcomings of proposed native title legislation. See also Larissa Behrendt, *Achieving Social Justice: Indigenous Rights and Australia's Future* (The Federation Press, 2003) especially 86–94.

24 Monaghan (n 1) 30.

Nonetheless, despite their usefulness in securing some Indigenous political goals, there are real and evident limitations to these demands, which do not fundamentally call into question the right of the settler state 'to inaugurate law on lands acquired through colonial settlement',[25] and they do not interrogate the implications of seeking inclusion and accommodation within colonial political and legal frames. Drawing on Fanon's analysis of the 'relationship between recognition and freedom in the master/slave dialectic of Hegel's *Phenomenology of Spirit*', Glen Coulthard (Yellowknives Dene First Nation) argues that

> in contexts where colonial rule is not reproduced through force alone, the maintenance of settler-state hegemony requires the production of . . . 'colonized subjects': namely, the production of the specific modes of colonial thought, desire, and behavior that implicitly or explicitly commit the colonized to the types and practices and subject positions that are required for their continued domination.[26]

Within this analysis, recognition given by the settler state is not an honouring of Indigenous sovereignty, and it is not a true delimitation of the state's power '*but rather [is] a field of power through which colonial relations are produced and maintained*'.[27] Coulthard, via Fanon, is ensuring that we attend to the structural nature of colonialism and, thus, 'the *structural* problem of colonial recognition'.[28]

The structural problem of colonial recognition becomes clear in the context of Indigenous rights claims. Despite the increased recognition of Indigenous rights (both domestically and internationally), the fundamental status of Indigenous peoples as colonised subjects remains. Scholars such as Marjo Lindroth see 'the rights of Indigenous peoples and the corresponding duties of states and other actors as inscribed in rationalities of governance, in practices of (neoliberal) power'.[29] This means that Indigenous rights are allowed only to the extent that the 'principles of neoliberal logics . . . are not prevented from functioning'.[30] Within this account of Indigenous rights, any

25 Pasternak (n 5) 146.

26 Glen Coulthard, *Red Skins, White Masks* (University of Minnesota Press, 2014) 16.

27 Glen Coulthard, *Red Skins, White Masks* (University of Minnesota Press, 2014) 17 (emphasis in original).

28 Glen Coulthard, *Red Skins, White Masks* (University of Minnesota Press, 2014) 16 (emphasis in original).

29 Marjo Lindroth, 'Indigenous Rights as Tactics of Neoliberal Governance: Practices of Expertise in the United Nations' (2014) 23(3) *Social & Legal Studies* 341, 343 (where neoliberalism is understood 'as a rationality of governance that is pervaded by the market logic of cost-effectiveness': 343).

30 Marjo Lindroth, 'Indigenous Rights as Tactics of Neoliberal Governance: Practices of Expertise in the United Nations' (2014) 23(3) *Social & Legal Studies* 346.

given Indigenous claim will survive or perish to the extent that the claim threatens the modern rationalities of neoliberal colonial governance.[31]

Louiza Odysseos goes further than this, arguing that the act of claiming human rights brings '*homo juridicus*' into being and renders it as 'partner' and 'predicate' to neoliberal governmentality.[32] This suggests that rather than merely delimiting the kinds of Indigenous rights liable to success or failure, Indigenous rights function as a method of co-option of Indigenous politics. This is commensurate with Foucault's argument that a right 'is both an instrument of, and vehicle for, the exercising of the multiplicity of dominations in society and the relations that enable their implementation'.[33] Foucault believed that although the power of the law diminished, it is merely one of many *tactics* employed 'to arrange things in such a way that, through a certain number of means, such and such ends may be achieved'[34] and that *rights* can be read as merely another tactic of power. It is therefore possible to read Indigenous rights as a tactic of settler colonial biopower, wherein

> the system of right and the judicial field are enduring channels for relations of domination and the many forms of techniques of subjugation. For this reason, right should not be understood as the establishment of legitimacy, but rather the methods by which subjugation is carried out.[35]

Not only does this position the Indigenous rights-claimer (and Indigenous politics more broadly) within neoliberal biopolitical processes of Indigenous domination, but these processes also work by eliminating Indigenous difference via their assimilationist functions.

We can also situate the failures of native title within the structural problem of colonial recognition. Native title narrowly defines the parameters of Indigenous sovereignty and interest in Country. As Aileen Moreton-Robinson (Koenpul) explains,

> What Indigenous peoples have been given, by way of white benevolence, is a white-constructed form of 'Indigenous' proprietary rights that are not epistemologically and ontologically grounded in Indigenous conceptions

31 See also Jeff Corntassel, 'Towards Sustainable Self-Determination: Rethinking the Contemporary Indigenous-Rights Discourse' (2008) 33 *Alternatives* 105.

32 Louiza Odysseos, 'Human Rights, Liberal Ontogenesis and Freedom: Producing a Subject for Neoliberalism?' (2010) 38(3) *Millennium: Journal of International Studies* 747, 772; see also Lindroth (n 29) 343.

33 Aileen Moreton-Robinson, *The White Possessive: Property, Power, and Indigenous Sovereignty* (University of Minnesota Press, 2015) 132.

34 Michel Foucault, 'Governmentality' in Graham Burchell, Colin Gordon and Peter Miller (eds), *Foucault Effects: Studies in Governmentality: With Two Lectures by and an Interview with Michel Foucault* (University of Chicago Press, 1991) 95.

35 Moreton-Robinson (n 33) 132; see also Michel Foucault, *Society Must Be Defended: Lectures at the Collége De France, 1975–6* (Picador, 2003) 27.

> of sovereignty. Indigenous land ownership, under these legislative regimes, amounts to little more than a mode of land tenure that enables a circumscribed form of autonomy and governance with minimum control and ownership of resources, on or below the ground, thus entrenching economic dependence on the nation state.[36]

Although there are suppositions present in this definition, which I implicitly call into question in the final section of this chapter, for the present purposes Moreton-Robinson's description accurately describes the ways in which '[t]here is a reflexive and unreflective tendency to automatically shift legal discourses involving indigenous [sic] actors into frameworks with diminished authorities'.[37] That is,

> the indigenous label, once applied to other political and legal discourses of the state, is a diminutive—it indicates that whatever compelling force the discourse may have outside the realm of indigenous politics, that legal weight is lesser in the indigenous context.[38]

Here, 'title' becomes 'native title' and suffers a diminution of the bundle of rights contained in the former.

The pragmatic appeal of rights and recognition-based approaches is clear; but it is also clear that such efforts have repeatedly failed to fundamentally alter the relationship between the settler state and Indigenous people. Ultimately, what remains largely unchallenged by these approaches are 'fundamental questions of jurisdiction, sovereignty, and authority',[39] which have the capacity to truly unsettle the australian settler state. This type of politics has helped secure our survival, but our *liberation* depends upon us turning away from the political and legal scaffolding imposed by the settler state.[40]

Indigenous Nation Building

Recognition- and rights-based approaches do not seek recognition of 'self-determination within settler colonial structures as a legal and political default'.[41] Rather, these approaches are articulated within the broader

36 Aileen Moreton-Robinson, 'Introduction' in Aileen Moreton-Robinson (ed), *Sovereign Subjects: Indigenous Sovereignty Matters* (Allen and Unwin, 2007) 4.

37 Danielle Delaney, 'Wearing Raven's Cloak: Law, Recognition, and Indigenous Identity' (PhD Thesis, University of Wisconsin-Madison, 2022) 1 <https://search.library.wisc.edu/digital/AF7AF2QWOUVSFW9B>.

38 Danielle Delaney, 'Wearing Raven's Cloak: Law, Recognition, and Indigenous Identity' (PhD Thesis, University of Wisconsin-Madison, 2022) 1 <https://search.library.wisc.edu/digital/AF7AF2QWOUVSFW9B>.

39 Monaghan (n 1) 30.

40 Monaghan (n 1) 30; see also Coulthard (n 26).

41 Gertz (n 22) 112.

politics of Indigenous refusal and Indigenous resurgence[42] and take form in efforts towards Indigenous nation building,[43] which can include the construction of Indigenous non-state legal orders[44] (these are typically operationalised within a framework of legal pluralism—i.e., alongside the legal system of the settler colonial state (and other Indigenous legal systems)) and other acts of self-determination not dependent on the accommodation of the settler state.[45] Such practices are diverse and, in some ways, less susceptible to co-option by the settler state and its attendant logics. Nonetheless, I do wish to hold them up to the fundamental edict of decolonisation to which I have already referred: do such efforts fundamentally alter the relation between the settler state and Indigenous people by rejecting the state's ability 'to inaugurate law on lands acquired through colonial settlement?'[46]

Janine Gertz (Gugu Badhun, Ngadjonj), in her work on Gugu Badhun nation building, argues for coexistence with the australian state via agitation 'for social, political, and legal change where new attitudes and laws are inclusive of Gugu Badhun definitions and perspectives of sovereignty and self-determination'.[47] Gertz argues that absent the revolutionary decolonial violence of Fanon, a 'more realistic program of *decolonisation*'[48] is needed; this program of decolonisation must 'rebuild jurisdiction that exist[s] alongside and outside the constituted order of the australian state in order to reject colonial assimilationist tactics'.[49] Like many other proponents of this approach, Gertz is clear that efforts undertaken in this vein need to be cautious about rebuilding in the likeness of the colonial state.[50] Following Taiaiake Alfred (Mohawk),[51] Gertz makes the case that because concepts such

42 See, e.g., Audra Simpson, 'On Ethnographic Refusal: Indigeneity, "Voice" and Colonial Citizenship' (2007) 9 *Junctures: The Journal for Thematic Dialogue* 67; Audra Simpson, *Mohawk Interruptus* (Duke University Press, 2014).

43 See, e.g., Gertz (n 22).

44 See, e.g., Hadley Friedland and Val Napoleon, 'Gathering the Threads: Developing a Methodology for Researching and Rebuilding Indigenous Legal Traditions' (2015) 1(1) *Lakehead Law Journal* 16; John Borrows and James Tully, 'Introduction' in Michael Asch, John Borrows and James Tully (eds), *Resurgence and Reconciliation: Indigenous—Settler Relations and Earth Teachings* (University of Toronto Press, 2018) 3.

45 See, e.g., Leanne Betasamosake Simpson, *Dancing on Our Turtle's Back: Stories of Nishnaabeg Re-Creation, Resurgence and a New Emergence* (ARP Books, 2011).

46 Pasternak (n 55).

47 Gertz (n 22) 83; see also Pasternak (n 55) 94: 'Indigenous Peoples' sovereignty will continue to be limited if our only strategy is to seek legal remedy of our situation within the current international and domestic colonial structures.'

48 Gertz (n 22) 83, emphasis in original.

49 Gertz (n 22) 83.

50 Gertz (n 22) 83, 180–81. See also Frantz Fanon, *The Wretched of the Earth* (Penguin Books, 1967); Frantz Fanon, *Black Skin, White Masks* (Grove Press, 1976); Simpson (n 45); Taiaiake Alfred, *Peace, Power, Righteousness: An Indigenous Manifesto* (Oxford University Press, 2nd ed, 2009).

51 Taiaiake Alfred, 'Sovereignty' in Joanne Barker (ed), *Sovereignty Matters: Locations of Contestation and Possibility in Indigenous Struggles for Self-Determination* (University of Nebraska Press, 2005) 33.

as sovereignty are socially constructed, they can be 'critically examined and purposefully *re*-constructed' to serve Indigenous liberatory ends.[52]

Within Indigenous nation building efforts, the Indigenous understanding of nation can be contrasted with Western ideas of the nation state. Where the nation state in the post-Westphalian political order is based upon 'European models of political and social organisation whose dominant defining characteristics are exclusivity of territorial domain and hierarchical, centralised authority',[53] Indigenous peoples have 'typically . . . been organised primarily by tribal or kinship ties, have decentralized political structures often linked in federation, and have enjoyed shared or overlapping spheres of territorial control'.[54] This latter sense of 'nation' is generally incorporated into Indigenous nation-building efforts. Indigenous nation building can be understood as a politic focused on

> [t]he assertion of genuine decision-making authority over lands and other natural resources held to be an Indigenous patrimony, over the internal affairs of Indigenous communities, over the nature and process of economic development on their lands, over cultural properties and the management of cultural heritage, over the organization of self-government, and over other matters that directly affect Indigenous welfare.[55]

This form of nationhood envisages 'a defined polity that holds and maintains a political identity as a distinct cultural group whose law, customs, and decision-making processes are drawn from their cultural and spiritual connections to a defined geographic territory'.[56] It typically involves the concept of (at least dual) citizenship and contemplates the design and implementation (or recognition and renewal) of Indigenous political constitutions.[57]

I appreciate the pragmatic approach that Gertz operationalises to further the political goals of the Gugu Badhun people, and I accept that the excavation of jurisdiction for an Indigenous legal and political order is a meaningful and powerful act of Indigenous resistance. However, I hold reservations about the desirability of an Indigenous future imagined in these terms or, at least, about calling such a future a decolonised one. First, this future (as a matter

52 Gertz (n 22) 83.

53 James Anaya, *Indigenous Peoples in International Law* (Oxford University Press, 2nd ed, 2000) 15.

54 James Anaya, *Indigenous Peoples in International Law* (Oxford University Press, 2nd ed, 2000) 15.

55 Stephen Cornell, 'Processes of Native Nationhood: The Indigenous Politics of Self-Government' (2015) 6(4) *International Indigenous Policy Journal*.

56 Gertz (n 22) 184.

57 In relation to this last point, see, e.g., Anna Dziedzic and Mark McMillan, 'Australian Indigenous Constitutions: Recognition and Renewal' (2016) 44(3) *Federal Law Review* 337.

of pragmatic politics) takes as a given the continued existence of the australian state and advocates for coexistence with it. To my mind, coexistence with this system is acquiescence to it. Decolonisation, as I suggest in the following section, is a project of dismantling—for everyone and for all lands—the colonial systems of domination that harm people and planet, premised as they are on subjugation, extraction and control. Second, the history of decolonisation elsewhere demonstrates the capacity for colonial power relations to continue in new forms even after it appears that the political and legal apparatus of colonisation has been removed (as Nelson Maldonado-Torres says, 'coloniality survives colonialism').[58] The implications of this, for me, speak to the necessity of understanding decolonisation to be a joint struggle directed towards the dismantling of the 'colonial world order established by European empires'.[59]

This task requires the development of a more critical relationship to recognisable forms of political power and greater attention to the 'broader politics of knowledge production'.[60] Such efforts will assist us in the necessary work of decolonising our minds and our political vision so that we attend to the 'epistemological foundation to the capitalist and imperial order'[61] that continues to operate and colonise while we are imagining our future. Central to this task is the recognition that the project of Western modernity, which has been a key element of colonising projects, is 'both a structure of power, and a mode of power'.[62] As Gennaro Ascione explains,

> As a structure of power, it is an ideology bounded to Western domination and white supremacy. . . . As a mode of power . . . it is implemented by multiple actors and subjectivities that are hierarchically distributed, moved by specific needs, put under determined pressures yet transversally positioned in front of meta-geographical dualisms such as Europe/Others, West/East, North/South, metropolis/colonies.[63]

58 Nelson Maldonado-Torres, 'On the Coloniality of Being: Contributions to the Development of a Concept' (2007) 21(2–3) *Cultural Studies* 240, 243.
59 Gurminder K Bhambra, 'Postcolonial and Decolonial Dialogues' (2014) 17(2) *Postcolonial Studies* 115, 119.
60 Gurminder K Bhambra, 'Postcolonial and Decolonial Dialogues' (2014) 17(2) *Postcolonial Studies* 115, 119.
61 Boaventure de Sousa Santos, João Arriscado Nunes and Maria Paula Meneses, 'Introduction: Opening Up the Canon of Knowledge and Recognition of Difference' in Boaventura de Sousa Santos (ed), *Another Knowledge Is Possible: Beyond Northern Epistemologies* (Verso, 2007) xix.
62 Gennaro Ascione, *Science and the Decolonization of Social Theory: Unthinking Modernity* (Palgrave Macmillan, 2016) 2.
63 Gennaro Ascione, *Science and the Decolonization of Social Theory: Unthinking Modernity* (Palgrave Macmillan, 2016) 2.

Delegitimising epistemological colonial rule attends to both this structure and mode. We can begin attending by emphasising the 'geopolitics of knowledge production'[64] by asking which knowledges we privilege[65] and moving beyond or 'towards different protocols of concept formation whose logic is not entirely inferable from the conceptual archive of the West and its epistemological architecture'.[66]

Although I concur with the view that concepts such as 'sovereignty', 'government', 'nation' and 'territory' are socially constructed, offering some potential for their recuperation and reshaping to meet more liberatory ends, I believe that a key task for decolonial thinkers is to allow ourselves the challenge of a truly radical vision of freedom. Such a vision asks to what extent do we need concepts borrowed or repurposed from the dominant strands of Western political theory to imagine a good collective life? Must we continue to entertain the existence of political entities—like the settler colonial nation state—premised as they are on domination, exclusion and extraction?

Decolonial Invitations

What I hope has come through in the previous section is that a commitment to a truly radical vision of decolonisation—one that takes seriously a rejection of the settler state's ability 'to inaugurate law on lands acquired through colonial settlement'[67]—necessarily contemplates the abolition of not only 'australia' and other settler colonial nation states but also the broader legal, political, economic and social systems that they operate within and by which they are sustained. In this section, I grapple with the implications of such a statement by offering a sketch of my current understanding of what this project entails and requires. I must emphasise that my thoughts continue to develop and evolve; this offering is intended not only as a provocation but also, more importantly, as an invitation, to engage the messy questions that emerge when we begin from a premise that is not rooted in the perpetuation of the colonial legal order.

Decolonisation, like abolition, must be understood as an expansive project of dismantling and building—and, like abolition, both projects occur simultaneously. What must be dismantled is the entirety of the 'totalising apparatus of state power'[68] that 'order[s] the relationships between particular

64 Walter Mignolo, *Local Histories/Global Designs: Coloniality, Subaltern Knowledges, and Border Thinking* (Princeton University Press, 2012) 89.

65 Margaret Kovach, *Indigenous Methodologies: Characteristics, Conversations, and Contexts* (University of Toronto Press, 2009) 75.

66 Ascione (n 62) 2.

67 Pasternak (n 5).

68 Monaghan (n 1) 31.

peoples, land, the "natural world", and civilisation'.[69] What must be built is the more contested question—indeed, it is perhaps the perennial question of a Left often preoccupied with the distinctions to be made among anarchist, communist and socialist models. Rather than engage this particular conversation in the limited space that remains, we can begin by dismantling and building at the locations that have been identified as sites of colonial, imperial and capitalist power—and that the building, at these sites, should begin in line with our collective desires.[70]

I want to distinguish the argument that I am making here from the variants of Indigenous political thought that are expressed in terms of an 'absolute Indigenous sovereignty' and premised on the cultivation of a 'scepticism of all things related to the Australian state viewed as illegitimate'.[71] The case that I am making here is not concerned with legitimacy and indeed goes further by asking us to consider whether the form of the nation state could survive the tearing down of all colonial structures. I think not. This is not a politics rooted in refusal but in a vision of a free life beyond the constraints imposed by Westphalian sovereignty.

To speak plainly, in a decolonial future, the political categories of 'Indigenous' and 'settler' should no longer exist because the structures that produce these categories will not exist. The dismantling of these structures requires a global decoloniality that would amount to a radically reconceptualised and reconfigured world. This vision—including its anarchic distaste for borders, the state and capitalism—flows naturally from the lessons that I have been taught about kinship and Country and our obligations to do life-sustaining work. That is, this vision emerges directly from an Indigenous epistemology, ontology and axiology. In saying this, I know that I am privileged to have been nurtured in ways not premised on domination and alienation but rather in ways that recognised our fundamental enmeshment with one another and all things. It is precisely this expansive understanding of our relationships that we cannot afford to lose through our participation in legal training and practice.

Colonialism—and through it, capitalism—structures our lives at every level. From the local, intimate and interpersonal to the national and international,

69 Eve Tuck and K Wayne Yang, 'Decolonization Is Not a Metaphor' (2012) 1(1) *Decolonization: Indigeneity, Education & Society* 1, 21.

70 Here, I am invoking Eve Tuck's plea for 'desire-based research' in Eve Tuck, 'Suspending Damage: A Letter to Communities' (2009) 79(3) *Harvard Educational Review* 409 and the injunction of Curley et al. to 'envision futures that account for everyday experiences and desires of Black and Indigenous peoples' in Andrew Curley et al., 'Decolonisation Is a Political Project: Overcoming Impasses between Indigenous Sovereignty and Abolition' (2022) 54(4) *Antipode* 1043, 1045.

71 Eddie Synot, 'Arresting the Tide of History: The Uluru Statement from the Heart', *TWAILR: Reflections #13* (29 January 2020) <https://twailr.com/arresting-the-tide-of-history-the-uluru-statement-from-the-heart/>.

the possibilities of our lives are determined by these overarching structures. Decolonisation, as I have said, is a political struggle over the 'fundamental questions of jurisdiction, sovereignty, and authority'[72] at each site where colonial and capitalist power occurs and is reproduced. From this, decolonisation is clearly, of necessity, connected to all struggles against imperialism, colonialism and capitalism, and serious consideration needs to be given to coalition building and the opening of intellectual and political pathways between Indigenous peoples and other radical actors. I do not believe that Indigenous sovereignty is ceded or abandoned when we imagine our future as enmeshed with the futures and freedoms of all other people. Rather, I believe that our sovereignty will be realised in tandem with the collective liberation of all people, animals and the planet from colonial and capitalist structures and that this requires more than the mere excavation of Indigenous jurisdictions that coexist with the systems and structures responsible for our dispossession and subjugation.

72 Monaghan (n 1) 30.

3

EVIDENCE GIVEN BY EDDIE CUBILLO TO THE YOORROOK JUSTICE COMMISSION

Eddie Cubillo and Jaynaya Dwyer

Introduction

Eddie Cubillo is a descendant of the Larrakia, Wadjigan and Central Arrente peoples. Dr Cubillo is recognised nationally and internationally for his experience and expertise in Indigenous governance and justice service delivery to First Nations Peoples. He is Director of the Indigenous Law and Justice Hub at Melbourne Law School. Dr Cubillo was Associate Dean of Indigenous Programs at Melbourne Law School beginning in 2020. He resigned in 2023 due to racism and a lack of cultural safety within the faculty. This chapter is an abridged version of his evidence given to the Yoorrook Justice Commission in its public hearings on the criminal justice system. The original outline of evidence can be accessed online through the Yoorrook Justice Commission website.[1]

The Need for Action

It is frustrating that no one seems to be listening to the recommendations made by previous royal commissions and inquiries relating to First Nations justice. Yoorrook needs to be different. It is critical not only to build a rapport with the affected communities before expecting people to provide sensitive testimony about these issues again but also to follow through with action. This has happened multiple times. But no one listens.

1 Dr Eddie Cubillo, 'Outline of Evidence of Dr Eddie Cubillo', *Yoorrook Justice Commission* (Outline of evidence, 15 December 2022) <https://yoorrookjusticecommission.org.au/public-hearing/public-hearings-12-to-16-december-2022/#evidence-container>. For a video recording of this evidence, see https://yoorrookjusticecommission.org.au/video/criminal-justice-system-hearing-day-8/.

DOI: 10.4324/9781003473404-4

I have previously written on the toll of successive inquiries on Indigenous people:

> I have thought long and hard about whether this practice of appointing bodies and then ignoring them is a deliberate strategy of distraction, designed to keep our people occupied and engaged with these serious problems, but always kicking a response down the road to some future government. Our human and material resources are already stretched thin. The demands made of us by these inquiries, especially on those who are already suffering, would only be worth it if they generated concrete action and meaningful system change. So far, they have not. They have resulted in a rehash and rewrite of recommendations and themes that have been emphasised and repeated in all these past inquiries.[2]

In the Royal Commission into Aboriginal Deaths in Custody ('RCIADIC') from 1987 to 1991, there is a whole chapter on racism in the report.[3] Very few people have read it. It examines all of the underpinning issues that affect our people and drive them into the criminal justice system. When revisiting these recommendations, we see that they have all been repeated many times by other inquiries but not implemented. There have been at least 500 First Nations deaths in custody since the RCIADIC handed down its final report in 1991.[4]

This inaction has even occurred as recently as the Australian Law Reform Commission report, *Pathways to Justice—Inquiry into the Incarceration Rate of Aboriginal and Torres Strait Islander Peoples*, from 2017.[5] This report has not been responded to or implemented by the current or former government.[6] It is quite current, and no one is even looking at it or implementing it. It has 35 recommendations designed to reduce the disproportionate rate of incarceration of Aboriginal and Torres Strait Islander people and improve community safety. There are more recommendations regarding State and Territory inquiries around children, education and the justice system. Many of the resulting reports have never been seen in the community or taken up by governments.

2 Eddie Cubillo, '30th Anniversary of the RCIADIC and the "White Noise" of the Justice System Is Loud and Clear' (2021) 46(3) *Alternative Law Journal* 185, 187.

3 *Royal Commission into Aboriginal Deaths in Custody* (Final Report, April 1991), vol 2, ch 12. See also vol 4, ch 28 <https://www.austlii.edu.au/au/other/IndigLRes/rciadic/national/vol4/>.

4 'Deaths in Custody in Australia', *Australian Institute of Criminology* (Real-Time Dashboard, 2024) <www.aic.gov.au/statistics/deaths-custody-australia>.

5 Australian Law Reform Commission, *Pathways to Justice—Inquiry into the Incarceration Rate of Aboriginal and Torres Strait Islander People* (Report No 133, December 2017) <https://www.alrc.gov.au/publication/pathways-to-justice-inquiry-into-the-incarceration-rate-of-aboriginal-and-torres-strait-islander-peoples-alrc-report-133/>.

6 See Law Council of Australia, 'Time for a Government Response to Pathways to Justice Report' (Media Release, 25 March 2021), noting that the lack of response has continued to the time of publication of this text in 2024.

We are always talking about these things and giving evidence, and no one listens. Governments act as though the inquiry itself *is* the action addressing these systemic issues rather than a preliminary exercise to inform evidence-based action. It is an indictment, and it is a 'kick the can down the road' exercise to keep Indigenous people happy. Everyone gets involved in royal commissions, and people hope for things to come out of them; but we have told these stories before, and no one listens.

This takes a real toll on Aboriginal people involved with these royal commissions and inquiries. I worked on the Don Dale Royal Commission as Director of Community Engagement. It was the job of the Don Dale Royal Commission to uncover where the systems had failed and make recommendations on how to improve the situation in the Northern Territory 'to provide a safer future for our children'.[7] We had a really short time period to act. We had six months initially, which was not even enough time to pull together staff, and it did not allow us to get the best people.

After the Don Dale Royal Commission and despite our recommendations, the government went the other way and introduced changes so that kids on the streets after certain hours would be taken away from their families.[8] We had just given them these recommendations on a silver platter—and we just got more punitive measures. Why do these processes and inquiries invest so much time, energy and money (and re-create the trauma for those involved) if the Government continually responds with more punitive measures?

Very few of our recommendations were implemented.[9] They even changed the bail and sentencing laws to make them harsher straightaway after the Don Dale Royal Commission.[10] Ultimately, the whole issue hinges on the political vote. The public thinks that 'tough on crime' works, even though the research and statistics tell us that this is not the case. Once you become incarcerated, you come out the other side and graduate to being a better criminal. We have been making these recommendations for 32 years, and something needs to change.

7 'The Protection and Detention of Children in the Northern Territory', *Royal Commissions* (Web Page) <www.royalcommission.gov.au/child-detention>.

8 Thalia Anthony and Eddie Cubillo, 'NT Laws Reproduce Carceral Politics Governing Aboriginal Children', *Arena* (8 April 2021) <https://arena.org.au/nt-laws-reproduce-carceral-politics-governing-aboriginal-children/>.

9 For information about the findings and recommendations of the Don Dale Royal Commission, see *Royal Commission and Board of Inquiry into the Protection and Detention of Children in the Northern Territory* (Final Report, November 2017) vol 1 <https://www.royalcommission.gov.au/child-detention>.

10 National Aboriginal and Torres Strait Islander Legal Service, 'Punitive New Bail Laws Have Already Led to Spike in Youth Custody Numbers' (Media Release, 24 June 2021) <www.natsils.org.au/wp-content/uploads/2021/06/NATSILS-Media-Release-N.T-Youth-Justice-Reforms.pdf>.

The Experiences of Indigenous Advocates

The work that Aboriginal people do as advocates takes a personal toll on us. It is difficult working towards change in a system that is so stacked against us. People do not appreciate the sacrifices made or the emotional toll of the work. We hear stories that cannot be unheard that often trigger our own trauma from our personal experiences.[11]

I have survived my advocacy work, but I am scarred. While working on the Don Dale Royal Commission, I saw the intrusion of these policies that continue to disrespect our values, our people and our culture that do not allow our people and our culture to address the problems that we know how to deal with.

After returning to the Northern Territory for the first time after participating in the Don Dale Royal Commission, I was treated with hostility by Indigenous people who did not see any indication of real positive change as a result of the Don Dale Royal Commission's investigation. Within hours of being home, I was confronted, subjected to obscenities and physically threatened in relation to my role on the Commission.[12]

Royal commissions have a considerable mental health impact on their staff. On the Don Dale Royal Commission, we were provided with counselling on the job, but you do not necessarily need it then because you are surrounded by people and debriefing with colleagues all of the time. When you are gone, you no longer get this support. You are in your family home, and no one understands what you have heard and what you know. My experience was that I needed psychological assistance after the Royal Commission was over, but I was told that this assistance was no longer provided. Former Commissioner Mick Gooda lobbied on my behalf to get further coverage. But by the time they got back to me with an answer, I had already engaged with my Aboriginal medical service, which provided me with assistance.

Indigenous people have a lot at stake when participating in this sort of advocacy. We have enormous responsibilities to our families, extended families and communities. It is not a game for us. It is our families' and our kids' lives that are at stake. Our people keep hearing promises, but these promises have not led to real change. This needs to come across in the recommendations made to government—namely, that it is important to implement and act on Yoorrook's recommendations and that implementation needs to be bipartisan.

11 Eddie Cubillo, 'On the Personal Toll for Indigenous Advocates and People When Governments Fail to Act', *Croakey Health Media* (online, 18 June 2018) <www.croakey.org/on-the-personal-toll-for-indigenous-advocates-and-people-when-governments-fail-to-act/>.

12 Eddie Cubillo, 'On the Personal Toll for Indigenous Advocates and People When Governments Fail to Act', *Croakey Health Media* (online, 18 June 2018) <www.croakey.org/on-the-personal-toll-for-indigenous-advocates-and-people-when-governments-fail-to-act/>.

The Racism in the Legal System

I have been impacted by trauma, colonisation and systemic racism. As an Indigenous person with white-settler law qualifications, I have heard in academic and legal institutions how the law is supposedly fair and just. This does not resemble what I have experienced in my own life. I have seen from experience in my personal life and on the Don Dale Royal Commission how unconscious bias plays a substantial role in impacting outcomes for Aboriginal people in the white-settler system. In the following, I share some stories of bias that I have personally experienced in the legal system to demonstrate that my qualifications and position do not protect me from blatant racism.

When I started as a lawyer in the Northern Territory, the first day that I arrived in court to represent clients, the court orderly asked me to move from where I was sitting to sit 'behind my lawyer'. She assumed, based on my appearance, that I must have been a client rather than a lawyer. I told her that I was the lawyer. A short while later, another orderly came over and asked me the same thing.

Twenty-two years later, the same thing happened at the Don Dale Royal Commission. I was sitting in court with another Indigenous lawyer. I told him that the court orderly was going to come over and ask if we are in the right place. Sure enough, the orderly came over a short time later to ask if 'we're on the list' and if we are in the right courtroom. My colleague showed them their Royal Commission ID, and we walked out laughing. Humor is the only way that we can cope with these things. We are angry and hurt, but it is so constant that you cannot do anything but laugh. How do we obtain justice when we are already judged based on the colour of our skin?

In my role as Associate Dean of Indigenous Programs at the Law School at The University of Melbourne, I was moving some boxes to a different office within the faculty. On my third run, a student asked me to come and clean up his coffee that had spilled. He thought that I was a cleaner based on my appearance and that I was carrying boxes. It happens all of the time—people will follow me on campus asking what I am doing there. It is difficult to accept the racism at the university. It is like a betrayal, working with a curriculum with such silence and omissions. Even worse is knowing that it will affect our students and that the students will carry it into their actions in the profession, perpetuating cultures of legal institutions that harm Aboriginal people.

Recently, I was pulled over by the police while driving in a wealthy eastern suburb of Melbourne. I have heard this described as the offence of 'driving while black'.[13] The police searched my car while I was sitting on the sidewalk

13 'Driving while black' is a slang term that refers to incidents of police racially profiling drivers of motor vehicles, implying that the driver's race is the primary reason for the stop. See Tamar Hopkins, 'Racial Profiling in Contemporary Australian Policing' (2020) 161 *Precedent* 4.

in the rain. During the search, they asked me what I was doing in this suburb and asked me how I afforded my car. I would have challenged the police officers' behaviour if I had not had the experiences that I have had. I know that, as a black man, you have to act a certain way to protect your safety. Throughout this ordeal, my anxiety was really high, even though I knew I had done nothing wrong.

These individuals' biases and decision-making mean that policies and laws affect Aboriginal people differently than the non-Aboriginal population. Aboriginal people are overrepresented in all areas of the criminal justice system. Our women are the fastest growing proportion of incarcerated people.[14] This has a particular impact on our family dynamics—men have been incarcerated for so long, and the women have been at home looking after the family unit. What happens now when our women are also being locked up?

The trial of Zachary Rolfe marked a historic moment in accountability for Aboriginal deaths in custody. Former Northern Territory police officer Zachary Rolfe was charged with murder, manslaughter and engaging in a violent act causing death for shooting 19-year-old Warlpiri man Kumanjayi Walker while on duty in the remote community of Yuendumu in November 2019. This was the first case of a police officer facing a murder trial for an Aboriginal death in custody in the Northern Territory since the RCIADIC.[15] When Rolfe was found not guilty of murder and other charges by an all-white jury, no Indigenous person thought that there would be a different result.

I attended the coronial inquest into Kumanjayi Walker's death[16] in Alice Springs to observe police officers giving evidence. The police officers basically all said that they had never heard or observed any racism in their workplace. But I also saw a police officer break ranks and give evidence about racism in the police force. The Police Commission told this officer that they would no longer represent him and that he would have to find his own lawyer. The blue line was really apparent with the police.[17]

14 Deirdre Howard-Wagner and Chay Brown, 'Increased Incarceration of First Nations Women Is Interwoven with the Experience of Violence and Trauma', *The Conversation* (online, 6 August 2021) <https://theconversation.com/increased-incarceration-of-first-nations-women-is-interwoven-with-the-experience-of-violence-and-trauma-164773>.

15 Thalia Anthony and Eddie Cubillo, 'Kumanjayi Walker Murder Trial Will Be a First in NT for an Indigenous Death in Custody. Why Has It Taken So Long?', *The Conversation* (online, 28 October 2020) <https://theconversation.com/kumanjayi-walker-murder-trial-will-be-a-first-in-nt-for-an-indigenous-death-in-custody-why-has-it-taken-so-long-148922>.

16 For further information on this case, see 'Kumanjayi Walker Coronial Inquest', *Department of the Attorney General and Justice, Northern Territory Government* (Web Page) <https://justice.nt.gov.au/attorney-general-and-justice/courts/inquests-findings/kumanjayi-walker>.

17 'Blue line' or 'thin blue line' refers to the code of silence among police officers and the tactics used to discourage individuals from whistleblowing or speaking out against the corruption and misconduct of other officers: Ann C Hodges and Justin Pugh, 'Crossing the Thin Blue Line: Protecting Law Enforcement Officers Who Blow the Whistle' (2020) 52(1) *UC Davis Law Review Online*.

At the part of the inquest that I attended, the majority of Indigenous people present did not enter the courtroom. I believe that this was because of the large police presence observing the proceedings. Instead, Indigenous people stayed in the park outside and waited for updates. There were, however, a lot of positives about how the inquest was run. The counsel assisting the coroner, Peggy Dwyer, did a good job engaging with Aboriginal people and preparing witnesses to tell their stories. Time was not wasted, and people were not left waiting for long. There was a unique Welcome to Country that provided an in-depth depiction of the Larrakia People and our lands.

The fact is, if you lock up vulnerable people, especially in a biased system, then the risk of a tragic death in custody increases.[18] If we want to reduce the number of Aboriginal deaths in custody, then we need to reduce the rates at which Aboriginal people are taken into custody. This was at the core of the recommendations from the RCIADIC. Custody should be used as a last resort, for the most serious situations, and only where necessary.

The Importance of Culture

Culture and kinship are strengths that help us survive these types of things. My parents separated when I was one. We lived with extended family. This enriched my cultural life and therefore supported my wellbeing. This arrangement is not afforded to our people in the same way anymore; we do not get to rely on kinship. We have people evaluating our home lives and what is 'best' or 'most suitable' for us. If it was not for staying with family, then I never would have survived the breakdown of my immediate family. It is traumatising each time that a family breakdown happens, but I was nurtured and guided by my cultural kinship practices, and my uncles took care of me.

Changing Curricula and Accreditation Standards

I am an academic staff member at the most prestigious law school in Australia. Four prime ministers and 14 High Court justices came out of this law school. It troubles me that most graduates have no understanding about Indigenous law. The reality is that there is no *real* push in the profession for systemic change. We have students coming out of sandstone universities who will become leaders. They need to have an understanding of Aboriginal issues.

When I was in New Zealand recently, I met university deans who spoke Te Reo Māori without blinking an eye. There is real Māori immersion in New Zealand throughout their curricula—there is an acceptance that Māori are

18 Eddie Cubillo, 'Aboriginal Deaths in Custody: NT's "Paperless Arrest" Police Powers Need Urgent Review', *Sydney Morning Herald* (online, 31 May 2015) <www.smh.com.au/opinion/aboriginal-deaths-in-custody-nts-paperless-arrest-police-powers-need-urgent-review-20150531-ghdf8u.html>.

Traditional Owners. They are a long way ahead of us. Furthermore, the regulator of legal curricula in New Zealand recently announced the introduction of a requirement that all law schools teach Tikanga Māori.

We get great turnout at our events at the Indigenous Law and Justice Hub at Melbourne Law School, and students have great engagement in our classes. Our students are eager to learn about First Peoples in Australia, but we are not giving them the information that they need to work effectively alongside Indigenous people in the justice system. Our profession must accept that we need continuous education on these issues. Our position is that, in the context of the small number of Indigenous academics, all teaching staff have a responsibility to teach Indigenous content proficiently, and we as an institution need to support teaching staff to accomplish this.

My experience is that in universities, we teach the law, but we do not teach the reality of the law much of the time. Additionally, my experience is that some teachers bring biases into the classroom. Their omissions and narratives dictate how they frame their subjects. By the time that the students get into practice, I fear that they will have it ingrained in their heads that Indigenous people are problematic and that they are trouble—not that they carry intergenerational trauma or have complex needs.

In December 2020, the Council of Australian Law Deans ('CALD') released a statement condemning the systemic discrimination that permeates the Australian legal system with respect to First Nations peoples.[19] The Council acknowledged the role that Australian legal education has played in supporting the law's systemic discrimination and structural bias against First Nations peoples. It called on all Australian law schools to work in partnership with First Nations peoples to give priority to the creation of culturally competent and culturally safe courses and programs.

Part of the problem is the regulation of legal education. In the Priestley 11,[20] which are the required core subjects to complete a law degree in Australia, not one of these subjects is Indigenous, and no content is required to be delivered through an Indigenous lens. As a result, many students study law for three or four years without being taught how the law systemically impacts First Nations peoples. The curriculum is racist, and it needs to change.[21] At

19 Council of Australian Law Deans, 'CALD Statement on Australian Law's Systemic Discrimination and Structural Bias Against First Nations Peoples' (3 December 2020) <https://cald.asn.au/blog/2020/12/03/cald-statement-on-australian-laws-systemic-discrimination-and-structural-bias-against-first-nations-peoples/>.

20 Law Admissions Consultative Committee, *Prescribed Academic Areas of Knowledge* (Law Admissions Committee, 2016).

21 Eddie Cubillo, 'Education: Indigenous Programs at Law School', *Law Institute Journal* (online, July 2022) <www.liv.asn.au/Web/Law_Institute_Journal_and_News/Web/LIJ/Year/2022/07July/Education__Indigenous_programs_at_law_school.aspx>.

Melbourne Law School, I am involved in a curriculum review that seeks to incorporate Indigenous content into the Juris Doctor. First, we approached Legal Method and Reasoning, a 10-day crash course on legal principles that all first-year students take. We have 'Indigenised' this subject and received a lot of good feedback. Now, we are focusing on the Priestley 11 so that students can get a glimpse of the predicaments of Indigenous people in this country. We have a small grant to 'train the trainer' in the law school on delivering Indigenous content, acknowledging that teaching staff need support to implement these changes.

We are also developing new elective subjects, including on-Country learning experiences for law students to enhance their understanding of First Nations peoples and the law.[22] Our aim is to ensure that all students have a baseline understanding of Indigenous experiences with the law and the skills for working safely with Indigenous clients while also providing opportunities for in-depth learning through specialisation.

I recommend that the CALD adopt a 12th Priestley unit on Indigenous history and law. I recommend something aligned with the call to action 28 of the Canadian Truth and Justice Commission:

> We call upon law schools in Canada to require all law students to take a course in Aboriginal people and the law, which includes the history and legacy of residential schools, the United Nations Declaration on the Rights of Indigenous Peoples, Treaties and Aboriginal rights, Indigenous law, and Aboriginal—Crown relations. This will require skills-based training in intercultural competency, conflict resolution, human rights, and antiracism.[23]

In line with the Canadian Truth and Justice Commission call to action 27,[24] I also recommend that lawyers be supported to work with Indigenous people through ongoing training and accreditation post-admission. As explained by Sandra Shutt, calls to action 27 and 28 show that 'there are substantive elements of the story of indigenous-settler relations that are essential for understanding what it means to be a legal advocate, law student, or lawyer today, and that gaps in existing knowledge have caused harm'.[25]

22 For information on one such subject, see 'Access to Justice on Country LAWS90257', *The University of Melbourne Handbook* (Web Page) <https://handbook.unimelb.edu.au/2023/subjects/laws90257>.

23 Truth and Reconciliation Commission of Canada, *Calls to Action* (2015) 3.

24 Truth and Reconciliation Commission of Canada, *Calls to Action* (2015) 3.

25 Sandra Shutt, 'TRC Offers a Window of Opportunity for Legal Education', *Canadian Lawyer* (15 June 2015) <https://www.canadianlawyermag.com/news/general/trc-offers-a-window-of-opportunity-for-legal-education/269823>.

I do not believe that there is appropriate regulatory incentive or market availability of ongoing professional development education concerning cultural capability and cultural safety for lawyers who work with Aboriginal and Torres Strait Islander people. This is a barrier to effective access to justice for Indigenous Victorians and is unsafe.

When New South Wales Legal Aid was led by Brendan Thomas, an Indigenous man, if you wanted to work there as a panel firm,[26] then you needed to have Indigenous accreditation, and they conducted evaluations and surveys with clients about how clients rated their practitioner. This accreditation and evaluation requirement should be mandated everywhere for lawyers working with Aboriginal people.

I was at the Australian Institute of Aboriginal and Torres Strait Islander Studies ('AIATSIS') conference in Queensland this year, and I heard two retired native title judges say that they did not have appropriate knowledge of Indigenous people when they were appointed as judges and that they were still learning towards the end of their tenure. Hearing this bolstered my determination that things need to change.

Solutions and Reforms

Australian people should have an understanding of the trauma that continues to affect Aboriginal people. These traumas and stories and the hiding from police will continue to happen until we see proper change. We need to start with this early in our education systems and carry it through to institutions such as universities. In Darwin, if you get on a plane and leave for the hospital, then people think that you are going there to die because you do not come back. These are real stories and experiences for our mob, our community. We need the broader public to understand these experiences and to get over the systemic and unconscious bias against our people. Many of us mob who take on the toll of working in Indigenous advocacy say the same thing in terms of asking other Australians to stand with us.

When the Northern Territory Government changed its bail and sentencing laws,[27] we wrote to them and said that this went against the recommendations from the Don Dale Royal Commission. We spoke to one local member at the time who had once supported us but voted for these changes anyway, and she replied that she listened to her constituents. She was worried about keeping her seat. This was really disappointing—we will not get anywhere

26 A panel firm is a legal service provider that contracts to provide legal services to legal aid clients.

27 National Aboriginal and Torres Strait Islander Legal Service (n 10).

until the wider public has a sympathetic view that Aboriginal people are not getting a fair opportunity in the justice system. We are only 3 per cent of the population, so we are not an impactful voting group. We rely on the public to keep government accountable.

The public wants to see 'tough on crime', but they do not understand that locking people up does not make them any safer. Our politicians do not understand this either. If we really want to make change, then this needs to be better understood. Biases and structural racism need to be accounted for. We all have them.

When we have new governments, we do not have a new bureaucracy. The people in it make the same racist decisions. The same people decide whether we get a welfare card or if our kids stay in our homes or not. This is where the issues are—the same people write the policies.

Accreditation

I would like to see it come from Yoorrook's recommendations that people working in the justice system need to understand Indigenous law and lore and have basic competencies and understanding to work safely with Indigenous people. The accreditation or continued professional development needs to be ongoing. Judges who work with Indigenous people also need this. This was the recommendation from the Canadian truth-telling commission.[28] If we get started in Victoria, then we can provide something for the rest of the country to emulate.

Reimagining Goals and Policies

Currently, the reality of the criminal justice system centres around control, coercion and punishment. A reimagined system would be more reformative and focused on rehabilitation by looking at the trauma and the factors that contribute to the behaviour in question.

If you can get rid of the recent bail and sentencing reforms and raise the age of criminal responsibility,[29] then changes will happen right away. There also need to be other options around sentencing—mandatory sentencing has impacted the independence of judges, and the separation of powers has been breached.

28 Truth and Reconciliation Commission of Canada (n 23).

29 In Australia, children as young as 10 years can be arrested, charged with criminal offences, detained and incarcerated. The Raise the Age Campaign is pushing for federal, state and territory governments to raise the age of criminal responsibility to at least 14 years old. See the Raise the Age Campaign website: <https://raisetheage.org.au/>.

Indigenous Legal Services

We need to appropriately fund Aboriginal and Torres Strait Islander Legal Services to enable access to justice for Indigenous people. The 'tough on crime' approach in Australia increases the work for Indigenous legal services, and they are not being provided with enough funding to manage the workload.[30] Aboriginal Legal Services are the most culturally safe place for Aboriginal people to go to, but there is very limited funding. Government policy has seen these services moved away from being community-controlled and pushed towards adopting standard corporate governance structures.

Treaty

With frameworks, the government can consider what it is willing to negotiate and relinquish in a treaty. But Indigenous people cannot accept an obligation that alleviates the government of its responsibilities.

The treaty should be a living document that is flexible enough to achieve the best outcomes for everyone. It can help build a respectful relationship between government and Indigenous people, as Indigenous voices need to be heard at every level. For better outcomes, we need to move to genuine self-determination and shift decision-making power to First Peoples. To help our people avoid the criminal justice and child protection systems, we need to address disadvantage, discrimination and disempowerment by improving outcomes in health, education, housing and employment. Change will happen when First Peoples are in control. The re-design of these systems must be part of the statewide treaty negotiations. First Nations peoples should be designing the systems that affect them.

The Victorian Government should make investments now to support First Peoples and experts to begin thinking about the redesign of these failing systems. This could be accomplished by resourcing the First Peoples' Assembly to work with Aboriginal community-controlled organisations[31] and their communities to develop aspirations and priorities to shift decision-making power to First Nations peoples.

30 Giovanni Torre, 'Funding Crisis Sees Aboriginal Legal Service Freeze Operations at 13 New South Wales Courts', *National Indigenous Times* (online, 15 May 2023) <https://nit.com.au/15-05-2023/5966/funding-crisis-sees-aboriginal-legal-service-freeze-operations-at-13-new-south-wales-courts>. See also Edward Cubillo, *What Does "Self-Determination" Mean in the Context of Legal Service Provision for Aboriginal and Torres Strait Islander Legal Services (ATSILS)?* (PhD Thesis, 2021) <https://opus.lib.uts.edu.au/handle/10453/156115>.

31 Aboriginal community-controlled organisations ('ACCOs') are incorporated bodies led by Aboriginal and Torres Strait Islander people, most often for the purpose of service provision to communities.

Recognition of Indigenous Laws

Aboriginal people have law that is not recognised as law or embraced as a source of meaningful justice in Australia. In my recent travels to New Zealand, I saw how Tikanga (which is Māori law and customary practices) is increasingly being incorporated into the common law and addressed by courts.[32] The Waitangi Tribunal has a broad scope in New Zealand to make findings and recommendations on historical and contemporary breaches of the treaty with First Nations people, including in relation to Tikanga. We are far from this in Australia. We need more writing from our people on legal pluralism models to enable the recognition of Indigenous laws and, if appropriate, some of its integration into the legal system.

The common law in Australia is meant to be flexible and reflect our communities' values. It should be able to evolve to accommodate the presence of Indigenous legal systems. Importantly, this needs to be conducted in a way that does not deny the validity of the law and culture that has evolved since first contact, as the current legal system so often does. Urban blackfellas have their cultural beliefs, practices and identities. It has been taught in history that the real blackfellas are those running around in underpants with a spear. But no culture is stagnant. Indigenous people have been adapting for years, and yet whitefellas expect us to stay the same.

The Need for Action

The Yoorrrook Justice Commission is the first formal truth-telling process concerning historical and ongoing injustices experienced by First Peoples in Victoria. Truth telling has long been acknowledged as a crucial component of the treaty process, and Aboriginal Victorians have called upon successive governments to establish a formal truth-telling entity for generations.

The Victorian Government committed to working towards a treaty in 2016 and passed the *Advancing Treaty Process with Aboriginal Victorians Act 2018* (Vic). In partnership with the First Peoples' Assembly of Victoria,[33] the Victorian Government established Yoorrook in 2021 to facilitate that truth-telling process.

The aims of Yoorrook are to establish an official public record of the impact of colonisation on First Peoples in Victoria; develop a shared understanding among all Victorians on the impact of colonisation and the diversity, strength and resilience of First Peoples' cultures; and make recommendations not only for healing, system reform and practical changes to laws, policy and

32 See *Peter Hugh McGregor Ellis v The King* [2022] NZSC 144.

33 The First Peoples' Assembly of Victoria is an independent representative body established to represent Traditional Owners of Country and Aboriginal and Torres Strait Islander peoples in Victoria on the pathway to a treaty in Victoria.

education but also for matters to be included in future treaties.[34] The Yoorrook Justice Commission has also set out to adopt culturally appropriate, trauma-informed, First Peoples-centred methods of information gathering in working towards these aims.

People have invested in telling their stories, but no one is told what the outcomes are. I have seen this happen before—but it should not happen. If you are lucky and have a laptop and wifi, then you might be able to download it. My hardcopies of reports of commissions of inquiry are like a doorstop—no one uses them. Communications need to be introduced in a way that is relevant and accessible. There needs to be follow-through and investment in the communication of recommendations to communities. Communities need to know what the recommendations are and any commitments by the government to implement them.

34 'What Will Yoorrook Do? Frequently Asked Questions', *Yoorrook Justice Commission* (Web Page) <https://yoorrookjusticecommission.org.au/faqs/>.

4

THE SHACKLES OF TERRA NULLIUS IN CHILD PROTECTION 'REFORMS'

Terri Libesman, Paul Gray and Kirsten Gray

Introduction

In this chapter, we examine the distribution of power across state child protection decision-making, which enables state actors to earnestly pursue 'reforms' to improve outcomes for First Nations children while simultaneously administering institutions that justify the perpetuation of trauma. We argue that the systemic violence of state child protection systems is thereby masked in good intentions, while First Nations families remain subject to powers that relentlessly inflict harm. We unpack aspects of the vast differences in perception and experience of procedural and substantive justice between First Nations and non-Indigenous institutional parties in child protection decision-making. Our commentary draws on examples from New South Wales, given our proximity to and deeper experience in this jurisdiction, as illustrative of the broader structural challenges underpinning the continued call of First Nations for system transformation in all jurisdictions.

In investigating these differences, we address three themes. The first is the alienation of First Nations families and communities from child protection systems and their common experience of such systems as violent.[1] This is despite the 'achievement' of law reforms, resulting from tireless First Nations-led advocacy over an extended period, which provide for participatory and procedural rights.[2] This theme of reform without change reveals

1 *After the Apology* (Pursekey Productions Pty Ltd, 2017).
2 Terri Libesman and Kylie Cripps, 'Aboriginal and Torres Strait Islander Children's Welfare and Well-Being' in Lisa Young, Mary Kenny and Geoffrey Monahan (eds), *Children and the Law in Australia* (LexisNexis Butterworths, 2nd ed, 2017) 308.

DOI: 10.4324/9781003473404-5

deep-seated colonial values that resist transformational change. We suggest that the ongoing foundational legal concept *terra nullius* remains unresolved post *Mabo v State of Queensland [No 2]* ('Mabo No 2')[3] and stymies effective child protection reforms.

One of the factors that makes state child welfare systems resistant to change is the inherent, yet unacknowledged, whiteness[4] that underpins such institutions, including children's courts where many child protection decisions are made. The second theme that we explore is how colonial perspectives are structurally prioritised when making decisions about the lives of First Nations children and young people and furthermore, why state child protection systems are resistant to change. 'Reforms' presented as strengthening procedural protections in individual matters either remain unimplemented or are revealed as reproducing the structures that have underpinned protectionist and assimilationist policies, privileging colonial perspectives in decisions about First Nations children.

The third and final theme that we address is the necessity of moving beyond piecemeal reforms to state child protection and court structures, with their focus on procedural justice, to reforms that offer transformational change. We propose that effective reforms require the transfer of child protection powers from state institutions to First Nations as an expression of their inalienable collective interest in their children's futures and their inherent authority to determine these futures free from the interference of the state.[5] This is necessary to attain legitimate and effective child protection authority and relatedly, institutions for First Nations families and communities.

Failed Cycles of Review and Reform

The findings from child protection research, reviews and inquiries since *Bringing Them Home*[6] provide consistent evidence of the importance of First Nations' self-determination in child protection law, policy, services and decision-making.[7] Equally consistent is evidence of the failure to enact recommendations from prior inquiries and where reforms have been enacted, of

3 *Mabo v State of Queensland [No 2]* [1992] HCA 23.

4 Aileen Moreton-Robinson, *The White Possessive: Property, Power, and Indigenous Sovereignty* (University of Minnesota Press, 2015) 15.

5 Megan Davis, *Family Is Culture: Independent Review of Aboriginal Children and Young People in Out-of-Home Care* (Report, November 2019)) ('*Family is Culture*') <https://dcj.nsw.gov.au/children-and-families/family-is-culture.html>.

6 National Inquiry into the Separation of Aboriginal and Torres Strait Islander Children from their Families, *Bringing Them Home* (Report, 1997) <https://humanrights.gov.au/our-work/projects/bringing-them-home-report-1997>.

7 National Inquiry into the Separation of Aboriginal and Torres Strait Islander Children from their Families, *Bringing Them Home* (Report, 1997) <https://humanrights.gov.au/our-work/projects/bringing-them-home-report-1997>.

the failure to implement these reforms, including legal entitlements.[8] The latter includes longstanding legal rights such as the Aboriginal and Torres Strait Islander Child Placement Principles ('Placement Principles'), including rights to participation in service delivery and child protection decision-making.[9] Community-based reports such as *Family Matters* continue to note the failure of governments to implement these principles in full and the need to strengthen national indicators beyond limited and sometimes misleading placement data.[10]

For example, although reporting has historically conflated placement with family (whether Aboriginal or not) and ongoing connections and enjoyment of culture, *Family Matters* reported that the proportion of Aboriginal children placed with Aboriginal family members declined substantially from 2013 (53.6 per cent) to 2022 (40.7 per cent), with little corresponding data about their enjoyment of cultural connections that underpin identity and resilience.[11] This misrepresents the broad spirit and intent of the Placement Principles for Aboriginal children to remain with their family, for their family and community to be involved in decisions about their lives, and through them, for Aboriginal children to be able to enjoy connections to their Aboriginal community and culture consistent with their rights and developmental needs. There have been proposals to improve the range of indicators to match this broad intent, including the development of a draft set of indicators in 2018, but many indicators are still 'under development'.[12] These failings coincide with enormous levels of increased child protection intervention in First Nations families over the past three decades, which is most pronounced at the most severe intervention: out-of-home care.[13]

This pattern of formal reform without change is illustrated by recent qualitative research that examines the implementation and breach of section 12 of the *Children and Young Person's (Care and Protection) Act 1998* (NSW) ('*Care and Protection Act*'). Section 12 provides for the participation of First

8 Davis (n 5); Teresa Libesman et al., *Aboriginal Participation in Child Protection Decision-Making in New South Wales* (Report, December 2023) ('*Aboriginal Participation in Child Protection Decision-Making*') <https://dcj.nsw.gov.au/children-and-families/family-is-culture.html>.

9 Libesman and Cripps (n 2) 318–26.

10 SNAICC, *Family Matters Report 2023* (2023) 19 ('*Family Matters*'). <https://www.snaicc.org.au/resources/family-matters-report-2023/>

11 SNAICC, *Family Matters Report* 2023 (2023) 19 ('*Family Matters*'). <https://www.snaicc.org.au/resources/family-matters-report-2023/>.

12 'Aboriginal and Torres Strait Islander Child Placement Principles Indicators', *Australian Institute of Health and Welfare* (Web Page, 7 May 2024) <www.aihw.gov.au/reports/child-protection/child-protection-australia-2021-22/contents/indicators/atsicpp-indicators>.

13 SNAICC (n 10) 19. 'Out of home care' refers to situations in which a child is removed from the family home and placed in foster care (where the child is placed with an unrelated foster parent), residential care (where the child is placed in a residential facility) or kinship care (where the child is placed with a trusted relative or community member).

Nations families, kinship groups, communities and community organisations in all significant child protection decision-making.[14] However, the research found routine breaches of section 12 across all stages of child protection intervention in First Nations families' lives.[15]

This research interviewed families, Children's Court magistrates, First Nations and non-Indigenous children's out-of-home care organisations, and care and protection lawyers about their understanding and experiences of section 12. Three key findings were made. First, family members felt largely bewildered and pained by their experiences with the child protection system. Many families felt so alienated and outside the law's protection that they believed state actors could do whatever they wanted and that families had no protection from the state intervening in their lives, including the ultimate power to remove their children.[16] Many reported leaving the Children's Court without knowing what had happened and feeling that their account of events was not heard.[17]

Second, Children's Court magistrates found section 12 'interesting'; despite its decades-long history in legislation, none were familiar with the provision, and none could recall it being used in their courts.[18] The research asked about the participation of Aboriginal organisations and community groups, and again, the magistrates thought that this was an interesting idea but consistently noted that this did not generally occur.[19] All participants observed that usually the parents and sometimes grandparents provided affidavits. The interviewed magistrates largely perceived their courts as fair, with families and the Department having a chance to be heard. They also mostly presented as wanting to make their courts an approachable place for Aboriginal participants.

Third, community organisations reported to the researchers that they seldom if ever participated in the Children's Court decision-making process and were unfamiliar with it. Sometimes, departmental workers consulted with them; some community organisations said that they were consulted numerous times about the same questions but rarely felt that their viewpoint was heard or if it was heard, it was not given weight or even considered in the decision-making.[20]

This research illustrates the disjuncture between the perceptions of non-Indigenous actors within child protection institutions and the First Nations families subject to the power of these institutions. The research

14 *Children and Young Persons (Care and Protection) Act 1998* (NSW) s 12.
15 Libesman et al. (n 8) 107.
16 Libesman et al. (n 8) 71–77.
17 Libesman et al. (n 8) 77–79.
18 Libesman et al. (n 8) 107.
19 Libesman et al. (n 8) 71–77.
20 Libesman et al. (n 8) 71–77.

findings concur with the findings of *Family is Culture*,[21] discussed later in this chapter, which found that misleading and untested evidence resulted in the removal of First Nations children from their families. Although the legitimacy of the child protection system is presumed by non-Indigenous judicial officers and other institutional participants, it lacks legitimacy for many First Nations families and communities.[22] There is a foundational lack of trust in the system.

The Paradox of Reform without Change

The paradox of recognition and non-recognition plays out through reforms that are recited as important but that are then minimised in practice. Reforms such as the participation rights guaranteed by section 12 of the *Care and Protection Act* are not substantially implemented. These reforms are largely procedural, intended to treat First Nations families and communities with greater dignity and respect, and purport to enhance the transparency and impartiality in child protection decision-making. If substantially implemented, then they would make the child protection system less discriminatory and fairer.

Actors within the system perceive child protection decision-making to be about the best interests of individual children, while many First Nations people experience child protection institutions as both individually and collectively discriminatory. That is, they perceive the child protection system as targeting not just them but also their family and community as a system of control.[23] Procedural justice would reduce unfairness, but it would not address the underlying alienation. This requires systemic and structural change.

Systemic and structural changes require that a second, more foundational paradox of inclusion and non-inclusion in child protection be addressed. This is the paradox of the recognition of rights to participation and 'self-determination', with the implicit presumption that these rights will, or even can, be implemented within the existing state child protection framework. Although common ground exists between First Nations and non-Indigenous understandings of care and protection of children—for example, that children must be free from physical, sexual and emotional abuse—there are also considerable differences in the meaning of key concepts

21 Davis (n 5).
22 Terri Libesman and Paul Gray, 'Self-Determination, Public Accountability, and Rituals of Reform in First Peoples Child Welfare' (2023) 18(1) *First Peoples Child and Family Review* 81.
23 Debra Swan and Jen Swan, 'Demanding Change of Colonial Child Protection Systems Through Good Trouble: A Community Based Commentary of Resistance and Advocacy' (2023) 18(1) *First Peoples Child and Family Review* 28.

such as the best interests of the child[24] and the requirements that are necessary to achieve this common goal. These differences reflect cultural values, experiences, and family and community structures that shape the very ways that societies and childhoods are understood and organised. Collectivist First Nations values differ markedly from the presumed whiteness that imbues contemporary state child protection systems. These values are founded in collective community differences.

Contemporary state child protection institutions recognise the need for procedural justice for First Nations families but resist implementing reforms to this end. Overcoming this resistance and inertia is critical to improving First Nations' child protection experiences, but this is not sufficient to achieve justice. Innovations such as the Victorian Koori family hearing day—Marram-Ngala Ganbu—provide an exemplar of how greater procedural justice within non-Indigenous child protection systems can be achieved. Established in 2016, Marram-Ngala Ganbu, which sits in Broadmeadows and Shepparton in the state of Victoria, provides a more supportive and appropriate environment for making child protection decisions with respect to First Nations children and seeks to address many of the elements that create a lack of cultural safety. The participants, who include family, extended family, child protection staff, family support services, lawyers and ACSASS (a Victorian First Nations service),[25] sit at a round table with the Children's Court magistrate. Families are assisted with accessing legal representation and family support services and understanding court proceedings. Proceedings are conducted informally, with fewer cases heard on a court day, which allows more time for matters to be heard. Marram-Ngala Ganbu has seen greater compliance with legal rights, including an increase in First Nations family participation in child protection proceedings, greater compliance with the Aboriginal Child Placement Principles and a more balanced inclusion of First Nations and departmental information, which is essential for optimal judicial decision-making.[26] Despite Marram-Ngala Ganbu's success in enabling a fairer implementation of state child protection laws, it has not been extended since its inception.

Procedural reforms will improve families' experiences in state child protection systems by making them less discriminatory and fairer, but they do not address the foundational *terra nullius* principle within child protection. The transfer of child protection authority to First Nations institutions is necessary to develop child protection services that embed First Nations values.

24 Wendy Hermeston, 'Safe, Protected . . . Connected? The Best Interests of Aboriginal Children and Permanency Planning in the NSW Care and Protection System' (PhD Thesis, University of Technology Sydney, 2021).

25 Lakidjeka—Aboriginal Child Specialist Advice and Support Service ('ACSASS').

26 Kerry Arabena et al., *Evaluation of Marram-Ngala Ganbu* (Report, November 2019) <https://www.childrenscourt.vic.gov.au/file/evaluation-marram-ngala-ganbu>.

Governments have committed to this transfer of authority to Aboriginal communities through *Safe and Supported: The National Framework for Protecting Australia's Children 2021–2031*.[27] However, as we have noted, governments have a poor record when it comes to realising the intent of reforms, particularly where those reforms challenge the authority of state systems over Aboriginal children, families and communities.

Colonial Mindsets in Judicial Institutions

The Australian judicial system is largely presided over by people from non-Indigenous backgrounds. As a system imported from England, this is not surprising, with Australian law imposed on top of enduring First Nations legal systems that have governed social structures on the continent for millennia. In contrast, the relatively recent imposition of western legal systems designed by, built for and exercised by non-Indigenous people in the service of colonisation has produced decisions and shaped knowledge through a prism of legal whiteness. These decisions have had at their heart the destruction of First Nations families, communities and way of life. This continues to be the prevailing experience of First Nations peoples.

The appointment of First Nations judicial officers offers some scope for reducing such alienation. Over the past five years, the number of Aboriginal and Torres Strait Islander people joining courts across the country as either judges or magistrates has been increasing. This includes recent appointments such as Lincoln Crowley to the Supreme Court of Queensland, Louise Taylor to the Supreme Court of the Australian Capital Territory, David Woodroffe to the Local Court in the Northern Territory, Michael Lundberg to the Supreme Court of Western Australia and Nathan Jarro to the District Court of Queensland.[28]

Of course, several First Nations trailblazers took up roles on the bench long before these recent appointments. Local Court Magistrate Patricia O'Shane,

27 Commonwealth of Australia, *Safe and Supported: The National Framework for Protecting Australia's Children 2021–2023* (2021) <www.dss.gov.au/sites/default/files/documents/12_2021/dess5016-national-framework-protecting-childrenaccessible.pdf>.

28 'The Honourable Justice Lincoln Crowley,' *Supreme Court Library Queensland* (Web Page) <www.sclqld.org.au/collections/explore-the-law/judicial-profiles/crowley-200364>; Matt Garrick, 'Decorated Former Lawyer David Woodroffe Formally Sworn in as Northern Territory's First Aboriginal Court Judge,' *ABC News* (online, 3 January 2023) <www.abc.net.au/news/2023-01-03/david-woodroffe-appointed-first-nt-indigenous-court-judge/101823466>; 'First Aboriginal Judge for ACT Supreme Court', *ACT Government* (Web Page, 26 July 2023) <www.act.gov.au/our-canberra/latest-news/2023/july/first-aboriginal-judge-for-act-supreme-court>; Supreme Court of Western Australia, 'Appointment of New Supreme Court Judge' (Media Statement, 21 September 2022); 'His Honour Judge Nathan Jarro', *Supreme Court Library Queensland* (Web Page) <www.sclqld.org.au/collections/explore-the-law/judicial-profiles/jarro-198282#:~:text=In%20March%202018,%20Judge%20Jarro,Honourable%20Justice%20Martin%20Moynihan%20AO>.

Magistrate Sue Gordon and District Court Judge Bob Bellear all held judicial roles in the 1990s and were the first Indigenous Australians to do so. Various other Aboriginal and Torres Strait Islander people have been appointed to judicial positions in magistrate and local courts, while Matthew Myers AM remains the only First Nations person to be appointed to the federal judiciary as a member of the Federal Circuit Court in 2012.[29]

Outwardly, these are important appointments—certainly not only for the individuals but also for their families and the First Nations community overall. At an institutional level, these appointments are important because they represent a point of difference in the exercise of judicial power, and they contribute to a judiciary that better reflects the community over which it exercises authority. They represent a fusion of knowledge of First Nations ways of knowing and doing alongside western legal expertise, and they bring these perspectives to bear at what Torres Strait Islander scholar Martin Nakata calls the 'cultural interface'[30] of the courtroom.

These perspectives are significant—they mark a subtle shift in the largely monocultural composition of the Australian judiciary and provide a means of imbuing legal decision-making with First Nations understandings of the law. This is an acknowledgement that the law, like all social institutions, is not neutral. Rather, it is informed by the personal backgrounds of individuals, knowingly and unknowingly, within broader socio-cultural structures, that underpin the standpoints of judicial officers. These appointments are significant for improved procedural and substantive justice outcomes, but as minority figures within a colonial system, their inclusion alone is insufficient to achieve transformative change.

The perspectives that First Nations judicial officers bring means that they are equipped with a deeper understanding of the issues affecting First Nations communities and are perhaps more likely to understand the importance of relevant legal provisions, such as section 12 discussed previously. The *Family is Culture* report made a similar point and noted the importance of judicial officers 'with specialised knowledge of Aboriginal culture and a proven ability to communicate and work with Aboriginal families', specifically, the appointment of Aboriginal magistrates to improve decision-making regarding Aboriginal children and families.[31] In the five years since, updates about the progress of these recommendations suggest that various actions have been undertaken to determine the need and benefit of specialist magistrates and that the appointment of specialist magistrates is 'on track'. However,

29 Department of Social Services, 'Australia's First Indigenous Federal Magistrate Welcomed' (Media Release, 10 February 2012) <https://formerministers.dss.gov.au/13588/australias-first-indigenous-federal-magistrate-welcomed/>.

30 Martin Nakata, 'The Cultural Interface' (2007) 36(S1) *The Australian Journal of Indigenous Education* 7.

31 Davis (n 5) 391.

these actions do not appear to have considered in any way this stated preference for Aboriginal magistrates, or magistrates with specialised knowledge of Aboriginal culture, to consider child protection matters that affect Aboriginal children.[32] Although many of the sitting First Nations judicial officers are in courts without child protection jurisdiction, the roles of both professional and cultural knowledge are pertinent to understanding the limitations of inclusion within courts.

In a criminal setting, this may mean a better understanding of the contextual factors for bail and sentencing and the available community support services. In a child protection setting, this will extend to understanding not only the interaction between First Nations communities and child welfare authorities but also the ongoing legacies of colonisation and the Stolen Generations. This deep understanding, founded in experience from the First Nations standpoint, may also bring with it an ingrained judicial scepticism when it comes to accepting departmental, police and, indeed, First Nations evidence on face value. This may mean that First Nations judicial officers are more likely to interrogate and ask questions. Former Aboriginal Magistrate Pat O'Shane was well known for her interactions with police while she was on the bench.[33]

Similarly, First Nations Federal Circuit and Family Court Judge Matthew Myers has been very public about the devastating impact of state child protection systems on First Nations families; he has cited the increase in the rate of removals since the Stolen Generations and the urgent need for reform,[34]

32 New South Wales Department of Communities and Justice, *Family is Culture Progress Report* (25 November 2020) 29 <https://dcj.nsw.gov.au/documents/children-and-families/family-is-culture/family-is-culture-response-progress-report-november-2020.pdf>; New South Wales Department of Communities and Justice, *Family Is Culture Progress Report* (May 2021) 78 <https://dcj.nsw.gov.au/documents/children-and-families/family-is-culture/family-is-culture-response-progress-report-may-2021.pdf>; New South Wales Department of Communities and Justice, *Family Is Culture Progress Report* (August 2021) 79 <https://dcj.nsw.gov.au/documents/children-and-families/family-is-culture/family-is-culture-response-progress-report-august-2021.pdf>; New South Wales Department of Communities and Justice, *Family Is Culture Progress Report* (February 2024) 41 <https://dcj.nsw.gov.au/documents/children-and-families/family-is-culture/February_2024_-_Family_is_Culture_Response_Progress_Report.pdf>.

33 Paul Tatnell, 'Calling Police 'F—ing' Pigs Not Offensive: O'Shane', *Sydney Morning Herald* (online, 7 May 2010) <www.smh.com.au/national/nsw/calling-police-fing-pigs-not-offensive-oshane-20100507-uiu8.html>; see also Tim Dick, 'Judges Rule O'Shane Was Right to Jail Bullying Man for Contempt', *Sydney Morning Herald* (online, 20 January 2007) <www.smh.com.au/national/judges-rule-oshane-was-right-to-jail-bullying-man-for-contempt-20070120-gdpab9.html>.

34 'Removal of Kids Horrifies Nation's Only Indigenous Federal Judge', *The Australian* (11 December 2014) <https://www.theaustralian.com.au/subscribe/news/1/?sourceCode=TAWEB_WRE170_a_GGL&dest=https%3A%2F%2Fwww.theaustralian.com.au%2Fnational-affairs%2Findigenous%2Fremoval-of-kids-horrifies-nations-only-indigenous-federal-judge%2Fnews-story%2Ffb2543c80d949061>.

including engaging directly with First Nations communities and using his influence to elevate their perspectives. During one interview on the *Law Report* in 2023, Judge Myers recounted an exchange with community members and described being 'scoffed' at for remarks that he had made about First Nations children having as many as ten placements during their time in out-of-home care.[35] The data were met with derision and commentary from the community that these figures were incorrect. Judge Myers discussed how he engaged with the community to explore in greater depth their perspectives and lived experiences of child welfare systems. The audience members indicated that the figures presented were very 'light'. One Aboriginal woman in the audience indicated to Judge Myers that she herself had experienced at least twenty placements during her time in care. It is hoped that Judge Myers continues to draw on the lived experiences of Aboriginal people to affect change and to apply a healthy scepticism when engaging with quantitative data that present a potentially narrow perspective about the lived realities of the First Nations children, families and communities affected by state child protection systems.

Judge Myers has also spoken up at conferences and in the media about the need for change, including suggesting that First Nations families consider utilising the Family Court jurisdiction instead of the Children's Court to obtain better outcomes.[36] This is worth consideration for families affected by contemporary child protection systems but does not address the dominating structures that perpetuate poor outcomes within child protection jurisdictions or the foundational paradox of ongoing *terra nullius*.

The judiciary has much to answer for regarding its complicity in the ongoing removal of First Nations children from their families. The considerable discretion afforded to judicial decision-makers provides significant opportunities to extend procedural fairness and demand that institutional actors meet a high threshold to justify state intervention and the separation of families. Alleged harms requiring intervention should be considered against the harms and poor outcomes associated with out-of-home care, and there should be much greater insistence on exhaustive efforts to create safety and preserve families so that removal is truly an intervention of last resort.[37]

Consistent with legislative mandates for the participation of Aboriginal families and communities in decision-making, such as section 12 of the *Care*

35 Damien Carrick, 'US Lawyer Faces Sanctions Over Chat GPT Use: What Family Courts Can Do for Indigenous Australians', *The Law Report* (ABC Radio National, 13 June 2023) <www.abc.net.au/listen/programs/lawreport/chatgpt-lawyer/102405786>.

36 Damien Carrick, 'US Lawyer Faces Sanctions Over Chat GPT Use: What Family Courts Can Do for Indigenous Australians', *The Law Report* (ABC Radio National, 13 June 2023) <www.abc.net.au/listen/programs/lawreport/chatgpt-lawyer/102405786>.

37 *Children and Young Persons (Care and Protection) Act 1998* (NSW) s 9(2)(c).

and Protection Act, the voices of First Nations families and communities must not only be sought by child protection workers but heard by judicial officers. If there is broad agreement about the need for different decisions to achieve better outcomes for First Nations children, then such efforts must reconsider issues of procedural justice in the context of necessary structural change. In the absence of structural change, we will see endless cycles of reform and legislative amendment without progress, further entrenching a system in which colonial knowledge and authority reign supreme at great cost to First Nations children and families.

Limitations of Colonial Systems in Judicial Decision-Making

It is important that there are now more First Nations judicial officers. They challenge the overwhelming whiteness of judicial institutions and the way that the law interacts with First Nations communities. However, as a minority group that forms less than 1 per cent of the overall judicial population, the extent to which such challenges are possible is limited. As much as First Nations judicial officers might bring their unique cultural standpoint to judging and are more likely to have knowledge of the legislative provisions aimed at reducing discrimination, their presence is not a panacea.

First Nations judges and magistrates are ultimately constrained to operate within the realm of state law. They cannot overturn decades of colonial decisions that have had a detrimental impact on First Nations peoples. They can challenge, but they cannot change the inadequacies and the structural racism within the policies and practices of child welfare systems. They cannot unilaterally implement the decades of reviews and inquiries aimed at addressing the overrepresentation of First Nations children in the child protection system. First Nations judicial officers by themselves cannot stem the tide of removals facing future generations of First Nations children. Although their contributions are important, they should not be overstated; First Nations judges and magistrates provide a way of shifting rather than piercing the whiteness that prevails in our courtrooms.

Achieving the transformational change that has long been envisioned by First Nations people requires more than the addition of First Nations judicial officers. Furthermore, state laws post-*Mabo* remain committed to retaining the 'skeleton of principle'[38] that developed from the law of England. The re-establishment of First Nations jurisdictions to oversee the rights and interests of First Nations children under First Nations laws and governance remains the catalyst for change that is necessary to reject the ongoing spectre of *terra nullius* in the child protection system.

38 *Mabo v Queensland [No 2]* (1992) HCA 23 [29] (Brennan J).

Colonial Mindsets in Child Protection Practice

Executive structures and practices are highly influential, both in terms of the experiences of children and families and in the judicial decision-making process. Reforms within these executive agencies have similarly focused on practice to 'improve' the quality of decisions and uphold the 'best interests' of children, including First Nations children. These include practice efforts to improve 'engagement' for family and community participation in decision-making, structures to provide 'independent' expertise to inform the court, such as Children's Court Clinics, and the appointment of children's legal representatives to advocate for their interests. Although these processes are well intentioned, they nevertheless offer little substantive change to the structural barriers that have characterised colonial interventions in First Nations families for more than two centuries.[39] Despite wide acknowledgement of the need for structural change, cycles of reform frequently reinforce the same flawed colonial logics and result in the same avoidable, poor outcomes.

Child protection practice standards emphasise the central role of family, community and culture, including cultural safety in achieving positive outcomes for children and young people.[40] Practice expectations include applying relevant international human rights instruments, such as the United Nations Declaration on the Rights of Indigenous Peoples ('UNDRIP').[41] UNDRIP requires working alongside First Nations families and adhering to the relevant rights-based legislative provisions and policies. In New South Wales, this includes the Aboriginal and Torres Strait Islander principles[42] and the Aboriginal Case Management Policy, a comprehensive policy document developed by the New South Wales Child, Family and Community Peak Aboriginal Corporation ('AbSec').[43]

39 Terri Libesman, Kate Ellinghaus and Paul Gray, 'Colonial Law and Its Control of Aboriginal and Torres Strait Islander Families' in Peter Cane, Lisa Ford and Mark McMillan (eds), *The Cambridge Legal History of Australia* (Cambridge University Press, 2022) 433.

40 New South Wales Department of Communities and Justice, *Practice Framework Standards for Child Protection and Out of Home Care Practitioners* (2020). <https://dcj.nsw.gov.au/documents/service-providers/deliver-services-to-children-and-families/child-protection-services/practice-framework-standards.pdf>.

41 *United Nations Declaration on the Rights of Indigenous Peoples*, GA Res 61/295, UN Doc A/RES/61/295 (2 October 2007, adopted 13 September 2007) <https://social.desa.un.org/sites/default/files/migrated/19/2018/11/UNDRIP_E_web.pdf>.

42 *Children and Young Person's Care and Protection Act 1998* (NSW) ss 11–14 ('*Care and Protection Act*').

43 'About the Aboriginal Case Management Policy', *New South Wales Government* (Web Page) <https://dcj.nsw.gov.au/service-providers/oohc-and-permanency-support-services/aboriginal-case-management-policy/aboriginal-case-management-policy-statement/about-acmp.html>.

However, statutory child protection officials are granted wide discretion in applying these standards and in determining how they contribute to child protection decision-making. In this way, decisions about the futures of First Nations children, individually and collectively, remain under the authority of state institutions and processes and often avoid scrutiny or oversight from First Nations communities.

As with the finding that key legislative provisions are routinely not applied by judicial officers, these legislative and policy settings are not reliably implemented in practice.[44] The discretion afforded to child protection officers and the deference shown to their perspectives by judicial officers[45] present a significant barrier to achieving just outcomes for First Nations children and their families and communities. For example, the *Family is Culture* review found examples of child protection officers' non-compliance with practice frameworks and legislation and numerous examples of practitioners presenting misleading evidence about families to justify child protection decision-making. The review noted that

> In light of the sheer number of policy documents, codes of conduct, legislative instruments and training materials that address the issue of the standard of evidence to be supplied to the Children's Court, the Review was perplexed to discover that FACS [the NSW Department of Family and Community Services] provided the Children's Court with misleading or untrue evidence in a significant proportion of the case files that were reviewed. The gravity of the occurrence varied on a case by case basis. While it is possible some of the mistakes and omissions could be attributed to human error, in some cases it was difficult to understand how the error could have occurred during the normal course of events.[46]

This has significant implications for the quality of decision-making regarding the future of First Nations children and for procedural justice being afforded to First Nations families and communities.

Certain decision-making processes and tools further entrench non-Indigenous frameworks and perspectives. This includes the continued use of imported safety and risk assessment tools despite criticisms from First Nations families, communities and researchers that they perpetuate inequalities and contribute to the over-representation of First Nations children forcibly removed from their

44 Davis (n 5); SNAICC (n 10); SNAICC—National Voice for Our Children, '*Family Matters Report 2022* (Report, October) (SNAICC, 2022) <https://www.snaicc.org.au/resources/family-matters-report-2022/>.

45 Elizabeth Fernandez et al., *A Study of the Children's Court of New South Wales* (Report, 2014).

46 Davis (n 5) 384.

families.[47] Such tools provide a façade of rigorous, valid assessment underpinning child protection decision-making by both child protection authorities and judicial officers that effectively marginalises First Nations perspectives and experiences. These tools also minimise the consideration of protective factors and other strengths present in First Nations families that contribute to experiences of safety for First Nations children.

Similarly, recent reforms to increase the use of 'family group conferencing' have been represented by state administrators as a key commitment to increasing the involvement of First Nations families and communities in decisions about their children.[48] However, their structural positioning emphasises accountability to child protection authorities rather than to the families and communities that they are ostensibly intended to empower. This is likely to compound the identified risks whereby family and community voices are co-opted and marginalised[49] while presenting a false narrative that families and communities have been afforded an opportunity to be meaningfully engaged and heard in decisions about their children.

Cycles of reform intended to strengthen safeguards for First Nations children and families tend to be co-opted by state child protection authorities, positioning First Nations children and families within systems in ways that marginalise their voices and recreate and reinforce colonial systems of intervention. For example, recent legislative changes in New South Wales require child protection authorities to provide timely and purposeful assistance to families to prevent unnecessary removals and increase the rate of restorations.[50] Although the foundation of this 'active efforts' standard emphasises the responsibility of state authorities to assist families, subsequent guidance about the new laws developed by the executive child protection agency clearly diminishes this intent by defining active efforts in accordance with existing rights rather than a new higher standard[51] that warranted the inclusion of

47 Jorge Branco, 'Indigenous Organisations Call for Child Safety Tool to Be Scrapped', *Nine News* (online, 17 January 2023) <www.9news.com.au/national/child-safety-nsw-indigenous-organisation-calls-for-racist-child-safety-tool-to-be-scrapped/15f2d936-4b5d-473a-92c9-8bb2009bcc4c>.

48 'Impact on Aboriginal Families', *NSW Department of Communities and Justice* (Web Page) <https://dcj.nsw.gov.au/service-providers/deliver-services-to-children-and-families/child-protection-services/shaping-a-better-child-protection-system/impact-on-aboriginal-families.html>.

49 Tarar Ney, Jo-Anne Stoltz and Maureen Maloney, 'Voice, Power and Discourse: Experiences of Participants in Family Group Conferences in the Context of Child Protection' (2013) 13(2) *Journal of Social Work* 184; cited in AbSec, *Shaping a Better Child Protection System—AbSec Submission* (2017) <https://drive.google.com/file/d/1ScJYz_3u80wq2kWvQ9QyUn989KJFrWxy/view?usp=sharing>.

50 'Understanding the Family Is Culture Laws', *New South Wales Department of Communities and Justice* (Web page) <https://dcj.nsw.gov.au/children-and-families/family-is-culture/new-laws.html>.

51 'Understanding the Family Is Culture Laws', *New South Wales Department of Communities and Justice* (Web page) <https://dcj.nsw.gov.au/children-and-families/family-is-culture/new-laws.html>.

stronger legislative provisions.[52] In reality, these 'reforms' merely recreate the same harmful practices that they were intended to prevent.

The establishment of Children's Court Clinics[53] and the appointment of Independent Legal Representatives[54] to advocate for the interests of children before the court reflect procedural 'reforms' that have arguably further reinforced the structures that undermine the rights and interests of First Nations children. These examples ostensibly serve the interests of children and families by ensuring access to adequate expertise in assessing the needs of children, determining how these needs might best be met, and providing children an independent voice in court processes. Such roles can be highly influential in judicial decision-making, as they are seen as impartial and objective.[55] However, these reforms also further entrench non-Indigenous perspectives and authority in the decision-making about First Nations children.[56] The expertise valued by the Children's Court Clinics is steeped in non-Indigenous knowledge systems despite these fields being implicated in past and ongoing systems of harm, and the known paucity of culturally valid theoretical frameworks and assessment tools is also a problem.[57] Such expertise presumes a similar epistemic *terra nullius* and fails to recognise the knowledge and practices that confer safety to raise generations of First Nations families. This false 'gap' is thus filled with ill-suited non-Indigenous frameworks and tools.

Similarly, although independent legal representatives play a significant role in representing the interests of First Nations children in court processes (particularly for infants and young children), there is no expectation that these representatives will have suitably demonstrated knowledge and awareness of the developmental needs of First Nations children or how their best interests are conceptualised by their community to inform the advocacy on their behalf. Rather, such legal representatives are empowered to make representations regarding the interests of First Nations children about which they may be entirely ignorant.[58] Although they are described as 'independent', their standpoint disproportionately represents non-Indigenous perspectives, and this informs their contributions to the judicial process, including their

52 Davis (n 5).

53 'Children's Court Clinic', *Children's Court New South Wales* (Web page) <https://childrenscourt.nsw.gov.au/care-and-protection/children-s-court-clinic.html>.

54 'Legal Representation for a Child or Young Person', *Department of Communities and Justice* (Web page) <www.facs.nsw.gov.au/families/legal/care-and-protection-proceedings/legal-representation>.

55 Fernandez et al. (n 45) 30.

56 Clare Tilbury, 'Obtaining Expert Evidence in Child Protection Court Proceedings' (2019) 72(4) *Australian Social Work* 392, 399.

57 Ash Wright et al., 'Attachment and the (Mis)apprehension of Aboriginal Children: Epistemic Violence in Child Welfare Interventions' (2024) *Psychiatry, Psychology and Law* 1.

58 Australian Law Reform Commission, *Seen and Heard: Priority for Children in the Legal Process* (Report, 8 November 1997) 13, 58 <https://www.alrc.gov.au/publication/seen-and-heard-priority-for-children-in-the-legal-process-alrc-report-84/>.

examination of child protection agency and 'expert' evidence concerning First Nations families and children.

Despite the apparent reforms to improve the quality of representation of First Nations families, child protection systems continue to privilege non-Indigenous expertise while simultaneously acknowledging that such judgments have underpinned systems of harm for generations. Furthermore, in our experience, when First Nations expertise is included, there remains a significant challenge in translating cultural concepts so that they are understood by non-Indigenous legal systems and decision-makers.[59] Once again, this emphasises the importance of First Nations judicial officers in child protection decisions.

These challenges highlight that state institutions—whether government authorities, 'experts' or judges—should not be considered 'independent' in matters regarding the integrity and survival of First Nations families as they share an interest in First Nations' dispossession and the dismemberment of First Nations families. Meanwhile, the recognition of the rights and interests of First Nations children predominantly depends on the professional and cultural humility of non-Indigenous 'experts'.

Many of these systems and professions have sought to improve their cultural awareness and cultural safety—whether in ongoing professional development or through the introduction of policy or practice standards. Such efforts are important but are ultimately limited: they may mitigate some of the harms associated with structural violence but cannot themselves achieve an end to this violence. Ending the violence is necessary for the collective safety of First Nations children, families and communities. In this way, the aim of achieving 'cultural safety' in state child protection systems is itself misleading because such systems are imbued with colonial violence. No amount of cultural awareness will render these systems 'safe' for First Nations children, families or communities.

Cultural safety and addressing this colonial violence require that the current approach to the exercise of child protection authority by state systems, including legislatures, government agencies and judiciaries, be discontinued. The legitimate authority of First Nations to govern themselves and determine the futures of their children, families and communities must be recognised. Although current policy frameworks have committed to some 'transfer' or 'delegation' of authority from the state to First Nations communities[60] and courts have taken positive steps to establish more inclusive settings,[61] care

59 James Beaufils, '"That's the Bloodline": Does Kinship and Care Translate to Kinship Care?' (2023) 58 *Australian Journal of Social Issues* 296.

60 Department of Social Services, *Safe and Supported: Aboriginal and Torres Strait Islander First Action Plan 2023–2026* (Australian Government, 2022).

61 'The Winha-Nga-Nha List Commences at Dubbo Children's Court', *Aboriginal Legal Service (NSW/ACT)* (Web Page, 7 September 2023) <www.alsnswact.org.au/the_winha_nga_nha_list_commences_at_dubbo_children_s_court>.

should be taken to ground reforms in Indigenous peoples' human rights to self-determination, autonomy, and self-governance. This requires an end of ongoing systems of violence rather than colonial states benevolently and conditionally sharing their authority with First Nations peoples.

Conclusion

The discord between, on the one hand, legislative and human rights commitments to participation and self-determination and, on the other hand, First Nations communities' and organisations' experiences within child protection systems requires the political will to address it. Although research, reviews and many participants in child protection systems express a commitment to Aboriginal peoples' rights to participation and self-determination, there is an enormous gap between good will (and good words) and what happens in practice. Child protection reforms are supposedly well-intentioned, but the cycles of harm that they recreate are foreseeable and, in this sense, should also be considered intentional outcomes of such policy settings.[62]

Alex Broom and colleagues note that in the context of social structures and institutions, 'some actions are more possible and, indeed, more highly and frequently rewarded than others'.[63] In relation to state child protection systems and practice, the grounding of decisions about First Nations children in interventionist and assimilationist frameworks remains 'more possible' and drives First Nations peoples' experiences of marginalisation, violence and harm. Decisions about the rights, interests and futures of First Nations children continue to be determined by non-Indigenous institutions, non-Indigenous processes and predominantly non-Indigenous people. Non-Indigenous knowledge systems and ideas of 'expertise' are continually prioritised and valued, despite the known role of these disciplines and experts thereof in past and ongoing harms experienced by First Nations peoples. Meanwhile, limited procedural reforms largely provide a façade of progress while simultaneously masking how these reforms recreate structural violence and resist deeper structural transformation.

This gap is evidenced in the failure to substantially implement reforms, such as the Aboriginal Child Placement Principles, and rights, such as those provided by section 12 of the *Care and Protection Act*. We argue that even if these reforms were to be implemented, there are limits to what can be achieved within state child protection systems. To attain child protection institutions that embed Aboriginal community and family values and that are accountable to Aboriginal individuals and communities, the foundational

62 Alex Broom et al., 'The Administration of Harm: From Unintended Consequences to Harm by Design' (2023) 43(1) *Critical Social Policy* 51.
63 Alex Broom et al., 'The Administration of Harm: From Unintended Consequences to Harm by Design' (2023) 43(1) *Critical Social Policy* 67.

terra nullius that grounds existing child protection frameworks needs to be rejected.

If we are to challenge the *terra nullius* mindsets in child welfare, then we must go beyond the procedural safeguards administered by non-Indigenous authorities and decision-makers. First Nations peoples must be empowered to make decisions grounded in their expectations of child-rearing and aspirations for the futures of their children. This is a critical foundation for all child protection systems—the expression of the collective interests of a community in the future of its children and through the children, the future of the community. This requires a transfer of child protection jurisdiction, on equal terms, to First Nations communities and institutions.

5

'WHO BUILT THIS FENCE?'

Regenerating Faculty Landscapes for Lasting Education Reform

Simon Young and Kirstie Smith[1]

Introduction

One of the greatest obstacles that we face in reforming legal education and research to better serve First Nations communities is the challenge of impermanence.[2] The many contributors to this book have inevitably had to pilot their work and insights through shifts (probably many) in university personnel, priorities, resources and strategies—shifts that can be almost tidal in frequency and that very often leave little trace of past worthy initiatives. All too frequently, we find ourselves back where we began.

The focus of this chapter is structural reform: the redesign and regeneration of faculty landscapes to better sustain pedagogical advances and to make the journey easier for those who might follow. Our own ideas and efforts are no more than the sum of observation, collation and collaboration—drawing on ideas suggested, tried and tested by others in law, in cognate disciplines or in overseas institutions. We have the opportunity of working at a young law school in a regional university, where the commitments to educational access, innovation and community development are not just ideological but very necessary parts of the business model. In this context, which we are

1 The authors acknowledge with gratitude and respect the Country and nations of our region—we are privileged to live and work on their lands and stand with them in our educational endeavours. We particularly honour the people who continue to care for and dedicate themselves to the Country of our law school teaching places—the Giabal and Jarowair peoples (and the broader Waka Waka Nation) and the Jagera, Yuggera and Ugarapul peoples, who continue their devotion to this Country, its air and its waterways in silence, with great patience and with enduring, unbreakable resilience.

2 See, e.g., Marcelle Burns, 'Are We There Yet? Indigenous Cultural Competency in Legal Education' (2018–19) 28(2) *Legal Education Review* 215, 218.

DOI: 10.4324/9781003473404-6

learning presents significant opportunities for First Nations education, we can stand on the shoulders of those who have accomplished so much elsewhere and shared their ideas (including the many contributors to this book). In this context, we can take the rare opportunity to re-imagine what a law school can be in this space.

The good news for those who are new to these challenges (or for those who are looking for new ways to step out of the institutional tides) is that it seems that much of the work to redesign and regenerate faculty landscapes can be conducted at the grassroots level in law schools themselves—early, efficiently, collaboratively, and somewhat irrespective of shifting institutional priorities. There is obvious work to be accomplished around program and course structures, First Nations student support and higher degree pathways. However, there is also much that can be done (and we suggest done first)[3] around physical and virtual spaces, staffing and workloading, readying and equipping colleagues, curating resources, cross-university and external collaborations, reciprocal community engagement and support, and (more broadly) brokering change to make more space for First Nations voices. This structural change recognises that we seek genuine and sustainable change rather than just the allocation of onerous and isolated responsibilities to existing or future First Nations staff.

This chapter is a practical one by design; we hope that it is a useful complement to the far deeper pedagogical and theoretical insights that emerge from this book. Our original idea was to explain our work as digging foundations for lasting reform in the educational greenfield of a young regional law school. However, we soon realised that we were for the most part writing about a more modest undertaking and an enduring shared challenge. Vanessa Fisher—of the Dungibara, Ewamin, Garumngar Jiman people of Cherbourg, Southern Queensland—once wrote, 'Who built this fence to keep me out?'[4] These lines now resonate very clearly for us in our university work. Our task is to help dismantle the institutional fences that run through and around our university endeavours. In this process, we seek to reunite our law school's purposes and lands with the wisdom and custodianship of our local First Nations communities. Our advantage is not an educational 'greenfield'—far from it, as we are all ultimately working in a 'colonised space in which the curriculum is organically oriented towards White studies at the expense of other knowledge'.[5] Our advantage is simply that in a young regional law school, the fences seem not to be so high.

3 Cf. Jeffery G Hewitt, 'Decolonizing and Indigenizing: Some Considerations for Law Schools' (2016) 33(1) *Windsor Yearbook of Access to Justice* 65, 70.

4 Vanessa Fisher, 'My Country' (1988) 7(1) *Social Alternatives* 46. The poet Vanessa Fisher—an important voice in our region—supported the University of Southern Queensland School of Law and Justice as part of a First Nations Advisory Board.

5 Yusef Progler, 'The Changing Face of the University and Knowledge' in Claude Alvares and Shad Saleem Faruqi (eds), *Decolonising the University: The Emerging Quest for*

This chapter, then, is a progress report on our own attempt to bring down some fences in preparation for the more concerted curriculum work to come. Our hope (and our experience so far) is that this work and the regeneration that flows from it not only makes enduring pedagogical reform easier and more meaningful but also can, in fact, make it somewhat inevitable. We are honoured to share our experiences in this book, while emphasising again at the outset that our own work flows from the wisdom and resilience of others who built foundations for us all.

Interim Principles

A core tenet of the successes that we have observed is that enduring curriculum reform is a slow and iterative process and perhaps, necessarily, a somewhat organic one. However, there is some urgency to the task of graduating more culturally aware lawyers,[6] and some of our law school colleagues will engage quickly when accessible content and/or course space presents itself. One way for a school or faculty to manage the early momentum is to agree (with guidance from a university's First Nations college and Aboriginal and Torres Strait Islander legal colleagues) on a set of 'interim' guiding principles.[7] These can serve not only as an accessible reminder of the importance of this work but also as something of a guard rail ('first, do no harm'). They can be distributed regularly at planning days and committee meetings and evolve as needed.

Interim principles can succinctly state the very clear imperatives that drive our work in this field: most obviously to support First Nations students, to build better legal professionals, to improve legal access and outcomes for First Nations communities and to meet contemporary employer expectations. There may also be university-specific responsibilities to acknowledge, for example, in the case of a regional university where the responsibility to provide opportunities for and connect with communities across great distances may be somewhat different to the responsibilities of universities concentrated in and around major cities. The principles themselves can draw on the significant existing scholarship, of which the contributors to this book are some of the most important architects. Emphasis can be placed on the

---

Non-Eurocentric Paradigms (Penerbit USM, 2012) 48, 50. See also Eddie Cubillo, 'Indigenous Programs at the Law School' (July 2022) *Law Institute Journal* 30; Bronwyn Fredericks, 'The Epistemology That Maintains White Race Privilege, Power and Control of Indigenous Students and Indigenous Peoples' Participation in Universities' (2009) 5(1) *Critical Race and Whiteness Studies* 1; James (Sakej) Youngblood Henderson, 'Postcolonial Indigenous Legal Consciousness' (2002) 1 *Indigenous Law Journal* 1.

6 See Cubillo (n 5).

7 See generally Universities Australia, *Guiding Principles for Developing Indigenous Cultural Competency in Australian Universities* (October 2011); Indigenous Cultural Competency for Legal Academics Program, *Final Report* (2019).

central importance of institutional and individual self-reflection,[8] the need for constructive and strengths-based approaches to Indigenous content (with respect for the complexity and sophistication of Indigenous legal systems)[9] and the importance of proper integration and coherence across courses. They can also highlight the importance of respecting the diversity of Aboriginal and Torres Strait Islander perspectives and experiences,[10] bringing First Nations voices to the content and engaging with local issues and communities (and place-based learning) wherever possible.[11] Furthermore, these principles can underline the importance of sensitivity to terminology, cultural protocols, research ethics and cultural and intellectual property rights. Colleagues might be reassured that expert support can and should be accessed and that it is very appropriate to build content incrementally as knowledge and self-reflection expand across programs.[12] Perhaps most importantly, interim principles can start and finish with the reminder that in pursuing this work, we must never lose our focus on the wellbeing of our First Nations students amid university targets. If this focus is lost, then all else counts for little.

In our own experience, carefully crafted interim principles can help hold open the space needed for the work ahead while structural foundations are laid. They also provide a clear rationale for (and inform) the structural work, can help build interest and commitment and can help protect the integrity of future initiatives. Moreover, the collaborations necessary to generate these principles—with First Nations colleges and legal colleagues—will begin to build the trust, cooperation and connections that will be so critical to all the work that follows.

Staffing and Staff Capabilities

Experiences across Australian law schools illustrate that a critical ingredient for sustained advances in curriculum and student support is personnel. Permanent identified positions for First Nations academics must be a fixed target

8 See, e.g., Marcelle Burns and Jennifer Nielsen, 'Dealing with the "Wicked" Problem of Race and the Law: A Critical Journey for Students (and Academics)' (2018–2019) 28(2) *Legal Education Review* 375.

9 See, e.g., Ambelin Kwaymullina, 'Teaching for the 21st Century: Indigenising the Law Curriculum at UWA' (2019) 29 *Legal Education Review* 1; Alison Jones, 'Dangerous Liaisons: Pākehā, Kaupapa Māori, and Educational Research' (2012) 47(2) *New Zealand Journal of Educational Studies* 100; John Borrows, 'Heroes, Tricksters, Monsters, and Caretakers: Indigenous Law and Legal Education' (2016) 61 *McGill Law Journal* 795, 797.

10 See, e.g., Burns (n 2) 225.

11 See, e.g., Annette Gainsford, 'Connection to Country—Place-Based Learning Initiatives Embedded in the Charles Sturt University Batchelor of Law' (2018–2019) 28(2) *Legal Education Review* 317; Val Napoleon and Hadley Friedland, 'An Inside Job: Engaging with Indigenous Legal Traditions Through Stories' (2016) 61 *McGill Law Journal* 725.

12 See, e.g., Kate Galloway, 'Indigenous Content in the Law Curriculum: Process and Structure' (2018) 28(2) *Legal Education Review* 331, 353.

in any structural reform.[13] It may take some time for university priorities and resources to align and deliver this, but the growing First Nations student numbers across the country and evolving external expectations of curriculum clearly confirm that this must be a key goal of our initiatives. Just as importantly, First Nations academics must be properly supported with position descriptions and workload arrangements that respect the multifaceted and often interdisciplinary nature of their teaching and research roles, their community obligations, their own family obligations and their specific importance in supporting students and colleagues.[14]

Faculty and school managers (and staff) must be ready for educational reform and understand its critical importance to properly support the role. The goal is not only the 'visibility' of First Nations peoples in staffing and curriculum but also, ultimately, the proper reflection of First Nations laws, knowledges, experiences and pedagogies in our programs.[15] Support networks for this significant work, and most importantly for the First Nations academics who will lead it, can be proactively built from connections with First Nations colleges and colleagues at other schools and collaborations between law schools. The past experiences of our leaders in this field confirm that building respect and sustained support for our First Nations law colleagues is a critical part of this journey.

Honorary and adjunct positions can also be valuable in building a culture of change and respect. Retired First Nations judges, magistrates and legal policy experts (and present practitioners from law or education) can bring deep experience to a law school, and adjunct/advisory appointments across law schools can help build close networks and diverse supervisory teams. Law schools might also consider additional new shared appointments—for example, with First Nations colleges—that will help build the collaboration and interdisciplinarity that are crucial to curriculum reform and community-led research agendas. Law schools can further actively advocate for and support First Nations appointments in other schools and organisational units. More broadly, law schools can build reciprocal relationships with various organisations and agencies—such as Aboriginal and Torres Strait Islander legal services, courts and community justice groups, specialist family law

13 See, e.g., Burns (n 2) 236.

14 See Asmi Wood and Nicole Watson, 'Mirror, Mirror on the Wall, Who Is the Fairest of Them All?' (2018) 28(2) *Legal Education Review* 263, 269–70.

15 Susan Bird, John Rawnsley and Ciprian Radavoi, 'True Justice Through Deep Listening on Country: Decolonising Legal Education in Australia' (2023) 19(4) *AlterNative: An International Journal of Indigenous Peoples* 892, 895. See also Irene Watson and Marcelle Burns, 'Indigenous Knowledges: A Strategy for First Nations Peoples Engagement in Higher Education' in Sally Varnham, Patty Kamvounias and Joan Squelch (eds), *Higher Education and the Law* (Federation Press, 2015) 41; Ambelin Kwaymullina and Blaze Kwaymullina, 'Learning to Read the Signs: Law in an Indigenous Reality' (2010) 34 *Journal of Australian Studies* 195.

services, land councils, Aboriginal corporations, legal aid services, or child and family 'official solicitors'—to create a rich source of content advice and student opportunity.

Building cultural capability and confidence in staff inevitably takes time, humility, some difficult conversations and regular reminders that in our work, we both reflect *and generate* legal directions.[16] Universities sometimes cycle through official cultural programs relatively quickly, which can lead to some repetition, confusion and/or the mistaken perception that cultural capability is a completable attribute rather than an ongoing journey.[17] However, in this respect, law schools can once again (at least in part) take their own lead. The building of strong relationships with local communities, First Nations colleagues (and colleges) and professional organisations working in relevant fields can open pathways for capacity building for staff (including on-Country learning). It is critical that this work towards capacity building is not left solely to existing or future First Nations colleagues.[18] They are not the ones who need to build capacity; moreover, much of this work is quintessentially a team task. Engaging all staff allows the opportunity for informed advocacy and a sense of collaboration and authenticity for both staff and students.[19] It properly recognises that most educators have themselves been deprived of First Nations perspectives and knowledge such that building the capacity of the team is essential.[20]

The old-fashioned idea of an existing non-Indigenous staff member taking responsibility as an 'Indigenous liaison' has some ongoing utility when the challenge of reform is initially understood as a structural one. Many elements of the incremental work explored in this chapter, particularly the building of connections and collaborations, can be commenced immediately with good will and the guidance of First Nations colleges and key advisors. As emphasised at the outset, these structural initiatives can make the important curriculum work easier and more meaningful and can help support our future First Nations colleagues. The 'liaison' or 'collaborations' role, where it is needed, must also be considered a university investment and should be properly recognised in workload and supported. Moreover, continuity is just as important in this role as it is in the longer-term endeavours. Of course, a key purpose of this initial role is to create space for and pursue the establishment of identified positions for which it can become a key support in the future.

16 Borrows (n 9) 799.
17 See Wood and Watson (n 14) 272–73.
18 Burns (n 2) 238.
19 Carrie Karsgaard, Thashika Pillay and Lynette Shultz, 'Facing Colonial Canada Through Pedagogies of Equity for First Nations: An Advocacy Education Project' (2022) *Journal of Curriculum and Pedagogy* 6.
20 Danielle Hradsky and Rachel Forgasz, 'Possibilities and Problems of Using Drama to Engage with First Nations Content and Concepts in Education: A Systematic Review' (2023) 50 *The Australian Educational Researcher* 965, 966.

Physical and Virtual Spaces

The tertiary education sector and our profession have in recent years embraced the practice of acknowledging Country. However, there is still space for leadership and a need for some diligence in this context. Genuine acknowledgement rather than rote repetition is a demonstration of true respect for traditional property rights through academic insistence that one's local region is not and was not empty space but that every land form or physical feature has a name, is known and is cared for by its local First Nations people.[21] First Nations legal academics, who carry the knowledge and burden of colliding legal histories, regularly offer the most inspiring acknowledgements—which are personal and with some specific attention to local places and significant events. We can take this example back to our own institutions. We can encourage those who lead events and meetings to acknowledge Country personally (rather than choosing a more 'appropriate' proxy), to step away from university scripts and to truly own the respect and gratitude that an acknowledgement embodies. It is hoped that our students will take this with them into their own careers and help to ensure that this vital practice endures in a meaningful way.

Traditional ownership and local histories can also be acknowledged in broader ways. For example, art and language can be respectfully introduced in physical and virtual university spaces. Concerning art, our own experience was that the existing university art holdings included an extensive collection of First Nations works that were not previously on regular display. Beyond this, strong connections with local communities (with reciprocity in research endeavours) can facilitate the purchased use or commissioning of local community art to feature on book covers, conference materials or project posters. Short agreements to protect cultural and intellectual rights are readily accessible. Strong community connections and sensitivity to local protocols can also facilitate the use of local language in appropriate ways, such as in resource collections or support portals for First Nations students.[22]

Particularly (but not exclusively) in regional universities, there may also be opportunities for the opening and sharing of university spaces and facilities. Universities can host community-driven events (on key issues such as child protection, community justice and the Uluru Statement[23]) and in this way, provide a safe space for open discussion and equality of voice. Moreover,

21 Kieran Dolin, 'Poetry and "Post-Mabo Lysis": John Kinsella on Property and Living on Aboriginal Land' (2021) 26(2) *Journal of the Theoretical Humanities* 32, 37.

22 UniSQ School of Law and Justice curates (under the title 'galangba'—'good place') a detailed list of internship/scholarship/job opportunities for First Nations students, alongside links to specific support services and news on local community events.

23 'Uluru Statement from the Heart' *The Uluru Dialogue* (Web Page) <https://ulurustatement.org/the-statement/view-the-statement/>.

local First Nations organisations, such as Community Justice Groups[24] or local corporations, might benefit from the occasional or regular use of meeting spaces on university grounds. A collaborative approach between universities and community groups and organisations can enhance the capacities of each and build tangible reciprocity. The necessary review and revitalisation of library collections, which will be important to later curriculum reform, can be pursued with these broader community uses in mind, and university libraries frequently have community borrowing plans available.

Relationships and Collaborations

At the beginning, middle and end of all of the 'landscape' reforms that we explore in this chapter are relationships.[25] Not the transactional relationships that tend to drive the corporate world, our profession and increasingly the tertiary sector, but long-term, respectful and reciprocal relationships built on trust, shared values and equality of voice. These relationships must necessarily start with listening and then listening again, and they must be allowed to help set the very first agendas for future initiatives.[26] In our experience, collaborations begin best with relationships rather than with projects, and it takes ongoing diligence to ensure that we prioritise genuine alliance and codesign and resist any deadline-driven return to seeking cultural 'rubber stamps' or 'ticks of approval'.

First and foremost are our own First Nations colleges and institutes. Any school or faculty has much to gain from a strongly forged partnership with its university's hub for First Nations teaching and research—and perhaps more to give than most might realise. In our experience, this partnership must begin from a clear understanding that: the First Nations college or institute is frequently under-resourced for an enormous range of cross-university and external responsibilities; its role is complex and multi-layered; specific professional or money-earning scientific disciplines are no more important than the First Nations colleges and institutes; and a university's long-term success very much depends on their success. Strong partnerships here can be a valuable way to strengthen, broaden and amplify our collective work. Most obviously, such partnerships can build a great synergy around curriculum

24 In Queensland, Community Justice Groups are an Aboriginal and Torres Strait Islander-run, community-based response to crime and justice-related issues. They take a person-centred approach to reduce crime, contact with the justice system and recidivism through cultural leadership and capabilities. Community Justice Groups are reflective of their communities, and their needs differ depending on the jurisdiction. It is helpful to consider this when contemplating an offer for meeting space or collaboration.

25 See broadly, e.g., Hannah Askew, 'Learning from Bear-Walker: Indigenous Legal Orders and Intercultural Legal Education in Canadian Law Schools' (2016) 33(1) *Windsor Yearbook of Access to Justice* 29.

26 Gainsford (n 11) 330.

development, community engagement and community co-designed research initiatives. Moreover, significant collaborations can be constructed around preparatory programs, student support and retention, the management and uptake of tutoring assistance schemes, targeted advertising of student opportunities, staff capabilities and confidence, and mutual support of junior staff and events.

The First Nations Pro Vice-Chancellor/Deputy Vice-Chancellor's office—to the extent that it operates independently of the colleges/institutes—is another potentially important partner, particularly as regards community engagement and events, recruitment, research directions and institutional level policy development. Moreover, building connections across traditional discipline boundaries can also be invaluable. These efforts can help us to properly embrace the inherent interdisciplinarity of First Nations teaching and research and build relationships for smoothly functioning cross-school research collaborations and co-supervision teams as new projects emerge. For us, this has been fruitful in fields such as climate resilience, cultural heritage, youth issues and allied health.

Critically important to our own law school efforts was the establishment of a First Nations legal advisory board, which consisted of First Nations practitioners, alumni and legal academics along with First Nations college representatives and local Traditional Owners.[27] Our grand designs were derailed somewhat by the arrival of COVID, but the advisory board has generously continued to provide invaluable advice on an ad hoc and individual basis for several years regarding priorities, resources, strategies and challenges encountered along the journey.

Beyond these critical partnerships, several other collaborations can be very helpful in sustaining momentum and building capacity. For us, the cross-law school network, drawn together particularly by the Indigenous Cultural Competency for Legal Academics Program,[28] continues to be a generous source of expertise and support. Connections with relevant professional bodies (such as ILAQ, ATSILS and AFLSQ[29]), individual legal professionals, specialised courts, Community Justice Groups and law firms keen to support this work at universities have also been valuable.

27 We are indebted to the original advisory board of Vanessa Fisher, Prof Tracey Bunda, Assoc Prof Kathryn Gilbey, Dr Ambelin Kwaymullina, Assoc Prof Marcelle Burns, Adj Prof Bevan Manthey, Dr Eddie Cubillo, Avelina Tarrago and Robyn Lui. The editors of this book (Prof Nicole Watson and Prof Heather Douglas), many of the book's contributors, and leaders at our university (including Prof Odette Best, Prof Benny Wilson, Prof Raelene Ward, Prof Celmara Pocock, Dr Cally Jetta, Emerson Zerafa-Payne, Paul Carmody, Tonia Chalk, Geoff Keating, Laurie-anne Parsons, Anna Jackson, Rachael Collins, Melanie Waters and Joshua Waters) have also been invaluable supporters of our law school initiatives.

28 See Indigenous Cultural Competency for Legal Academics Program (n 7).

29 Indigenous Lawyers Association of Queensland; Aboriginal and Torres Strait Islander Legal Service; Aboriginal Family Legal Services Queensland.

Community Connections

Ultimately, what may prove to be most important to the sustainability of educational reforms is a law school or faculty's own connections with local communities and community organisations (built with guidance and coordination from senior First Nations colleagues).[30] Genuine, reciprocal relationships can result in diverse collaborations on various activities including local events, discussion days or elder/youth support projects. In our own experience, these relationships can evolve into solid partnerships whereby a law school is simultaneously engaging with local knowledge to enhance teaching capacity and providing broad support to communities around issues such as native title, cultural heritage, constitutional recognition, community justice, water negotiations, social enterprise structures, tenure issues and business planning. Moreover, these partnerships can unearth research opportunities and new research teams.

Appropriate remuneration for specific community contribution is, of course, essential.[31] However, a law school's deeper support for communities can take a variety of forms, such as co-authoring legal reform submissions, offering informal meetings and workshops on legal developments and processes, commissioning community art (as discussed previously), voluntarily participating in site regeneration, or sponsoring/hosting (or participating in) community events and discussions. In terms of more legally focussed support, law school clinics can play a potentially significant role in improving community legal outcomes while simultaneously helping to produce more practice-ready and culturally aware students and building relationships with local community legal services. Non-practising law school members can also play an important role by drawing on connections to find relevant legal advice, brokering pro bono support from local or larger firms, ensuring access to good information about complaint avenues and processes and finding appropriate business planning advice where needed.

Our own hope is that the interest and opportunity flowing from reciprocal community engagement, together with cross-disciplinary collaborations and the building of postgraduate pathways (discussed below), might, in the longer term, evolve into a regionally focused First Nations legal research centre that can pursue projects co-designed with local communities.[32] In the meantime, embracing cross-disciplinary issues and partnerships helps us contribute constructively to large cross-university projects involving the climate, heritage mapping, youth support, site revival, agricultural innovation and (of course) broader pedagogical change.

30 See Gainsford (n 11) 321; Napoleon and Friedland (n 11) 725.

31 Burns (n 2) 241.

32 See Annette Gainsford, 'Embedding Indigenous Knowledges in the Design of the Higher Education Curriculum: An International Study in Law Education' (PhD thesis, Charles Sturt University, 2021).

Student law societies may well have their own initiatives underway and be seeking to engage independently with local community groups. Schools and faculties can support these initiatives in various ways. Easy, low-cost methods include attending student initiatives or events, encouraging or assisting connections between community groups and student initiatives that align, and cross-advertising events or initiatives that might be useful or interesting. Additionally, law schools can provide space (real or virtual) for students to listen to community elders and grassroots organisers about community initiatives where engagement is helpful for communities. These collaborations provide real context for students and can present powerful examples of self-determination and innovation. They provide space for students within and around their learning to develop genuine appreciation for local First Nations perspectives and experiences. Assisting student organisations and student law societies in this way gives them some ownership of their broader responsibilities as the next generation of lawyers while modelling collaboration and the importance of respectful community connection.

First Nations Student Support

One of our most important tasks is building informed and sustained support for our First Nations students.[33] This would have warranted earlier discussion in this chapter, but it seems to flow in large part from the initiatives and institutional self-reflection already discussed. However, practical steps can start early: in regional outreach around study choices for high school and mature-aged students; in flexible program design to better accommodate students navigating community, work and/or family obligations; and in the establishment of or participation in preparatory programs. Collaboration with First Nations colleges or institutes is invaluable in ongoing student support, particularly in providing students with immediate personal in-school connections, tutorial assistance and appropriate proactive support for progression. Support will look different for each student and can be time-based, technological or centred around academic literacy. First Nations colleges can provide tailored advice on the needs of particular students.

Connecting students to broader networks of fellow students and mentors can also be an important part of the exercise. It is relatively easy to collate opportunities for First Nations scholarships, internships, competitions and graduate positions in an accessible place—perhaps alongside critical study support resources and details of local community events. But we have often

33 For important discussions of student experiences, see, e.g., Wood and Watson (n 14); Heather Douglas, 'The Participation of Indigenous Australians in Legal Education 1991–2000' (2001) 24 *University of New South Wales Law Journal* 485; Melanie Schwartz, 'Retaining Our Best: Imposter Syndrome, Cultural Safety, Complex Lives and Indigenous Student Experiences of Law School' (2018–2019) 28(2) *Legal Education Review* 293.

found (particularly in the regional context) that ostensibly good opportunities may be inaccessible to students juggling distance and community, work and family obligations. Law schools might be able to encourage the revision of program guidelines, offer additional support to students in these contexts and/or broker supporting bursaries and prizes (e.g., from local law firms). Some low-hanging sources of income might also be considered for these purposes, including royalties on edited book collections, continued professional development ('CPD') income or educational support built in to funded projects. Broader university outreach programs appear to be increasingly active in establishing First Nations student scholarship funds (e.g., endowment funds) to which law schools can both contribute and lay claim.

A critical next step in our First Nations student support efforts is the building of attractive and well-supported higher degree by research ('HDR') pathways, whether they be with our own universities or our collaborators. HDR opportunities can be advertised via First Nations resources sites (discussed earlier), and several other building blocks can be put in place early for these purposes. First, as explored previously, well-established connections with other schools and faculties can help accommodate the inherent interdisciplinarity of many First Nations research priorities, and connections across universities can help counter the unfortunately still small number of senior First Nations legal academics. These established connections mean supervisory expertise can be quickly assembled (and with a strong likelihood of smooth functioning). Cross-disciplinary and/or cross-university research centres can greatly assist in this regard.

Second, it is vital that channels are established for immediate consultation with First Nations colleges or institutes in response to HDR inquiries by First Nations students or on First Nations issues. Experienced and well-meaning colleagues may still not immediately see the need for this. However, the contemporary dictates of ethical research and the importance of providing First Nations students with appropriate access to Indigenous research methodologies mean that the consultation should be automatic. Just as importantly, relevant supervisors in schools can and should be supported in appropriate training on Indigenous research methodologies—not because they should necessarily take the lead but so they might better understand the sophistication and importance of these emerging frameworks and contribute well in a supervisory team.

On more logistical matters, First Nations HDR positions can of course be built into funded research projects, and this could further help in building community collaborations. Moreover, projects with community partners can be bolstered by HDR projects designed around their priorities. In turn, HDR students can be supported in various ways beyond the usual progress reports and supervisory 'check-ins'. Access to cultural support is important (if it is not already built securely into the supervisory team). Furthermore, it is important to consider context and career goals in project design: intentions to enter academia, government policy roles or community-focused organisations each carry different implications for preferred HDR outcomes (in terms of the breadth of study, methodology and publications). Law schools could consider joining forces with cognate disciplines to produce published collections of First Nations HDR student work. Students can also be supported by 'communities of practice'[34]—a model of mutual student support with which all of us are familiar from our own postgraduate studies. One step forward is the possibility, referred to earlier, of an Indigenous law research centre to support and unite established and emerging researchers in the field.

Brokering Change

There are many less tangible actions that a law school can take to help regenerate broader university landscapes. In simple administrative terms, law schools can actively engage in university-wide First Nations teaching, research and reconciliation committees and working groups. Just as importantly, they can advocate for First Nations representation on other university committees and initiatives (and help ensure that these voices are genuinely and proactively listened to). Law schools can also be ready to assist in a variety of administrative processes such as relevant recruitment panels and organisational centre reviews. Perhaps most importantly, on the administrative side, we (as lawyers) can draw on our natural justice and transactional instincts to help ensure that 'everyone is in the room' when important decisions are made. These less tangible administrative activities, which effectively pursue and harness influence at the university level, can amplify the work of all of our First Nations academics and be an attraction in the recruitment of First Nations lawyers seeking to make an impact for the broader benefit of their communities.

More broadly, working in partnership with First Nations colleges/institutes (or guided by them), law schools can play a significant role in organising, facilitating and supporting university and community events on contemporary topics of importance to communities. Closer to home, they can ensure sustained attention to First Nations speakers and issues in the law school's public lectures, research seminars and planning days. Law schools and First Nations colleges/institutes can also work together to secure adjunct appointments and the conferral of honorary awards for key First Nations professionals, policy drivers and community leaders. These appointments and conferrals can further support teaching, research and engagement initiatives.

Law schools can contribute to the research space in a variety of ways beyond building their own community-focused research and partnerships. First, they can advocate for the inclusion of First Nations perspectives in

34 See Etienne Wenger, *Communities of Practice: Learning, Meaning and Identity* (Cambridge University Press, 1998).

large cross-disciplinary projects. As previously mentioned, in our work, this has been successful in projects concerning climate resilience, water, drought and agricultural innovation. Second, they can actively support First Nations college/institute initiatives to connect and coordinate the (often vaguely intersecting) research on First Nations issues that is conducted across schools and research centres. Third, they can seek to help support emerging First Nations scholars outside the school by assisting them in confirmation processes, helping to include them in publication and grant teams and creating opportunities for showcasing and disseminating their research.

With respect to teaching, law schools can be active in supporting (and perhaps piloting) First Nations college/institute initiatives on student orientation and support, career advice, cross-school liaison, etc. Invaluable teaching partnerships can be built to both enrich law programs and help ease the significant demands on college/institute resources. Moreover, close partnerships with First Nations colleges/institutes can create ready-packaged joint contributions (from law and First Nations scholars) that are available to other disciplines, for example, in the environmental management space. It is critical that we very proactively ensure that First Nations academics have appropriate workload recognition in any teaching programs (and of course in engagement and research activities).[35]

Curriculum

At this point, we should put away our landscaping tools and hand this discussion back to the deeper thinkers in this book. However, it is our hope and hypothesis (and fortunately our experience so far) that the structural initiatives that we discuss will help make enduring curriculum reform not only easier but also, in fact, a natural and inevitable evolution.

Along with many law schools and consistently with the statements of the Council of Australian Law Deans[36] and Universities Australia,[37] we have express program objectives concerning Indigenous perspectives prominently built into our educational aspirations for both Bachelor of Laws and Juris Doctor students. However, visibility of program objectives is just the first of many steps in dismantling the hegemony and myths, at the heart of the legal curriculum, that inhibit the building of a culturally safe space and progressive learning environment for First Nations students and academics alike.[38]

35 Burns (n 2) 239.

36 Council of Australian Law Deans, *CALD Statement on Australian Law's Systemic Discrimination and Structural Bias against First Nations Peoples* (Council of Australian Law Deans, 2020) <https://cald.asn.au/first-nations-peoples/>.

37 See Universities Australia (n 7).

38 Peter Prince, 'Our Natives Have No Constitutional Right to Equal Privileges with White People' in Kate Bagnall and Peter Prince (eds), *Subjects and Aliens: Histories of Nationality, Law and Belonging in Australia and New Zealand* (ANU Press, 2023) 119, 149.

For our part, we have various elective subjects 'in production'. These include a First Nations-led First Nations Peoples and Law subject for which we are reviewing precedents on content and approach; this will highlight First Nations laws and knowledges as encompassing the oldest and most enduring legal system in human history. Also in development are a new subject on Murri courts and sentencing led by a retired First Nations magistrate (now an adjunct professor) and an expanded native title subject that will seek to closely engage with the Traditional Owners and communities with which we have been building partnerships. We are also in discussions with nearby law schools about a shared course 'shell' to help us jointly host visiting international Indigenous scholars. We are steadily building an equivalent focus in our criminology programs, including through the existing subject 'Race, Diversity, Crime and Justice'. Our law school clinic is actively building connections with community legal services and increasingly acts as a conduit for internships and job opportunities, and our close partnership with our College for First Nations is producing some innovative (joint) cross-teaching in other disciplines.

Beyond these specialised initiatives and now with a First Nations-led team in place, we will slowly and steadily build momentum on the critical task of reviewing our core subjects. So far, this exercise has been somewhat organic for us, as we focused chiefly on the broader landscaping work. However, we have been learning that the exercise relies on a range of strategies: building staff engagement and 'buy in', lateral thinking to achieve viability in crowded content schedules and virtual teaching spaces, incremental tenacity and patience, some opportunism (e.g., when courses come up for review for other reasons) and, of course, collaboration. We are making small but positive steps and hope to embark on a coordinated program of work across core subjects in the near future by utilising the partnerships and resources that we have been building, trying different strategies for a local fit and drawing on the extraordinary collective wisdom of the contributors to this book and our trusted advisors.

A number of the peripheral initiatives referred to earlier in this chapter will, we hope, endure and support well our emerging curriculum projects. These include a review of library holdings and maintaining a First Nations student resources site that will include links to topical issues and local events. Most important, of course, is our ongoing investments in key (permanent) positions and the partnerships that we are seeking to steadily build. These investments and partnerships will (we hope) provide firm footing for enduring pedagogical change that might help reverse the role of Australian legal education in perpetuating structural bias against First Nations people. We seek to work deeply and as urgently as the task permits to help safeguard the next generation of Australian lawyers against rising nationalism, populism, misinformation and the disenfranchisement of minority voices.

Conclusion

This is our modest beginning. We are honoured to have the opportunity to share our experiences (to date) in the company of the other contributors to this important book. The context of a young regional law school seems to present some significant opportunities to test and advance the work in which we are all engaged. Most importantly, it provides us with the opportunity to lay foundations at the beginning of an institutional history. However, our writing and reflection revealed very clearly to us that this was not, and could never be, an institutional greenfield and that there was nothing grand or new about our work. We are, for the most part, just engaged (in our own little corner) in the shared endeavour of seeking to remove the old colonial fences that inhere in and around all of our educational institutions. Whether our brand of fence removal will have some enduring impact at our own university remains to be seen. But we are certainly building partnerships and aspirations that we never considered possible in academia. We hope that we can build a law school where our First Nations colleagues and local communities feel respected, honoured and keen to work with us to educate their treasured young people and build law graduates who are all a little more fit for purpose.[39] Most of all, we hope that our law school will never return to the start of the journey—that the change that we seek is now in the water.

Given the failure of the Australian constitutional referendum on whether to create a Voice to Parliament to represent Indigenous communities,[40] the year 2023 will, we fear, live somewhat infamously in Australian history. It seems unlikely that universities can somehow pivot magically to ensure that such mass distribution of misinformation on law and legal history will never happen again. However, it seems to us that we can certainly work harder to better hold up our part of the sky. Our own journey is built on the wisdom, strength and labour of others—and we hold closely to some key lessons that they have shared. These are the tenets that drive our work. What reflection do our First Nations students see of themselves in our law schools?[41] How do we, first and foremost, make more space for First Nations voices and ensure that they are listened to?[42] Moreover, returning to the wisdom of our local elder, who built these fences[43] that keep the wisdom and custodianship of communities from our law school endeavours?

39 See Burns (n 2) 217; Sarah Marsden and Sarah Buhler, 'Lawyer Competencies for Access to Justice: Two Empirical Studies' (2017) 34(2) *Windsor Yearbook of Access to Justice* 186, 190–92.

40 Kirstie Wellauer, Carly Williams and Bridget Brennan, 'Why the Voice Failed', *ABC Online* (16 October 2023) <https://www.abc.net.au/news/2023-10-16/why-the-voice-failed/102978962>.

41 Wood and Watson (n 14); and earlier, Nicole Watson, 'Indigenous People in Legal Education: Staring into a Mirror Without Reflection' (2005) 6(8) *Indigenous Law Bulletin* 4.

42 Kwaymullina (n 9); Gainsford (n 11) 321.

43 Fisher (n 4) 46.

6

CHALLENGES AND STRATEGIES FOR INCORPORATING INDIGENOUS LAWS AND HISTORIES ACROSS LEGAL EDUCATION CURRICULUM

Annette Gainsford, Alison Gerard and Emma Colvin[1]

Introduction

Embedding Indigenous perspectives in legal education can pose a number of challenges for law schools. As Larissa Behrendt observes, '[w]e cannot create a place of subversion and transformation within the academy without creating a culturally safe place.'[2]

Although Indigenous strategies in higher education at a national and institutional level provide strategic intent, these strategies fall short of offering knowledge and advice on how Indigenous content can be embedded. For Indigenous academics, students and guest lecturers, cultural safety is a pivotal element and consideration. Building cultural safety into the inclusion of Indigenous perspectives across legal education is an authentic way to prepare students for the legal profession and is central to any transformation in higher education.

More than a decade ago, the Indigenous Higher Education Advisory Council led Universities Australia to adopt a whole-of-sector approach to

1 We acknowledge the traditional custodians of the lands on which this book chapter was written, particularly the lands of the Wiradyuri and Ngunnawal. We acknowledge Aboriginal and Torres Strait Islander peoples as the sovereign peoples of this land that we now call Australia. We express our gratitude and respect to the Elders-in-Residence across our respective university campuses for their guidance as part of our professional development in the areas of curriculum, research and governance.

2 Larissa Behrendt, 'Indigenous Storytelling: Decolonizing Institutions and Assertive Self-Determination: Implications for Legal Practice' in Jo-Ann Archibald Q'um Q'um Xiiem, Jenny Bol Jun Lee-Morgan and Jason De Santolo (eds), *Decolonizing Research: Indigenous Storywork as Methodology* (Zed Books, 2019) 175 quoted in Amy Thunig and Tiffany Jones, '"Don't Make Me Play House-N***er": Indigenous Academic Women Treated as "Black Performer" within Higher Education' (2021) 48 *Australian Education Research* 397, 415.

DOI: 10.4324/9781003473404-7

embedding Indigenous perspectives in curricula and implementing an Indigenous graduate attribute for all courses.[3] These Guiding Principles and Best Practice Framework[4] documents from 2011 were supplemented by two Indigenous Strategies in 2017–2020 and 2022–2025. The progress of these recommendations has been slow, particularly for law schools.[5] Australian approaches to embedding Indigenous perspectives in legal education vary considerably, with mixed outcomes.[6] A common obstacle is the default attitude and expectation of law schools that Indigenous academics will take on the role of Indigenous curriculum development.[7] However, Indigenous legal academics frequently find the interface between the Indigenisation of curriculum and their research program far from their chosen path as law academics.

Examining the ways that law schools can influence transformational change in embedding Indigenous perspectives brings into focus two levers that we explore in this chapter. The first lever encompasses the institutional strategies that can support law schools to fulfil their commitments. Most universities should now have their own Indigenous curriculum policy or education strategy, but many are not properly embedded in governance frameworks or adequately resourced. The second lever involves the potential role of the legal profession admission standards. Despite repeated calls over many decades for legal education to include various forms of cultural awareness and cultural competence,[8] there is no requirement to demonstrate professional capabilities to work effectively with and for Indigenous peoples and communities before graduation or for admission as a legal practitioner. This silence puts Australia at odds with legal education standards in Canada[9] and

3 Marcelle Burns, 'Towards Growing Indigenous Culturally Competent Legal Professionals in Australia' (2013) 12(1) *International Education Journal: Comparative Perspectives* 226, 228.

4 Universities Australia, *National Best Practice Framework for Indigenous Cultural Competency in Australian Universities* (October 2011) 4 <www.universitiesaustralia.edu.au/uni-participation-quality/Indigenous-Higher-Education/Indigenous-Cultural-Compet#.XGXB-OJKgb0>.

5 Marcelle Burns, Anita Lee Hong and Asmi Wood, *Indigenous Cultural Competency for Legal Academics Program* (Final Report, 2019) <https://ltr.edu.au/resources/ID14-3906_Burns_FinalReport_2019.pdf>.

6 Alison Gerard, Annette Gainsford and Kim Bailey, 'Embedding Indigenous Cultural Competence: A Case Study' in Kevin Lindgren and Francis Kunc (eds), *The Future of Australian Legal Education: A Collection* (Thomson Reuters, 2018) 323.

7 Burns, Lee Hong and Wood (n 5) 18.

8 See *Royal Commission into Aboriginal Deaths in Custody* (National Report, 1991) vol 1, 295.

9 Scott Franks, 'Sustaining Progress in Indigenous Legal Education', *The Canadian Bar Association* (11 October 2022) <https://nationalmagazine.ca/en-ca/articles/the-practice/legal-education/2022/sustaining-progress-in-indigenous-legal-education>.

Aotearoa (New Zealand).[10] Legal professional accreditation standards 'are strong drivers of the content in law curriculum' and could thus mandate change in law schools.[11] For universities without a robust Indigenous curriculum framework—centrally or within the law school—the development of legal profession admission standards may provide direction and guidance on quality standards for curriculum development and ongoing professional development for legal practitioners.[12]

In the first part of this chapter, we substantiate our use of 'cultural safety' and examine its critical importance in the process of embedding Indigenous perspectives in Australian law schools. We then closely examine an institutional strategy that can support law schools to decolonise their curricula. Finally, we examine how industry standards have developed in the health profession to capture key learnings and offer pathways for developing professional admissions standards in law. These will serve to guide law schools—and hold them accountable—in embedding Indigenous perspectives by using culturally safe practices.

Cultural Safety in Legal Education

One of the key challenges in incorporating Indigenous perspectives into legal education is the consideration of staff and students' cultural safety. This also includes Indigenous community or industry stakeholders who partner in the design, development, and delivery of legal education. The term 'cultural safety' was originally coined by Māori nurse, anthropologist and writer Irihapeti Ramsden and is now widely used in the scholarship on teaching and learning.[13] However, there is ambiguity and at times, discord about what is meant by 'cultural safety'. Often, 'cultural safety' will appear in policies and guidelines but will not be defined. Where definitions are outlined, there are different perspectives on what cultural safety means.[14]

Maryann Bin-Sallik observed 20 years ago that challenges to 'formal Indigenous participation within the higher education sector . . . have revolved around issues of "cultural safety"'.[15] She is clear that there is a 'moral obligation' to provide a culturally safe space for teaching and research at

10 'New Tikanga Māori Requirements', *New Zealand Council of Legal Education* (Web Page) <https://nzcle.org.nz/>.
11 Burns, Lee Hong and Wood (n 5) 22.
12 Burns, Lee Hong and Wood (n 5) 22.
13 BJ Newton, 'Creating Cultural Safety as an Aboriginal Teacher in a Class of Non-Aboriginal University Students' (2021) 74 *Australian Social Work* 4.
14 See Burns (n 3) 226 for a discussion of these definitions in professions.
15 Maryann Bin-Sallik, 'Cultural Safety: Let's Name It!' (2003) 32 *The Australian Journal of Indigenous Education* 21.

universities.[16] She advocates using the term 'cultural safety' as a movement away from Western notions of equal opportunity and asserts that cultural safety 'is a term that all cultural groups can relate to and it does not have connotations of special treatment'.[17]

We recognise that terminology is always in flux. Language is powerful and can reproduce inequality.[18] We continue to use 'cultural safety' in this work because we draw on literature that defines and uses this term, and we believe that it captures the inherent requirements for transformation, as stated by Larissa Behrendt at the beginning of our chapter. In any case, we believe the underpinning concepts that inform cultural safety have much in common with other definitions, such as cultural humility and cultural competence. Acknowledging that further work needs to be done on defining cultural safety and how it is used in the context of teaching and learning in higher education, for this chapter, we have centred on Robyn Williams' definition[19] to encapsulate how we see cultural safety being potentially operationalised in the classroom. Williams' definition of cultural safety centres Indigenous identity and considers culturally unsafe practices as anything that is experienced as an assault on identity. A culturally safe environment provides social and emotional safety, a shared commitment to respect one another and a mutual understanding of how to work together.[20]

It has long been documented that law schools can be sites of cultural tension and outright hostility for Indigenous academics and students.[21] Despite movements to address this—for example, through the work of the Indigenous Cultural Competency for Legal Academics Program ('ICCLAP')[22]—and positive changes whereby Indigenous students in Australian law schools have enjoyed greater participation and success in recent years, Indigenous students continue to have culturally unsafe experiences. Melanie Schwartz found that such experiences result in

> alienation and 'imposter syndrome'—an intrusive feeling of non-belonging; and a related issue of the need for more institutional regard for the complex

16 Maryann Bin-Sallik, 'Cultural Safety: Let's Name It!' (2003) 32 *The Australian Journal of Indigenous Education* 25.

17 Maryann Bin-Sallik, 'Cultural Safety: Let's Name It!' (2003) 32 *The Australian Journal of Indigenous Education* 27.

18 Aileen Moreton-Robinson, *The White Possessive: Property, Power and Indigenous Sovereignty* (University of Minnesota Press, 2003).

19 Robyn Williams, 'Cultural Safety: What Does It Mean for Our Work Practice?' (2008) 23 *Australian and New Zealand Journal of Public Health* 213.

20 Robyn Williams, 'Cultural Safety: What Does It Mean for Our Work Practice?' (2008) 23 *Australian and New Zealand Journal of Public Health* 213. See also Anne Eckermann et al., *Binang Gooj: Bridging Cultures in Aboriginal Health* (University of New England, 1994).

21 Asmi Wood and Nicole Watson, 'Mirror, Mirror on the Wall, Who Is the Fairest of Them All?' (2018) 28(2) *Legal Education Review* 16.

22 Burns, Lee Hong and Wood (n 5).

lives of Indigenous students, including cultural or family obligations and high levels of stress in students' personal lives.[23]

Fernando and Bennett highlight the risk of secondary trauma to Indigenous students because of the curriculum content.[24] For Newton,[25] cultural safety is critical for First Nations educators, not just students. There is a risk of trauma to staff, and we need to consider the cultural safety of both staff and students. Newton provides her perspective as an Aboriginal woman teaching mainly non-Aboriginal social work students. She notes that she started by feeling vulnerable in the classroom but developed a 'safe and collaborative learning and teaching experience'.[26] In creating culturally safe spaces, we need to reconsider subtle expectations placed on Indigenous staff to share their personal stories when the same expectations are not presumed of non-Indigenous staff.[27] It is evident that a culturally safe working and learning space is vital in the process of Indigenising education curricula generally, with many documented examples of unsafe cultural practices in law schools in particular, including some experiences of these practices shared by other authors in this book.[28] Although examples of culturally unsafe practices are numerous and transforming law schools may be a lengthy process, the goal should always be to make law schools 'safer'.[29] We next examine how this can be achieved through institutional and school-level strategies for decolonising legal education.

Institutional and Law School Strategies to Decolonise Legal Education

Currently, law schools in Australia are investigating ways to 'transform' legal education to counteract the dominant Western curriculum. This transformational change comes with a number of challenges that involve the workload and cultural safety of Indigenous academics.[30] Whole-of-university

23 Melanie Schwartz, 'Retaining Our Best: Imposter Syndrome, Cultural Safety, Complex Lives and Indigenous Student Experiences of Law School' (2018) 28(2) *Legal Education Review* 1, 2.
24 Terrina Fernando and Bindi Bennett, 'Creating a Culturally Safe Space When Teaching Aboriginal Content in Social Work: A Scoping Review' (2019) 72(1) *Australian Social Work* 47, 50.
25 Newton (n 13).
26 Newton (n 13) 4.
27 Thunig and Jones (n 2).
28 See Chapter One: Introduction by Heather Douglas and Nicole Watson and Chapter Two: Evidence Given by Eddie Cubillo to the Yoorrook Justice Commission by Eddie Cubillo and Jaynaya Dwyer.
29 Jeff Corntassel and Virginia Drywater-Whitekiller, 'Learning on and From the Land: Indigenous Perspectives on University Land-Based Learning Pedagogies' in Cornel Pewewardy, Anna Lees and Robin Zape-tah-hol-ah Minthorn (eds), *Unsettling Settler Colonial Education: The Transformational Indigenous Praxis Model* (Teachers College Press, 2022) 99.
30 See Burns, Lee Hong and Wood (n 5) 17.

approaches have been found to contain the potential to eliminate direct pressure on faculties and academics. In 2019, the final report of the ICCLAP highlighted that university-wide strategies and faculty commitment were critical success factors for including Indigenous cultural competency in curricula.[31] The report states that 'Indigenous cultural competency must become core university business'.[32] Notably, only half of Australia's law schools responded to the Indigenous-led ICCLAP survey. Another survey of Indigenous cultural competency undertaken about the same time by two non-Indigenous University of New South Wales (UNSW) law academics had a response rate of 90 per cent.[33]

Institutional strategies to support the decolonising of legal education take on many different forms across Australian universities. One such strategy is the embedding of an Indigenous graduate attribute, which was identified as a critical success factor in the ICCLAP report. Of the Australian law schools that participated in the ICCLAP survey, only two universities include an Indigenous graduate attribute in their courses. One university that includes an Indigenous graduate attribute as a university-wide strategy is the University of Technology Sydney ('UTS'). It states that 'UTS graduates will have knowledge of Indigenous Australian contexts to inform their capability to work effectively for and with Indigenous Australians across their professional discipline'[34] through the inclusion of an Indigenous course intended learning outcome. Implementation of the Indigenous graduate attribute is further supported by the Indigenous Graduate Attribute Curriculum Framework approved by the UTS Academic Board in March 2022. The framework was developed in alignment with the Australian Qualification Framework criteria of knowledge, skills and application. This includes 'knowledge of cultural, historic and contemporary contexts that influence the lives of Indigenous Australians'; skills to 'examine the nature of the profession and critically reflect on the intersection between Indigenous Australian engagement, experience and achievement within the profession'; and application of 'knowledge and skills relating to Indigenous Australian contexts to inform capabilities to work for and with Indigenous Australians within a professional context'.[35]

31 Burns, Lee Hong and Wood (n 5) 17.

32 Burns, Lee Hong and Wood (n 5) 19.

33 Harry Hobbs and George Williams, 'The Participation of Indigenous Australians in Legal Education, 2001–18' (2018) 42(4) *University of New South Wales Law Journal* 1294.

34 'Graduates Attributes', *University of Technology Sydney* (Web Page) <www.uts.edu.au/research-and-teaching/learning-and-teaching/uts-model-learning/graduates-attributes>.

35 'Graduates Attributes', *University of Technology Sydney* (Web Page) <www.uts.edu.au/research-and-teaching/learning-and-teaching/uts-model-learning/graduates-attributes>, and see Australian Qualifications Council, *Australian Qualifications Framework* (Australian Qualifications Framework Council, 2nd ed, 2013) <https://www.aqf.edu.au/framework/australian-qualifications-framework>.

The Indigenous Graduate Attribute Curriculum Framework provides a guide for individual faculties to develop curricula according to national and institutional priorities. It is also aligned with the courses' accreditation process to provide governance and proper oversight on quality and compliance and to ensure the cultural safety of curriculum content and assessments. University-wide support for embedding Indigenous content in different law courses is reinforced by the role of Associate Dean of Indigenous Teaching and Learning, held currently by Annette Gainsford, the lead author of this chapter. The Associate Dean carries the university-wide Indigenous graduate attribute portfolio and leads a centralised Indigenous Teaching and Learning Team. The team comprises six education academics who provide faculty outreach support and all of the institutional frameworks and resources housed in the Office of the Pro-Vice-Chancellor of Indigenous Leadership and Engagement.

This form of institutional support assists the law school in designing and developing Indigenous graduate attribute content for embedding in law courses, with the university-wide and centralised focus relieving some of the Indigenous curriculum tensions within the law school. The benefits of such an approach include institutional governance and accountability that enable a consistent and transparent methodology to embedding Indigenous content in law courses. This ensures that the specific curriculum is informed and supported by a framework that is designed to enable constructive alignment among the Indigenous course's intended learning outcome, the Indigenous graduate attribute content, and the assessment that is needed to ensure that the Indigenous graduate attribute is achieved. This learning and teaching scaffold enables students to graduate with professional capabilities to work with and for Indigenous Australians when they graduate from law school.

To support the Indigenous graduate attribute process, the centralised Indigenous Teaching and Learning Team facilitates professional development workshops for faculty academics, including the Indigenous Cultural Capability Workshop and the Culturally Safe Indigenous Teaching and Learning Practices Workshop. This approach applies the directive from Universities Australia's *Indigenous Strategy 2022–2025* and learning from the ICCLAP report that professional development is crucial to the success of embedding Indigenous cultural competence.[36] Both professional development workshops are facilitated by Indigenous academics and involve Indigenous teaching and learning pedagogies such as yarning circles. Professional development is further supported through the International Indigenous Community of Practice, founded and led by one of this chapter's authors, Annette Gainsford, where academics can join seminars and learn from others.

36 Burns, Lee Hong and Wood (n 5) 19.

Professional development opportunities are specifically aimed at increasing the capacity of academics to design, develop and deliver Indigenous graduate attribute-focused content. This university-wide strategy empowers the law school to work collaboratively with the Indigenous Teaching and Learning Team on Indigenous curriculum and access professional development on culturally safe subject delivery. This centralised method again alleviates some of the workload pressure for Indigenous academics in faculties and enables the law school to produce graduates with the knowledge and skills to work with and for Indigenous Australians across the legal profession. In the next section, we review how industry standards can further support law schools to embed Indigenous perspectives in curricula.

Leveraging Industry Standards to Embed Indigenous Perspectives

In the foreword to *Indigenous Legal Judgments*, Megan Davis writes that '[l]aw reform is about imagination'.[37] It 'requires you to imagine that the world *can* change. It requires a leap of faith that the institutions built to deliver the change can deliver, even those institutions that have let down our people and abandoned our people.'[38] In re-imagining this transformational path for higher education, we also note the sage warning of Alison Whittaker in her contribution to *Indigenous Legal Judgments*: 'It's very easy to reveal the structural racism of settler law—it's very hard to imagine a way out of it that doesn't replicate that structure.'[39] In this section, we imagine how law accreditation bodies can mandate Indigenous content in higher education programs and make Indigenous cultural competence a standard for admission as a legal practitioner. We begin by determining where we are now to map the path to structural change.

Australian Law School Standards and Indigenous Perspectives

Despite repeated calls over many decades for legal education to include various forms of cultural awareness and cultural competence,[40] there is no requirement to demonstrate Indigenous cultural competence before graduation or admission as a legal practitioner. This absence puts Australia at odds with legal education standards in Canada and now Aotearoa

37 Megan Davis, 'Foreword' in Nicole Watson and Heather Douglas (eds), *Indigenous Legal Judgments: Bringing Indigenous Voices into Judicial Decision Making* (Routledge, 2021) xvi.

38 Megan Davis, 'Foreword' in Nicole Watson and Heather Douglas (eds), *Indigenous Legal Judgments: Bringing Indigenous Voices into Judicial Decision Making* (Routledge, 2021) xvi.

39 Nicole Watson and Heather Douglas, 'Introduction' in Nicole Watson and Heather Douglas (eds), *Indigenous Legal Judgments: Bringing Indigenous Voices into Judicial Decision Making* (Routledge, 2021) 4.

40 *Royal Commission into Aboriginal Deaths in Custody* (National Report, 1991) vol 1; Burns, Lee Hong and Wood (n 5).

(New Zealand).[41] As Eddie Cubillo writes, 'Aboriginal and Torres Strait Islander laws and jurisprudence [are] excluded from the Priestley 11'.[42]

The ICCLAP, led by Marcelle Burns and referred to previously, was initiated to promote the inclusion of Indigenous cultural competence in legal education. The goal of the program was to consult with legal academics and stakeholders to identify knowledge gaps and professional development needs, develop guiding principles, pilot some modules and resources and establish a practice community in legal education. The ICCLAP's initial finding was that 'there was little evidence to show that ICC [Indigenous cultural competency] had been incorporated into Bachelor of Laws Programs'.[43] The ICCLAP Final Report acknowledged that legal accreditation standards drive content, and stakeholders proposed that peak bodies be lobbied, champions among lawyers and judges be identified, and Closing the Gap targets include Indigenous cultural competence to ensure that Indigenous perspectives are embedded in law curricula.[44] The ICCLAP ultimately recommended that a working party be established to 'develop a strategy to lobby legal admissions authorities and professional associations to include ICC in legal accreditation and academic standards'.[45] This working party was underway as of 2023.

We note two further developments since the ICCLAP concluded that are relevant to accreditation standards in legal education. The first is the redrafted Priestleys project initiated by the Law Admissions Consultative Council ('LACC'). The Prescribed Areas of Knowledge, published by the LACC and known as the 'Priestley 11', lists the subjects and areas of knowledge that must be included for the accreditation of law degrees across Australia. In 2018–19, the LACC sought to lead a process of redrafting the Priestley 11 requirements to more closely align them with the Threshold Learning Outcomes for law degrees and the Tertiary Education and Quality Standards Authority ('TEQSA')[46] standards generally.[47] At the time, teams of teachers who could assist in the redrafting were identified, and they developed new learning outcomes to replace the Priestley 11. It is unknown who assisted in the redrafting and whether any of the academics were Aboriginal and Torres Strait Islander people. In the new draft, Indigenous content was included in constitutional and property law. The LACC proposal was deferred in 2020, with the LACC website stating that this occurred as the Council of Australian Law Deans ('CALD') was undertaking its own review of the curriculum.[48]

41 Franks (n 9); 'New Tikanga Māori requirements' (n 10).
42 Eddie Cubillo, 'Indigenous Programs at Law School' (July 2022) *Law Institute Journal* 30, 31.
43 Burns, Lee Hong and Wood (n 5) 10.
44 Burns, Lee Hong and Wood (n 5) 10.
45 Burns, Lee Hong and Wood (n 5) 10.
46 TEQSA is the regulator of tertiary education in Australia.
47 Law Admissions Consultative Committee, *Redrafting the Academic Requirements for Admission* (Legal Services Council, 2019) 2.
48 Cubillo (n 42) 34.

The second notable development was the redrafted CALD Australian Law School Standards.[49] In 2020, the standards were updated in consultation with the Working Party on First Peoples Partnership,[50] an initiative established to fulfil a recommendation of the ICCLAP. The revised standards include specific reference to the following:

- curriculum, expressed as 'Aboriginal and Torres Strait Islander perspectives on and intersections with the law'[51]; and
- library resourcing, namely, 'primary and secondary comparative material from other legal systems, including oral artefacts from Aboriginal and/or Torres Strait Islander legal systems, which are the subject of study in the Law School and are adequate to support the School's teaching and research programs'.[52]

The CALD standards also now include a series of explanatory notes that foreground the Universities Australia recommendations relating to Indigenous cultural competency as a graduate attribute and reference the ICCLAP report, the 'Behrendt Report'[53] and Universities Australia frameworks.[54] They also assert that assessment strategies must exist and draw attention to employment strategies specifically for Indigenous staff. Additionally, in terms of consultation, Aboriginal and Torres Strait Islander knowledge-holders are specifically mentioned, alongside other industry bodies. Despite these two developments, law is still far from other disciplines such as health, where industry requirements mandating Indigenous perspectives in the curriculum are in place. We now turn to examine these professions to determine what they might offer us to accelerate the commitment to embedding Indigenous perspectives and improving the professional capabilities of law graduates and lawyers to work effectively for and with Indigenous peoples.

49 Council of Australian Law Deans, *Australian Law School Standards with Guidance Notes* (2020) <https://cald.asn.au/wp-content/uploads/2024/04/Australian-Law-School-Standards-v1.3-30-Jul-2020.pdf>. No active certification process exists for the Standards.

50 Council of Australian Law Deans, *Working Party on First Peoples Partnership—Terms of Reference* (2020) <https://cald.asn.au/first-nations-peoples/>.

51 Council of Australian Law Deans, *Working Party on First Peoples Partnership—Terms of Reference* (2020) 5.

52 Council of Australian Law Deans, *Working Party on First Peoples Partnership—Terms of Reference* (2020) 9.

53 The Behrendt Report was a sector-wide report recommending that universities build the Indigenous cultural competence of staff and students. See Larissa Behrendt et al., *Review of Higher Education Access and Outcomes for Aboriginal and Torres Strait Islander People* (Final Report, 2012) <https://www.education.gov.au/aboriginal-and-torres-strait-islander-higher-education/review-higher-education-access-and-outcomes-aboriginal-and-torres-strait-islander-people>.

54 Larissa Behrendt et al., *Review of Higher Education Access and Outcomes for Aboriginal and Torres Strait Islander People* (Final Report, 2012) 17–18.

Learning from Other Disciplines and Professions

Professional industry bodies in health are contributing to significant changes not only in curriculum and accreditation requirements for universities but also in the regulation of health practitioners. The National Registration and Accreditation Scheme was established over a decade ago to ensure that health practitioners Australia-wide were subject to the same education, training and quality control standards.[55] Known as the 'National Law', the scheme is hosted by the state of Queensland and is adopted in each state and territory.[56]

Following Indigenous-led advocacy and coordination, amendments to the National Law in October 2022 introduced a new objective to 'build the capacity of the Australian health workforce to provide culturally safe health services to Aboriginal and Torres Strait Islander Peoples'.[57] It also introduced a new guiding principle that the National Law ensure the development of 'a culturally safe and respectful health workforce' that is responsive to Indigenous peoples' health needs and 'contributes to the elimination of racism in the provision of health services'.[58] These reforms are then operationalised through national boards, such as the Nursing and Midwifery Board of Australia. The principal regulator for health professions, the Australian Health Practitioner Regulation Agency ('AHPRA'), works in concert with national boards to ensure that practitioners have the appropriate training and qualifications to practice.

The reforms to the National Law, which centre the capacity building of the health workforce to deliver culturally safe and respectful health services, are the culmination of Indigenous-led whole-of-sector approaches that offer insights for the legal profession and legal education. During 2016–17, the Aboriginal and Torres Strait Islander Health Strategy Group was formed as a strategic partnership among key stakeholders, including Indigenous health leaders, experts and organisations and leaders from national boards, accreditation authorities, and AHPRA.[59] The Aboriginal and Torres Strait

55 Queensland, *Parliamentary Debates* (Legislative Assembly, 12 October 2022) 2636 (YM D'Ath, Minister for Health and Ambulance services) 2636.

56 Council of Australian Governments, *Intergovernmental Agreement for a National Registration and Accreditation Scheme for the Health Professions* (2008) <https://www.ahpra.gov.au/documents/default.aspx?record=WD10%2F36&dbid=AP&chksum=NwgooGtzxb6JjNBIEP9Lhg%3D%3D>.

57 *Health Practitioner Regulation National Law and Other Legislation Amendment Act 2022* (Qld) s 3(2).

58 *Health Practitioner Regulation National Law and Other Legislation Amendment Act 2022* (Qld) s 3A(2)(a)(aa) (i) and (ii).

59 APHRA and National Boards, *The National Scheme's Aboriginal and Torres Strait Islander Health and Cultural Safety Strategy 2020–2025* (2020) <https://www.ahpra.gov.au/About-Ahpra/Aboriginal-and-Torres-Strait-Islander-Health-Strategy/health-and-cultural-safety-strategy.aspx>.

Islander Health Strategy Group privileges self-determination and is a joint decision-making body, as distinct from an advisory body.[60] It developed two significant documents to direct the sector's approach.

First, in 2018, the National Scheme Aboriginal and Torres Strait Islander Health Strategy—Statement of Intent[61] was signed by 15 national health practitioner boards, AHPRA, accreditation authorities and Aboriginal and Torres Strait Islander health sector experts and organisations. The Statement of Intent outlined a common vision and values statement on achieving health equity between Indigenous and non-Indigenous Australians by 2031. While noting the absence of an agreed national definition of cultural safety, it defined cultural safety as 'the individual and institutional knowledge, skills, attitudes and competencies needed to deliver optimal health care for Aboriginal and Torres Strait Islander Peoples'.[62] This reflects the principles outlined in Ramsden's definition discussed earlier in this chapter.

The second major contribution of the Strategy Group was *The National Scheme's Aboriginal and Torres Strait Islander Health and Cultural Safety Strategy 2020–2025* ('*Health and Cultural Safety Strategy*') aimed at eliminating racism from health care. This five-year strategy was the cornerstone of efforts to amend the National Law.[63] This strategy was written by Indigenous leadership business ABSTARR Consulting, which engaged with Aboriginal and Torres Strait Islander organisations and representatives throughout the strategy's development.[64] The *Health and Cultural Safety Strategy* is endorsed by over 40 organisations, including the accreditation authorities that oversee education and training for future health practitioners and those regulating all current practitioners. The Strategy Group provides continued oversight of the strategy.[65]

A baseline definition of cultural safety produced by the Strategy Group, in collaboration with the National Health Leadership Forum,[66] appears in the

60 APHRA and National Boards, *The National Scheme's Aboriginal and Torres Strait Islander Health and Cultural Safety Strategy 2020–2025* (2020) 5.

61 'Aboriginal and Torres Strait Islander Health Strategy—Statement of Intent', *AHPRA & National Boards* (Web Page) <www.ahpra.gov.au/About-Ahpra/Aboriginal-and-Torres-Strait-Islander-Health-Strategy/Statement-of-intent>.

62 'Aboriginal and Torres Strait Islander Health Strategy—Statement of Intent', *AHPRA & National Boards* (Web Page) <www.ahpra.gov.au/About-Ahpra/Aboriginal-and-Torres-Strait-Islander-Health-Strategy/Statement-of-intent>.

63 'Aboriginal and Torres Strait Islander Health Strategy—Statement of Intent', *AHPRA & National Boards* (Web Page) <www.ahpra.gov.au/About-Ahpra/Aboriginal-and-Torres-Strait-Islander-Health-Strategy/Statement-of-intent>.

64 Ann Cheffers, 'First Nations-led Health Strategy Makes Cultural Safety Priority One for Indigenous Patients', *ABSTARR Consulting* (Web Page, 3 March 2020) <https://abstarr.com/first-nations-led-health-strategy-makes-cultural-safety-priority-one-for-indigenous-patients/>.

65 APHRA, *Aboriginal and Torres Strait Islander Health Strategy* (Web Page) <www.ahpra.gov.au/About-Ahpra/Aboriginal-and-Torres-Strait-Islander-Health-Strategy.aspx>.

66 The National Health Leadership Forum comprises leading Aboriginal and Torres Strait Islander health and wellbeing organisations and members.

Health and Cultural Safety Strategy. Cultural safety is defined in the Strategy as follows:

> Cultural safety is determined by Aboriginal and Torres Strait Islander individuals, families and communities. Culturally safe practise is the ongoing critical reflection of health practitioner knowledge, skills, attitudes, practising behaviours and power differentials in delivering safe, accessible and responsive healthcare free of racism.[67]

This definition appears alongside several guiding principles and requirements that set out what health practitioners must do to ensure that the provision of health services is culturally safe and respectful. This includes acknowledging the impacts of colonisation and systemic racism and their far-reaching effects on the health of individuals and communities, addressing their own biases, privileging self-determination and fostering a safe work environment.

Nursing and midwifery were the first to implement the cultural safety objectives in their professional codes of conduct.[68] The Congress of Aboriginal and Torres Strait Islander Nurses and Midwives ('CATSINaM') was particularly active in lobbying for the government to embed cultural competency and safety in the National Law.[69] In 2018, CATSINaM produced a joint statement with the Nursing and Midwifery Board of Australia ('NMBA') to stipulate that their codes 'must clearly communicate the requirement for cultural safety'.[70] The codes of conduct now contain the following definition of cultural safety:

> [The] **Cultural safety** concept was developed in a First Nations' context and is the preferred term for nursing and midwifery. Cultural safety is endorsed by the Congress of Aboriginal and Torres Strait Islander Nurses and Midwives (CATSINaM), who emphasise that cultural safety is as important to quality care as clinical safety. However, the 'presence or absence of cultural safety is determined by the recipient of care; it is not defined by the caregiver' (CATSINaM, 2014, p. 9[71]). Cultural safety is a

67 AHPRA and National Boards (n 59) 9.

68 Eleanor Milligan et al., 'Achieving Cultural Safety for Australia's First Peoples: A Review of the Australian Health Practitioner Regulation Agency-Registered Health Practitioners' Codes of Conduct and Codes of Ethics' (2021) 45 *Australian Health Review* 398.

69 AHPRA and National Boards (n 59) 19. For a review of the criticisms and success stories in embedding Indigenous perspectives in nursing and midwifery, see Claudia Virdun et al., 'Working Together to Make Indigenous Health Care Curricula Everybody's Business: A Graduate Attribute Teaching Innovation Report' (2013) 46(1) *Contemporary Nurse* 97.

70 NMBA, 'NMBA and CATSINaM Joint Statement on Culturally Safe Care', *Nursery and Midwifery Board Ahpra* (February 2018) <www.nursingmidwiferyboard.gov.au/Codes-Guidelines-Statements/Position-Statements/joint-statement-on-culturally-safe-care>.

71 CATSINaM, *Towards a Shared Understanding of Terms and Concepts: Strengthening Nursing and Midwifery care of Aboriginal and Torres Strait Islander Peoples* (CATSINaM, 2014).

> philosophy of practice that is about how a health professional does something, not [just] what they do. It is about how people are treated in society, not about their diversity as such, so its focus is on systemic and structural issues and on the social determinants of health. Cultural safety represents a key philosophical shift from providing care regardless of difference, to care that takes account of peoples' unique needs. It requires nurses and midwives to undertake an ongoing process of self-reflection and cultural self-awareness, and an acknowledgement of how a nurse's/midwife's personal culture impacts on care. In relation to Aboriginal and Torres Strait Islander health, cultural safety provides a de-colonising model of practice based on dialogue, communication, power sharing and negotiation, and the acknowledgment of white privilege. These actions are a means to challenge racism at personal and institutional levels, and to establish trust in healthcare encounters (CATSINaM, 2017b, p. 11[72]). In focusing on clinical interactions, particularly [the] power inequity between patient and health professional, cultural safety calls for a genuine partnership where power is shared between the individuals and cultural groups involved in healthcare. Cultural safety is also relevant to Aboriginal and Torres Strait Islander health professionals. Non-Indigenous nurses and midwives must address how they create a culturally safe work environment that is free of racism for their Aboriginal and Torres Strait Islander colleagues.[73]

These detailed notions are then integrated into the code of ethics, alongside the professional standards and the code of conduct. Cultural safety has been the centrepiece of the reforms, which aim to make quality improvements to patient safety by directing a course of action for AHPRA, national boards and accreditation authorities that regulate current and future health practitioners.

Indigenous and non-Indigenous health leaders have developed a framework that recognises cultural safety as intrinsic to the health of individuals and communities and prioritises its realisation in governance frameworks that train future health professionals and regulate current practitioners. It also demonstrates the privileging of self-determination through governance structures that emphasise joint decision-making powers by using Indigenous organisations as a resource to provide leadership. CATSINaM has its own company, website, board of directors and strategic plan for 2023 to 2028. The Strategic Plan sets out the commitment of CATSINaM to leadership and

72 CATSINaM, *The Nursing and Midwifery Aboriginal and Torres Strait Islander Health Curriculum Framework (Version 1.0)* (2017).

73 CATSINaM, *Position Statement: Embedding Cultural Safety across Australian Nursing and Midwifery* (2017); NMBA, *Code of Ethics Midwifery* (2018) 17.

advocacy by enhancing stakeholders' understanding of culturally safe nursing and midwifery practice and investing in culturally safe education.[74] Additionally, CATSINaM is funded to support the Leaders in Indigenous Nursing and Midwifery Education Network with $2.51 million from 2022–23 to 2025–26.[75] This forms part of the Closing the Gap implementation measures. There is no equivalent body in legal education or the legal profession, and this leadership work needs to be utilised to be effective and sustainable.

Conclusion

Progress in implementing the Universities Australia whole-of-curriculum approach to Indigenous cultural competence has been slow for legal education. This chapter has provided insights on two strategies to accelerate this transformation. First, strong institutional frameworks are critical to embedding Indigenous perspectives sustainably and to an appropriate standard. They can also alleviate the cultural workload of Indigenous academics in faculties and bolster cultural safety for academics, students and industry and community partners.

Second, cultural safety is central to the embedding of Indigenous perspectives in law curricula so that workplaces, classrooms and legal services can be experienced respectfully and without racism. Professional standards in law have a significant influence on legal curricula and thus have the potential to shape legal education to ensure that Indigenous perspectives are embedded authentically and in culturally safe ways to enable all graduates to work effectively with and for Indigenous peoples.

At this stage, legal education and the legal profession are a long way from developing a legal admission standard that reflects the professional capabilities that lawyers need to work with and for Aboriginal and Torres Strait Islander peoples. Engaging an Indigenous business such as ABSTARR to consult with individuals and communities could be a vital step. Drawing on the example from health, an Indigenous-led, whole-of-sector approach is required to create change. The health sector also shows the importance of developing a common definition of cultural safety early in the process. This cannot be retrofitted. What cultural safety means in the classroom and the profession needs to be developed through processes that privilege Indigenous experts and stakeholders. Given that law is heavily influenced by

74 'CATSINaM Strategic Plan 2023–2028', *CATSINaM* (Web Page) <https://dgc5bd.a2cdn1.secureserver.net/wp-content/uploads/2023/11/CATSINaM-Strategic-Plan-2023-2028_FINAL.pdf>.

75 'Closing the Gap Implementation Measures', *National Indigenous Australians Agency* (Web Page) <www.niaa.gov.au/indigenous-affairs/closing-gap/implementation-measures/leaders-indigenous-nursing-and-midwifery-education-network-linmen>.

accreditation standards, updating these standards will provide another impetus for law schools to embrace the embedding of Indigenous perspectives as core business. Current legal practitioners will then be subject to the same education and quality standards as future law graduates. Transformational change in legal education is only possible through culturally safe pathways. This chapter has explored the types of institutional approaches that can support and sustain change at multiple levels within universities.

PART II

Changing Thinking through Theory

7

STORYTELLING—THE POWER OF FIRST NATIONS JURISPRUDENCE

Larissa Behrendt

Introduction

In my first year of law school, we were taught how to find cases in the law journals that populated the law school library. Finding cases and learning citations was a practical introduction to the concept of the doctrine of precedent, which was preserved because things that were written down had a status. There was an inherent legitimacy in the way that what was written in one law book, decades or over a century ago, could provide guidance to how disputes should be decided today. It was still open to interpretation, but this written word seemed to have its own authority.

In this mundane exercise, the process of colonisation was reinforced, not only by imposing the British legal system on Aboriginal and Torres Strait Islander lands but also by bleeding into our subconscious the notion that what is written is more sacred, is wiser and more powerful than knowledge that is passed down orally. These books were presented with a status that reasserted the authority of the British legal system and undermined the authority of the sovereignty, laws and governance structures of my own people.

At the time I started my law degree, no Aboriginal and Torres Strait Islander rights to land were recognised. Pre-Mabo, Australian law, in what was a self-confessed 'legal fiction', had structured an argument that the country had been claimed by the British under the notion of *terra nullius*—a land without people or government. Therefore, when I was taught property, the class began with a dismissal of the rights to land of Aboriginal people. For a whole year, we studied the way that British—and, therefore, Australian—law operated, given surety of title. No one was challenged to think about how Aboriginal people were dispossessed or to consider the consequences of this dispossession.

DOI: 10.4324/9781003473404-9

Luckily, I also had the benefit of an education in the community of Redfern. While growing up in Sydney, I was engaged with the community in Redfern. To me, it was a place of deep intellectual movements that spoke of 'sovereignty' and 'land justice' and a place where the concept of self-determination had manifested in practical ways, specifically, with the first Aboriginal legal service, the first Aboriginal medical service, and a strong commitment to community control.[1] There was a disconnect between what I understood about the legal conquest of Australia from my education in Redfern and what I was taught in class at law school.

The increasing number of First Nations people within the academy, including in law schools, has seen these assumptions that were once presented as a given being scrutinised and challenged. As part of the transformation, new ways of seeing, analysing and understanding are being introduced. A foundational example of this shift, and the first practical iteration of Indigenous standpoint theory that I read, was Worimi man and historian John Maynard's *Fight for Liberty and Freedom*.[2] The book not only investigated and brought to life an important period of history and the role of the Australian Aboriginal Progressive Association but also detailed the role in this movement of Maynard's grandfather, Fred Maynard. It struck me that Maynard's scholarship was stronger for leaning into his family history. I would hear non-Indigenous historians disparage Maynard's work as lacking objectivity, but what, I wondered, is objectivity anyway, especially when one is writing about the history of a country where the colonisation process is ongoing?

Strong critique of the role that property law played—and continues to play—in the colonisation of Australia is now a part of law school curricula because of First Nations legal scholars such as Nicole Watson,[3] Jason de Santolo,[4] Irene Watson[5] and Asmi Wood,[6] as well as critical scholars including Aileen Moreton Robinson.[7] The approach to colonial curriculum

1 Gary Foley, 'Black Power in Redfern: 1968–1972', *The Koori History Website* (Web Page, 2001) <https://kooriweb.org/foley/resources/pdfs/228.pdf>.

2 John Maynard, *Fight for Liberty and Freedom: The Origins of Australian Aboriginal Activism* (Aboriginal Studies Press, 2007).

3 Nicole Watson, *Aboriginal Women, Law and Critical Race Theory: Storytelling from the Margins* (Palgrave, 2021).

4 Jo-Ann Archibald Q'um Q'um Xiemm, Jenny Lee Morgan and Jason De Santolo (eds), *Decolonizing Research: Indigenous Storywork as Methodology* (Zed Books, 2019); *Warburdar Bununu* (Brown Cabs, 2019) <https://watershieldfilm.com/>.

5 Irene Watson, *Aboriginal Peoples, Colonialism and International Law: Raw Law* (Taylor and Francis, 2014).

6 Asmi Wood, 'Self-Determination Under International Law and Some Possibilities for Australia's Indigenous Peoples' in Laura Rademaker and Tim Rowse (eds), *Indigenous Self-Determination in Australia: Histories and Historiography* (ANU Press, 2020) 26.

7 Aileen Moreton Robinson, *The White Possessive: Property, Power and Indigenous Sovereignty* (University of Minnesota Press, 2015). See also Aileen Moreton Robinson, *Talkin' Up to the White Woman: Indigenous Women and Feminism* (University of Queensland Press, 2000).

is also challenged by scholars including Marcelle Burns[8] and Annette Gainsford[9] and by the Indigenous Legal Judgments project led by Nicole Watson.[10] Through the work of this generation of scholars, the law school curriculum has been fundamentally altered.

Through this scholarship, and the increased First Nations presence within the legal academy, there has been further development of Indigenous methodologies such as standpoint theory. Standpoint theory provides not only a methodological framework that assists with decolonising approaches but also a research framework to locate the researcher in relation to the research. In this way, standpoint theory reflects the First Nations worldview of interconnectedness. It acknowledges that we understand the world better when we understand how one thing is related to something else. It provides for an articulation of the relationship between the First Nations scholar and the colonial legal system.

The Western academic tradition assumes neutrality or objectivity by a scholar. It treats subjectivity with suspicion. In contrast, Indigenous approaches to knowledge understand that where you are placed—your positioning or your 'standpoint'—will fundamentally influence the way that you see the world. The Indigenous standpoint recognises up front that we, as individuals, are shaped by our cultures, cultural values and experiences with society's institutions. This is true regardless of one's background, and it challenges those who do not reflect on the values, biases and assumptions that they bring to their work. In this way, Indigenous standpoint theory plays an important role in challenging assumptions around neutrality that are actually a way of reinforcing power structures of colonisation and patriarchy.

The Standpoint of First Nations Lawyers

Standpoint theory also helps us understand the different perspectives and worldviews of law students and lawyers. It recognises that when a person walks into a law school, they bring with them their own prejudices and assumptions about the way that the world works. For First Nations law students, we enter law school with the historical relationship between law and colonisation—and its on-going role—as part of our lived experience.

An awareness of the ongoing impact of the removal policy, the history of dispossession and the over-representation in the criminal justice system

8 Marcelle Burns, 'Are We There Yet? Indigenous Cultural Competency in Legal Education' (2018) 28(2) *Legal Education Review* 29.

9 Annette Gainsford, Marcus Smith and Alison Gerard, 'Accrediting Indigenous Australian Content and Cultural Competency within the Bachelor of Laws' (2021) 31(1) *Legal Education Review* 59.

10 Nicole Watson and Heather Douglas (eds), *Indigenous Legal Judgments: Bringing Indigenous Voices into Judicial Decision Making* (Routledge, 2021).

provides a more sceptical, less trusting view of the operation of laws. It is already understood that the law plays a role in reinforcing power structures. Law is approached with a critical eye; its assumptions are interrogated, and its concepts of 'equity' and 'fairness' are challenged. This equates to greater engagements with law reform, the use of strategic litigation and challenges to what the concepts of 'justice', 'fairness' and 'equity' mean.

In bringing this experience to the law classroom and then, to the profession, First Nations people engage another Indigenous methodology—that of storytelling. In this way, Indigenous methodology that places research in context provides an opportunity to relate to the nature of this context, and this is most effectively accomplished through the act of narrative or story. The relation of life story and experience not only becomes an important context for Indigenous scholars but also plays an important role in the academy.[11]

Lived experience can provide a counter-narrative to assumptions within colonial law made by those who are uncritical and unquestioning about the way that the law operates. A diversity of counter-narratives that question and prod the operation of laws is important. But it is through the experiences of First Nations people that the ongoing role that the law continues to play in colonisation can be illuminated.

Storytelling as a Transformative Legal Practice

Storytelling illuminates experiences that are often at the margins. It allows for the comparison of experience at a depth at which issues that are conceived at an abstract level—child removal, contact with the criminal justice system and racism—remain within a human context. Storytelling achieves two things in this context: it is an assertion of our sovereignty, *and* it counters the colonial narratives and stories that have spread across our lands. Reasserting our stories on our land is a way of reasserting our ownership. This is an important role within the academy, in spaces that have been unwelcoming and alienating for First Nations people and in disciplines that have privileged colonial perspectives over Indigenous ones. It is also important in the context of academic institutions that have sought to research First Nations people and our cultures and have used such research in ways that are unethical and that undermine the interests and wellbeing of Indigenous subjects or deprive them of the intellectual property rights to their knowledges.

In this way, storytelling, and the oral tradition of First Nations' cultures in Australia, pose a threat to the power structures that the legal system protects. Accordingly, the colonial legal system's privileging of the written word

11 See the influential work of Jo-Ann Archibald on storytelling. Jo-Ann Archibald, *Indigenous Storywork. Educating the Heart, Mind, Body and Spirit* (UBC Press, 2008); Archibald Q'um Q'um Xiiem et al. (n 4).

over oral traditions has an additional implication that effectively privileges the colonial perspective over those of First Nations. For example, evidence from settler diaries, although rife with misunderstanding and prejudice, has been given more weight than the oral history of traditions, language, stories and practice that can be traced back thousands of years.[12] Traditional stories around the country, for example, identify climactic shifts such as sea rise and volcanic activity.[13]

As I have argued elsewhere, there are many reasons to be sceptical about imposed legal systems that are clearly colonial and now attempt to normalise the laws of our country. We know that they were a tool in the colonisation process. Our laws were dismissed by colonial states, and they used their legal systems to try and legitimise this. They did not want to recognise our legal systems because to do so would be to recognise our sovereignty, our culture and our connection to our land. Colonial institutions such as the legal system therefore build in a wilful blindness about these elements of Indigenous culture.[14]

It is important to consider that, just as First Nations' experience provides a narrative, what are presented as neutral facts or unquestioned assumptions about the colonial legal system are also constructs or stories. The 'doctrine of discovery' was a rule created by colonising nations about the circumstances in which they were entitled to occupy land. Ignoring the role of greed, riches and power, the narrative created involved a grant by God (through papal bulls or permission) to take lands from heathens and to civilise them.[15] Much brutality was committed in the name of 'civilising the natives.'

This narrative was extended into the Australian context through the construction of *terra nullius*, whereby the Aboriginal and Torres Strait Islander nations' deep connections to land—which were evidenced by stories—were ignored. Instead, the colonial legal system created a self-confessed 'legal fiction', that is, a story of settlement of land over which no one had a claim. This legal fiction remained comfortably ensconced in Australian law until 1992, when the High Court decided in the *Mabo* case that there was a form of Aboriginal title or native title that was retained by Indigenous nations in certain circumstances. Until then, the concept of *terra nullius* was used to justify the claim of absolute title over Indigenous lands in Australia by the

12 *Members of the Yorta Yorta Aboriginal Community v Victoria* (2002) 214 CLR 422.

13 This story was part of the Budj Bim claim for their UNESCO Heritage Listing. It is naturally interconnected with other parts of the cultural landscape. 'Budj Bim Cultural Landscape', *UNESCO World Heritage Convention* (Web Page) <https://whc.unesco.org/en/list/1577/>.

14 Larissa Behrendt, 'Indigenous Story-Telling: Decolonising Institutions and Assertive Self-Determination: Implications for Legal Practice' in Archibald Q'um Q'um Xiiem et al. (n 4) 175.

15 Robert James Miller et al., *Discovering Indigenous Lands: The Doctrine of Discovery in the English Colonies* (Oxford University Press, 2010).

British and then, the Australian state. Although the doctrine of *terra nullius* was overturned in relation to native title, the High Court was clear that there was no recognition of rights to self-government or recognition of Aboriginal sovereignty that naturally flowed from overturning this fiction.[16]

In disconnecting our land from our governance system, the Court used the narrative tool of metaphor. It described a skeleton, saying that Aboriginal rights can only be recognised by the colonial legal system to the extent that their recognition does not fracture the skeleton of the law[17]—that is, recognition only to the extent that it does not disturb the colonial power balance. To this end, native title exists only after all other titles have been considered, which ensures its minimal impact on the established colonial property regime.

Stories of connection to Country, of songlines unbroken, of languages still spoken and of songs, dances, paintings and stories that are forms of proving custodianship of land under First Nations law have been dismissed and deemed not to hold any legal weight.[18] They cannot be accepted because they are not in a legal reference. The threat that this proof of cultural connection poses to the colonial order has to be neutralised. Therefore, the colonial legal system is dismissive of storytelling because it is deeply challenged by it. Disconnecting law from story disconnects law from personal story. Storytelling humanises. It gives voice to people.

Like my First Nations colleagues, I became a lawyer to change the world. I found, instead, that the practice of law made me feel like a cog in a system. I moved to academia to focus on law reform and found, particularly in the spaces of child protection and criminal justice, that the evidence base is too often dismissed by policy-makers and law-makers. The roll-out of the Northern Territory Intervention, which was against the evidence base,[19] was further proof that ideology and political point-scoring will undermine important attempts at law reform. This is not to say that court work has no role to play. It is crucial. Strategic litigation, particularly class actions, are important strategies for shifting the law. Law reform is still achieved by providing an evidence base for unjust outcomes and templates for what works. But these can be complemented by the role of storytelling.

Over the years, my understanding of what it means to be an advocate has evolved. It started with seeing it solely as a role where I speak for those who cannot speak for themselves, translating their stories into a form acceptable

16 *Mabo v Queensland [No 2]* (1992) 175 CLR 1, 46 (Brennan J).

17 *Mabo v Queensland [No 2]* (1992) 175 CLR 1, 46 (Brennan J) [28]–[30] (Brennan J). Justice Brennan's judgment contains the metaphor of the skeleton of the common law and the need to not break it.

18 Asmi Wood, 'Law and Native Title' in Larissa Behrendt et al. (eds), *Aboriginal and Torres Strait Islander Legal Relations* (Oxford University Press, 2nd ed, 2019) 167.

19 Jon Altman and Melinda Hinkson (eds), *Coercive Reconciliation: Stabilise, Normalise, Exit Aboriginal Australia* (Arena Publications, 2007).

to the legal system through which they are moving. However, over time, through the community members with whom I have had the privilege of working, I have come to understand that another important part of being an advocate is recognising the times when I should be speaking for a client versus the many times it would be better and more powerful to hear the stories from the people themselves. Advocacy should also be about making space for those who have been marginalised and silenced in the system so that they can regain their power and their voice.

This lesson first came from the families that we worked with in the Bowraville community. Over a period of several months during the summer of 1990–1991, three Aboriginal children—Colleen Walker, aged sixteen years, Evelyn Greenup, aged four years and Clinton Speedy Duroux, aged sixteen years—were murdered on the Aboriginal reserve on the edge of the town of Bowraville in New South Wales. When the children first went missing, their parents knew that something was wrong, but when they took their complaints to the police, they were not taken seriously.

Only after Clinton's body was found a few weeks after his disappearance did police start to investigate, but instead of sending in homicide detectives, they sent investigators who had child welfare experience. There has only ever been one suspect in this case—a white man who engaged in a pattern of behaviour that involved bringing alcohol onto the reserve, putting drugs in the alcohol and sexually assaulting young Aboriginal women. He had allegedly attempted this on Colleen, on Evelyn's mother and on Clinton's girlfriend. He was charged, but the failings in the police investigation resulted in his acquittal. The police overlooked critical evidence during the period in which they did not take the disappearances seriously.

The families of Colleen, Evelyn and Clinton have fought to have the case brought back to court and get a conviction. When I was approached by Colleen's aunt to see what could be done to assist them, the families had already been engaged in a twenty-year struggle. I had always been aware of this case: the murders occurred while I was in law school, and they symbolised to me, as an Aboriginal young person, the very deep failings of our criminal justice system. Aboriginal men and women were being locked up at disproportionate rates for offences such as being drunk in public and swearing, but a white man who allegedly murdered three Aboriginal children could walk free. It was part of the historical and contemporary context that I brought with me into the classroom and into the legal profession.

The Bowraville families had noticed that the only times there had been movement in their case were the two occasions in which the mainstream media had published stories about them. Could we, they asked, create our own documentary to once again raise the profile of the case? They were right. This was not a case that could be best defined by legal arguments. This was a case about getting justice for three sets of parents whose children had been murdered and about putting a serial child killer behind bars—and this was a more compelling argument than any legal one. A documentary in which the parents could speak for themselves was a powerful way to emphasise this important concept by putting the story into the words of the parents; no lawyer could argue the rightness of this case as powerfully as they could.[20]

Another avenue that we pursued was to call for a parliamentary inquiry.[21] Although there had never been such an inquiry into a case like Bowraville, the families decided to lobby for one. They did this successfully.[22] One of the first steps taken by the New South Wales Legislative Council Standing Committee on Law and Justice was to watch the documentary, *Innocence Betrayed*, to get a sense of the story and the families and to hear their point of view. Then, the committee members went to Bowraville and spent time with the families before asking a single question for the inquiry.

When the Standing Committee on Law and Justice delivered its findings, every member of the committee spoke with passion about the need to obtain justice in this case. What was striking was how each committee member said something like, 'As a parent, I could not imagine how I would feel if this would have happened to my child' or 'I put myself in their shoes'. It was a testament to the power of hearing the stories of those who have been most betrayed by the system. No one was caught up in the legal semantics. Law-makers understood that this was, at its heart, a case where parents wanted justice for their murdered children. Who can turn away from that?

Developing a Storytelling Jurisprudence

Innocence Betrayed set a template for other documentaries and how I would approach them.

After the Apology[23] was a collaboration between Aboriginal grandmothers who were fighting to have their grandchildren placed in their care and the Aboriginal community control sector that has been instrumental in advocating for policy changes to reduce the number of First Nations children in out-of-home care.

Working in this space, it is easy to see how policy failures and individual prejudices create injustices that often see Aboriginal children removed in circumstances where they should not be removed. Even in circumstances where removal is necessary, guidelines are not followed, and the Indigenous

20 *Innocence Betrayed* (Jumbunna/NITV/Frontyard Films, 2014).

21 The Jumbunna team includes Jason De Santolo, who leads the Land Justice Hub, and Craig Longman, who leads the Strategic Litigation Team.

22 Legislative Council Standing Committee on Law and Justice, Parliament of New South Wales, *Family Response to the Murders in Bowraville* (Report No 55, 6 November 2014) <https://www.parliament.nsw.gov.au/committees/inquiries/Pages/inquiry-details.aspx?pk=2131>.

23 *After the Apology* (Pursekey Productions, 2017) <https://aftertheapology.com/>.

Child Placement Principle is not utilised.[24] The system is also under-resourced and imbalanced. More emphasis and resources are put into removal than into early intervention and reunification. The national figures, which show that Aboriginal children are in out-of-home care at higher rates than their non-Indigenous counterparts in every jurisdiction in Australia, are a testament to the fact that this is a systemic problem with historical roots.[25]

Law reform in this space is difficult. Many people assume that if child protection departments are involved in a case, there must be a reason. But ask those who work in child protection or who have been caught up in it, and they will tell you that there are systemic problems and failings that lead to tragic individual cases. It is difficult to get movement on the reforms needed and challenging to explain how there is still prejudice in a system in which poverty is interpreted as neglect.

After the Apology was an attempt to bring actual cases where injustice had occurred to the public's attention and to show a pattern. It captured real instances of wrongful removal: children removed due to suspected neglect but then found to have had medical conditions that were exceptionally well-managed and a child removed and transferred interstate for suspected neglect when the source of the child's distress was bullying from within the school. The women—mostly grandmothers—who were the main protagonists in the film not only were strong advocates for their own cases but also had worked to try and secure systemic reform. When one hears their stories in their own words, the case is clearly made that the system is failing Aboriginal children and their families. However, the film was also a chance to highlight what actually works. The examples of a father and a young mother who were both being supported by the Mallee District Aboriginal Services ('MDAS') showed through moving stories the role that the Aboriginal community-controlled sector plays in providing early intervention, community placements and the road to restitution and reunification that government departments cannot and do not provide.

Adding to the marginalisation experienced by those who have been wronged by the system is a legal prohibition in all jurisdictions of identifying children who are subject to a care order. Although this is a good policy

24 For information about this principle, see 'Aboriginal and Torres Strait Islander Child Placement Principle', *SNAICC* (Web Page) <www.snaicc.org.au/our-work/child-and-family-wellbeing/child-placement-principle/>.

25 For the most up to date data on child removal, see 'Family Matters Report 2023', *SNAICC* (Web Page) <www.snaicc.org.au/our-work/child-and-family-wellbeing/family-matters/>. See also Teresa Libesman and Paul Gray, 'Self-Determination, Public Accountability, and Rituals of Reform in First Peoples Child Welfare' (2023) 18(1) *First Peoples Child and Family Review* 81; Paul Gray, 'First Nations Reimagining of Child Welfare Key to Addressing Ongoing Disparities' (2021) 50(3) *Australian Bar Review* 466; James Beaufils, 'That's the Bloodline': Does Kinship and Care Translate to Kinship Care?' (2023) 58(2) *Australian Journal of Social Issues* 259.

position to ensure that a child's privacy is protected, it means that when the department makes a mistake, there is little ability for those affected to hold it to account. Animation in the documentary provided a tool to ensure that the legal prohibition and its public policy purpose were respected. At the same time, it provided a mechanism for mothers and grandmothers who have had their children wrongfully removed to speak about what had happened to them. Thus, the film contained four animated vignettes, specifically, stand-alone short films that chronicled the experiences of four Aboriginal women in their own words.

Another aspect of the self-determination approach adopted in *After the Apology* is the use of only First Nations experts. This not only is a way of showcasing the work done at the coalface but also reinforces that First Nations people are best placed to identify the problems and craft the solutions to the issues that face our community. One of these experts was Andrew Jackomos, the Victorian Commissioner for Aboriginal Children and Young People, who undertook a review in 2015 of 100 cases of Aboriginal children in protective services.[26] This review noted that it was a regular occurrence that his staff would find family or kin of children within a few minutes of looking for them on Facebook in cases where the department had said they had not been able to find them in years.

The stories in the film showcased how even though the Aboriginal Child Placement Principle highlights the need for connection to extended family, Aboriginal grandparents are finding themselves deemed 'unacceptable' as carers. This has occurred even when they had no issues or departmental involvement bringing up their own children, were employed, owned their own homes and did not take drugs or consume alcohol. Their grandchildren were being placed in the homes of non-Indigenous people instead. In the context of seeing the Aboriginal Child Placement Principle so systematically ignored, it is difficult not to draw the conclusion that there is a mix of unconscious bias and overt racism affecting decision-making within child protection departments. What is needed is First Nations voices, First Nations perspectives, First Nations solutions and First Nations experts.

These same principles were employed in *Maralinga Tjarutja*,[27] a film about the impact of nuclear tests on the Aboriginal people whose Country was contaminated. The film came about because the Maralinga Tjarutja people had been approached for approval for a television series about the nuclear testing to be filmed on their land. In a sign of their sophistication and savvy, they said that they would only grant this permission if the broadcaster

26 Benjamin Preiss and Miki Perkins, '"Shocking Failures" in Child Protection for Aboriginal Kids: Report', *The Age* (online, 26 October 2016) <www.theage.com.au/national/victoria/shocking-failures-in-child-protection-for-aboriginal-kids-report-20161026-gsazg7.html>.

27 *Maralinga Tjarutja* (Blackfella Films, 2020) <http://blackfellafilms.com.au/project/maralinga-tjarutja/>.

(the ABC) also produced a documentary that captured their story (since the television series did not). They also stipulated that their documentary had to be screened in a prime-time spot before the television series.

When I was approached to direct the project, my first step was to meet with the community with no cameras. I was there just to hear how they wanted their story told. While listening, it became apparent that the nuclear testing, although a most virulent form of colonisation, was only a part of the story. The story began with the long custodianship of the Country by people who had made the desert their home.

The story of disruption started not at the time of the nuclear testing but when the railway came through in the 1910s. During this period, the waterhole at Ooldea was contaminated. This had been the reliable water source that had maintained life in the area for thousands of years, and it took only several years for it to be destroyed by the colonisers. Because of the contamination, the mission at Ooldea was closed. But because the nuclear testing was about to take place, people were moved away from their lands and sent south to a town called Yalata. This resulted not just in relocation to someone else's Country—the change to a colder climate caused many of the old people to die.

However, this was also a story of strength and reclamation. After the testing, the traditional owners fought for recognition of what had happened to them and sought compensation. Today, they live back on Country, caring for it as they always have. To this end, the film opens and closes with scenes of the rangers from Oak Valley looking after the land. Jeremy Lebois and Mima Smart, the heart of the story, travel to the South Australian Museum to reclaim copies of photographs that had been lodged there. The albums, with photographs of the Ooldea Mission, contained images of relatives, ancestors and significant community figures. The repatriation saw the women in the Yalata community travel to the place where the old camp was and relive the memories of the impact of the move. In the Oak Valley community, the images triggered memories of an Ooldea song and dance that was then taught to the children. In the end, the testing itself is only one part of an ongoing colonisation process, but not even nuclear testing could break the connection that the Maralinga Tjarutja people have to their Country. The telling of this story brought more stories to life and continued to keep the culture strong.

Creating space for Jeremy and Mima to tell the stories of their community was a process that meant structuring the story in the way that they wanted to tell it. The railway, and the ills that it brought, was their first disaster. The closure of the mission was the second; the nuclear testing just the third. But Oak Valley is proud of what it has built—the ranger program, the school, an Aboriginal medical service, housing and other infrastructure. I felt that it was not only necessary to tell the story in the way that the community would tell it but also important to capture their tone in telling it: not anger and outrage, but steely determination, pride in culture and a reverence for the ancestors who fought to get the Country back and who campaigned for repatriation and for, to the extent possible, decontamination.

Storytelling and Self-Determination—A Framework

Indigenous storytelling is the counter-narrative to colonisation. Indigenous story deconstructs and shifts power.[28] Working with the Bowraville families, the women fighting to have their children and grandchildren returned and the Maralinga Tjarutja community has shown the power of storytelling to change hearts and minds. It has also shown how creating a space for people to tell their own stories can assist in regaining agency and reasserting their own power—things that their experience in the legal system has stripped them of. Storytelling can create a space for self-determination.

Over time, we have developed a framework for this in our own creative, research and legal practice: a self-determination framework that moves our voices from the margins and places them in the centre. This should be a guiding part of our process, and we have developed a self-determination framework that takes this into account.

The first question that we must ask ourselves as researchers is how is this research building the capacity of the community? The second is how can we mobilise the resources of the university to do the work that the community needs done? In thinking about storytelling as a methodology, the questions that we ask are

- What is the human impact of the law/policy?
- Who has the power/who is powerless?
- Who needs to be empowered to speak?
- Who has the real authority to speak? WHOSE STORY is it?
- How can we help them tell the story?

In our work at Jumbunna,[29] we have sought to ensure an integration of research, practice (through litigation) and storytelling (through new media). Our best work occurs when we integrate all three, mostly because of the way that storytelling enriches our advocacy.

28 See Michelle H Raheja, *Reservation Reelism: Redfacing, Visual Sovereignty, and Representations of Native Americans in Film* (University of Nebraska Press, 2013).

29 'Jumbunna Institute for Indigenous Education and Research', *University of Technology Sydney* (Web Page) <www.uts.edu.au/research/jumbunna-institute-indigenous-education-and-research>.

A Final Reflection

I do not see my legal and academic work and my creative practice as two separate things. They are inextricably bound. They form different strategies for decolonising our laws and institutions by challenging dominant narratives and attempts to silence. Moreover, they are assertions of sovereignty, that is, a continual project that makes space for First Nations culture, laws, lore, perspectives, voices and agency.

The role of a First Nations advocate must be to challenge the power structures within the system. However, it is also important to reflect upon how the power that each of us has gained as we have navigated our way through the colonial world can be used to create space to bring others from the margins in to have a voice, to have their say and to tell their story. Storytelling impacts both the speaker and the listener. It prompts you to think deeply about the concept of self-determination, not just as an abstract idea, but as a transformative framework with practical applications that should fundamentally shift colonial mindsets and power arrangements. It should also provide a framework to nourish and strengthen the world's oldest, continuous living cultures.

8

GENRE OUTLAW

Ruby Langford Ginibi

Suvendrini Perera[1]

Introduction: Against a Gubbaising Order

Ruby Langford Ginibi opens her introductory essay for the inaugural issue of the journal *Law/Text/Culture* with a story about a Lebanese-Australian woman, Ramya, ringing to ask her for assistance with a homework assignment that her son had been asked to complete on Aboriginal customary law. 'I was flabbergasted', Ginibi writes:

> How ironic it was that the education system now wanted to know about Aboriginal law when in fact we were dispossessed of our own land, and that we urban Kooris were forced to assimilate and give up our languages and culture and become like white people. We were forced to conform to their laws and standards, the invaders of our country.[2]

Aboriginal law, reified, delimited and qualified by the patronising adjective 'customary', becomes one of the forms of knowledge through which

1 The late Bundjalung writer Ruby Langford Ginibi was a staunch friend and mentor to me over several decades. She edu-ma-cated me, as a young non-white migrant, to my responsibilities towards the Aboriginal owners of the land. Her edu-ma-cation has been formative in my personal and professional life. This chapter is dedicated to her memory. This chapter draws substantially on two previously published pieces: Suvendrini Perera and Joseph Pugliese, 'White Law of the Biopolitical' (2012) 3(1) *The Journal of the European Association of Studies on Australia* and Suvendrini Perera, 'Having Trouble with the Law: Racialised Punishment and Testimonies of Resistance' in Margaret Thornton (ed), *Romancing the Tomes: Feminism, Popular Culture and the Law* (Cavendish, 2002) 113. I thank both publications for allowing me to reproduce text from these sources.

2 Ruby Langford Ginibi, 'Aboriginal Traditional and Customary Laws' (1994) 1(1) *Law/Text/Culture* 8.

DOI: 10.4324/9781003473404-10

non-Anglo migrants are schooled as national subjects and inducted within an order of normative white citizenship that is founded on the denial of the very possibility of Aboriginal law. In her response, Ginibi challenges the relegation of Aboriginal law to the status of a colonial trophy within the education system. Mounting her own campaign of counter education, or *edu-ma-cation*,[3] of Ramya, her Lebanese-Australian interlocutor, and her wider readership, Ginibi uncompromisingly reminds us of the racialised foundations, structures, operations and effects of Australian law and its violent imposition of what she named elsewhere a 'gubbaising' (a Koori term for 'whitening') order. This uncompromising opposition to gubbaising law is at the heart of her projects as a writer, historian and edu-ma-cator.

Ginibi's analysis of the homework assignment on Aboriginal customary law is illuminated by Dylan Rodriguez's discussion of 'the "multiculturalization" of white supremacy'.[4] In the US context, Rodriguez discusses how a 'normative civic whiteness' is produced through

> ongoing and complex relations of hierarchy, discipline, power and violence that have come to oversee the current and increasingly incorporative 'multicultural' modalities of white supremacy wherein 'people of color' [and other racialised groups] are selectively and incrementally solicited, rewarded, and absorbed into the operative functionings of white supremacist institutions (e.g., the military, police, schools) and discourses.[5]

Normative civic whiteness works 'aggressively' as a form of 'biopolitical power'. It 'creatively transposes the technologies of racism and white supremacy on to alternate (i.e., "nonwhite") racial identifications and embodiments' as it also operates punitively to establish and reproduce the sites and institutions that uphold Australia as a racialised nation-state.[6] The 'discursive and material expansion' of the regime of normative civic whiteness and the production of a 'white civilian ontology' form the basis of the 'contemporary hegemony of law and order and its materialization into a "way of life"'.[7] Whiteness thus enmeshes with law in securing and reproducing colonial and racist forms of biopower that affects the embodied subjects who are its targets.

3 The Koori word 'edu-ma-cate' has a particular significance in Ginibi's work, underscoring the distinctiveness of the Indigenous knowledge being imparted. See Suvendrini Perera, '"You Were Born to Tell These Stories": The Edu-ma-cations of Doctor Ruby' (1998) 17(1) *Meridian* 15.

4 Dylan Rodriguez, *Forced Passages: Imprisoned Radical Intellectuals and the U.S. Prison Regime* (University of Minnesota Press, 2006) 25.

5 Dylan Rodriguez, *Forced Passages: Imprisoned Radical Intellectuals and the U.S. Prison Regime* (University of Minnesota Press, 2006) 25.

6 Dylan Rodriguez, *Forced Passages: Imprisoned Radical Intellectuals and the U.S. Prison Regime* (University of Minnesota Press, 2006) 25.

7 Dylan Rodriguez, *Forced Passages: Imprisoned Radical Intellectuals and the U.S. Prison Regime* (University of Minnesota Press, 2006) 25.

Ruby Langford Ginibi's writings throughout the 1990s stand as stubbornly dissonant and resistant at all levels to the regime of normative civic whiteness established as a national 'way of life'. This begins with the biopolitical ordering of sexuality, family and domesticity and the relentless disciplining of aberrant bodies and subjectivities that she confronts in her two earliest books *Don't Take Your Love to Town*[8] and *Real Deadly*.[9] In her two subsequent volumes, *My Bundjalung People*[10] and *Haunted by the Past*,[11] Ginibi tracks the violent operations of law and order through what she termed the 'White Injustice System'.

I understand Ruby Langford Ginibi's production to be an exemplar of what Nicole Watson identifies as 'Indigenous women's outlaw culture' in her book *Aboriginal Women, Law and Critical Race Theory*.[12] 'Indigenous women's outlaw culture is manifest in a spectrum of relationships with the law', Watson writes, as she identifies two specific dimensions of this culture: 'removing one's self outside of the law and operating within the parameters of the law'.[13] *Haunted by the Past* operates from a position outside the law: at one level, it directly confronts and refutes the law in the form of 'the white injustice system'; at another level, it confronts the unwritten laws that order civic whiteness and its norms of genre, gender, class and race.

Ginibi's efforts are thus a body of work that stands as powerful in its dissonance, as writings of Indigenous women's outlaw culture. Defying the readings of her work that have situated her as a black counterpart of the classic Aussie battler, Ginibi refused to be confined to the realm of literature. 'I haven't discovered fiction yet,' she repeatedly declared, 'I'm too busy writing the truth.'[14] As forms of truth-telling, Ginibi's writings take their place in a tradition of Aboriginal women's documentations and testimonies of Australia's history, and they expound the myriad ways in which, from the outset of colonisation, Aboriginal women have acted as agents of outlaw culture.

Genealogies of Aboriginal Incarceration

The following are the opening lines of *Haunted by the Past* in a chapter titled 'Beginnings':

> When does Nobby's story begin? With his birth . . . ? Or further back with my struggles as an Aboriginal woman raising nine children mostly on my own?

8 Ruby Langford Ginibi, *Don't Take Your Love to Town* (University of Queensland Press, 1988).
9 Ruby Langford Ginibi, *Real Deadly* (Angus & Robertson, 1992).
10 Ruby Langford Ginibi, *My Bundjalung People* (University of Queensland Press, 1994).
11 Ruby Langford Ginibi, *Haunted by the Past* (Allen & Unwin,1999).
12 Nicole Watson, *Aboriginal Women, Law and Critical Race Theory: Storytelling from the Margins* (Palgrave, 2021).
13 Nicole Watson, *Aboriginal Women, Law and Critical Race Theory: Storytelling from the Margins* (Palgrave, 2021) 45.
14 Ruby Langford Ginibi, 'Voicing the Land' [1997] *Notes and Furphies* 117.

> Or maybe Nobby's story starts even earlier than that in the 1880s, when my family went to live on Box Ridge Mission after their traditional lands were taken over by the first squatters up in the north of New South Wales. Thinking about it, I'd say Nobby's story has its roots way back. . . . It's part of a bigger historical picture and a longer story. . . . This story continues today.[15]

From these opening lines, Ginibi signals an animating principle of the text, the dynamic between past and present, from the earliest stages of colonisation to the era of 'reconciliation' initiated in the 1990s. The beginning of Nobby's story, as the passage tells us, cannot be separated from a 'bigger picture and a longer story' that starts with the removal of her Bundjulung people to Box Ridge mission. The chapter describes Ginibi's childhood on the mission:

> Miss Hiscocks was the mission manager when I was a kid. Later, she became the matron of that infamous Cootamundra Girls' Training Home where they trained the stolen children to be serviced out as slaves, which ended with a national inquiry that John Howard has never apologised for. He gets gagged on the word 'sorry'.[16]

Written in the late 1990s, when the revelations of the inquiry into the Stolen Generations of Aboriginal children were beginning to be publicly acknowledged, *Haunted by the Past* inserts the narrative of Nobby's incarceration as a 16-year-old boy into the history of Aboriginal institutionalisation, a history that includes foster homes, missions and schools, as well as prisons. As her reference to then Prime Minister John Howard and his refusal to apologise on behalf of the government emphasises, Ginibi's story is at the same time a narrative of contemporary Australia as a society that sanctions and continues the colonising and genocidal practices of the past.

The temporal shifts between past and present in the text are paired with shifts in the genre and texture of the writing. Immediately after the passage quoted previously, Ginibi goes on to reference a passage from *Bringing Them Home*,[17] the official report from the Human Rights and Equal Opportunity Commission's inquiry into policies and practices of child removal:

> We may go home, but we cannot relive our childhoods. We may reunite with our mothers, fathers, sisters, brothers, aunties, uncles, communities, but we cannot relive the 20, 30, 40 years that we spent without their love and care, and they cannot undo the grief and mourning they felt when we

15 Ginibi, *Haunted by the Past* (n 11) 1.

16 Ginibi, *Haunted by the Past* (n 11) 6.

17 Australian Human Rights Commission, *Bringing Them Home: Report of the National Inquiry into the Separation of Aboriginal and Torres Strait Islander Children from their Families* (Australian Human Rights Commission, 1997) 10 ('*Bringing Them Home*') <https://humanrights.gov.au/our-work/projects/bringing-them-home-report-1997>.

> were separated from them. We can go home to ourselves as Aboriginals, but this does not erase the attacks inflicted on our hearts, minds, bodies and souls, by caretakers who thought their mission in life was to eliminate us as Aboriginals.[18]

The text then returns from the larger story to Ginibi's own story:

> Even today people like the matron Miss Hiscocks do not take responsibility for what they did to our Aboriginal people, as they state they 'were only doing their jobs'.[19]

The passages loop from past to present, from report to autobiography, personal to public, tracing institutional links through the movements of Miss Hiscocks from Box Ridge to Cootamundra, linking the various forms of institutionalisation of Indigenous peoples, and making powerful connections between collective and personal stories of home, loss and return. All of these instantiate various forms of haunting as the past and the present, the personal and the political and the intimate and the collective leak and seep into one another. Precisely as hauntings, they refer both to the unspoken spectres of colonial violence that continue to trouble Australia as the new century dawns, and to unacknowledged histories of collective trauma and psychic wounding that are perceived only in the register of individual criminality, as antisocial acts to be punished.

The connections that Ginibi makes between different forms of institutionalisation of Aboriginal people can be illuminated by Angela Davis's theorising, in the US context, of a genealogy of 'racialised punishment'. Davis sketches a genealogy that

> would accentuate the links between confinement, punishment and race. At least four systems of incarceration could be identified: the reservation system, slavery, the mission system, and the internment camps of World War II. Within the U.S. incarceration has thus played a pivotal role in the histories of Native Americans and people of African, Mexican and Asian descent. In all these places people were involuntarily confined and punished for no other reason than their race or ethnicity.[20]

In *Haunted by the Past*, Ginibi provides her own racialised genealogy of the Australian prison system, showing that since colonisation, the history of the institutionalisation and incarceration of Indigenous peoples has taken

18 Ginibi, *Haunted by the Past* (n 11) 6.
19 Ginibi, *Haunted by the Past* (n 11) 6.
20 Angela Davis, 'Racialized Punishment and Prison Abolition' in Joy James (ed), *The Angela Y. Davis Reader* (Blackwell, 1999) 96, 97.

varied forms: expulsion away from traditional country to distant camps and reserves; incarceration in detention centres or penal settlements for people deemed 'uncooperative', including migrants and refugees; and the systematic forced removal of children for confinement in missions for indentured servitude and assimilation.

Writing Back to the Law

In insisting on the connections between different forms of incarceration and institutionalisation, *Haunted by the Past* provides its own alternative genealogy of the Australian prison system. Going even further, Ginibi's book positions itself as a direct intervention in— and a talking back to—the machinery of Australian law. This occurs at both the macro and micro levels in the text. At the macro level Ginibi constantly comments on and contextualises the legal judgments against her son and other Aboriginal men by pointing out the lie of a 'justice system' based on the paramount injustice of colonisation and the role of the police in implementing and maintaining this system. Here, the text outlines ground more systematically mapped by, among others, Chris Cunneen, and reveals the structural and institutional links between the 'processes of colonisation and criminalisation, and in particular the role of the police in that process'.[21] At the local and micro levels, Ginibi continually identifies the levels of documented corruption in the New South Wales police force at the time, challenging the authority of the police and judges as custodians of law and order.[22]

At a further level, Ginibi repeatedly engages in an (unequal) dialogue with the law in its various manifestations. As an author, she points out the punitive consequences of talking back to the law, identifying the excisions that had to be made to the book for fear of legal action. She writes of her inability to 'include all the facts as I know them or write about all the people that have died. I have had to cut back on some details I think you all should know. That's the white fella's law for you, aye?'[23] In addition to exposing the gaps demanded by 'white fella's law', the text narrates two even more direct attempts by Ginibi to intervene in the (in)justice system.

In the first of these scenes, as Nobby is arrested and taken to Annandale police station in inner Sydney, Ginibi confronts the arresting sergeant with the knowledge and authority of her role as a researcher and edu-ma-cator of the law:

> I told the sergeant who I was and I said I was writing the story of my son's life, about the years he had given to the prison system. I told him . . . that

21 Chris Cunneen, *Conflict, Politics and Crime* (Allen & Unwin, 2001) 3.
22 Ginibi, *Haunted by the Past* (n 11) 24, 65, 68.
23 Ginibi, *Haunted by the Past* (n 11) 78.

> I'd been researching Aboriginal deaths in custody. I told him it was a big shame on Australia that the killing times are still with us. . . . The police sergeant couldn't give a damn. I could see that it annoyed him to even try to explain to me (a black woman) what was happening to my son.[24]

The disjunction here is between Ginibi as the author/edu-ma-cator who researches, records and analyses Aboriginal deaths in custody and Ginibi as the police sergeant sees her: 'a black woman' unworthy of even a response to a query about her son, let alone without any power to question his actions. The disjunction between these two positions is one that plays out again and again in *Haunted by the Past*: between Ginibi as a black woman placed outside the law of white settler society and the position from which she repeatedly attempts to engage with the law, authorised by her sovereignty as an Indigenous subject and as a recognised writer and scholar.

A more extended exchange along the same lines is detailed in the last section of *Haunted by the Past*, when Ginibi is recognised by a judge after Nobby, once again in trouble with the law, is brought before a court:

> The judge recognised me there and said 'I've read your writing Mrs Langford, I admire your writing.' I was so disgusted . . . that I stood up and said 'You couldn't have been listening very much to what I've been writing about, Your Honour.'[25]

Ginibi follows up this exchange by writing a letter to the judge, again explaining Nobby's history and attaching copies of her books to add weight to her words. Although permission was withheld to publish the judge's response in *Haunted by the Past*, Ginibi summarises it for her readers and proceeds to speak back to the judge for several pages of the book:

> I really wanted to include the judge's reply to my letter in this book, but he wouldn't give permission . . . I was very offended by some of the things he said. He didn't mean to offend me but some of his remarks and the language he used did. He addressed me by my first name in a paternalistic way as if he were a personal friend, which he is not. And every time he referred to Aboriginal people, which was on numerous occasions, he always used a small 'a'. . . . He returned by postpak my three books which I had sent to his chambers to edu-ma-cate him.[26]

In sending the judge copies of her book, Ginibi operates from a position that seeks to enter an exchange with the 'white fella's law' from her own position

24 Ginibi, *Haunted by the Past* (n 11) 142.
25 Ginibi, *Haunted by the Past* (n 11) 164–65.
26 Ginibi, *Haunted by the Past* (n 11) 169.

as an Aboriginal authority on law. The judge's rejection of Ginibi's books graphically represents his repudiation of the possibility of any such exchange; it is a refusal to recognise an Aboriginal woman as an interlocutor of 'white fella's law', let alone the possibility of being 'edu-ma-cated' by her.

The judge's refusal to recognise Ginibi as an interlocutor is by no means the end of her attempts to speak back to Australian law. *Haunted by the Past* constitutes her defiant response to the judge and embodies her determination to hold his law to account. In this way, she insists on the value of her family's story as a *public* story and makes her role as Nobby's mother count as a *public* role, one which entitles her to speak with a weight of authority beyond that of the individual. *Haunted by the Past* represents Ginibi's return, as an established author, to the 'gubbaised' materials of her first book, reworking them in ways that make her political and narrative position more pronounced and staking their claim as history. She argued in a 1997 essay:

> My first book, *Don't Take Your Love to Town*, has been in the [NSW] Higher School Certificate curriculum for the last five years, educating white and multicultural Australia . . . I'm amazed that it has never been used as a historical text: it has been used in the themes Aboriginal experience, family, cultural identity, and many others, but never in a historical context.[27]

Rather than falling short of her previous achievement of 'classic' Australian status (as Philip Morrissey argued in a highly critical contemporary review, which is discussed later in this chapter), in *Haunted by the Past*, Ginibi invites us to revisit her award-winning autobiography *Don't Take Your Love to Town* as truth-telling history.[28] In this way, she resists the disciplining and categorising normativity of both law and literature. The refusal of Ginibi's later books, in particular, to conform to the laws of white civic order—its norms of genre, gender, class and race—perhaps account for their being made invisible in subsequent decades.

Genre Trouble: Rewriting Literature, History and the Law

In *Haunted by the Past*, Ginibi situates the story of her son Nobby's repeated terms in jail with the life stories of her family, newspaper accounts and official evaluations of his case. These are interwoven, in turn, with stories and poems of other Indigenous men in prison. The names John Pat, Robert Walker, Charlie Michaels, Eddie Murray, David Gundy and Daniel Yock have become only too familiar in a national register of pain and injustice

27 Ginibi, 'Voicing the Land' (n 14) 117.
28 Philip Morrissey, 'Writing from Behind Bars' (2000) *Australian Book Review* 20.

through the toll of Aboriginal deaths in custody. Two landmark documents frame the text: the *Bringing Them Home* report[29] on the inquiry into the Stolen Generations and the volumes of the Royal Commission into Aboriginal Deaths in Custody.[30]

Through the incorporation of extracts from these reports into her text, along with newspaper cuttings and brief biographies of other incarcerated Aboriginal men, *Haunted by the Past* exceeds the confines of the classic autobiography. It also confronts us with the limits of the autobiographical framework or of an individual's 'personal' story for understanding the racialised experience of imprisonment and 'trouble with the law'. *Haunted by the Past* thus also opens up questions of genre and articulates new forms of subjectivity and collectivity to serve politicised ends.

Questions of genre—that is, of reception, interpretation and reading—are, as Chandra Mohanty points out, inescapably political:

> Third World women's narratives are not in themselves evidence of decentering hegemonic histories and subjectivities. It is the way in which they are read, understood and located institutionally which is of paramount importance. After all the point is not just 'to record' one's history of struggle, or consciousness, but *how* they are recorded; the way we read receive, and disseminate such imaginative records.[31]

In the case of *Haunted by the Past*, its reception, its location in disciplinary and generic terms and its representation, dissemination and publicisation through the key institutions that instruct and direct us how to read are all significant.

Many of these points are crystallised in a review published in the *Australian Book Review* ('*ABR*'). The publication had an institutional location and weight in Australian public life that authorised the views expressed and helped determine how, or indeed whether, a text would be read. In this instance, the review, titled 'Writing from Behind Bars', was doubly authorised by the description of the reviewer, Philip Morrissey, as an 'Aboriginal writer living in Melbourne'. Two extracts from the review are telling:

> Nobby and his problems with the law . . . were an important aspect of Ginibi's earlier work *Don't Take Your Love to Town*. While that book is an Australian classic . . . *Haunted by the Past* does not have the same

29 *Bringing Them Home* (n 17).

30 *Royal Commission into Aboriginal Deaths in Custody* (National Report, April 1991) ('*RCIADIC*').

31 Chandra Mohanty, 'Cartographies of Struggle: Third World Women and the Politics of Feminism' in Chandra Mohanty, Lourdes Torres and Ann Russo (eds), *Third World Women and the Politics of Feminism* (Indiana University Press, 1991) 34.

> degree of complexity and affective richness: in consequence though we learn a lot about Nobby, he remains an oddly insubstantial figure.[32]

In a second passage, Morrissey writes that

> Underlying Ginibi's concern for Nobby is the real fear that he will end up one more Aboriginal man dying in custody, and to *illustrate* this possibility she provides short biographies of several Aboriginal men who . . . don't make it out alive.[33]

Morrissey's review makes it critical to distinguish between the genre of autobiography/biography under which the text is officially classified and the category to which it more closely belongs: as a testimonial or life writing.[34] Lisa Lowe describes testimonial writings as forms of narrative

> that are not merely representational, disconnected from 'real' political life; neither are the[y] . . . transparent records of histories of struggle. Rather these forms, life stories, oral histories, histories of community, literature—are crucial forms that connect subjects to social relations. To consider testimony and testimonial as constituting a 'genre' of cultural production . . . extends the scope of what constitutes legitimate knowledges to include . . . forms and practices that have been excluded from both empirical and aesthetic modes of evaluation.[35]

Located between the empirical and the purely aesthetic or literary, *Haunted by the Past* has most in common with these forms of witness-bearing and truth-telling, that is, with testimony, rather than with more familiar works of autobiography, for example, with a text such as Sally Morgan's *My Place*,[36] one of the first books by an Indigenous author to have achieved best-seller status in Australia in the lead-up to the bicentenary celebrations of the colonial invasion in 1988. In the *ABR* review cited previously, Ginibi's first book, *Don't Take your Love to Town*, also published at the time of the 1988 bicentenary, is used as an aesthetic yardstick against which to measure *Haunted by the Past*, which was published 10 years later in a very different climate.

32 Morrissey (n 28).
33 Morrissey (n 28), emphasis added.
34 See, e.g., Phillipa Sawyer, 'Fictions of White Australia Identity: Land and Community in Contemporary Australian Women's Life Narratives' (MA Thesis, La Trobe University, 1996).
35 Lisa Lowe, 'Work, Immigration, Gender: New Subjects of Cultural Politics' in Lisa Lowe and David Lloyd (eds), *The Politics of Culture in the Shadow of Capital* (Duke University Press, 1997) 356.
36 Sally Morgan, *My Place* (Fremantle Press, 1987).

Morrissey elevates *Don't Take your Love to Town* to the status of an 'Australian classic', a description that removes it from a category of specifically Aboriginal writing and relocates it within an—albeit reconstructed—Australian canon. Compared with *Don't Take your Love to Town*, *Haunted by the Past* is found wanting in the literary humanist values of 'complexity' and 'affective richness', while Nobby is found lacking as a fleshed out, rounded character: 'an oddly insubstantial figure'.

The implicit hierarchies of genre that frame the review preclude it from pursuing a more interesting line of inquiry about *why* the text might be less interested in presenting fully rounded characters as demanded by the novelistic conventions of Western autobiography. The change from Ginibi's initial working title, 'Nobby's Story', to *Haunted by the Past* offers a clue, suggesting a progressive realisation that the individual (auto)biographical framework proves inadequate to the narrative and political imperatives of the text. Similarly, where the reviewer sees the stories from the Royal Commission as 'short biographies' provided to 'illustrate' a point, in a different critical framework, these may be understood not as mere 'illustrations' but as interweavings into the text that allude to the collective nature of the experience of prison for young Aboriginal men.[37]

The interconnectedness between Nobby's story and those of other Aboriginal men in custody is underlined in a powerful and complex scene at the end of *Haunted by the Past* in which Ginibi describes Nobby's wedding:

> [A]s they were getting into the car, something distracted me and made me look on the top of the car. I was struck dumb! There was a circle of faces I knew very well! The spirits of John Pat, Robert Walker, Charlie Michaels, Eddie Murray, David Gundy and Daniel Yock! They were callin out to Nobby, sayin, 'On ya brother. You survived the brutal jails. . . . Go in peace, and live for all of us.' And then Nobby looked up and waved, and I knew he's seen them too![38]

'*Live for all of us*.' Here, instead of a story of individual success or the overcoming of adversity, the traditional subject of autobiography, Ginibi writes Nobby's moment of success as simultaneously marking a deep, collective and systemic loss. The litany of familiar names of men who have died in custody carries the weight of the collective stories of those who did not make it, and they are woven into the fabric of Nobby's happier story. The success narrative of an individual 'crossing the boundaries' of the prison system is destabilised by the simultaneous presence of these other stories, a literal haunting.

37 Francesca Bartlett has suggested that the personal stories given to *Bringing Them Home* and *RCIADIC* need to be understood as Australian examples of testimonial writing. See Francesca Bartlett, 'Public Stories of the Stolen Generations' (PhD Thesis, La Trobe University, 1999).

38 Ginibi, *Haunted by the Past* (n 11) 178–79.

Although Morrissey's review establishes a qualitative difference between Ginibi's first book, *Don't Take Your Love to Town*, and her mature production in *Haunted by the Past*,[39] I identify a strong continuity between them in the ways that both books exceed the demands of humanist autobiography. The publication of *Don't Take Your Love to Town* in the bicentennial year, 1988, inevitably shaped both its production and reception. Later, Ginibi was to deplore attempts to 'gubbaise', or whiten, her work by its Anglo-Australian editor and publisher. The desire to promote the book as a text of reconciliation and to present its narrator as a simple, all-Australian type can obscure *Don't Take Your Love to Town's* uncompromising politics and unsparing representation of the devastating consequences of poverty and racism.

Equally 'gubbaising' are ongoing efforts by critics to fit the text into existing literary categories. Attempts to recruit *Don't Take Your Love to Town* into the battler genre associated with canonical Australian authors ignore the fact that the literary construct of the battler, a product of the nationalist 1890s, is from its inception an ideologically loaded and racially marked figure. Its consolidation as an icon of Australianness, which was quickly reinforced by advertising and popular culture, corresponds with the establishment of the federated white Australian state in 1901. The recurrence of this figure 100 years later in the rhetoric of Pauline Hanson's One Nation Party[40] and John Howard's Liberal Party[41] suggests the extent to which, far from being an inclusive image of the struggling people in our society, the battler remains a figure of the ethnocentric Anglo-Australian imagination.

Rather than the heroic, white, usually male battler of 'the bush', a key construct of the Anglo-Australian imagination, the figure addressed by *Don't Take Your Love to Town* is the urban Aboriginal woman with her children. Rejecting the individualism of the battler genre, Ginibi's text is concerned with the collective, historically and socially produced conditions of Aboriginal families in urban Australia. The hostile forces that she contends with are not of an indiscriminating, apolitical 'nature' but rather the systematically racist policies and practices of the state in housing, employment, education and, most urgently, law and the criminal (in)justice system. In this sense, *Don't Take Your Love to Town* itself is a text that breaks with the narrative conventions of traditional autobiography by quoting extensively from documentary sources and chronicling, not the development or success of an

39 Morrissey (n 28).

40 Pauline Hanson is an Australian political figure and founder of the One Nation Party. See Nick Baker, 'Please Explain: The History of Pauline Hanson's One Nation Party', *SBS* (online, 30 April 2019) <www.sbs.com.au/news/article/please-explain-the-history-of-pauline-hansons-one-nation-party/bpt8rxpxn>.

41 John Howard was the Prime Minister of Australia from 1996 to 2007. He is remembered by Indigenous communities for his dismantling of the policy of self-determination and his refusal to apologise to the members of the Stolen Generations. See Nakari Thorpe, '7 Legacies of John Howard's Government', *NITV* (online, 3 March 2016) <www.sbs.com.au/nitv/the-point/article/7-legacies-of-john-howards-government/qj915w31j>.

individual self, but a complex and intermeshing, inescapably political, *collective* story that necessarily exceeds the confines of the narrowly personal. The text's inclusion of statistics and other non-literary materials on Aboriginal men in custody reinforces Ginibi's insistence on the representational, historical and truth-telling nature of her story.

The collective and relational subjectivity of the narrator in *Don't Take your Love to Town* thus also draws on a conceptual and historical understanding more adequately addressed by the genres of life-writing or testimonio. As Philippa Sawyer has shown, critics attempting to read *Don't Take Your Love to Town* according to the canons of Anglo-American autobiography have, not surprisingly, sometimes found themselves out of their depth.[42] As previously suggested, it appears that in *Haunted by the Past*, Ginibi, now an established author, returns to and reworks the 'gubbaised' materials of her first book. Rather than falling short of her previous achievement of 'classic' Australian status, *Haunted by the Past* perhaps invites us to revisit *Don't Take Your Love to Town*.

The contemporary reception and dissemination of *Haunted by the Past* reveal a degree of reluctance to acknowledge the wider, specifically political claims of Ginibi's story or to read it as anything more than the tale of a single family. Significantly, this reluctance is couched in terms of a 'natural' scepticism aroused by the author's gendered positionality. In the *ABR*, Ginibi is described as 'an indulgent mother' whose maternal affection leads her to overlook the possibility of her son's responsibility for his own actions—and, by extension, the responsibility of the other men discussed in the book.[43] This view is reinforced, perhaps even more damagingly, on the back cover of *Haunted by the Past* by the publisher's blurb referring to a writing told with the 'bias of mother love'. In both cases, positioning Ginibi as (only) a mother immediately depoliticises her analysis and undercuts the authority of her parallel roles as writer, researcher and social critic.

The title of the *ABR* review, 'Writing from Behind Bars', takes on an added layer of meaning in this context and is suggestive of a partiality in the author's vision obscured by its own bars of love. The reviewer states the following:

> As I understand it 53% of the Aboriginal men whose deaths were investigated by the Royal Commission were being held for crimes of violence against women. The values which sustain prisoners' rights to safe and humane treatment in custody are equally applicable to victims of crime; *deaths in custody and criminal acts are separate issues which need to be understood on their own terms*. They meet in *Haunted by the Past* because

42 Sawyer (n 34).
43 Morrissey (n 28).

> Ginibi insists on *personalising* and to some extent *romanticising* stories of individual men rather than sustaining a political analysis of the impact of racism and colonialism on Aboriginal life.[44]

The operative words in this quotation are 'personal' and 'political', which are posed here as mutually exclusive. Ginibi is seen as 'personalising' the prisoners' stories at the expense of a 'political analysis'. A more accurate description might be that the text *reconfigures* the boundaries between personal and political, showing them as intertwined and inextricable. Rewriting the 1970s feminist adage, Ginibi reveals not only that the personal is political but also that the political is personal. Ginibi's positionality in the text is irreducible to a singular role—'mother', 'Indigenous social critic', 'autobiographer' or 'writer'; her attempts to edu-ma-cate the judge, for example, are a consequence of the multiple positions that she occupies as an Indigenous woman, as Nobby's mother, and as a nationally famous Koori writer and edu-ma-cator.

The reviewer's reference to a narrative of 'victims' rights' and the charge of 'personalising and to some extent romanticising stories of individual men' reveal how a rhetoric of 'crime', 'individual responsibility' and victimhood can work to obscure and depoliticise questions of the criminalisation of racialised populations. 'Crime', as Davis indispensably points out, 'is . . . one of the masquerades behind which "race" with all its menacing ideological complexity, mobilizes old public fears and creates new ones.'[45] The mobilisation of a narrative of victims' rights shuts down the argument with the 'obvious' answer that the proper place for the criminal is prison. The carceral logic of the reviewer seems to render a focus on gender and a focus on race mutually exclusive: Ginibi's focus on the racialised incarceration of Aboriginal men is seen as dismissing, or by implication perhaps even condoning, the men's sexual violence against women. But is the reinscription of black men as sexual predators a productive way to address questions of sexual violence, most of it directed at black women? Whereas factors of gender and race need to be considered in their complex historical configurations, in the opinion of the reviewer, prison appears to function once more as the receptacle for the social ills of a racist and sexist system.

The assertion by the reviewer that 'deaths in custody and criminal acts are separate issues which need to be understood on their own terms' suggests that 'the criminal act' exists in isolation.[46] However, 'deaths in custody and criminal acts' are emphatically not 'separate issues' but intimately and

44 Morrissey (n 28) (emphasis added).

45 Angela Davis, 'Race and Criminalization: Black Americans and the Punishment Industry' in Joy James (ed), *The Angela Y Davis Reader* (Blackwell, 1998) 61, 62.

46 Morrissey (n 28).

structurally connected through the historical relationship between the police and Indigenous peoples. A simplified understanding of crime as a self-evident category—what we 'know'—ignores factors such as the over-policing of Indigenous people in contemporary Australia and continuing histories of colonisation, racism and criminalisation.

It is precisely the circulation of historically generated, racialised fears of Black men that Ginibi attempts to circumvent in her narrative. Her account is less blindly 'romanticising' than an attempt to humanise Nobby in his experiences of a dehumanising prison system:

> Pauline . . . went out to see him but came back runnin back in tears, cryin, 'Quick, Mum! Come and talk to im! He's kickin and swearin at em. . . . I hurried out to the station wagon starting to cry myself and pleading, 'Come on son, please behave' . . . . Looking at him made my heart bleed as he was handcuffed with only a smock and a pair of jockettes on. . . . I screamed out, 'Where's his clothes? He's a human being y'know!' Nobby was spitting and kicking at the police as they manhandled him out of the station wagon. His eyes were wild like a terrified lost animal.[47]

This clear-eyed, precise description reads less as 'bias', 'indulgence' or sentimentality than as a moment of empathy for a young man terrorised by the law.

Reading texts as testimonials, Lowe argues, can 'displace the categorizing drive of disciplinary formations':

> While specifying the difference between forms, this understanding of cultural production troubles both the strictly empirical foundations of social science and the universalising tendencies of aesthetic discourse. In this mode we can read testimony . . . as a complex mediating genre that selects, conveys and connects 'facts' in particular ways without reducing social contradiction or compartmentalising the individual as a site of resolution. Likewise we can read literary texts like the novel not merely as the aesthetic framing of a 'private' transcendence, but as a form that may narrate the dissolution or impossibility of the private domain. . . . In this sense cultural forms of many kinds are important media in the formation of oppositional narratives and crucial to the imagination and rearticulation of new forms of subjectivity, collectivity and practice.[48]

Situated within a 'complex mediating genre', *Haunted by the Past* enables the formation and articulation of new subject and speaking positions for

47 Ginibi, *Haunted by the Past* (n 11)152.
48 Lowe (n 35) 356–57.

both writer and reader. Through the medium of life story, it connects subjects to social relations and 'personal' stories to collective histories, making visible the systemic and insitutionalised ways in which the law and the prison implicate and impinge on particular racialised groups. Placed in this context, *Haunted by the Past* enables space for articulating new sites, subjectivities and solidarities of struggle against the forms of racialised punishment produced and reproduced as part of the common sense of Australia's *civic* whiteness as a 'way of life'. As a text that speaks back to the 'disciplinary and categorizing drives' of both law and literature, it produces alternative critical and interpretive positions, clears new spaces and creates unexpected sites for readers at different institutional and disciplinary locations.

Coda

Between the Royal Commission of 1991 and the writing of this chapter in 2024, there have been over 500 deaths of Aboriginal people in custody.[49] Cleveland Dodd, aged 12 years, Ricky-Lee Cound, aged 22, and David Dungay, aged 25, are only some of the young men whose names have become all too familiar in the media, alongside the names of Aboriginal women who have died in custody, including Auntie Tanya Day and Ms Dhu. 'The killing times are still with us' Ginibi wrote, confronting the police sergeant in *Haunted by the Past*.[50] Her words resonate with those of Laura Cound, the mother of Ricky-Lee, a quarter century later:

> Ricky died at the hands of the prison system. A racist system that sees too many young Aboriginal men enter and not enough leave. . . . We have stood with too many families, Aboriginal families, who have lost their sons, sisters, fathers in custody. These families like ours, are broken by these deaths. The system has failed us all.[51]

49 Amanda Porter, 'Quantifying an Australian Crisis: Black Deaths in Custody', *The University of Melbourne* (Web Page, 13 April 2023) <https://pursuit.unimelb.edu.au/articles/quantifying-an-australian-crisis-black-deaths-in-custody>.

50 Ginibi, *Haunted by the Past* (n 11) 142.

51 Giovanni Torre, 'Family of Young Noongar Man Who Died in Custody Urges Inquest to Shine Spotlight on Systemic Crisis', *National Indigenous Times* (online, 8 May 2024) <https://nit.com.au/08-05-2024/11279/family-of-young-noongar-man-who-died-in-custody-urges-inquest-to-shine-spotlight-on-systemic-crisis>.

9

RELATIONALITY AS AN INDIGENOUS TEACHING PRAXIS IN LEGAL EDUCATION

Marcelle Burns

Introduction

Over recent decades, there has been a growing commitment within the Australian higher education sector to include Indigenous knowledges and cultural competency in the curriculum.[1] As a Gomeroi-Kamilaroi First Nations woman, my experience of working in legal practice was that many well-intentioned lawyers who were committed to social justice lacked the knowledge and skills needed to develop effective working relationships with their Indigenous clients.[2] After eight years of working as a solicitor, I came to the legal academy with a 'mission' to ensure that law graduates were better prepared to work with and for Indigenous peoples in their future careers.[3] Consequently, I have developed and taught a number of subjects on Indigenous peoples and the law within both the Bachelor of Laws and Bachelor of

1 Indigenous Higher Education Advisory Council/Universities Australia, *Guiding Principles for Developing Indigenous Cultural Competency in Australian Universities* (Universities Australia, 2011a) and *National Best Practice Framework for Indigenous Cultural Competency* (Universities Australia, 2011b). More recently, the *Universities Australia Indigenous Strategy 2022–2025* makes a commitment to eliminate racism, develop anti-racism strategies and promote cultural safety at universities at 14 and 46–9. See also Marcelle Burns, Anita Lee Hong and Asmi Wood, *Indigenous Cultural Competency for Legal Academics Program* (Final Report, 2019).

2 I worked as a criminal lawyer with the Aboriginal Legal Service (NSW/ACT) Limited from 2000 to 2008 and for most of this time, was the only Indigenous lawyer employed by the service.

3 Marcelle Burns, 'Towards Growing Indigenous Culturally Competent Legal Professionals in Australia' (2013) 12(1) *International Education Journal: Comparative Perspectives* 226.

DOI: 10.4324/9781003473404-11

Indigenous Studies programs at various universities.[4] Over this time, I have developed what I call an 'Indigenous relational pedagogy' in teaching students about the often fraught relationship between First Peoples and the Australian legal system. This chapter outlines my pedagogy and teaching praxis using an Indigenous relational approach.

One of the fundamental aspects of this work is teaching students, both First Nations and non-Indigenous, about the colonial history of Australia and the ongoing forms of colonialism that persist today. This necessarily involves an aspect of truth telling—teaching students about the Frontier Wars,[5] child removal policies[6] and the exploitation and dispossession of Indigenous lands[7] to develop students' understanding of how historical policies inform the current relationship between First Peoples and the Australian nation state. Teaching mixed cohorts of First Nations and non-Indigenous students also presents a challenge to design learning activities and assessments that speak to the diverse experiences of our students and support their personal and academic growth. It is also important to create culturally safe learning spaces for *all students* so that they can explore this difficult subject matter in a supportive and non-judgmental environment, irrespective of their cultural background.[8]

Teaching the history of colonisation in Australia tends to invoke feelings of shock, shame and guilt in non-Indigenous students. For Indigenous students, learning this knowledge may validate their personal, family and community history and experience. For some Indigenous students, it may reveal the insidious nature of colonial policy and the suppression of Aboriginal culture and identity, as many are still learning about their Indigenous ancestry. For all students, learning about colonisation can be a challenging and emotional experience because it may call into question fundamental 'truths' that had been hitherto accepted. It can also be emotional because of the violent and inhumane treatment of Indigenous Australians, which arguably no longer accords with contemporary human rights or community values.

4 Southern Cross University, Bachelor of Laws and Bachelor of Indigenous Studies (Indigenous law major) (1996–2014); Queensland University of Technology, Bachelor of Laws (2008–2014); University of New England, Bachelor of Laws (2015–2022).

5 See, e.g., Henry Reynolds, *Forgotten War* (NewSouth Publishing, 2013).

6 National Inquiry into the Separation of Aboriginal and Torres Strait Islander Children from their Families, *Bringing Them Home* (Report, 1997) <https://humanrights.gov.au/our-work/projects/bringing-them-home-report-1997>.

7 Larissa Behrendt et al., *Aboriginal and Torres Strait Islander Legal Relations* (Oxford University Press, 2nd ed, 2019) 3–18.

8 Cultural safety has been defined by Williams as 'an environment that is spiritually, socially and emotionally safe, as well as physically safe for people; where there is no assault, challenge or denial of their identity, of who they are and what they need. It is about shared respect, shared meaning, shared knowledge and experience of learning together'. Robyn Williams, 'Cultural Safety—What Does It Mean for Our Work Practice?' (1999) 23(2) *Australian and New Zealand Journal of Public Health* 213.

The challenge for legal educators is how to teach about colonisation (and its ongoing forms) in ways that are not disempowering but that will motivate students to become advocates and allies for change.

In this chapter, I discuss relationality as an Indigenous teaching pedagogy and praxis. Part One establishes what I call an 'Indigenous relational pedagogy' informed by Indigenous philosophical and knowledges[9] approaches. Part Two presents how I deploy relationality as a teaching praxis by using two examples from my experience—discussion forums and reflective journals. It also describes student feedback on these activities and assessments and how I developed my pedagogy in response to this feedback. Part Three draws conclusions from this analysis. It is argued that using an Indigenous relational approach to teaching this content enables students to develop an understanding of the historical context of colonisation and recognise its ongoing forms. Students can also gain an appreciation of themselves as cultural beings with agency and power to effect change and become ethical and culturally responsive practitioners in their respective disciplines.

Part One: An Indigenous Relational Pedagogy

My teaching pedagogy applies an Indigenous knowledges approach that emphasises 'relationality'[10] and 'reciprocity'.[11] It is also informed by an 'Indigenous anti-racist pedagogy' that aims to 'reveal contradictions between dominant ideologies and [A]boriginal subjugation' and promote Indigenous self-determination.[12] Indigenous pedagogical approaches require students to engage with Indigenous epistemologies and perspectives, deconstructing their own cultural situated-ness and requiring critical self-reflection.[13] In my teaching, I privilege Indigenous knowledges and perspectives and use Indigenous narratives to 'stimulate dissonance'—that is, 'psychological discomfort from incompatibility between behaviour and beliefs'.[14] Wain argues that this approach is effective in 'providing triggers for self-reflection on assumptions

9 Here, I intentionally use knowledges in the plural to reflect the diversity of First Peoples.

10 Aileen Moreton-Robinson, 'I Still Call Australia Home: Indigenous Belonging and Place in a White Post-Colonizing Society' in Sara Ahmed et al. (eds), *Uprootings/Regroundings: Questions of Home and Migration* (Berg Publishers, 2004) 34.

11 Irene Watson, 'Kaldowinyeri-Munaintya: In the Beginning' (2000) 4(1) *Flinders Journal of Law Reform* 6.

12 Robert Regnier, 'Warrior as Pedagogue, Pedagogue as Warrior: Preliminary Reflections on Aboriginal Anti-Racist Pedagogy' in Roxana Ng, Pat Staton and Joyce Scane (eds), *Anti-Racist, Feminism, and Critical Approaches to Education* (Greenwood Publishing Group, 1995) 67.

13 Jane Williamson and Priya Dalal, 'Indigenising the Curriculum or Negotiating the Tensions at the Cultural Interface? Embedding Indigenous Perspectives and Pedagogies in a University Curriculum' (2007) 36(S1) *The Australian Journal of Indigenous Education* 52, 51–58.

14 Toni Wain, *Creating Cultural Empathy and Challenging Attitudes through Indigenous Narratives* (Final Report, 2013) 10.

and values, as well as broader issues of social justice' and leading students to recognise their unconscious biases in a non-threatening environment.[15]

I embrace the philosophy that 'adult learning is enhanced when learning builds upon students' individual experiences and when students regard their learning as relevant'.[16] Therefore, I take a student-centred approach to teaching that aims to situate student learning within their experience. This makes learning meaningful to students by drawing on their existing knowledge to anchor new concepts and to reveal gaps in their knowledge.[17] I also recognise the need to both challenge and support student learning in cross-cultural contexts and the potential for student resistance and 'discomfort' to be used pedagogically to create transformative learning experiences.[18] Throughout my teaching practice, I build 'relationality' with and between students to support their learning and promote 'reciprocity' to develop shared responsibility for learning and advancing Indigenous self-determination.

Although relationality is not necessarily a novel pedagogical approach, from an Indigenous perspective, there are some key differences in the way that it is understood and deployed. In teaching and pedagogical practice, relational teaching has been described as teachers getting to know their students as a pre-condition for their future learning or as a remedial measure to engage difficult students.[19] Relational pedagogy has also been described as a way of students getting to know one another by telling their own stories, so we, as teachers, can 'draw invisible lines [and] get them to relate to each other'.[20] In this section, I outline key aspects of Indigenous knowledges and relationality as pedagogy.

First, it must be acknowledged that First Nations and Peoples are diverse, and they embrace inclusivity and co-existence.[21] This is evidenced on this

15 Toni Wain, *Creating Cultural Empathy and Challenging Attitudes through Indigenous Narratives* (Final Report, 2013) 10–11.
16 Marlene Le Brun and Richard Johnstone, *The Quiet Revolution: Improving Student Learning in Law* (Law Book Company, 1994) 100.
17 Phil Race, *The Lecturer's Toolkit: A Practical Guide to Assessment, Learning and Teaching* (Routledge, 5th ed, 2019) 35–36.
18 Susan Bryant, 'The Five Habits: Building Cross-Cultural Competence in Lawyers' (2001) 8 *Clinical Law Review* 58–59; David Hollinsworth, 'Unsettling Australian Settler Supremacy: Combating Resistance in University Aboriginal Studies' (2016) 19(2) *Race, Ethnicity and Education* 426.
19 Andrew Hickey and Stewart Riddle, 'Performative Enactments of Pedagogy in the Classroom: Strategies and Tactics of Relationality' (2023) *Pedagogy Culture and Society* 6.
20 Alexander M Sidorkin, 'Toward a Pedagogy of Relation' (2000) *Faculty Publications, Rhode Island College* 6–7.
21 Irene Watson, 'Settled and Unsettled Spaces: Are We Free to Roam?' in Aileen Moreton-Robinson (ed), *Sovereign Subjects: Indigenous Sovereignty Matters* (Routledge, 2007) 15; Ambelin Kwaymullina, 'Aboriginal Nations, the Australian Nation-State and Indigenous International Legal Traditions' in Irene Watson (ed), *Indigenous Peoples as Subjects of International Law: Raw Law* (Routledge, 2018) 1, 1–2; Lester-Irabinna Rigney, 'Indigenous Australian Views on Knowledge Production and Indigenist Research' in Julian E

continent,[22] now known as Australia, where over 250 First Nations language groups were co-existing prior to British colonisation. Such diversity was embraced and celebrated, with respect for differences integral to First Peoples' laws and culture.[23] Consequently, it is not possible to articulate a 'universal' First Nations position or standpoint. Rather, I outline some common philosophical themes expressed by First Peoples in the Australian context.

Second, First Peoples' worldviews emphasise the 'inter-connectedness' of all living things,[24] which is also described as 'relationality'[25] and 'relatedness'.[26] Relationality means that the self is not understood as an atomistic individual but in the context of our relationships to our kin, Country and creation ancestors.[27] Such relationships also extend to other living entities, including waterways, plants, climate, skies and spirits.[28] For Karin Martin, relationality can also be understood as a causal effect—that is, a direct response to an action or event and its consequences or result.[29] Therefore, relationality as a pedagogy and teaching praxis can help students understand the complex social, cultural and legal factors that have influenced colonisation and its ongoing forms over time.

First Peoples' knowledges are also seen as 'relational' and collectively owned.[30] Relationality and respect for diversity also appreciate that all knowledges are 'socially situated, partial and grounded in subjectivities and experiences of everyday life'.[31] Relationality is emphasised in this context through the need to articulate and understand our own positionality and relationship to others. This is consistent with Aboriginal protocols of acknowledging Country and identifying kinship connections to inform social

---

Kunneir and Nomalungelo Goduka (eds), *Indigenous Peoples Wisdom and Power: Affirming Our Knowledge Through Narratives* (Ashgate, 2006) 39; Karin Martin and Booran Mirraboopa, 'Ways of Knowing, Being and Doing: A Theoretical Framework and Methods for Indigenous and Indigenist Research' (2003) 27(76) *Journal of Australian Studies* 207.

22 Kwaymullina, 'Aboriginal Nations' (n 21).

23 Martin and Mirraboopa (n 21) 207.

24 Watson (n 12); Ambelin Kwaymullina, 'Seeing the Light: Aboriginal Law, Learning and Sustainable Living in Country' (2005) 6(11) *Indigenous Law Bulletin* 12.

25 Moreton-Robinson (n 10).

26 Karin Martin, *Please Knock Before You Enter: Aboriginal Regulation of Outsiders and the Implications for Researchers* (Post Pressed, 2008) 66; Martin and Mooraboopa (n 21) 205.

27 Karin Martin, *Please Knock Before You Enter: Aboriginal Regulation of Outsiders and the Implications for Researchers* (Post Pressed, 2008) 76; Mary Graham, 'Some Thoughts about the Philosophical Underpinnings of Aboriginal Worldviews' (2008) 45 *Australian Humanities Review* 182–83.

28 Martin and Mirraboopa (n 21) 207.

29 Martin (n 26) 69.

30 Bagela Chilisa, *Indigenous Research Methodologies* (Sage, 2012) 21.

31 Aileen Moreton-Robinson and Maggie Walter, 'Indigenous Methodologies in Social Research' in Maggie Walter (ed), *Social Research Methods: An Australian Perspective* (Oxford University Press, 2006) 2.

relations and behaviours.[32] Therefore, our 'standpoint' is significant because it informs how we view the world and our place within it.[33] Standpoint theory also recognises that all knowledges are historically, socially and culturally contingent.[34] Standpoint also sheds light on power relations and how knowledge is produced.[35] Jay Phillips articulates an 'Indigenous pedagogical standpoint' that invites consideration of our inter-subjectivity and the 'deconstruction of the epistemological conditions under which Indigenous peoples are "known"'.[36] According to Phillips, teaching Indigenous content without a relational pedagogy may simply perpetuate 'essentialising' and 'deficit discourses' about Indigenous peoples.[37] Therefore, an Indigenous relational approach is important to 'unpacking' how students' knowledge about Indigenous peoples has been shaped. Importantly, it also helps students make the transition from being 'knowers' to 'learners'.[38]

In the Canadian context, Indigenous pedagogies apply the concept of relationality in curriculum by creating opportunities 'that emphasize learning in relationships with fellow students, teachers, families, members of the community, and the local lands'.[39] Relationality is also linked to the principle of 'holism' because all things are related in Indigenous worldviews.[40] Holism embraces the idea that there are four interconnected dimensions of knowledge common to Indigenous epistemologies—emotional, spiritual, cognitive

32 Moreton-Robinson (n 10).

33 Alison Wylie, 'Why Standpoint Matters' in Sandra Harding (ed), *The Feminist Standpoint Theory Reader* (University of California Press, 2000) 341.

34 Alison Wylie, 'Why Standpoint Matters' in Sandra Harding (ed), *The Feminist Standpoint Theory Reader* (University of California Press, 2000) 341.

35 Allan Ardill, 'Australian Sovereignty, Indigenous Standpoint Theory and Feminist Standpoint Theory' (2013) 22(2) *Griffith Law Review* 315, 325.

36 Jay Phillips, 'Indigenous Australian Studies, Indigenous Standpoint Pedagogy, and Student Resistance' in Jo Lampert (ed), *Oxford Encyclopedia of Global Perspectives on Teacher Education* (Oxford University Press, 2019) 3.

37 Jay Phillips, 'Indigenous Australian Studies, Indigenous Standpoint Pedagogy, and Student Resistance' in Jo Lampert (ed), *Oxford Encyclopedia of Global Perspectives on Teacher Education* (Oxford University Press, 2019) 3. Scott Gorringe describes deficit discourse as a 'mode of thinking that frames and represents Aboriginal identity in a narrative of negativity, deficiency, disempowerment. When all the thinking, all the conversations and all the approaches are framed in a discourse that sees Aboriginality as a problem, very little positive movement is possible.' Scott Gorringe, 'Aboriginal Culture Is Not a Problem. The Way We Talk About It Is', *The Guardian* (online, 15 May 2015) <www.theguardian.com/commentisfree/2015/may/15/aboriginal-culture-is-not-a-problem-the-way-we-talk-about-it-is>.

38 Gordon Pon, 'Cultural Competency as New Racism: An Ontology of Forgetting' (2009) 20(1) *Journal of Progressive Human Services* 59.

39 Asma-Na-Hi Antoine et al., *Pulling Together: A Guide for Indigenization of Post-Secondary Institutions*' (BCcampus Open Publishing, 2018) 16 <https://opentextbc.ca/indigenizationcurriculumdevelopers>.

40 Asma-Na-Hi Antoine et al., *Pulling Together: A Guide for Indigenization of Post-Secondary Institutions*' (BCcampus Open Publishing, 2018) 16 <https://opentextbc.ca/indigenizationcurriculumdevelopers>.

and physical—which are inseparable and need to be nurtured for human development and wellbeing.[41] Consequently, Indigenous pedagogies focus on the whole person and emphasise not only academic and cognitive development but also emotional, social and spiritual growth.[42] Learning activities therefore need to provide opportunities for students to learn from and with one another and to explore these different knowledge dimensions. The way that I have employed the concepts of relationality and reciprocity is outlined later.

Degrees of Separation

My pedagogy for teaching Indigenous peoples and the law is also informed by social science research on the relationship between Indigenous and other Australians. The *Australian Survey of Social Attitudes* 2007 ('AUSSA') found that although 68 per cent of Australians recognise that Indigenous peoples are not treated equally to other Australians, and 52 per cent agreed that injustices against Indigenous peoples are not just in the past, only 45 per cent agreed that further government assistance is required to address Indigenous disadvantage.[43] However, one of the most worrying findings of this study was that only 9 per cent of people surveyed have daily contact with Indigenous Australians.[44] Some 46 per cent of respondents did not know any Indigenous people at all.[45] Yet many Australians have 'opinions' about Indigenous peoples! This suggests that most Australians form their views about Indigenous people from what they see in the media and discussions with their peers rather than from genuine engagement with Indigenous people. This survey has not been replicated, but more recent research is consistent with these findings. The application of the Implicit Association Test to the Australian context revealed that three out of four Australians hold explicit bias against Indigenous Australians.[46] Although subjects on Indigenous peoples and the law are not compulsory in Bachelor of Laws programs (students must self-select to undertake this study), there is no reason to assume that student attitudes towards Indigenous peoples are vastly different in this respect.

41 Asma-Na-Hi Antoine et al., *Pulling Together: A Guide for Indigenization of Post-Secondary Institutions'* (BCcampus Open Publishing, 2018) 16 <https://opentextbc.ca/indigenizationcurriculumdevelopers>.

42 Asma-Na-Hi Antoine et al., *Pulling Together: A Guide for Indigenization of Post-Secondary Institutions'* (BCcampus Open Publishing, 2018) 17.

43 Australian Survey of Social Attitudes 2007, reported in Maggie Walters and Chris Anderson, *Indigenous Statistics: A Qualitative Research Methodology* (Routledge, 2016) 102.

44 Australian Survey of Social Attitudes 2007, reported in Maggie Walters and Chris Anderson, *Indigenous Statistics: A Qualitative Research Methodology* (Routledge, 2016) 103.

45 Australian Survey of Social Attitudes 2007, reported in Maggie Walters and Chris Anderson, *Indigenous Statistics: A Qualitative Research Methodology* (Routledge, 2016) 102.

46 Siddharth Shirodkar, 'Bias against Indigenous Australians: Implicit Association Test Results for Australia' (2019) 22(3–4) *Journal of Australian Indigenous Issues* 3.

Therefore, it is important that students learn to critically analyse the information that they have received to date about Indigenous peoples and even 'un-learn' any myths or misconceptions that they may have. An understanding of relationality is important here to emphasise the connections between knowledge 'about' First Peoples and our position in Australian society, both historically and in the present.[47] These insights resonate strongly in the aftermath of the unsuccessful constitutional referendum on the Aboriginal and Torres Strait Islander Voice to Parliament, with widespread claims of misinformation and its impact on the outcome.[48] Clearly, there is much more work to be done in this respect.

Part Two: Relationality as a Teaching Praxis

In this section, I discuss how I have employed relationality as a teaching praxis in subjects on Indigenous peoples and the law. I outline how I have used relationality in the design of learning activities and assessment: through discussion forums (both face-to-face and online) and reflective journals. My engagement with relationality as a teaching praxis has been developed over many years and has been refined over time through my own reflective practice and in response to student feedback.

Discussion Forums

In the subject LAW149 Indigenous Legal Issues,[49] I used relationality as a teaching praxis in the design and assessment of discussion forums, both face-to-face and online. My initial attempts at engaging students in large group discussions on Indigenous legal issues proved difficult due to sensitivities about 'political correctness' and students not wanting to be perceived as getting it 'wrong' or causing 'offence'. After the first offering of LAW149 in 2010, I introduced small discussion groups as a way of increasing student engagement and building relationality with and between students. The discussion forum was assessed and had two aspects: student leadership role (10 per cent) and general discussion participation (5 per cent).

47 Phillips (n 36) at 3 states as follows: 'The key question for an ISP framed learning space shifts is not, "What do students need to know about Indigenous peoples and experiences?" but rather, "Where does my knowledge come from and what is its purpose and impact on the way I relate to, and form, understandings about Australian history and Indigenous Australian peoples and experiences?"

48 The Voice Referendum was defeated with a 'No' vote of 60.06 per cent—see '2023 Referendum Results', *Australian Electoral Commission* (Web Page) <https://results.aec.gov.au/29581/Website/ReferendumNationalResults-29581.htm>. See, e.g., Bridget Brennan, 'With the Defeat of the Voice Referendum, It's the Beginning of the End of a Bruising Era in Black Politics', *ABC News* (online, 16 October 2023) <www.abc.net.au/news/2023-10-16/voice-referendum-defeat-indigenous-response/102977272>.

49 Taught at Queensland University of Technology from 2010 to 2014.

For the discussion forums, students were placed into groups of six, with each student assigned a 'leadership' role for one of the tutorial topics.[50] Tutorial questions were provided to give structure to the discussion. During class, the tutor would drop into each group for up to 10 minutes to observe the discussions and ask questions of the leader and group. The session would conclude with each leader reporting back to the whole class on the key points from their discussion and raising any issues for further consideration and/or explanation. This aspect of the tutorial provided a neat summary of the key points and helped to identify issues that were problematic or troublesome for students. Relationality was reinforced across groups and with the students and teacher through lively discussion and critique.

Most non-Indigenous students came to the study of these units to learn 'about' Indigenous peoples and culture; they also came with a limited understanding of themselves as cultural beings.[51] There is a perception that 'culture' belongs to the Indigenous 'other' and that white Australians have no culture.[52] Indigenous students are also diverse in terms of their culture and connection to Country and are therefore often keen to learn about their heritage and culture through their studies.[53] It is well recognised that to develop students' competence to work effectively with Indigenous Australians, students must have the 'ability to critically reflect on one's own culture and professional paradigms in order to understand its cultural limitations and effect positive change'.[54] Thus, helping students to understand how their own culture (and its limitations) may impact communication with Indigenous peoples is an important step towards developing cultural competency. The diversity of Indigenous peoples in the Australian context also makes it relevant for Indigenous students to prepare themselves to work with and for other Indigenous groups whose cultural norms may differ from their own.

In the first tutorial discussions, students were asked to identify their own cultural background and share this with the group. Many non-Indigenous students responded that they were 'just Australian', so further probing was necessary to get them to articulate just what this meant. This inevitably led to

50 This model was adapted from my former colleagues, Marett Leiboff and Mark Thomas, 'The Articulate Student: Engaged Student Interaction in the Learning of Legal Theory' in Ian Wells et al. (eds), *Online Learning and Teaching (OLT) 2004 Conference Proceedings. Exploring Integrated Learning Environments* (Teaching and Learning Support Services, Queensland University of Technology, 2004) 113.

51 Bryant (n 18) 59.

52 WEH Stanner, *White Man Got no Dreaming: Essays 1838–1973* (ANU Press, 1965–1991).

53 This is not intended to diminish the cultural identity of Indigenous peoples but rather to acknowledge that estrangement from culture is often part of the 'Indigenous experience' due to government policies of forced removal of children, integration and assimilation, which constituted cultural genocide. See generally National Inquiry into the Separation of Aboriginal and Torres Strait Islander Children from their Families (n 6) Chapter 13.

54 Universities Australia, *National Best Practice Framework for Indigenous Cultural Competency* (n 1).

a discussion about cultural norms and rules and language—what behaviour is accepted or not and protocols for engagement. Analogies were also drawn with 'legal culture' and the language, dress, rules and protocols that students were learning in law school to be able to operate effectively as legal professionals.[55] In this way, a relational approach enabled students to recognise themselves as cultural beings—operating within multiple cultural contexts at different times.[56] It also helped students to understand that law is not an objective and neutral phenomenon but rather is culturally determined.

What really impressed me about the student leaders was their diligence in preparing for the task and their generosity in sharing information and what they had learnt—well beyond the prescribed readings and course materials. Perhaps this was because all students knew that they would be leaders at some point and would be judged by their peers. However, I believe that the small group discussion format was an effective way of building relationality by providing a framework for students to support one another and fostering a community of learners. It also promoted reciprocity between students, who were both givers and receivers of information and knowledge. The supportive and non-judgmental environment made discussions about Indigenous peoples and the law less daunting for students and helped them to develop an understanding that we all share responsibility for addressing racism and injustice. It also fostered deep rather than superficial learning of the content due to the sharing of information and meaningful exchange generated both between students and with academic staff.

Student feedback on the small group discussions was positive, with many students reporting that these provided a safe environment to explore some of the more complex and challenging issues presented in the subject. The following comment from the 2012 student evaluation survey bears this out:

> The structure of the tutorials was very interesting. Starting with guided questions in groups of peers, then pooling our comments at the end. I think the topics covered were very complex and confronting, and potentially controversial, and this structure made people more comfortable and allowed us to 'grow' our ideas and opinions.[57]

In the 2013 unit evaluation, students were asked focused questions on the discussion forum assessment as follows:

- The small group discussions provided a supportive learning environment for me to explore the unit content—response 4.28 out of 5.
- The student leadership roles encourage all students to participate in discussion forums—response 4.05 out of 5.[58]

55 Bryant (n 18) 70.
56 Bryant (n 18) 59.
57 LWB149, LEX Survey 2012.
58 LWB149, Unit Evaluation 2013.

Some of the comments received were as follows:

> [S]tudent leadership roles encourage students to participate and voice their opinions and views, and also to be able to see certain issues from different perspectives and points of view.
>
> The group discussion allowed me to know other people's opinions and I can actually engage in the discussions.
>
> Loved small tutorial groups, it's much easier to get comfortable and contribute meaningfully to the topic![59]

This feedback supports a relational pedagogical approach and demonstrates how it helped create a safe learning environment for students to explore complex issues in relation with their peers (and academic staff).

Relationality and Reflective Journals

Another way of building relationality in my teaching praxis has been through a reflective journal assessment in both LWB149 and LAW164.[60] Reflective writing in legal education has most commonly been used in the context of work integrated learning and/or professional placements to document student learning and reflect on ethical and professional issues.[61] Reflection has been recognised to be important in developing the self-management skills that are included in the Threshold Learning Outcomes ('TLOs') for the Bachelor of Laws program. TLO 6—self management—states that law students should develop the ability to 'reflect on and assess their own capabilities and performance, and make use of feedback as appropriate, to support personal and professional development'.[62] Self-reflection is also an effective tool to promote psychological health and wellbeing in law students and to develop emotional intelligence and resilience in legal practice.[63] In my teaching praxis, I have used self-reflection to develop students' understanding of colonisation (which was often lacking) and self-awareness of how their culture (and its limitations) may impact effective communication with First Peoples in their personal and professional lives.[64]

59 LWB149, Unit Evaluation 2013.

60 LAW164 2010–2014; LAW149 2017–2022.

61 Judith McNamara, Tina Cockburn and Catherine Campbell, *Good Practice Guide (Bachelor of Laws): Reflective Practice* (Australian Learning and Teaching Council, 2013) 3.

62 Sally Kift, Mark Israel and Rachael Field, *Learning and Teaching Academic Standards Project: Bachelor of Laws Learning & Teaching Academic Standards Statement* (Australian Learning & Teaching Council, December 2010); McNamara et al. (n 61) 2–3.

63 McNamara et al. (n 61) 1.

64 For a discussion of how reflective journals have also been used to engage students in reflection on race and the law, see Marcelle Burns and Jennifer Nielsen, 'Dealing with the "Wicked"

The reflective journal assessment had two key learning objectives. The first was to get students to reflect on their prior knowledge of colonisation and the Stolen Generations as a way of getting them to critically question where their prior knowledge about Indigenous peoples comes from and how it influences their understanding of Indigenous peoples today. This necessarily involves some 'unpacking' of students' prior understanding, with the aim of making students more aware of how their views of Indigenous peoples have been formed and the limitations of their knowledge. This approach is consistent with Phillips' Indigenous standpoint pedagogy (discussed earlier) and a relational approach to student learning. Importantly, self-reflection in this context also allows students to critically analyse contemporary discourses about Indigenous peoples and to evaluate, and be receptive to, new information—especially from Indigenous peoples. From a pedagogical perspective, the first instalment of the journal enabled academic staff to gain a snapshot of students' prior knowledge of colonisation. It also provided a process to build relationality with students by engaging with their reflections and giving feedback on how they could develop and deepen their understanding. Second, the journal was designed to get students to apply what they have learnt to outline strategies for developing effective working relationships with Indigenous peoples.[65] Marking this aspect of the journal gave academic staff an opportunity to assess the extent to which students' understanding had grown and to support further learning through constructive feedback.

Students were given detailed 'Reflective Journal Information' that set out the rationale, learning objectives and assessment criteria. Guiding questions were included to give students a starting point for their reflection, as many students were not familiar with this type of assessment. The 4Rs Model of Reflective Thinking was used to provide a clear structure for the journal.[66]

Problem of Race and the Law: A Critical Journey for Students (and Academics)' (2019) 28(2) *Legal Education Review* 375.

65 LAW164 Reflective Journal Information, T1 2022 set out the learning objectives as follows: 'In this unit the reflective journal assessment is designed to support students in their learning by engaging in a process of deep thinking to: gain an understanding of the historical, social, legal and political context of the British colonisation of Australia; gain an understanding of the ideologies, beliefs and legal doctrines that supported the British assertion of sovereignty in Australia; compare these beliefs, ideologies and doctrines to your own values and/or life experience; reflect upon your own prior knowledge of these issues, including identifying gaps in your knowledge; gain an understanding of First Peoples' experiences and interactions with the Anglo-Australian legal system—both historical and contemporary; identify potential barriers to effective communication with First Peoples; [and] consolidate your learning of the above issues by articulating strategies to develop effective working relationships with First Peoples in your future career.'

66 Mary Ryan, 'The Pedagogical Balancing Act: Teaching Reflection in Higher Education' (2013) 18(2) *Teaching in Higher Education* 144. See also 'The 4Rs Model of Reflective Thinking', *QUT DRAW Project* (Web Page) <www.citewrite.qut.edu.au/assets/docs/4Rs-for-students-page1-v1.5.pdf>.

The 4Rs Model outlines key steps in the reflective writing process that students were required to demonstrate:

- Reporting—describing the issue/event on which you are reflecting;
- Relating—comparing the issue/event to your own experience, knowledge and values;
- Reasoning—developing your understanding about the issue/event with reference to relevant materials and literature; and
- Reconstructing—explaining how what you have learnt will inform your future learning and/or professional practice.

The Reflective Journal Information acknowledged that the subject matter may be confronting, that for many students, it may be the first time that they have been exposed to this information, and that it was 'okay not to know'. What was important, however, was that students document their thinking about why this may be the case and consciously work towards learning more so that they are better informed. The instructions also acknowledged that the content may provoke an emotional response in students and that the journal provided a process to work through their feelings and deepen their understanding on an intellectual level. In this respect, the reflective journal engaged students in affective learning by getting them to consciously consider the traumatic impacts of colonisation and develop their emotional intelligence to work more effectively with First Nations peoples in their future careers. For First Nations students, it was also acknowledged that the content may be deeply personal and distressing, with the reflective journal providing a process to explore some of the impacts of colonisation, with a view toward personal, family and community healing. Students were also encouraged to reach out to the Unit Coordinator if they were struggling with any of the unit content.

The first instalment of the journal was due in Week 3, with a focus on students reflecting on colonisation and child removal policies (500 words; worth 10 per cent). This aspect of the journal was designed according to First Year Curriculum principles, as a low-stakes assessment due before the Higher Education Loan Program (HELP) census date.[67] The second instalment of the journal was due later in the teaching period so that students could draw upon theoretical materials and substantive legal issues to demonstrate their understanding of the strategies to develop effective working relationships with First Peoples (1500 words; worth 30 per cent).[68]

In the first instalment of the journal, the vast majority of non-Indigenous students discussed how little they knew about colonisation and the Stolen

67 Kathy Egea, '6 Principles of First Year Curriculum: Assessment', *LX at UTS* (Blog Post, 10 November 2022) <https://lx.uts.edu.au/blog/2022/11/10/6-principles-of-first-year-curriculum-assessment/>.

68 LAW164 2022. The weighting of this assessment varied from 10 per cent initially to 30 per cent over time.

Generations. This has been a consistent theme for about 90 per cent of non-Indigenous students over time. They were genuinely shocked about frontier violence and the forced removal of children. Students expressed feelings of shame at the treatment of Indigenous peoples. As the journal instructions acknowledged, the unit content may provoke an emotional response—which it evidently did. Of course, I could have simply told students that their knowledge of colonisation was probably quite limited, but enabling them to come to this conclusion themselves opened them up to becoming more critically aware of the limitations of their knowledge. The better students questioned why they were not aware of these events from their socialisation or prior education. This was significant in getting students to understand the hegemonic power of social institutions such as schools and the media that represent dominant group interests (and consequently, how colonial power is reproduced). It also helped students to appreciate how all knowledge is socially constructed and partial. Most importantly, it helped show students that what they thought they knew about Indigenous peoples was not always accurate and that they must therefore question received information concerning its truthfulness and reliability. For Indigenous students, the journal provided a vehicle to explore the policies impacting their families over time; for many, this helped explain the challenges facing Indigenous communities in terms of intergenerational trauma and its ongoing effects.

In the second instalment of the journal, students were asked to reflect not only on how what they have learnt will inform their future practice but also on strategies for developing effective working relationships with Indigenous peoples. Although the majority of students could outline key Indigenous cultural and communication issues that may affect the client–lawyer relationship, fewer non-Indigenous students discussed how their own culture may impact effective engagement with Indigenous peoples. This indicated that some non-Indigenous students were more comfortable speaking about race and the 'other'. They were also effectively distancing themselves from ongoing forms of colonialism and feelings of guilt.[69] Better students were able to articulate both an understanding of themselves as cultural beings and an understanding of 'white privilege', which was important to developing their cultural competency.[70] These students also reported having an 'epiphany' or 'light-bulb' moments that were transformative learning experiences. The reluctance to engage with 'race' was overcome to an extent when I introduced materials on anti-racism, which were well received and gave students positive strategies to become effective allies and agents for change.[71]

69 Hollinsworth (n 18).

70 Peggy McIntosh, 'White Privilege: Unpacking the Invisible Knapsack' (July/August 1989) *Peace and Freedom Magazine* 10; Anne Barton, 'Going White: Claiming a Racialised Identity Through the White Australia Policy' (2011) 7(23) *Indigenous Law Bulletin* 16.

71 See Victoria Health, *Choosing to Act: How Victorians Can Prevent Race Based Discrimination and Support Cultural Diversity* (2013); 'Challenging Racism Project, Bystander Anti-Racism',

Student Feedback on the Journals

Student feedback on the reflective journals has been mostly positive, but, notably, there was some resistance to the reflective journals as a form of assessment. Some students simply did not see the relevance of reflection to their legal studies and preferred more traditional forms of assessment, such as legal problem-solving or essays.[72] Other feedback from students was that I was not using reflective journals 'properly'. There was also a perception that the reflective journal was simply a 'stream of consciousness' and did not require any referencing at all. As one student from the 2017 unit evaluation observed,

> Marcelle faced several uncooperative students who offered her no respect for her knowledge or capacity to teach the unit, based entirely on their inability to grapple with different teaching methods (reflective journals) and subsequently took this frustration out on her. She handled these complaints professionally and continued to teach the unit with the same unwavering passion and depth of knowledge.[73]

This feedback highlights the novelty of reflective writing as a form of assessment in legal education. It also demonstrates student resistance to Indigenous pedagogies that may differ from other forms of learning and assessment and the associated 'cultural load' that Indigenous academics often face in using (and sometimes) defending them.[74] My pedagogy on the use of reflective journals has adapted in response to this feedback. The Reflective Journal Instructions have been refined over time to address these concerns, and student complaints about the journal have significantly reduced.[75]

Western Sydney University (Web Page) <www.westernsydney.edu.au/challengingracism/challenging_racism_project/our_research/bystander_anti-racism>.

72 LAW164 Student Unit Evaluation 2017 TRI1; LAW164 Student Unit Evaluation 2018 TRI1. I did not teach the unit in 2019.

73 LAW164 Student Evaluation of Teaching, 2017 TRI1.

74 'Cultural load' is understood in the context of the workplace as the 'invisible workload employers knowingly or unknowingly place on Aboriginal and Torres Strait Islander employees to provide Indigenous knowledge, education and support'. See Nina Sivertsen, Courtney Ryder and Tahlia Johnson, 'Easing the Cultural load for [I]ndigenous People in the Workplace', *Law Society Journal* (online, 2 February 2023) <https://lsj.com.au/articles/easing-the-cultural-load-for-indigenous-people-in-the-workplace/>.

75 In 2021, there were no complaints about the reflective journal in the unit evaluation, and the unit was rated 4.35 out of 5—LAW164 Student Unit Evaluation 2021 TRI1. In 2022, one student complained that the requirement for referencing was not provided at the beginning of the unit (which I strongly contest) and that it was 'not a true reflective journal'. The unit was rated 4.61 out of 5—LAW164 Student Unit Evaluation 2022 TRI1.

There is, however, evidence that the reflective journal was effective in building relationality with students. As one Indigenous student put it,

> My cultural awareness and identity has grown and given me the opportunity to delve into my Indigenous heritage to reduce cultural isolation in [a] mainstream law faculty.[76]

This statement confirms the value of reflective writing to building relationality and providing a supportive learning environment for Indigenous students. The challenges (and rewards) of reflective writing were also evident in the following feedback from a non-Indigenous student:

> Thank you for your considered comments on my reflective journal part A. . . . Your comments are a help to me as I finish drafting Parts B and C. I thought I should let you know that this is by far the hardest piece of writing I have done for this degree, or in fact any of my other degrees. . . . I nearly pulled out of this course because I found it very personally challenging. But I am very glad I stuck with it.[77]

This feedback shows the power of reflective journals to build relationality with students by providing thoughtful and constructive feedback to support their learning. Another student highlighted how the subjective focus of the reflective journal was important in supporting their personal growth and self-awareness:

> There are not enough units in [XXX] Law degree that has [sic] a 'subjective' approach to learning. It helps to reflect on your own growth. It's good practice to take for in the legal profession . . . you need to have a subjective understanding to determine the extent it influences you.[78]

Overall, this feedback demonstrates how the reflective journal assessment was effective in getting students to engage with the complex conditions of colonisation (historical and continuing). The reflective journal also challenged and supported students in their learning and developed their self-awareness and emotional intelligence.

Although personally, I found marking the reflective journals quite fascinating, my colleagues did not always share this experience and often found the journals difficult to assess. This issue was addressed with markers in two ways. The first was emphasising the subjective nature of reflection and how

76 LAW149, reflective journal, 2009—used with the student's consent.
77 Unsolicited student email, 24 April 2018—LAW164 T1, 2018 (copy on file with the author).
78 LWB149 Unit Evaluation 2014.

in some respects, personal reflection cannot be 'wrong'; the second was reinforcing the 4Rs Reflective model to assess the *quality* of student reflection, especially the higher-order reflective skills such as 'reasoning' and 'reconstruction'. Here, the 4Rs Reflective model provided an effective framework for markers to make a quantitative judgment about the student's reflective writing without diminishing the personal stories shared.

From a teaching perspective, the reflective journal was instrumental in building relationality with students by sharing stories, providing feedback, giving direction for their future study and supporting them in their learning. An Indigenous relational pedagogical approach was important to achieving these learning outcomes, which are critical to building students' capability to develop effective working relationships with Indigenous peoples in their future careers and to become more culturally competent legal practitioners.

Part Three: Conclusions

Indigenous relational pedagogy is an important element of teaching subjects on Indigenous peoples and the law. In my experience, a relational approach has been effective for developing students' understanding of the complex historical, social and cultural context of colonisation and its continuing forms and effects. A relational approach can also engage students in deconstructing the epistemological conditions under which Indigenous peoples are 'known' and how knowledge 'about' Indigenous peoples is produced. These insights are essential for students to gain an appreciation of the discursive nature of legal knowledge and how it informs relations between Indigenous peoples and the Australian legal system.

Using a relational approach is also effective in developing students' understanding of themselves as cultural beings and how their own cultural norms may influence their communication and relationships with Indigenous peoples in their future careers. Reflective journals enable academics to develop relationships with their students by sharing stories and providing feedback to give direction for their future learning. It also provides a process for students to explore their feelings about colonisation and the treatment of Indigenous peoples in a way that builds their emotional intelligence and capacity to work effectively with Indigenous peoples. Relationality as a teaching praxis provides a framework to create culturally safe and supportive learning environments to enhance student learning in what is often perceived as a politically charged learning context.[79] Moreover, for academics, it can be incredibly rewarding to employ relationality as a transformative teaching praxis that enables our students to grow—both personally and professionally—in relation to ourselves and one another.

79 Andrew Trounson, 'Indigenous Focus at Unis Raises "Cultural War" Worry', *The Australian* (Sydney, 16 January 2012) 2.

10

DECOLONISING THE COMMON LAW

Beyond Colonial Thinking

Pekeri Ruska and Jennifer Nielsen

Introduction

Learning in Australian law schools focuses on the common law, a British tradition of principles and maxims that determine and allocate rights, freedoms and privileges.[1] This tradition was applied to Australia through a violent invasion that denied the ancient and inherent law ways of these lands.[2] British law silenced its violent theft of lands and waterways by applying a fiction, terra nullius, to deem the First peoples legally 'no-one', inferior and devoid of advanced polities, social structures and laws.[3]

Ever since, Aboriginal elders, activists and scholars have decried the common law's racist claim that its 'patriarchal white sovereignty',[4] as Goenpul scholar Aileen Moreton-Robinson names it, overrides their sovereignty and authority to speak for Country. They also expose how a racist ideology

1 Australian Law Reform Commission, *Traditional Rights and Freedoms—Encroachments by Commonwealth Laws* (Report 129, 2015) 29–32 <https://www.alrc.gov.au/wp-content/uploads/2019/08/alrc_129_final_report_.pdf>.

2 See Irene Watson, *Aboriginal Peoples, Colonialism and International Law—Raw Law* (Routledge, 2015); Aileen Moreton-Robinson, 'The Possessive Logic of Patriarchal White Sovereignty: The High Court and the Yorta Yorta Decision' (2004) 3(2) *Borderlands e-Journal*.

3 Irene Watson, 'Re-Centring First Nations Knowledge and Places in a Terra Nullius Space' (2014) 10(5) *AlterNative* 508. Though the High Court rejected the application of terra nullius to Australia in *Mabo v Queensland [No 2]* (1992) 175 CLR 1 ('*Mabo [No 2]*'), it instead enunciated the 'act of state doctrine' to 'explain' the legitimacy of the British Crown's acquisition of sovereignty: Aileen Moreton-Robinson, 'The Possessive Logic of Patriarchal White Sovereignty: The High Court and the Yorta Yorta Decision' (2004) 3(2) 18–19 (Brennan CJ). Professor Watson observes this doctrine as simply terra nullius in another guise. Watson, 'Re-Centring First Nations Knowledge' (n 3).

4 Moreton-Robinson, 'The Possessive Logic of Patriarchal White Sovereignty' (n 2).

DOI: 10.4324/9781003473404-12

propels the common law's tide of history like rank flesh hanging from its skeletal framework.[5] This ideology is manifest not only in the discrimination, racism and violence that causes a cumulative and often lethal impact on Aboriginal peoples' daily lives[6] but also in the epistemic violence by which Aboriginal peoples' worldviews and law ways are downgraded as somehow lesser, not real knowledge, not real law and not real philosophy.[7] Though we now speak of *Australian* common law,[8] this original racist ideology persists. It is present in both the common law's tempered, self-serving language ('people [who] have been *physically separated* from their traditional land and have *lost* their connexion with it' and the '*abandoning* of laws and customs based on tradition')[9] and its claims to an 'objective' and unbiased justice[10] that silences the past and the contemporary colonial havoc that it creates.[11]

Nonetheless, the rights, freedoms and privileges bestowed by Australian common law are celebrated for protecting individuals against state interference with the exercise of their rights.[12] The relationship to land is viewed through this lens of *rights*, specifically, property rights, a 'legal relationship with a thing [land]' and the 'degree of power' recognised as permissible to exercise over this thing.[13] Sitting like a 'trump card',[14] property rights are 'inherent' in Australian common law and protected from 'control or diminution, save only *by the laws of the land*'.[15]

And that creates the following paradox:[16] Australian common law rights depend on laws and law stories that *are not of these lands*.[17] British law

5 *Mabo [No 2]* (n 3) 43.

6 Watson, *Aboriginal Peoples, Colonialism and International Law* (n 2); Moreton-Robinson, 'The Possessive Logic of Patriarchal White Sovereignty' (n 2).

7 Aileen Moreton-Robinson, 'The White Mans's Burden: Patriarchal White Epistemic Violence and Aboriginal Women's Knowledge within the Academy' (2011) 26(70) *Australian Feminist Studies*. See also Osca Monaghan, 'Milirrpum v Nabalco Pty Ltd' in Nicole Watson and Heather Douglas (eds), *Indigenous Legal Judgments* (Routledge, 2021) 24, and Monaghan's chapter in this book.

8 We use this term to denote both Australian case law and statutory laws.

9 *Mabo [No 2]* (n 3) 59–60.

10 Larissa Behrendt, 'Indigenous Storytelling—Decolonising Institutions and Assertive Self-Determination: Implications for Legal Practice' in Jo-Ann Archibald Q'um Q'um Xiiem, Jenny Bol Jun Lee-Morgan and Jason De Santolo (eds), *Decolonising Research: Indigenous Storywork as Methodology* (Zed Books, 2019) 175, 179.

11 Irene Watson, 'Power of the Muldarbi, the Road to Its Demise' (1998) 11 *Australian Feminist Law Journal* 28.

12 See Australian Law Reform Commission (n 1) ch 7 and Beth Gaze and Melinda Jones Law, *Liberty and Australian Democracy* (Law Book Co, 1990).

13 *Yanner v Eaton* (1999) 201 CLR 351, 365–66 (Gleeson CJ, Gaudron, Kirby and Hayne JJ).

14 Gaze and Jones (n 12) 480.

15 Australian Law Reform Commission (n 1) 461 [18.8], citing Blackstone (emphasis added).

16 'The ideological scaffolding underpinning all property law in Australia is the belief in the superiority of Western ways of being in relation to the land', Monaghan (n 7) 28.

17 Moana Jackson, 'Decolonisation and the Stories in the Land', *E-Tangata* (online, May 9 2021) <https://e-tangata.co.nz/comment-and-analysis/moana-jackson-decolonisation-and-the-stories-in-the-land/>.

had no authority to supplant Aboriginal laws that were, and are, held by Country[18]—the 'Land is the law', and all meaning comes from it.[19] Kombumerri and Wakka Wakka philosopher Dr Mary Graham explains that

> The land is a sacred entity, not property or real estate; it is the great mother of all humanity. . . . The land, and how we treat it, is what determines our human-ness. Because land is sacred and must be looked after, the relation between people and land becomes the template for society and social relations.[20]

Aboriginal law ways and stories are relational and rest upon a 'custodial ethic' in which '*ownership is a social act and therefore a spiritual act*'.[21] The very health of a place is dependent upon the people of this place; Country needs people, and people need Country.[22] Accordingly, the philosophical focus of the relationship with land is about peoples' connection/*responsibility/obligation* to Country/to land/to kin.[23]

Under Australian common law, the relationship to land is reduced to a 'bundle of rights'[24] that operate within a hierarchy of being that divides body from mind and spirit and divides humans from non-human beings and from the physical and spiritual environment.[25] It struggles to translate the relational, spiritual and interdependent philosophy inherent in Aboriginal relationships to Country or convey the deep responsibilities to care for Country and protect cultural integrity for future generations.

Given this, Tanganekald, Meintangk Boandik scholar Irene Watson asks why 'would one bother to seek justice within a framework that perpetuates injustice?'[26] Watson's question should provoke us to reflect upon and upset the epistemologies and implicit values of the Australian common law. Of course, this work demands more than recognising perspective[27] or even

18 Watson, *Aboriginal Peoples, Colonialism and International Law* (n 2). See also Daniel Lavery, 'Renovating the Orthodox Theory of Australian Territorial Sovereignty' (2022) 45(2) *UNSW Law Journal* 499.
19 Mary Graham, 'Some Thoughts About the Philosophical Underpinnings of Aboriginal Worldviews' (1999) 3(2) *Global Religions, Culture, and Ecology* 105, 106.
20 Mary Graham, 'Some Thoughts About the Philosophical Underpinnings of Aboriginal Worldviews' (1999) 3(2) *Global Religions, Culture, and Ecology* 105, 106.
21 Mary Graham, 'Some Thoughts About the Philosophical Underpinnings of Aboriginal Worldviews' (1999) 3(2) *Global Religions, Culture, and Ecology* 114, 117.
22 Michael Shawn Fletcher, Untitled (Keynote address, A Profound Reorganising of Things: An International Conference, 14 November 2023) <https://arts.unimelb.edu.au/australiancentre/a-profound-reorganising-of-things>.
23 Graham (n 19) 114; Watson, *Aboriginal Peoples, Colonialism and International Law* (n 2).
24 *Yanner v Eaton* (n 13) 366 & 373 (Gleeson CJ, Gaudron, Kirby and Hayne JJ).
25 Graham (n 19) 113–15.
26 Watson, *Aboriginal Peoples, Colonialism and International Law* (n 2) 46.
27 Margaret Davies, *Asking the Law Question* (Thomson Reuters, 4th ed, 2017) 234.

a 'turn to culture'.[28] What we must do, Watson says, is decolonise the law by dissolving and thinking beyond the white colonial 'right way of knowing' intrinsic in Australian colonial common law and its methodologies and philosophies.[29] The work of decolonisation is to re-centre Indigenous voices and law.

In this chapter, we ask can Australian common law be decolonised? Can we navigate beyond the common law's colonial vision and de-centre its Eurocentric epistemological perspectives? If we truly de-centre and dissolve its 'right' thinking, then what will be left—and will this be worth saving? What new traditions of thinking and being might emerge through respectful engagements with Aboriginal worldviews and law ways?

Our purpose is to provoke discussion about this task and what might be involved in taking a 'decolonial turn'. To give context to our discussion, we focus on decolonising Australian cultural heritage laws, specifically, the *Aboriginal and Torres Strait Islander Heritage Protection Act 1984* (Cth) ('*ATSIHPA*'). We examine this decolonial turn by asking questions provoked by 'storytelling' as a methodology.[30] From the outset, we acknowledge that such a task is beyond the scope of one chapter in this text. Nonetheless, we see value in starting the 'unlearning' needed to decolonise law because it may lead us towards the possibilities of a future that 'had not existed before'.[31]

Decolonising Law

The Decolonial Turn

Decolonisation can be described as 'a plurality of ways of understanding the world' that should engender 'a multiplicity of knowledge frameworks', 'not simply those of the Global North'.[32] This means disentangling knowledge production and de-centring 'Eurocentric forms of knowledge for understanding and explaining the world and the place of human beings in it'.[33] This

28 See Jennifer Nielsen, 'The Problem with Research' in Dorota Gozdecka and Anne Macduff (eds), *Feminism, Postfeminism and Legal Theory: Beyond the Gendered Subject* (Routledge, 2019) 117.

29 Watson, 'Power of the Muldarbi' (n 11) 28 & 30.

30 Behrendt (n 10).

31 Irene Watson, 'Aboriginal Sovereignties' in Suvendrini Perera (ed), *Our Patch* (Network Books, 2007) 23, 26.

32 Boaventura de Sousa Santos, Sabelo Ndlovu-Gatsheni and Crain Soudien, 'Critical Reflections on the Place of the University in the 21st Century' (2022) 118 *South African Journal of Science* (Special issue: Radical Reason), Art. #14835, 1, citing Walter Mignolo, 'Coloniality and Subalternity' in I Rodriguez (ed), *The Latin American Subaltern Studies Reader* (Duke University Press, 2001) 224.

33 Boaventura de Sousa Santos, Sabelo Ndlovu-Gatsheni and Crain Soudien, 'Critical Reflections on the Place of the University in the 21st Century' (2022) 118 *South African Journal of Science* (Special issue: Radical Reason), Art. #14835, 1, 1, citing Walter Mignolo,

is an epistemic process that must also dismantle 'the structures of oppression that continue to work to justify the subjugation' of Indigenous peoples and other 'historically marginalized communities'.[34] This demands that we engage in the significant task of *unlearning*,[35] a task that requires humility, reflexivity,[36] truth-telling and 'non-Eurocentric' critical thinking about 'the possibilities of a different reality . . . an anti-capitalist, anti-colonialist, and an anti-patriarchal society . . . [with] no place for relativism'.[37]

Also vital is standpoint. Standpoint frames the legal actor's way of looking at the world and what they regard as important and significant, and it informs what they do and how they do it.[38] Despite the 'neutral, objective and impartial' method of doctrinal common law, our legal knowledge is mediated by who we are, our history and our cultural and social contexts. Our lived experiences are significant to what we apply as law and how we apply it.[39] Acknowledging standpoint is a step towards truth-telling, not only to challenge the Western (legal) claim to objectivity and neutrality but also to shed light on how knowledge is 'produced'.[40] Accordingly, we briefly share our respective standpoints to acknowledge the different modes of critical thinking and reflexivity that we bring to our writing process.

Pekeri

I am a Goenpul[41] woman from Terrangerri [North Stradbroke Island]. In my research, I exercise a Goenpul women's standpoint, drawing on the framework of Australian Indigenous women's standpoint.[42] Furthermore, as theorised by Moreton-Robinson, Indigenous women's standpoint is 'constituted

'Coloniality and Subalternity' in I Rodriguez (ed), *The Latin American Subaltern Studies Reader* (Duke University Press, 2001) 224.

34 Chaumtoli Huq, 'Decolonizing Objective Theory: Race and Coloniality in US Contract Law' in Foluke I Adebisi, Suhraiya Jivraj, and Ntina Tzouvala (eds), *Decolonisation, Anti-Racism and Legal Pedagogy—Strategies, Successes, and Challenges* (Routledge, 2024) 69, 69–70.

35 Watson, *Aboriginal Peoples, Colonialism and International Law* (n 2); Nielsen (n 28).

36 Kate Ogg, 'Decolonising Civil Procedure: Court Process as Continuing Colonisation and Tool for Indigenous Justice' in Foluke I Adebisi, Suhraiya Jivraj and Ntina Tzouvala (eds), *Decolonisation, Anti-Racism and Legal Pedagogy—Strategies, Successes, and Challenges* (Routledge, 2023) 164, 167.

37 De Sousa Santos et al. (n 32) 5.

38 Marrett Leiboff and Mark Thomas, *Legal Theories: Contexts and Practices* (Lawbook Co, 2009) 516.

39 See Marcelle Burns and Jennifer Nielsen, 'Dealing with the "Wicked" Problem of Race and the Law: A Critical Journey for Students (and Academics)' (2018) 28(2) *Legal Education Review* 1, 16–19.

40 Alison Wylie, 'Why Standpoint Matters' in Sandra Harding (ed), *The Feminist Standpoint Theory Reader* (University of California Press, 2000) 341, 339–51. See also Huq (n 34).

41 Goenpul is one of the three tribal groups that make up the 'Quandamooka people'.

42 Aileen Moreton-Robinson, 'Towards an Australian Indigenous Women's Standpoint Theory: A Methodological Tool' (2013) 78 *Australian Feminist Studies* 331.

by our sovereignty and constitutive of the interconnectedness of our ontology (way of being); our epistemology (our way of knowing) and our axiology (our way of doing)'.[43] Identifying one's standpoint 'enables us to acknowledge and to own our biases and to explicitly acknowledge our obligations to legitimise Indigenous experiences through our research'.[44]

While studying law at university, I could never truly relate to the theories and practices of the common law, which I was required to know and articulate to graduate. These structures did not correspond with the values of law and Country instilled in me by my family. However, I graduated from law school and have since endeavoured to engage my skills to assist Aboriginal people in navigating the colonial legal system, as a process to seek justice and a mechanism for truth-telling.

I am currently working on my PhD and am considering the various ways in which Quandamooka people have engaged in strategies of resistance to exercise sovereignty. One of the strategies that I examine is how Quandamooka people engage their voices to navigate the common law system. This exploration delves into their pursuit of justice, resistance against state sovereign powers and concurrent assertion of Quandamooka sovereignty.

My interest in co-authoring this chapter stems from my experiences protecting cultural heritage within Quandamooka Country. Through these processes, I have learnt what cultural heritage protection mechanisms look like in practice within colonial law. I engage with these systems by integrating my legal qualifications with my understanding of Quandamooka Country, alongside the continuous teachings from my elders.

Jennifer

I grew up amidst the 1960s civil rights movement in the United States, but my consciousness of race and whiteness emerged only because of the observations and challenges to white privilege by non-white peoples around me. It began when the Aboriginal law students who I met in Law School opened my eyes to law's hegemonic white culture. Later, it was made suddenly personal when a Yolŋu scholar and friend urged me to read the then-recent Cheryl I Harris article, 'Whiteness as Property'.[45] These, and many experiences that followed, have provoked a continuous journey of reflection, unlearning and cultural humility.

So many years later, I now recognise on whose Country I was born (Boonwurung), live (Quandamooka) and work (both Bundjalung and Yugambeh).

43 Aileen Moreton-Robinson, 'Towards an Australian Indigenous Women's Standpoint Theory: A Methodological Tool' (2013) 78 *Australian Feminist Studies* 340.

44 Crystal McKinnon, 'Expressing Indigenous Sovereignty: The Production of Embodied Texts in Social Protest and the Arts' (PhD Thesis, La Trobe University, 2018).

45 Cheryl I Harris, 'Whiteness as Property' (1993) 106(8) *Harvard Law Review* 1707.

As a white teacher and researcher, these days, I acknowledge my standpoint because there are important limitations on the knowing and subject position that I bring to the critique of law. My research applies critical race and whiteness theory within a framework informed by Indigenous scholarship on colonialism, self-determination, whiteness and racism. My intent is to effect anti-colonial and anti-racist strategies by exposing the tendency of mainstream Australian law to privilege 'white' interests. Moreover, I work reflexively and actively[46] to open spaces in which Indigenous and non-Western epistemologies can meet and disrupt my own.[47]

The purpose of our acknowledgement of our standpoints is to recognise that our respective ontologies have been shaped differently by our individual life experiences and social positions to inform how we understand law, colonialism, race and racism. It is also to acknowledge that we are socially constructed and positioned differently as 'racialised' subjects, which indelibly marks how we experience race and law in our daily lives. Our experiences and knowledge of 'law' are not, and simply cannot be, the same.[48]

Resurgence and an Ethic of Restoration

To us, decoloniality must aim for the right of all people but fundamentally for Indigenous people to have their culture and history acknowledged and respected and to live their life in accordance with their own cultural values without discrimination, appropriation, forced assimilation, ridicule or violence.[49]

For guidance, we turn to the honoured Māori legal theorist Moana Jackson:

> 'Decolonisation' . . . could be replaced with the ethic of restoration . . . to replace colonisation not by merely deconstructing or culturally sensitising the attitudes and power structures that it has established, but by restoring [protocol] that allows for balanced relationships based on the need for [clan] and [language group/nation] independence upon which any meaningful interdependence must rest. . . .
>
> Restoration (like colonisation) is also a process, not an event, and it will require a change of mind and heart as much as a change of structure . . . such transformations must confront the implacability of a power unjustly taken. . . .

46 Nielsen (n 28).
47 Aileen Moreton-Robinson, *Talkin' Up to the White Woman—Indigenous Women and Feminism* (University of Queensland Press, 2000), xxv.
48 See Burns and Nielsen (n 39).
49 Johanna Turunen, 'European Cultural Heritage and the Politics of Decolonisation' (2022) 12 *Tahiti* 107, 108–09.

> Stories for and about transformation rely on honesty about the misremembered stories and the foresight to see where different stories might lead.
>
> That is the ethic of restoration. It offers the chance, or challenge, to clutch truth and justice for 'future flowerings'.[50]

Stories are important in law. Since invasion, Australian common law has privileged its own narratives, tenaciously countering Aboriginal peoples' law stories of their deep connection to these lands.[51] This 'misremembering' is infused within[52] and has infused racism[53] within the canon of law told and written in judges' decisions and the volumes of legislation passed by the parliaments each year. To decolonise, we need to bring 'honesty' to Australian common law's 'misremembered stories' by re-centring Aboriginal law ways and stories. How can we bring honesty to the system of cultural heritage protection?

Larissa Behrendt explains that storytelling is important to decolonisation because '[r]easserting our stories . . . is a way of reasserting our ownership'—'it takes our voices from the margins and puts them in the centre'.[54] To use storytelling as methodology, she says that we should ask the following:

- What is the human impact of the law/policy?
- Who has the power/who is powerless?
- Who needs to be empowered to speak?
- Who has the real authority to speak?
- Whose STORY is it?
- How can we help storytellers enact the intent of the story?[55]

It is useful to deploy Behrendt's questions to unlearn the 'colonial (dis)order' that damages Aboriginal law ways and the 'terra nullius driven colonial culture' that infects our thinking and practice of law.[56] We aim to ask how/if Australian common law can centre Aboriginal peoples' law stories and how to learn/relearn and restore Aboriginal law ways.

Using storytelling as methodology, in the next section, we attempt a decolonial engagement with Australian common law by pursuing 'honesty about the misremembered stories' to gain 'foresight' about where these stories might lead.[57] We approach this in a generic way, though in practice, the questions would be adapted to the needs and specific knowledges of each group of Aboriginal people and knowledge holders. It is true that the

50 Jackson (n 17).
51 Behrendt (n 10) 176–78.
52 Behrendt (n 10).
53 Watson, 'Re-Centring First Nations Knowledge' (n 3) 515.
54 Behrendt (n 10) 178, 183–84. See also Behrendt's chapter in this book.
55 Behrendt (n 10) 178, 183–84.
56 Watson, *Aboriginal Peoples, Colonialism and International Law* (n 2) 46.
57 Jackson (n 17).

incommensurability between Australian common law and Aboriginal law ways feels simply impossible to navigate. Yet we are heartened by Osca Monaghan who writes, 'in the words of the anarchists, "another world is possible", and it is in its imaginings that we must begin'.[58]

Re-Membering the Stories

What Is the Human Impact of These Laws?

Cultural heritage is generally understood as telling (at least part of) a story about cultural identity:

> [It] links the past, the present and the future as it encompasses things inherited from the past that are considered to be of such value or significance today, that individuals and communities want to transmit them to future generations.[59]

Australian laws provide a range of statutory schemes to recognise and protect diverse forms of Aboriginal cultural heritage, although tangible and movable forms attract the greatest protections.[60] The heritage rights created can be recognised only by reference to Aboriginal peoples' laws and customs, which indicates at least a recognition that Aboriginal relationships to land and Country are intrinsically place-based. For instance, section 4 of the *ATSIHPA* aims to protect 'from injury or desecration' and preserve 'areas and objects in Australia and in Australian waters, being areas and objects that are of particular significance to Aboriginals in accordance with Aboriginal tradition'.

However, these laws have long been criticised for their colonial ethos and the 'danger' that sites will be chosen for protection through 'Eurocentric values and notions of what makes a place important'.[61] Libby Porter explains that 'critical awareness of the limitations' of cultural heritage laws is needed because these regimes remain 'embedded in Western world views about social change, what constitutes culture, whose knowledge is valued and how cultural heritage should be managed'.[62]

58 Monaghan (n 7) 31.

59 Farida Shaheed, *Report of the Independent Expert in the Field of Cultural Rights* (March 2011) [5] https://www.refworld.org/reference/themreport/unhrc/2011/en/89535.

60 See, e.g., *Protection of Movable Cultural Heritage Act 1986* (Cth).

61 Aliza Taubman, 'Protecting Aboriginal Sacred Sites: The Aftermath of the Hindmarsh Island Dispute' (2021) 19(2) *Environmental and Planning Law Journal* 140, 142. And see, Pekeri Ruska and Jennifer Nielsen, 'Reorganising the law to understand and protect all forms of cultural heritage' (2024) *Settler Colonial Studies* https://doi.org/10.1080/2201473X.2024.2419185

62 Libby Porter, 'Heritage Management' in Sue Jackson, Libby Porter and Louise C Johnson (eds), *Planning in Indigenous Australia from Imperial Foundations to Postcolonial Futures* (Routledge, 2018) 195, 196.

The *ATSIHPA*'s protections apply to tangible objects, Aboriginal remains (that is, bodies or any parts of a person's body) and intangible[63] forms of cultural heritage within significant areas, as section 3 designates, that are significant in accordance with

> the body of traditions, observances, customs and beliefs of Aboriginals generally or of a particular community or group of Aboriginals, and includes any such traditions, observances, customs or beliefs relating to particular persons, areas, objects or relationships.

But these traditions, observances, customs and beliefs—these Aboriginal law ways—are complex, alter with time and place and involve a multiplicity of methods to define and understand the relationships to land and cultural heritage. Victor Steffenson, a descendant of the Tagalaka clan, explains this complexity:

> When we look at the sky, the sea, the land, and all its resources, every single living thing contains its own categories of knowledge. Within that, there are many qualities that practically interconnect us to those resources in more ways than any of us can understand. The old people have a lore that says every living thing is to be respected and considered to be as important as any other. Everything has a special role and useful purpose that creates one living system. When all of the categories of knowledge are laid out into their fields, they create the form of a knowledge map.
>
> It is through the knowledge map that all our responsibilities and relationships with the natural world and each other are made visible.[64]

Australian common law struggles with this complexity because it atomises cultural heritage into component parts and disconnects it not only from the people who belong to it but also from their living culture.

Typically, cultural heritage rights and protections must outweigh the 'benefits' of 'development' to be recognised, are usually discretionary only and arise only when cultural heritage is under threat of injury or desecration. For example, the declaratory relief created by the *ATSIHPA* cannot be sought *unless* a threat arises.[65] Moreover, these laws may not prevent damage—and

63 See 'Intangible Heritage', *UNESCO World Heritage Convention* (Web Page) <https://whc.unesco.org/en/faq/40>.

64 Victor Steffenson, 'Putting the People Back into the Country' in Jo-ann Archibald Q'um Q'um Xiiem, Jenny Bol Jun Lee-Morgan and Jason De Santolo (eds), *Decolonizing Research: Indigenous Storywork as Methodology* (Zed Books, 2019) 224, 228.

65 *Aboriginal and Torres Strait Islander Heritage Protection Act 1984* (Cth) ('*ATSIHPA*'), 'Part II—Protection of Significant Aboriginal Areas and Objects'.

may even permit it.[66] This is damningly exemplified by Rio Tinto's destruction of the rock shelter at Juukan Gorge, resulting from an act that was legitimate under Western Australian cultural heritage legislation.[67] No remedy available through colonial law could ever recover the value and significance of Juukan Gorge that was lost by the Puutu Kunti Kurrama and Pinikura people. This loss is immeasurable and was caused by a company that acknowledged that its 'work culture was too focused on business performance and not enough on building and maintaining relationships with Traditional Owners'.[68] Under Aboriginal law ways, this would never be permitted.[69]

Likewise, cultural heritage laws impose minimal consequences (if any) for damaging or interfering with cultural heritage. The *ATSIHPA* makes it an offence to contravene a provision in a declaration[70] but creates no basis for financial (or other) compensation[71] or other relief or any penalties for damage, interference with or threat of injury to Aboriginal cultural heritage. Admittedly, some of these penalties are available under state cultural heritage laws, but ultimately, the human impact related to the loss of or permanent damage to cultural heritage is unknowable in Australian common law.[72]

Given this picture, what steps can be taken to re-centre Aboriginal law stories to decolonise these laws and change their human impact on Aboriginal communities? A priority is to restore holistic Aboriginal conceptions of cultural heritage. Wuthathi, Yadhaighana and Meriam lawyer Terri Janke provides insight on how this can be explained:

> [T]he intangible and tangible aspects of the whole body of cultural practices, resources and knowledge systems that have been developed, nurtured and refined . . . by Indigenous people and passed on by Aboriginal people as part of expressing their cultural identity.[73]

66 Examples include the Crown's 'recurrent exercise of a paramount power' or the 'tide of history' that washes away the relationship's foundation, that is, 'any real acknowledgment of traditional law and any real observance of traditional customs'. *Mabo [No 2]* (n 3) 58, 60.

67 Joint Standing Committee on Northern Australia, Parliament of Australia, *A Way Forward: Final Report into the Destruction of Indigenous Heritage Sites at Juukan Gorge* (Final Report, October 2021).

68 'Juukan Gorge', *Rio Tinto* (Web Page) <www.riotinto.com/en/news/trending-topics/juukan-gorge>.

69 Irene Watson, 'Aboriginal Relationships to the Natural World: Colonial "Protection" of Human Rights and the Environment' (2018) 9(2) *Journal of Human Rights and the Environment* 119; Graham (n 19) 115.

70 *ATSIHPA* (n 65) ss 22, 23.

71 Cf. *ATSIHPA* (n 65) s 28.

72 There 'is no aporia through which the sovereignty of First Nations and the essence of their spiritual and material connection to country can be recognised' or understood by Australian common law. Greta Bird and Jo Bird, 'First Nations Cultural Loss: Whiteness and the Timber Creek Judgment' (2021) 1 *Legalities* 68, 72.

73 Cited by Porter (n 62) 195.

Decolonising these laws also depends on restoring the Aboriginal law ways in which the relationship to Country is foundational—any action taken on Country must be lawful and consistent with these law ways. Finally, a shift is needed to re-centre Aboriginal relationships, interests and priorities as the objectives that cultural heritage laws serve.

Who Has the Power/Who Is Powerless?

The responsibility (and power) to administer Australian cultural heritage laws typically remains vested with government.[74] An Aboriginal person or group seeking to protect their relationship to land and cultural heritage holds no authority or power within this system—they are simply an 'applicant' sitting in a subordinated position to the state. The power structure that they face can be overwhelming, particularly given that grants of relief may be discretionary. For instance, under the *ATSIHPA*, the Minister *may* grant declaratory relief but is never obliged to do so.[75]

Though the Minister's (and their delegates') actions and decisions are amenable to judicial review, this is a limited process directed only at the quality of the decision-making processes, not the 'correctness' of the decision or its consequences.[76] Applications are costly and put applicants at risk of adverse costs orders, and even if they are successful, they may do little more than ensure a Minister re-makes a bad decision through a 'more correct' process.

From an Aboriginal worldview, it is nonsensical to put a minister of government in charge of decision-making about the care and protection of cultural heritage and of Country. Experience shows that they do not have the necessary expertise and knowledge and that they do not exercise their responsibilities through a 'custodial ethic'.[77] Such knowledge and expertise—and, thus, authority—reside only with those who are in proper relationship to that Country, that place. Aboriginal control over decision-making regarding cultural heritage is therefore essential.[78]

Re-centring Aboriginal authority and re-asserting the stories of Country and ways of being in relationship to a place would deconstruct and shift

74 Cf. *Aboriginal Cultural Heritage Act 2003* (Qld), which creates an Aboriginal Cultural Heritage Body to oversee and administer the laws. But see Queensland Government, 'Finalising the Review of Queensland's Cultural Heritage Acts' (Options Paper, December 2021).

75 The *ATSIHPA* provides that the Minister *may* make a declaration: ss 9(1), 10(1), and 12(1).

76 'Reviewing Government Decisions', *Caxton Legal Centre* (Web Page) <https://queenslandlawhandbook.org.au/the-queensland-law-handbook/your-rights-and-responsibilities/complaints-about-government-administrative-law/reviewing-government-decision/>.

77 Graham (n 19) 107–08, 112–13, 116.

78 Lauren Butterly, Ambelin Kwaymullina and Blaze Kwaymullina, 'Opportunity Is There for the Taking: Legal and Cultural Principles to Re-start Discussion on Aboriginal Heritage Reform in WA' (2017) 91 *Australian Law Journal* 367.

the power relationships that operate within the cultural heritage system.[79] Authority would lose its essence of 'colonial power' and shift to an ethic of custodianship and custodial obligation. A decolonised system of cultural heritage laws would recognise and operate on these bases.

Who Needs to Be Empowered to Speak?

When a development is proposed, the dominant voices are those of developers and proponents.[80] They unveil architecturally designed buildings and proclaim job creation and 'benefits' for the community. Rarely do we hear the voices of the Aboriginal peoples whose Country is the subject of this proposed development. In fact, typically, we hear nothing about the Aboriginal law stories for that Country until the knowledge holders are forced to reveal them in response to the threat of damage to their Country's cultural integrity.[81]

The due diligence procedures required under some cultural heritage processes may seek and secure agreement from Aboriginal peoples, but the destruction of Juukan Gorge exposes the inadequacy of the existing legal safeguards in place to protect Aboriginal cultural heritage, particularly intangible forms. 'Consultation' processes may 'hear' the concerns of an Aboriginal group or family, but they do not treat these concerns as law or knowledge. Rather, they are viewed as 'perspectives' to be balanced against competing interests—that is, the economic 'benefits' to be gained by the community (at large) by allowing development. For instance, under the *ATSHIPA*, the Minister may 'consider matters such as the effects of making a declaration [to protect cultural heritage] on the proprietary or pecuniary interests of persons other than the applicant'.[82]

Cultural heritage laws permit land to become 'enslaved and a consumable which is traded or sold in and out of existence'.[83] By permitting the destruction of Country and its sacred areas and stories, Australian common law remains an inherently violent colonial force that favours capitalist objectives and individual wealth rather than the Aboriginal custodial ethic. It echoes the story of terra nullius—the land is empty, belongs to no one and is there for

79 See Watson, 'Re-Centring First Nations Knowledge' (n 3).

80 Taubman (n 61) 147; Kylie Lingard et al., 'Are We There Yet? A Review of Proposed Aboriginal Cultural Heritage Laws in New South Wales, Australia' (2021) 28 *International Journal of Cultural Property* 107, 110.

81 See Taubman (n 61) 150.

82 Australian Government, *The Aboriginal and Torres Strait Islander Heritage Protection Act 1984: General Guide* (Department of Climate Change, Energy, the Environment and Water, 2023) 5 <www.dcceew.gov.au/sites/default/files/documents/atsihp-act-general-guide.pdf>.

83 Irene Watson, 'Buried Alive' (2002) 13 *Law and Critique* 256, 257.

the taking.[84] This logic is maintained by suppressing the counter-narratives contained in Indigenous knowledges.

When Aboriginal peoples speak in these consultation processes—these colonised spaces—their voices are 'captured, ricocheted, distilled'. As Watson asks, 'Where does that voice of our old people go?'[85] When Aboriginal peoples share their stories and their knowledge, they are doing so to enact their responsibilities to care for and protect Country and all that exists within it—*it is an act of law*. Thus, the decolonial work needed is to re-centre Aboriginal voices, not because they carry perspective or evidence, *but because they carry law*.

Who Has the Real Authority to Speak?

Australian common law grants 'standing' to speak in relation to a thing or problem to those with an interest or right in this thing. In cultural heritage matters, this is typically mediated through relationships to land. Under Australian common law, this relationship includes *rights* to the *productive, economic and useful value* of property: 'the right to use or enjoy . . . to exclude others, and the right to sell or give away'.[86] It grants those holding property a significant right to influence what is permitted on their land.

Under Aboriginal law ways, Aboriginal people are related to Country through bloodline connection to place and, in some circumstances, through marriage rights. In turn, Aboriginal people have obligations—rather than simply the right—to speak for Country. The ongoing impacts of colonisation make meeting these responsibilities fraught, which does not change through the grant of native title. Watson explains that native title does not return control to the people with proper authority to speak and care for Country:

> Native title does not free me to be who I am, a being of my people's own Raw Law. It is the killer of Raw Law because native title continues to dispossess from cycles of Nunga being . . . [and] will legalise the further, future rape of ruwe [country]'.[87]

Using the native title system to identify who speaks for Country 'potentially excludes certain Aboriginal people who may be knowledge holders and custodians of cultural heritage' within an area.[88] Determining who has the

84 Moreton-Robinson, 'The Possessive Logic of Patriarchal White Sovereignty' (n 2).

85 Irene Watson, 'Settled and Unsettled Spaces: Are We Free to Roam?' in Aileen Moreton-Robinson (ed), *Sovereign Subjects* (Routledge, 2007) 15.

86 Australian Law Reform Commission (n 1) 464 [18.20].

87 Watson, *Aboriginal Peoples, Colonialism and International Law* (n 2) 19; Jennifer Nielsen, 'Intervention: Lawful Destruction, Native Title and Epistemicide' (2022) 2(1) *Legalities* 46.

88 Queensland Government (n 74) 18.

authority to speak for Country will ensure that the correct story is being told. Decolonisation involves understanding that speaking for Country is not a generic obligation or right. To guarantee that the integrity of cultural heritage is protected, only the *right people* can speak for Country.[89]

Whose Story Is It?

Section 10 of the *ATSIHPA* creates a mechanism to apply for a declaration to protect cultural heritage. It requires applicants to provide evidence about why the area they need protected is a 'significant Aboriginal area', which means that they must put on record their stories that explain their deep connection with place.

However, Aboriginal knowledges are rarely treated as having intrinsic validity and credibility in legal processes and must be corroborated by and tested against white forms of knowledge such as anthropological and archaeological evidence.[90] There is a tendency in Australian common law processes to treat Aboriginal peoples' oral testimony (i.e., knowledge and law) as 'less credible' than the knowledge shared by 'experts', such as anthropologists and archaeologists.[91] Taubman also reports that 'many Aboriginal heritage claims are lost on procedural grounds because of the need to "prove" such knowledge through mechanisms of objective rationality'.[92]

Likewise, those who do not share secret or sacred information as early as possible in these processes may be accused of fabricating knowledge simply to oppose development. However, 'from the Aboriginal perspective late disclosure of tradition . . . is actually to be expected in the case of genuine sacred information of importance'.[93] Such expectations reflect a racist and deep-seated disrespect for Aboriginal knowledges and for Aboriginal peoples as authoritative and knowledgeable, and they signal the need to deconstruct and dissolve within legal thinking the 'white systemic ignorance which enables racism to influence knowledge production'.[94]

Aboriginal peoples hold the stories of place: stories that are embedded in songlines and woven by Aboriginal peoples into the 'everyday' of their lives. These stories possess the crucial and reliable evidence of the significance of their connection to place. In sharing their stories, Aboriginal peoples are

89 Eloise Schnierer, *Caring for Culture: Perspectives on the Effectiveness of Aboriginal Cultural Heritage Legislation in Victoria, Queensland and South Australia* (New South Wales Aboriginal Land Council, 2010) 33–34.
90 See Moreton-Robinson, 'The Possessive Logic of Patriarchal White Sovereignty' (n 2).
91 Behrendt (n 10) 176–78; Irene Watson, 'Indigenous Peoples' Law-Ways: Survival against the Colonial State' (1997) 8 *Australian Feminist Law Journal* 39, 51–52.
92 Taubman (n 61) 153.
93 Taubman (n 61) 150.
94 Watson, 'Re-Centring First Nations Knowledge' (n 3) 515.

asserting that they are still present, have not left and will always remain connected to their ancestral lands—that is, they re-assert their sovereignty and their ongoing lawful relationship to their lands. To decolonise cultural heritage laws, we must ask who is empowered to speak and whose knowledge is deemed (most) valuable? Do the laws treat Aboriginal people as experts when they share their generational knowledge about place? If not, then why not?

How Can We Help Storytellers Enact the Intent of the Story?

For Aboriginal peoples, maintaining their law across a violent colonial frontier is difficult enough, and 'the process of translating First Nations laws into a colonial court [and parliamentary] system has its own set of impossibilities'.[95] It is a very difficult thing to share law stories connected to place as 'evidence'—rather than as law and knowledge—in processes such as an application under section 10 of the *ATSIHPA*. Often, these stories contain cultural knowledge that can be shared only with a certain sector of an Aboriginal group (e.g., women's and men's business) and carry responsibilities to Country, humans and non-humankind. Transgressing the boundaries about how law stories can and should be shared, such as sharing women's business with men, causes great distress and harm to Aboriginal peoples.[96]

Under Aboriginal law ways, stories are shared for many different reasons, such as to teach their significance and transfer them through the generations. For example, Pekeri shares this example:

> I teach my children that a tree is never just a tree, but is connected to our breath, our jubbins (food for teething babies), parrots (sustenance), our shade, our markers of birthing places, our firewood etc. Without that tree, these resources diminish.

Decolonised laws would ensure that stories may only be told and shared—or not shared—through the ways that they can be, as permitted by Aboriginal law ways. They would also ensure that decision-makers have the right knowledge and understanding to respect, hear and apply the law that these stories contain.

Decolonisation anticipates that Aboriginal peoples' rights and responsibilities to speak for Country can never be supplanted, particularly not to favour colonial development and individual wealth.[97] It must achieve the 'free, prior and informed' authority to determine what can and *what cannot* happen

95 Watson, *Aboriginal Peoples, Colonialism and International Law* (n 2) 46.
96 See Taubman (n 61).
97 Nielsen (n 87) 50.

on Country, rather than merely provide a 'right to negotiate'.[98] As Watson cautions,

> It is important to note that consent could not be given to the theft and damage to land and the natural world, for these are acts which are against Aboriginal laws' core values and epistemologies, which centre a relational approach to land.[99]

Concluding Remarks

We have applied storytelling as a methodology to cultural heritage legislation to begin a decolonial process that seeks a different reality. The reality sought is one in which Aboriginal peoples' culture and history are valued and respected and all Aboriginal people live their lives in accordance with our/their own cultural values without fear of discrimination, appropriation, assimilation, ridicule or violence. We aim to restore Aboriginal sovereignties and protocols to ensure the balanced relationships needed between clan and language groups and with all non-human kin. We seek to move beyond colonial modes of thinking and practice by re-centring and restoring ancient and ongoing Aboriginal law ways and ways of knowing and being.

What this makes possible is profound because it gives voice to the otherwise voiceless—we are starting to hear the right story being told by the right people about their place. As Behrendt explains,

> The colonial legal system is dismissive of storytelling because it is deeply challenged by it. Disconnecting law from story disconnects law from personal story. Storytelling humanises. It gives voice to people. An important part of the decolonization process, especially as we work in the structures of the dominant culture like the legal system, is to advocate for broader law reform but to never lose sight of the colonial law's dominating power. And one way to subvert the dominant colonial legal system is to rely upon our traditional laws and their values and processes to guide our advocacy.[100]

Australian law must do better to protect cultural heritage, but this is not a simple, overnight task. Decolonising the common law's ideology and effect is time-intensive, involving multiple layers and generational shifts, requiring

98 The right to negotiate is a procedural right that enables native title holders to be consulted in relation to certain developments that may affect native title. See 'The Right to Negotiate', *National Native Title Tribunal* (Web Page) <www.nntt.gov.au/futureacts/Pages/Negotiation.aspx>.

99 Watson, 'Aboriginal Relationships to the Natural World' (n 69) 121.

100 Behrendt (n 10) 180.

'systemic change' and demanding 'actions from everyone'.[101] However, it is entirely feasible that these 'impossibilities' can be overcome. The character of our (legal) relationship with land and place can transform from a relationship of possession and exploitation to one of care and obligation—which are the responsibilities that would emerge by being in a lawful connection with place.

We leave you to ponder this question: once decolonised, what would be left of the Australian cultural heritage laws? And of this, what would be worth saving? To Asmi Wood, 'true' decolonisation

> must require the fracturing of or perhaps even 'shattering' of the current legal system 'as is' because it supports the colonial structure, including the oppressive racist elements of law and its associated institutions.[102]

At what cost do we continue to avoid decolonising Australian common law? The endgame of colonisation will be the death of us all.[103]

101 Turunen (n 49) 107.

102 Asmi Wood, 'Unmasking Indigenous Invisibility: Reforming and Decolonising the Pedagogy of Terra Nullius' in Foluke I Adebisi, Suhraiya Jivraj and Ntina Tzouvala (eds), *Decolonisation, Anti-Racism and Legal Pedagogy—Strategies, Successes, and Challenges* (Routledge, 2024) 149, 159.

103 Fletcher (n 22); Harriet Mercer, 'Colonialism: Why Leading Climate Scientists Have Finally Acknowledged Its Link with Climate Change', *The Conversation* (online, 22 April 2022) <https://theconversation.com/colonialism-why-leading-climate-scientists-have-finally-acknowledged-its-link-with-climate-change-181642>.

11

LEGAL EDUCATION AND FIRST NATIONS TEACHING AND LEARNING METHODOLOGIES

Storytelling/Yarning, Deep Listening and Lived Experience

Narelle Bedford[1]

Introduction

First Nations peoples are the holders of wisdom, storytellers and knowers of the truth. With a culture dating back 60,000 years in Australia, the First Nations systems for the transfer of knowledge are the original methodologies of teaching and learning. First Nations teaching and learning methodologies are a powerful example of the importance of honouring culturally diverse practices and increasing the understanding of different approaches that can be taken in teaching and learning—including in legal education.

First Nations teaching and learning methodologies must be prioritised in modern higher education, specifically, in legal education, for at least four reasons: first, to decolonise teaching and learning and open it to a wider range of sources and knowledge; second, to raise awareness of more First Nations' standpoints and voices; third, to increase the relevance of higher education to First Nations peoples; and fourth, to redress the dominance of settler-colonial voices and practices and reduce the inequities that a legal system founded on them has wrought on First Nations peoples.

1 Wallawani. My name is Narelle Bedford, and my mum is Jackie Bedford. She is a saltwater woman, a Yuin woman from Ulladulla on the South Coast. She spent her life honouring her culture and serving the community where she lived. She is wise but did not have the opportunity to complete much of high school. She instilled in me that education was a pathway to make a difference. I honour her in this analysis and all that she has taught me—especially to be culturally respectful of all First Nations cultures. I pay my respect to all First Nations people who have cared for ancient lands and passed on their knowledge and wisdom throughout generations. They are the original teachers and learners, and their culture is resilient and will always be.

DOI: 10.4324/9781003473404-13

The need for action with respect to First Nations peoples and legal education has been recognised by the Council of Australian Law Deans ('CALD') in its public statement published on 3 December 2020, which formally recognised Australian law's systemic discrimination and structural bias against First Nations peoples.[2] The statement acknowledges 'the part that legal education has played in supporting, either tacitly or openly, the law's systemic discrimination and structural bias against First Nations peoples'.[3] This position, as declared by the most senior legal educators throughout Australia, was featured in the Australian Law School Standards, developed by CALD, which were updated in July 2020 to include new areas of knowledge required for law degrees. The standards now include a statement that the law curriculum will 'develop knowledge and understanding of Aboriginal and Torres Strait Islander perspectives on and the intersections with the law'.[4]

To succeed in the process of decolonisation, legal education must seek to delink existing teaching and learning methods from practices that have erased, oppressed, racialised, minimised or dehumanised First Nations peoples and their experiences in the Australian legal system. This chapter argues that First Nations teaching and learning methodologies have an important role to perform in the decolonisation of legal education. This analysis considers three specific examples of First Nations teaching and learning methodologies that can be integrated into legal education: storytelling and yarning, deep listening and lived experience. Instilling these methodologies will assist in decolonising legal education and move it away from practices focused on arguments, adversarialism and dominance. This is because it is not only the law that is taught but also the way that it is taught that needs to be decolonised.

This chapter adopts a broad conception of legal education and argues that it should be understood as encompassing both initial legal qualifications and continuing professional development obligations. Developments

2 'CALD Statement on Australian Law's Systemic Discrimination and Structural Bias against First Nations Peoples', *Council of Australian Law Deans* (Web Page, 3 December 2020) <https://cald.asn.au/blog/2020/12/03/cald-statement-on-australian-laws-systemic-discrimination-and-structural-bias-against-first-nations-peoples/>.

3 'CALD Statement on Australian Law's Systemic Discrimination and Structural Bias against First Nations Peoples', *Council of Australian Law Deans* (Web Page, 3 December 2020) <https://cald.asn.au/blog/2020/12/03/cald-statement-on-australian-laws-systemic-discrimination-and-structural-bias-against-first-nations-peoples/>.

4 Council of Australian Law Deans and the Australian Law School Standards Committee, *Australian Law School Standards with Guidance Notes* (30 July 2020) 2.3.3 <https://cald.asn.au/wp-content/uploads/2020/07/Australian-Law-School-Standards-v1.3-30-Jul-2020.pdf>. See also Annette Gainsford, Marcus Smith and Alison Gerard, 'Accrediting Indigenous Australian Content and Cultural Competency within the Bachelor of Laws' (2021) 31 *Legal Education Review* 59.

in international praxis and reforms implemented to decolonise legal education in Aotearoa/New Zealand and Canada have achieved major progress compared to the nascent steps undertaken to date in Australia. This chapter reviews these developments and concludes that Australia needs to take urgent action to decolonise its legal education and make it more inclusive. The imperative for Australian law schools and continuing legal education providers to embed Indigenous cultural competency in legal education will only continue to gain strength in the future. The sooner that this action can begin in a thoughtful manner, the sooner that legal education will be improved. This chapter should be viewed as a contribution towards this goal.

The First Nations Teaching Methodology of Storytelling and Yarning

In Australia, it is accurate to record that First Nations peoples, collectively, have an emphasis on oral practices for the transmission of knowledge.[5] Both storytelling and yarning are long-practised methods of cultural knowledge sharing in First Nations communities worldwide and are customary in Aboriginal and Torres Strait Islander communities. There are transformative benefits to be gained from expanding the use of First Nations storytelling and yarning in higher education, as both are active teaching and learning processes that engage cultural humility and awareness and build deeper understanding.[6]

Legal education in particular presents meaningful opportunities for engaging with First Nations teaching and learning methodologies, such as storytelling and yarning, as part of a transformative learning experience for law students.[7] First Nations storytelling and yarning are authentic forms of what academics call narrative discourse.[8] Narrative discourse enables empathetic consideration of personal experiences.[9] It generally provides increased opportunities for effective participation and inclusion of those delivering the narrative or those to whom the narrative relates.[10]

5 See, e.g., Elaine Rabbitt, 'Indigenous Australian Oral Stories Contribute to the Australian Reconciliation Process' (2013) 35 *The Oral History Association of Australia Journal* 23.

6 Annette Gainsford and Su Robertson, 'Yarning Shares Knowledge: Wiradyuri Storytelling, Cultural Immersion and Video Reflection' (2019) 53(4) *The Law Teacher* 500.

7 Annette Gainsford and Su Robertson, 'Yarning Shares Knowledge: Wiradyuri Storytelling, Cultural Immersion and Video Reflection' (2019) 53(4) *The Law Teacher* 500.

8 Jane B Baron, 'The Many Promises of Storytelling in Law: An Essay Review of Narrative and the Legal Discourse: A Reader in Storytelling and the Law' (1991) 23 *Rutgers Law Journal* 79.

9 Richard Delgado, 'Storytelling for Oppositionists and Others: A Plea for Narrative' (1989) 87(8) *Michigan Law Review* 2411.

10 Richard Delgado, 'Storytelling for Oppositionists and Others: A Plea for Narrative' (1989) 87(8) *Michigan Law Review* 2411.

In a modern Australian context, the term 'yarning' may be more culturally appropriate than 'storytelling', as yarning is grounded in the everyday language of Aboriginal people and Torres Strait Islanders. Yarning can be defined as a talk or conversation that involves the sharing and exchange of information between two or more people, socially or more formally.[11] As Dawn Bessarab and Bridget Ng'andu state, '[t]o have a yarn is not a one-way process but a dialogical process that is reciprocal and mutual'.[12] Unlike storytelling, yarning does not carry the potential implication of being fictional or invoking the possibility of a made-up tale, which might wrongly be a connotation associated with storytelling. Additionally, yarning entails the practice of inclusivity so that many voices can be heard rather than an implied focus on one person 'telling' an audience their story/knowledge.

First Nations narrative discourse can be a powerful tool for transforming traditional thinking and modulating ingrained conceptions of reality. Richard Delgado has identified that a principal obstacle to reform generally is the 'majoritarian mindset', and narrative discourse can be a powerful counterbalance to dominant paradigms.[13] The traditional reliance on dominant paradigms has a particular resonance in the discipline of law, which builds knowledge through an established doctrine of precedent, whereby future approaches are based on, and bound by, past decisions of superior courts operating within a legal hierarchy.[14]

In the process of decolonising the legal system, it is significant to note that First Nations narrative discourse often contains accounts of events that may not otherwise be recorded in official government records or accord with these records. Historically, First Nations narrative discourse has not formed part of the official discourse in the Australian legal system. Thus, efforts to decolonise the legal system and legal education should embrace First Nations narrative discourse as a method of involving a greater diversity of knowledge. Although the mechanism to finally overturn *terra nullius*[15] was litigation, for Australian First Nations peoples, other mechanisms, such as royal commissions, coronial inquiries and other inquiries/reports, have provided more opportunity to focus on issues of concern to First Nations. In their more inquisitorial approach, these institutions use practices that diverge from courts and more closely mirror the learning and teaching methodologies of First Nations peoples.

11 Dawn Bessarab and Bridget Ng'andu, 'Yarning About Yarning as a Legitimate Method in Indigenous Research' (2010) 3(1) *International Journal of Critical Indigenous Studies* 37, 38.

12 Dawn Bessarab and Bridget Ng'andu, 'Yarning About Yarning as a Legitimate Method in Indigenous Research' (2010) 3(1) *International Journal of Critical Indigenous Studies* 38.

13 Delgado (n 9) 2412.

14 See Stephen Gageler and Brendan Lim, 'Collective Irrationality and the Doctrine of Precedent' (2014) 38(2) *Melbourne University Law Review* 525.

15 *Mabo v State of Queensland [No 2]* (1992) 175 CLR 1.

It is therefore unsurprising that, in Australia, positive momentum to incorporate First Nations storytelling has been found in royal commissions, coronial inquiries and other inquiry/report mechanisms. However, there are more opportunities for courts and other justice institutions such as tribunals to be forums that could be welcoming of First Nations storytelling or yarning. This approach should likewise be adopted in higher education institutions delivering legal education.

Best practice shows that in the use of storytelling and yarning, it is essential to be faithful to the language used by the person or person concerned.[16] Retaining authenticity of voice is an important practice to ensure that these First Nations teaching and learning methodologies are respectful towards those willing to share their stories and knowledge. Authenticity generates pride in First Nations ways of knowing, being and doing and creates cultural safety for the inclusion of Aboriginal and Torres Strait Islander people. Similarly, it is essential to record that authentic yarning is always a relational and non-hierarchical experience. Indeed, this explains why, in Aboriginal and Torres Strait Islander cultures, there is often use of the term 'yarning circles'.

Having outlined why it is useful to adopt First Nations methodologies, this analysis now offers two examples where this has been effectively achieved in an Australian legal context. The first example, less recent but better known, is the report *Bringing Them Home*.[17] The second is more recent but perhaps less well known. It is a case involving Aboriginal people living in a remote community and their quest for habitable housing. Both examples could be integrated into legal education as case studies that could then be used as prompts for storytelling/yarning experiences of students.

Bringing Them Home contains searing firsthand accounts of the experiences of Aboriginal and Torres Strait Islander peoples and the devastating trauma of the Stolen Generations laws and policies. Long silenced, this history has now entered the awareness of all Australians, resulting in shared understanding of the term 'Stolen Generations'. The standpoint of this chapter is informed by my family, which is full of our own stories from our own lived experience, including my mum's decades working as a case officer for Link-Up NSW.[18] Re-reading these narrative accounts is still deeply impactful.[19]

16 See, e.g., Kendra L Rieger et al., 'Elevating the Uses of Storytelling Methods within Indigenous Health Research: A Critical, Participatory Scoping Review' (2023) 22 *International Journal of Qualitative Methods* 1.

17 National Inquiry into the Separation of Aboriginal and Torres Strait Islander Children from their Families, *Bringing Them Home* (Report, April 1997) ('*Bringing Them Home*') <https://humanrights.gov.au/our-work/projects/bringing-them-home-report-1997>.

18 'Who Are Link-Up (NSW)?', *Link-Up (NSW)* (Web Page) <www.linkupnsw.org.au/>.

19 Narelle Bedford, 'Storytelling in Our Legal System: Healing for the Stolen Generations' (2019) 45 *Australian Feminist Law Journal* 321.

The inquiry, which ultimately led to the report, took oral and written evidence from 535 Aboriginal and Torres Strait Islander people,[20] in addition to evidence from numerous Aboriginal and Torres Strait Islander organisations. *Bringing Them Home* recorded that Aboriginal and Torres Strait Islander witnesses required personal and psychological support during the inquiry process and afterwards 'because of the traumatic nature of their memories and the inevitably confronting task of relating them to strangers'.[21] This case study demonstrates the emotional toll that yarning about traumatic events can take on those affected and the need for care to ensure that those most at risk are not re-traumatised.

The crucial work of the national Aboriginal and Torres Strait Islander-controlled organisation the Healing Foundation is highly influential and offers a voice of experience on the power of yarning to assist with healing after traumatic events if approached in a culturally informed manner.[22] In 2021, the Healing Foundation released a major report titled *Making Healing Happen*,[23] which aimed to restore dignity to those who have suffered from the Stolen Generation laws and policies by recognising the centrality of self-determination and the strengths of First Nations cultures in healing historical trauma. Integrating both *Bringing Them Home* and *Making Healing Happen* into legal curricula will increase awareness of the discriminatory impact that law can have despite its underlying intentions. It would also counter the stigma of victimisation by showing that Aboriginal and Torres Strait Islander people are the best-placed to formulate and advocate strength-based reforms.

The second example of the importance of storytelling in a legal context concerns an application that was made to the Northern Territory Civil and Administrative Tribunal ('NTCAT') under the *Residential Tenancies Act 2018* (NT) by multiple residents from the remote Aboriginal community of Ltyentye Apurte (also known as Santa Teresa).[24] The matter raised fundamental issues of tenants' rights to safe and properly maintained 'habitable' housing, with the necessary services functioning, in a remote community.

20 *Bringing Them Home* (n 17) Ch 1.

21 *Bringing Them Home* (n 17) 16.

22 *Healing Foundation* (Web Page) <https://healingfoundation.org.au/>. I express my profound respect for the important work of the Healing Foundation, a national Aboriginal organisation working with and supporting Stolen Generations families and communities still dealing with intergenerational trauma.

23 *Making Healing Happen* (Report, May 2021).

24 *Various Applicants from Santa Teresa v Chief Executive Officer (Housing) (No 2)* [2019] NTCAT 7.

In the NTCAT decision, Member McCrimmon explained as follows:

> 70 initiating applications against the Chief Executive Officer (Housing) (the 'Respondent') were filed in the Tribunal by the Applicants' representative, Mr Danial Kelly. Mr Kelly is a solicitor with the Australian Lawyers for Remote Aboriginal Rights. All 70 Applicants live in the town of Santa Teresa. Santa Teresa is an Aboriginal community located approximately 85 kilometres from Alice Springs, Northern Territory.[25]

Member McCrimmon further recorded that

> one of the lead Applicants was aged in her late 70s and speaks very little English. She also does not read English. Her first language is Eastern Arrente. At the hearing she gave evidence through an interpreter.[26]

Among the community members, she was not the only applicant who required interpreting services. Of course, courts and other tribunals in Australia also utilise interpreters, but this matter highlights the importance of authentic first-person storytelling for marginalised people within the legal process. Legal education needs to highlight that vulnerable and marginalised groups in our society must be well served so that they can be heard at the point when they come into contact with the Australian justice system.

The subsequent litigation history in the Ltyentye Apurte matter demonstrates the significance of the issues at stake. The NTCAT's decision to award compensation was appealed by the Northern Territory Government to the Northern Territory Supreme Court. Blokland J increased the amount of compensation awarded to the residents to $10,200.[27] Again, the Northern Territory Government appealed. The Northern Territory Court of Appeal allowed the appeal on a technical legal point that damages should not be awarded for disappointment and stress that was consequential to the breach of a tenancy agreement.[28] Finally, special leave to appeal to the High Court was granted, and the High Court delivered its judgment in the matter in November 2023, affirming the NTCAT's power to award damages for disappointment and stress.[29]

The value of the stories told by the applicants through interpreters—such as not having a back door on their house for 68 months—over five years—helped

25 *Various Applicants from Santa Teresa v Chief Executive Officer (Housing) (No 2)* [2019] NTCAT 7 [1].
26 *Various Applicants from Santa Teresa v Chief Executive Officer (Housing) (No 2)* [2019] NTCAT 7 [29].
27 *Young & Conway v Chief Executive Officer, Housing* [2020] NTSC 59.
28 *Chief Executive Officer (Housing) v Young* [2022] NTCA 1.
29 *Young v Chief Executive Officer (Housing)* [2023] HCA 31.

to resolve the critical legal questions of whether there is a human right to habitable housing and whether there is a power to compensate for this through an award of damages. This case study shows that authentic storytelling at all levels of the Australian justice system, such as the NTCAT, may be called upon to determine complex legal matters that may ultimately be worthy of the High Court's attention.

Storytelling and yarning is a First Nations methodology that can be incorporated into legal education with benefits in topical areas such as climate change. For example, the different perspectives recounted by an Aboriginal Senior Counsel, highlighting the divergence in burning-off practices between Indigenous and non-Indigenous people, were relayed in an article titled 'First Nations Peoples, Climate Change, Human Rights and Legal Rights'.[30] Specifically, this article explained how listening to the stories of Indigenous people through a native title claim process highlighted important knowledge. Through story, Elders had explained to one of the authors, a lawyer, that 'summer was the proper time to burn as the snakes and goannas . . . would be alert and able to get out of the way'.[31] This was contrasted with non-Indigenous burning practices, which were implemented during winter when many reptiles were dormant and therefore likely to perish if burning occurred.

In moving to embed First Nations narrative discourse in legal education, there is a fine line between appreciation and appropriation. First Nations narrative discourse cannot be respectfully appreciated by simply dropping a story from another culture into an already crowded curriculum. Instead, genuine and thoughtful efforts must be guided by First Nations cultural advisors so that the 'voice' of First Nations peoples is heard and prioritised.[32] Equally, it is not proper for non-Indigenous people to tell their version of what they believe are First Nations stories. Instead, a culturally appropriate person could be invited to lead the yarning (with appropriate recompense, such as payment to acknowledge the benefits of their wisdom and value of their time). Alternatively, with guidance from First Nations cultural experts, materials and other recordings of First Nations peoples sharing their knowledge and wisdom could be utilised so that this knowledge is heard from the authentic voices and not paraphrased or recast.

Similarly, modestly adopting a discursive or discussion-based approach to legal education is not a deeply authentic implementation of First Nations teaching and learning methodologies. For example, structural changes in

30 Narelle Bedford, Tony McAvoy and Lindsey Stevenson-Graf, 'First Nations Peoples, Climate Change, Human Rights and Legal Rights' (2021) 40(3) *University of Queensland Law Journal* 371.

31 Narelle Bedford, Tony McAvoy and Lindsey Stevenson-Graf, 'First Nations Peoples, Climate Change, Human Rights and Legal Rights' (2021) 40(3) *University of Queensland Law Journal* 373.

32 See, e.g., Gainsford and Robertson (n 6).

how legal education is delivered, such as shifting from passive lectures to interactive seminars, is not by itself a satisfactory manner of adopting First Nations teaching and learning practices. Care needs to be taken that First Nations teaching and learning methodologies are not appropriated to justify managerial changes in law schools and the broader higher education sector.

Any attempts to embed First Nations teaching and learning methodologies must also be sensitive to the dangers of entering into a deficit discourse. To effectively decolonise legal education, it is essential that 'strong stories' of First Nations resilience and truth are heard.[33] Stories should challenge any stereotypical assumptions that might be unconsciously carried by non-Indigenous law students.

The First Nations Teaching Methodology of Deep Listening

A natural complement to storytelling and yarning is the First Nations cultural practice of deep listening, as yarning is not a one-way process but a dialogical and reciprocal process. Thus, there is an inextricable link between the First Nations teaching methodology of storytelling and yarning and that of deep listening. To have an effective impact, storytelling and yarning rely upon a willingness to listen by the others engaged in the process.

Deep listening calls upon a requirement for 'still awareness', which is somewhat reminiscent of the practice of *Dadirri*. *Dadirri* is a word, concept and spiritual practice that derives from the Ngan'gikurunggurr and Ngen'giwumirri languages of the Aboriginal people of the Daly River region in the Northern Territory.[34] It is a cultural skill founded on respect and waiting. Similar cultural practices of deep listening exist in many Aboriginal and Torres Strait Islander nations.[35]

Deep listening decentres the non-speaker through quiet, contemplative observation, and it can provide the foundation for transformative learning.[36] In its true form, deep listening has a spiritual form and is explained as

> To know me is to breathe with me, to breathe with me is to listen deeply, to listen deeply is to connect. It is a sound, the sound of deep calling to

33 Although not in a legal context, see, e.g., Barbara Wingard, Carolynanha Johnson and Tileah Drahm-Butler, *Aboriginal Narrative Practice: Honouring Storylines of Pride, Strength and Creativity* (Dulwich Centre, 2015).

34 Miriam-Rose Ungunmerr-Baumann et al., 'Dadirri: An Indigenous Place-Based Research Methodology' (2022) 18(1) *AlterNative* 94.

35 See, e.g., Susan Bird, John Trevor Rawnsley (Larrakia, Anmetjerre), and Ciprian Radavoi, 'True Justice through Deep Listening on Country: Decolonising Legal Education in Australia' (2023) 19(4) *AlterNative* 892.

36 Laura Brearley and Treahna Hamm, 'Spaces between Indigenous and Non-Indigenous Knowledge Systems: Deep Listening to Research in a Creative Form' in Anna-Christina Engels-Schwarzpaul and Michael A Peters (eds), *Of Other Thoughts: Non-Traditional Ways to the Doctorate: A Guidebook for Candidates and Supervisors* (Sense Publishers, 2013).

> deep, down the deep inner springs inside us, we call on it and it calls on us.[37]

Deep listening emphasises the importance of respect and relationality in the listening process, getting the story right and being in right relationship with all involved and Country. It requires self-reflection by learners to develop their awareness of history, place and the ongoing impacts of trauma. Deep listening must be conducted in a trauma-informed manner. Best practice deep listening should therefore prioritise respect for the person imparting knowledge and honour the dignity of all engaged in the transmission of knowledge.

Deep listening is best when it occurs on Country so that the spiritual experience is enhanced by the connection to Country. Ideally, implementing deep listening in legal education would move the physical location of legal education away from the classroom and onto Country. This is not achieved merely by simplistic measures to hold classes 'outdoors': it must be thoughtfully implemented with appropriate guidance and permissions sought and obtained to be on Country that has a connection to the issues to be listened to. Susan Bird and her colleagues analysed an on-Country experience gained from walking in the mangroves of Ludmilla, a suburb of Darwin; visiting significant cultural sites in Kakadu National Park, Northern Territory; and speaking with community leaders in the small First Nations community of Gunbalanya, North West Arnhem, Northern Territory. They concluded that if important cultural aspects of deep listening (such as trauma-informed practices) are 'ignored, practitioners and educators risk reproducing colonial models'.[38]

Legal education presents many different opportunities for fostering the Aboriginal and Torres Strait Islander teaching and learning methodology of deep listening. Another example is the specifically designed listening experiences embedded in a cultural awareness clinic for law students, where 'a key design feature of . . . engagements is to position students as active listeners through observation and to develop the skills necessary for deep listening'.[39]

Opportunities for deep listening in legal education will need to be actively pursued, with assistance sought from local First Nations peoples, communities or organisations in identifying and making culturally respectful arrangements. Similarly to the guidance provided earlier with respect to storytelling/yarning, it is essential that there is cultural respect shown for this wisdom

37 Julieann Coombes and Courtney Ryder, 'Walking Together to Create Harmony in Research: A Murri Woman's Approach to Indigenous Research Methodology' 2020 15(1) *Qualitative Research in Organizations and Management: An International Journal* 58.

38 Bird et al. (n 35) 895.

39 Narelle Bedford et al., 'Developing Indigenous Cultural Competency in Law: Clinical Legal Education as a Method for Getting It Done' (2024) 34(1) *Legal Education Review* 111–132.

through appropriate acknowledgement, timelines and recompense (such as payment in advance) and that it is developed in a full, true and equitable partnership with relevant communities.

The goal of deep listening should be to hear and appreciate rather than to formulate a response or offer potential solutions. Deep listening should be an engaging and generative process whereby listeners are encouraged to evaluate their own standpoints and privileges and develop an awareness of any unconscious biases. Deep listening empowers First Nations people to be the architects of their own solutions to complex legal problems, informed by the broader social context in which these problems manifest. It can act as a counter to paternalistic tendencies wherein law students and lawyers expect themselves to provide advice and solve problems.

As an inherently relational practice, deep listening also ensures cultural safety for First Nations peoples by de-centring law students and involving them in non-judgmental engagement and interactions. Simultaneously, it can also help to build the cultural safety, comfort and confidence of First Nations law students, who might otherwise experience legal education as 'outsiders'. To enable knowledge transmission, it is not just the person imparting knowledge who must be accorded respect but all persons participating in the learning experience.

When implemented, deep listening experiences will provide a counter to the 'incredibly fast-paced world of legal practice' and take students into a space where they '[have] the time to listen, reflect and learn'.[40] Deep listening also mitigates concerns that traditional legal education can lack context and become too abstract in nature. A commitment to deep listening is consistent with recent pleas for lawyering to become more 'relational' and emphasise that listening skills are a core legal competency.[41]

The First Nations Teaching Methodology of Lived Experience

The third methodology of First Nations peoples that could be beneficially implemented in legal education is lived experience. First Nations people have experienced, either directly or within their family, the impact of government laws, practices and policies on Indigenous peoples. These transgenerational knowledges and personal impacts, together with insights into government decisions and policies, form a unique perspective[42]—a lived experience—

40 Bird et al. (n 35) 898.

41 Susan L Brooks, 'Listening and Relational Lawyering' in Debra L Worthington and Graham D Bodie (eds), *The Handbook of Listening* (Wiley, 2020).

42 Judy Atkinson, Jeff Nelson and Caroline Atkinson, 'Trauma, Transgenerational Transfer and Effects on Community Wellbeing' in Nola Purdie, Pat Dudgeon and Roz Walker (eds), *Working Together: Aboriginal and Torres Strait Islander Mental Health and Wellbeing Principles and Practice* (Commonwealth of Australia, 2014).

that should be a vital source for legal educators. The Black Dog Institute, a non-governmental organisation specialising in mental health, has developed a definition of lived experience for Aboriginal and Torres Strait Islander communities:

> Recognis[ing] the effects of ongoing negative historical impacts and or specific events on the social and emotional wellbeing of Aboriginal and Torres Strait Islander peoples. It encompasses the cultural, spiritual, physical, emotional and mental wellbeing of the individual, family or community.[43]

It is essential that recountings of First Nations lived experience should not be placed in a subordinate position or considered an inferior source to anthropological reports, official government records or legal standards of evidence. The changed perspective and value accorded to lived experience assists to de-stigmatise different interpretations of the Australian legal system. Therefore, when lived experience is integrated into legal education, it can reorient perceptions and deepen the understanding that the legal system may have unintended impacts on different people. Lived experience can effectively demonstrate that the human rights of First Nations peoples can be challenging to defend in a legal system that has historically not been open or accessible to First Nations people.

Lived experience can also bring the harsh reality of the Australian legal system and its impacts on Aboriginal and Torres Strait Islander people to life for non-Indigenous law students. This may be the first reorientating experience for such students. Exposure to lived experience of the Australian legal system is necessary for building empathy and countering racism, whether conscious or unconscious. The Indigenous Law and Justice Hub at The University of Melbourne stated in a submission to the Yoorrook Justice Commission that 'the absence of adequate regard to First Nations experiences in legal education has real impacts on Aboriginal and Torres Strait Islander peoples' experiences of settler law, and in turn their life chances'.[44] The authors argue that the legal profession must engage in 'existential reflection on the role of the profession as agents of colonisation',[45] and this reflection must be extended to an examination of the role of legal education in creating future legal professionals. By itself, however, this will not be sufficient to 'achieve the

43 Black Dog Institute, 'Lived Experience Definition released for Aboriginal and Torres Strait Islander Communities' (Media Release, 1 December 2020) <www.blackdoginstitute.org.au/media-releases/lived-experience-definition-released-for-aboriginal-and-torres-strait-islander-communities/>.

44 Indigenous Law and Justice Hub, *The University of Melbourne, Submission to the Yoorrook Justice Commission* (8 February 2024) 4 <https://law.unimelb.edu.au/__data/assets/pdf_file/0006/4851303/Final-Legal-Education-Reforms-for-First-Nations-Justice58.pdf>.

45 Indigenous Law and Justice Hub, *The University of Melbourne, Submission to the Yoorrook Justice Commission* (8 February 2024) 4 <https://law.unimelb.edu.au/__data/assets/pdf_file/0006/4851303/Final-Legal-Education-Reforms-for-First-Nations-Justice58.pdf>.

shift in professional culture and practice which is necessary'.[46] Incorporating lived experience into legal education must be undertaken carefully. It cannot be simply an overarching statement of disadvantage that engenders a sense of helplessness but instead must offer First Nations-led solutions and case studies demonstrating the importance of self-determination and community engagement to achieve tangible outcomes.

The Scope of Legal Education to be Decolonised

This chapter adopts a broad conception of legal education and argues that it should be understood as encompassing both law school studies and continuing professional development obligations. This is because legal education needs to span the entirety of a practitioner's career to ensure that they retain expertise in the modern evolution of the law and have the necessary skills to provide advice in increasingly complex disputes and transactions. Therefore, both initial legal qualifications and continuing professional development need to be decolonised.

Domestic law reforms can draw inspiration from other comparable common law systems in countries that have tackled the concept of legal pluralism and First Nations law. Developments in international praxis and reforms implemented to decolonise legal education in Aotearoa/New Zealand, Canada and South Africa are examined in this section. In all three countries, major progress has been achieved compared to the nascent steps undertaken in Australia.

In 2021, the New Zealand Council of Legal Education ('NZCLE') amended the regulations prescribing the content of the law degree in Aotearoa/New Zealand to include teaching and assessment of Tikanga Māori—specifically, a new compulsory law course on Tikanga Māori (Māori Laws and Philosophy). Existing compulsory law courses will also include relevant content on Tikanga Māori.[47] The NZCLE defines Tikanga Māori as Māori laws and philosophy, but the broad scope of Tikanga Māori has been explained by Te Aka Matua O Te Ture/the Law Commission of New Zealand, in its report on Māori Custom and Values, as 'the closest Māori equivalent to concepts of law and custom'.[48]

46 Indigenous Law and Justice Hub, *The University of Melbourne, Submission to the Yoorrook Justice Commission* (8 February 2024) 4 <https://law.unimelb.edu.au/__data/assets/pdf_file/0006/4851303/Final-Legal-Education-Reforms-for-First-Nations-Justice58.pdf>.

47 See 'New Tikanga Māori Requirements', *New Zealand Council of Legal Education* (Web Page) <https://nzcle.org.nz/>. For background context, see also Carwyn Jones, 'Indigenous Legal Issues, Indigenous Perspectives and Indigenous Law in the New Zealand LLB Curriculum' (2009) 19 *Legal Education Review* 257.

48 Te Aka Matua O Te Ture/the Law Commission of New Zealand, *Māori Custom and Values in New Zealand* (Study Paper 9, March 2001) 2.

The mandatory requirements for including Tikanga Māori in the law curriculum will be progressively introduced starting in 2025. There are six law faculties in Aotearoa/New Zealand, all of which jointly commissioned research to commence culturally respectful preparations. Led by the Te Kaupeka Tātai Ture (Faculty of Law) at Te Whare Wānanga o Otāgo (Otago University), the research highlighted the need to restructure the law curriculum on the basis that Aotearoa/New Zealand is a bijural, bicultural and bilingual legal system.[49] Thus, there is evidence grounded in research of the necessity to recognise Tikanga Māori as a foundational component of the legal system in Aotearoa/New Zealand and consequently, in its legal education. The research report concluded that '[t]here can be no systemic change to how we understand law in a contemporary Aotearoa New Zealand if we do not teach it differently in our law schools'.[50]

In Canada, the Final Report of the Truth and Reconciliation Commission ('TRC') stated that 'there has to be awareness of the past, acknowledgement of the harm that has been inflicted, atonement for the causes, and action to change behaviour'.[51] The TRC concluded by issuing 94 distinct Calls to Action. This was a deliberate and significant terminological choice, as a call to action is future-focused and achievement-oriented, in contrast to the more traditional term associated with inquiries—recommendations. The latter can be viewed as invoking the status of a mere suggestion for consideration.

In considering the role of lawyers and how to better educate them, the Canadian Truth and Reconciliation Commission critically noted that

> [t]he lack of sensitivity that lawyers often demonstrated in dealing with residential school Survivors resulted, in some cases, in the Survivors' not receiving appropriate legal service. These experiences prove the need for lawyers to develop a greater understanding of Aboriginal history and culture as well as the multi-faceted legacy of residential schools.[52]

49 Jacinta Ruru et al., *Inspiring National Indigenous Legal Education for Aotearoa New Zealand's Bachelor of Laws Degree, Phase One* (Issues Paper, 2021).

50 Jacinta Ruru et al., *Inspiring National Indigenous Legal Education for Aotearoa New Zealand's Bachelor of Laws Degree, Phase One* (Issues Paper, 2021) 46.

51 Government of Canada/the Truth and Reconciliation Commission of Canada, *Honouring the Truth, Reconciling for the Future: Summary of the Final Report of the Truth and Reconciliation Commission of Canada* (Report, 2015) 6–7. See also Jeffrey G Hewitt, 'Decolonizing and Indigenizing: Some Considerations for Law Schools' (2016) 33 *Windsor Yearbook Access to Justice* 65.

52 Government of Canada/the Truth and Reconciliation Commission of Canada, *Honouring the Truth, Reconciling for the Future: Summary of the Final Report of the Truth and Reconciliation Commission of Canada* (Report, 2015) 6–7. See also Jeffrey G Hewitt, 'Decolonizing and Indigenizing: Some Considerations for Law Schools' (2016) 33 *Windsor Yearbook Access to Justice* 168.

The national body coordinating all law societies in Canada, the Federation of Law Societies of Canada, was urged in Call to Action 27 to

> ensure that lawyers receive appropriate cultural competency training which includes the history and legacy of residential schools, the United Nations Declaration on the Rights of Indigenous Peoples, Treaties and Aboriginal Rights, Indigenous law and Aboriginal-Crown relations. This will require skills-based training in intercultural competency, conflict resolution, human rights, and anti-racism.[53]

Likewise, in Call to Action 28, all Canadian law schools were similarly called upon 'to require all law students to take a course in Aboriginal people and the law'.[54] Both calls to action have received support from professional bodies and multiple faculties of law, and implementation has been progressed by provincial-level law societies and individual law faculties, but there has been some debate and division. For example, the Law Society of Alberta held a vote of all members in 2023 on whether to continue the recent mandatory requirement for all lawyers to undertake a free, five-hour online course in cultural competency or be sanctioned with suspension. Ultimately, the mandatory requirement was retained by a majority of votes.[55]

Less controversial has been the reform of legal education at the initial qualification stage. For example, the University of Victoria in British Columbia has designed and now offers a joint degree program in *Canadian Common Law and Indigenous Legal Orders*, which is claimed to be the first of its kind in the world.[56] First Nations teaching and learning methodologies are embedded in this program, with 'the land as one of the classrooms'—that is, a full term in each of the third and fourth years is conducted on Country, 'immersed in community-led field schools'.[57]

53 Government of Canada/the Truth and Reconciliation Commission of Canada, *Honouring the Truth, Reconciling for the Future: Summary of the Final Report of the Truth and Reconciliation Commission of Canada* (Report, 2015) 6–7. See also Jeffrey G Hewitt, 'Decolonizing and Indigenizing: Some Considerations for Law Schools' (2016) 33 *Windsor Yearbook Access to Justice* 65.

54 Government of Canada/the Truth and Reconciliation Commission of Canada, *Honouring the Truth, Reconciling for the Future: Summary of the Final Report of the Truth and Reconciliation Commission of Canada* (Report, 2015) 6–7. See also Jeffrey G Hewitt, 'Decolonizing and Indigenizing: Some Considerations for Law Schools' (2016) 33 *Windsor Yearbook Access to Justice* 168.

55 See 'Call to Action # 27', *Indigenous Watchdog* (Web Page) <www.indigenouswatchdog.org/cta/call-to-action-27/>.

56 See 'Joint Degree Program in Canadian Common Law and Indigenous Legal Orders (JD/JID)', *University of Victoria* (Web Page) <www.uvic.ca/law/admissions/jidadmissions/index.php>.

57 'Joint Degree Program in Canadian Common Law and Indigenous Legal Orders (JD/JID)', *University of Victoria* (Web Page) <www.uvic.ca/law/admissions/jidadmissions/index.php>.

Turning to South Africa, the Truth and Reconciliation Commission found that

> [b]oth the Judiciary and the Magistracy, as well as the organised legal profession, were locked into an overwhelmingly passive mindset which characterised the judgements of the bench in the face of injustices of apartheid, and the reaction of the professions to such injustices.[58]

On legal education, the Commission specifically recommended the following:

> Law schools review their courses to ensure that the interests of all South Africans are served. Consideration must be given to increasing practical training and/or the introduction of compulsory community service as requirements for graduation. Law students [should] be given a greater understanding of human rights law and more intensive training in legal ethics.[59]

These particular conclusions of the Commission speak to the absolute need for legal education to extend beyond initial legal qualifications and into the ongoing professional development requirements for all practitioners (including members of the judiciary and magistracy in any training provided to them). An overwhelmingly passive mindset within the legal profession could be a risk facing any legal system, but if legal education has been decolonised and students and practitioners have cultural awareness skills gained through the deployment of First Nations methodologies, then this risk will be mitigated. The recommendations highlight that opportunities for decolonisation can occur not only in compulsory law subjects but also in law electives and legal clinic placements.

In the South African context, Michele Van Eck argues that the decolonisation of legal education must entail 'shedding the colonial yoke of exclusive western ideologies and thinking' and requiring a transformed, inclusive educational approach that incorporates 'local African traditions, customs and ideologies that existed prior to colonial imposition'.[60] She argues that 'decol-

58 *Truth and Reconciliation Commission of South Africa* (Report, 1998–2003) vol 5, ch 8, 254. See also Fiona C Ross, 'On Having Voice and Being Heard: Some After-Effects of Testifying Before the South African Truth and Reconciliation Commission' (2003) 3(3) *Anthropological Theory* 325.

59 *Truth and Reconciliation Commission of South Africa* (Report, 1998–2003) vol 5, ch 8, 254. See also Fiona C Ross, 'On Having Voice and Being Heard: Some After-Effects of Testifying Before the South African Truth and Reconciliation Commission' (2003) 3(3) *Anthropological Theory* 324–25.

60 Michele Van Eck, 'Decolonising Legal Education in South Africa: Is It Time to Press the Reset Button?' (2020) 2(1) *Journal of Decolonising Disciplines* 1.

onisation cannot be achieved merely as a change in legal education alone: it requires an ideological shift in the country's legal framework'.[61]

This review of developments in Aotearoa/New Zealand, Canada and South Africa adds further potency to the arguments for reforms to occur in Australia. Developments in other nations should not, however, be considered as the only or best available methods to decolonise legal education. Each nation must develop its own processes to be in harmony with the needs and wishes of First Nations peoples. Adoption of the teaching and learning methodologies used by First Nations peoples is one mechanism to help in the process of decolonisation.

The imperative for Australian law schools and continuing legal education providers to embed Indigenous cultural competency in legal education will only continue to gain strength. The sooner that this action can begin in a well-considered manner, the sooner that legal education in Australia will be improved and strengthened.

Conclusion

First Nations methodologies must be accorded greater priority in Australian legal education, and a culturally respectful process of decolonising legal education must be undertaken. Calls for First Nations knowledges and cultural sensitivity to be included in legal education are already loud in Australia and will continue to grow louder. A global praxis for such reforms is already occurring, with major developments in Aotearoa/New Zealand, Canada and South Africa. Australia needs to take urgent and considered action.

First Nations teaching and learning methodologies can and should be implemented in legal education. Storytelling and yarning, deep listening and lived experience should be embedded to enhance cultural respect and awareness in non-Indigenous students. The process of embracing these methodologies must be guided by those willing to share their cultural expertise, both inside and outside the institutions. In seeking this guidance, legal educators should be mindful of the cultural load that could be placed on First Nations academics, which is already considerable. It would be unreasonable to set further burdens on these academic staff. At the same time, non-Indigenous staff may be reluctant or unable to appropriately practise the recommended methods in the classroom. This is not easily solvable in the current context of legal education, but important reforms always require dedication and long-term commitment to be advanced and implemented. The ultimate goal of the decolonisation of legal education is crucial to ensure a

61 Michele Van Eck, 'Decolonising Legal Education in South Africa: Is It Time to Press the Reset Button?' (2020) 2(1) *Journal of Decolonising Disciplines* 4, 11, 21.

First Nations-responsive legal system in the future populated by legal professionals equipped with cultural awareness and appropriate skills.

The task of decolonising the Australian legal system cannot rest solely on reforms in legal education. Systemic reform of the entire legal profession, in all its aspects, must be undertaken. However, legal education presents a concrete place to start this crucial and necessary process. Legal education has the potential for lasting impacts as future generations of legal professionals become equipped to make an effective contribution to improving the experiences of First Nations people in the legal system.

PART III

Applying an Indigenous Lens to Law School Curricula

12

TEACHING STUDENTS TO APPRECIATE THE SIGNIFICANCE OF THE PLAINTIFF'S ABORIGINALITY IN INTENTIONAL TORTS CASES

Nicole Watson

Introduction

Racism was so ingrained in Queensland in the 1960s and 1970s that discrimination was a daily experience for most Aboriginal and Torres Strait Islander people. One was jeered at in the street, harassed by police officers and watched with eagle eyes in the supermarket. Many were incarcerated on reserves where they were dehumanised in myriad ways. Inmates were punished for nonsensical transgressions, such as the 'offence against discipline', which could be committed by being 'idle, careless or negligent at work'.[1] Those who had the courage to move to the capital of Brisbane were often confronted by the ignorance of their new neighbours.[2]

The conservative government of Premier Johannes Bjelke-Petersen was resolute in maintaining the oppression of Indigenous people. Activists who challenged the racism of the Bjelke-Petersen Government, such as my late father, Sam Watson, were vulnerable to intimidation by the state's police force. They also became targets of Patrick Killoran, the authoritarian Director of the Department of Aboriginal and Islander Affairs. As a child, I grew up hearing stories of Killoran's practice of keeping Aboriginal families under surveillance. It was an experience that Dad knew well.

1 *The Aborigines and Torres Strait Islanders' Regulations of 1966* (Qld) Regulation 70; see John Chesterman and Brian Galligan, *Citizens Without Rights: Aborigines and Australian Citizenship* (Cambridge University Press, 1997) 172.

2 'Protests on Hotel Use', *The Canberra Times* (online, 17 May 1974) <https://trove.nla.gov.au/newspaper/article/110778708?searchTerm=Aboriginal%20and%20hostel%20and%20Brisbane>.

DOI: 10.4324/9781003473404-15

At the age of seventeen, Dad was called to Killoran's office. Killoran revealed that he was aware that Dad would be attending university the following year and warned of harsh consequences should he associate with any 'undesirables'.[3] Many years later, Dad described this exchange as having the 'fear of God'[4] struck into him. But Dad was undeterred and continued to speak out against injustice. It was not long before he received his first physical blow from a police officer, being pummeled in the head while demonstrating against the *Aborigines' and Torres Strait Islanders' Affairs Act of 1965* (Qld) that, among other things, empowered Killoran to order the removal of Indigenous people to and between reserves.[5] Over time, the violence worsened, and on at least one occasion, Dad almost lost his life. This attack was alluded to in *Tribune*, the former newspaper of the Communist Party of Australia. In the middle of an article on an anti-racism conference is a photograph of my nineteen-year-old father.[6] His smile is at odds with the caption, which notes that he had recently been hospitalised after a savage beating by police officers.

Although Dad had been the victim of horrific abuse, he never attempted to bring the culprits to justice. Even had he been able to secure the services of a solicitor, it would have been his word against the police officers'. Despite his justifiable cynicism towards the legal system, Dad later encouraged me to study law. My favourite subject at university was Torts; I was captivated by the intentional torts of battery, assault and false imprisonment, which exposed me to cases in which police officers were held accountable for acts of violence perpetrated on Indigenous people.

One such decision was *Henry v Thompson*,[7] which originated in a vicious attack in a watchhouse in Normanton, approximately 2,000 kilometres north-west of Brisbane. Today, students may also learn about the more recent decision, *Bulsey v Queensland*.[8] In this case, the appellants were subjected to a terrifying raid in the early hours of the morning. Although the plaintiffs were victorious, the judgments in both cases were problematic because the Aboriginality of the plaintiffs was of only peripheral relevance, if acknowledged at all. By treating race as tangential, the judgments obscured the reality that violence inflicted on Indigenous people by police officers is not an

3 'Emperor for Life: Killoran's Queensland', *ABC Listen* (Australian Broadcasting Corporation, 10 June 2012) <www.abc.net.au/listen/programs/hindsight/emperor-for-life3a-killoran27s-queensland/4037300>.

4 'Emperor for Life: Killoran's Queensland', *ABC Listen* (Australian Broadcasting Corporation, 10 June 2012) <www.abc.net.au/listen/programs/hindsight/emperor-for-life3a-killoran27s-queensland/4037300>.

5 *Aborigines' and Torres Strait Islanders' Affairs Act of 1965* (Qld) s 34.

6 Denis Freney, 'Q'land Racism Conference a Milestone', *Tribune* (online, 8 February 1971) 10, <https://trove.nla.gov.au/newspaper/article/237867852?searchTerm=Q%27land%20Racism%20Conference%20a%20milestone>.

7 [1989] 2 Qd R 412.

8 [2015] QCA 187.

aberration—it is a normal occurrence rooted in a history in which the police were used as conduits of the state's violent policies.

This chapter provides a means for students to build their awareness of the significance of plaintiffs' Aboriginality in intentional torts cases by developing a reading practice that is conscious of the narratives that are privileged in judgments and those that have been erased. It is divided into three parts. Part One unpacks the history of the interactions between Indigenous people in Queensland and police and introduces the concept of 'reading back, reading Black'.[9] Part Two applies a 'reading back, reading Black' lens to *Henry v Thompson*, and Part Three similarly interprets the judgments of the Queensland Court of Appeal in *Bulsey v Queensland*.

Part One: Aboriginality, Police and the Intentional Torts

In this part, I discuss why relationships between Indigenous people and police are atypical, having been shaped by histories in which police officers were instrumental in the state's most oppressive Indigenous policies. Although the issues raised in this discussion are applicable to other Australian states and territories, it is concerned only with Queensland. I then discuss how the educational experiences of all students can be enriched by an appreciation of the significance of the plaintiff's Aboriginality in intentional torts cases before unpacking the practice of reading back, reading Black.

Indigenous People and Police

For much of our shared history, police officers have been at the forefront of colonisation. From the mid-nineteenth century to the early twentieth century, Native Police operated in different parts of Australia, including Queensland. Akin to Special Forces,[10] the Native Police had the singular purpose of annihilating Indigenous resistance to dispossession. Under the direction of white officers, Aboriginal troopers carried out the notorious 'dispersals', a euphemism for mass murder.[11] In Queensland alone, an estimated 40,000[12] people were slaughtered.

Aboriginal women had a range of experiences with the Native Police. Some formed long-term relationships with troopers, while others were raped

9 Bennett Capers, 'Reading Back, Reading Black' (2006) 35(1) *Hofstra Law Review* 9.

10 Jonathan Richards, *The Secret War: A True History of Queensland's Native Police* (University of Queensland Press, 2008) 8.

11 Jonathan Richards, *The Secret War: A True History of Queensland's Native Police* (University of Queensland Press, 2008) 15.

12 Deborah Richards, 'Independent Commission of Inquiry into Queensland Police Service Responses to Domestic and Family Violence', *A Call for Change* (2022) 212 ('*Richards Inquiry*').

and killed when deemed no longer useful.[13] Orphans on the frontier were especially vulnerable. Historians have described accounts of babies becoming gifts[14] and children who were sold into bondage.[15] For the most part, colonial authorities turned a blind eye to such atrocities.

The Native Police ceased to operate by the early twentieth century. By then considered to be on the verge of extinction, Aboriginal people were detained on reserves where they could quietly expire. This new policy of 'protection' found expression in the *Aboriginals Protection and Restriction of the Sale of Opium Act 1897* (Qld). In the absence of court supervision, any Aboriginal person could be seized and taken to a reserve,[16] where they would be stripped of personal autonomy. Once again, police officers were the conduits through which the protection policy was fulfilled. As regional protectors, police officers exercised control over where Aboriginal people could live, whom they could work for and how their wages were spent and were empowered to remove Aboriginal children from their families.[17]

Queensland's legislation that enabled the invasive regulation of Indigenous people was subject to numerous overhauls in the decades that followed the passage of the *Aboriginals Protection and Restriction of the Sale of Opium Act 1897* (Qld).[18] A common thread of the different Acts was the authoritarian control over Aboriginal people on reserves, effected by Queensland's Indigenous affairs bureaucracy in conjunction with police.[19] One of the most violent means of suppressing Indigenous dissent was forcible removal. Most notoriously, this power was used by Patrick Killoran on 15 November 1963 to dispossess the residents of the township of Mapoon, whose lands were to be mined for bauxite.[20] In the middle of the night, police officers seized families at gunpoint, and their homes were set alight.

In the capital of Brisbane, Indigenous people had greater autonomy, but they were still vulnerable to police harassment. In his memoir, Aboriginal

13 Jonathan Richards, 'The Native Police of Queensland' (2008) 6(4) *History Compass* 1024, 1033.

14 David Marr, *Killing for Country: A Family Story* (Black Inc, 2023) 311.

15 David Marr, *Killing for Country: A Family Story* (Black Inc, 2023) 311.

16 *Aboriginals Protection and Restriction of the Sale of Opium Act 1897* (Qld) s 9.

17 Anti-Discrimination Commission of Queensland, *Aboriginal People in Queensland: A Brief Human Rights History* (2017) 12 <www.qhrc.qld.gov.au/__data/assets/pdf_file/0013/10606/Aboriginal-timeline-FINAL-updated-25-July-2018.pdf>.

18 *Aboriginals Preservation and Protection Act 1939* (Qld); *Aborigines' and Torres Strait Islanders' Affairs Act of 1965* (Qld); *Aborigines Act 1971* (Qld); *Torres Strait Islanders Act 1971* (Qld).

19 Ross Fitzgerald, *A History of Queensland from 1915 to the 1980s* (University of Queensland Press, 1984) 517.

20 Stefan Armbruster, 'Forced Aboriginal Removal "Forgiven, Not Forgotten"', *SBS News* (online, 15 November 2013) <www.sbs.com.au/news/article/forced-aboriginal-removal-forgiven-not-forgotten/u6it4mogl>.

Legal Service solicitor Paul Richards reflected that in the 1970s, Indigenous people could be arrested for merely being out in public at night:

> One of the first cases for the voluntary service was a seventeen-year-old apprentice from Cherbourg. He was walking along Queen Street at a time when police still enforced the old rules of a 6.00 pm curfew and 'keeping the natives out of town'. The police in those days were still operating on the basis that the 'boundary streets' in Brisbane were intended to be the boundaries beyond which Aboriginal people would not pass into the city.
>
> This young man was a teetotaller, a quiet, shy and polite person. He found himself charged with resisting arrest and obscene language, the usual charges with which the police would bully Aboriginal people; hence the Aboriginal reference to police as 'the bullymen'.[21]

Rather than being forgotten, such episodes linger in the collective memory of Indigenous communities. The Commission of Inquiry into Queensland Police Service Responses to Domestic and Family Violence heard that distrust of the Queensland Police Service was 'engrained' in Indigenous families and communities.[22] This history has also impacted the culture of the force. The Inquiry heard allegations of the use of racist language by police officers,[23] the bullying of Indigenous staff[24] and a closed Facebook group that contained nauseating racist posts.[25] It concluded that racism was a 'significant problem' within the Queensland Police Service and that the organisation had not 'consistently dealt with racist conduct in an appropriate manner'.[26]

Why Should Torts Students Learn about Race?

Having established that relationships between Indigenous communities and police are informed by violent histories, one may ponder why such matters should have a place in Torts courses. The answer is that the education of all students is enhanced when they engage with the social context of judgments. Such engagement allows students to grasp how the law operates in practice. It may also empower students to consider important questions, such as whether torts judgments should express community abhorrence of racism. They may also be encouraged to question how well the law of torts serves the most marginalised members of our society.

21 Paul Richards, *Adventures with Agitators: Stories of Indigenous Australia* (MoshPit Publishing, 2019) 50.
22 *Richards Inquiry* (n 12) 212.
23 *Richards Inquiry* (n 12) 226.
24 *Richards Inquiry* (n 12) 229.
25 *Richards Inquiry* (n 12) 228.
26 *Richards Inquiry* (n 12) 235.

When intentional torts cases are sanitised of social context, there is also a risk that Indigenous students will feel pressure to dissociate from the experiential knowledge of their communities. Some students will have grown up hearing stories of elders who suffered the indignity of having to seek official sanction to marry or spend their own money. All will have some familiarity with publicised cases in which Indigenous people suffered preventable deaths in desolate watchhouse cells. Such stories have taught them that the law is not applied equally to all.

In the years that followed the commencement of the Black Lives Matter Movement, some American scholars reflected on the harms caused by the erasure of race from legal education. One such reflection that is pertinent to this chapter was written by Professor Shaun Ossei-Owusu,[27] who apologised to minority students for the disjuncture between 'the law on the books and what they see in the criminal justice system'.[28] At a time when police officers were killing innocent citizens such as Breonna Taylor with impunity, Black students were expected to remain 'emotionally desensitized'.[29] Ossei-Owusu termed the injury that resulted from this disjuncture 'spirit-murder'. The term 'spirit-murder' was coined by Professor Patricia Williams to describe the collective impacts on the victim's psyche of everyday racism, which was 'no less than the equivalent of body murder'.[30] Just as Professor Ossei-Owusu's students experienced spirit-murder through the decoupling of 'racial realities'[31] from their education, I suspect that many Indigenous students are traumatised when the lived experiences of their families and communities are disavowed in the classroom.

Reading Back, Reading Black

Students may develop an awareness of issues of race by borrowing from a practice called reading back, reading Black,[32] which was created by Bennett Capers, the Stanley D and Nikki Waxberg Professor of Law at Fordham University. This revolutionary approach to interpreting judgments was inspired

27 Shaun Ossei-Owusu, 'For Minority Law Students, Learning the Law Can Be Intellectually Violent', *ABA Journal* (online, 15 October 2020) <www.abajournal.com/voice/article/for_minority_law_students_learning_the_law_can_be_intellectually_violent>.

28 Shaun Ossei-Owusu, 'For Minority Law Students, Learning the Law Can Be Intellectually Violent', *ABA Journal* (online, 15 October 2020) <www.abajournal.com/voice/article/for_minority_law_students_learning_the_law_can_be_intellectually_violent>.

29 Shaun Ossei-Owusu, 'For Minority Law Students, Learning the Law Can Be Intellectually Violent', *ABA Journal* (online, 15 October 2020) <www.abajournal.com/voice/article/for_minority_law_students_learning_the_law_can_be_intellectually_violent>.

30 Patricia Williams, 'Spirit-Murdering the Messenger: The Discourse of Fingerpointing as the Law's Response to Racism' (1987) 42(1) *University of Miami Law Review* 127, 151.

31 Ossei-Owusu (n 27).

32 Capers (n 9).

by literary scholars such as Edward Said, who revealed how stereotypes of peoples in the Middle East embodied in popular texts justified imperialism and colonisation.[33] The practice of reading back, reading Black similarly exposes an additional layer of meaning to the text—one that is cognisant of how judgments 'contribute to an ideology of race and racial hierarchy'.[34]

To read back a judgment is akin to jurors who ask for specific testimony to be repeated so that it can be mulled over in their deliberations. Likewise, Capers asks for judgments to be re-read 'not only contextually, but also critically, sensitive to the stated and the unstated, the revealed and the concealed, and the meaning to be gleaned from both'.[35] When one takes the extra step of reading Black, one applies a lens that is 'attuned to the frequencies and registers of race'.[36]

Capers applies this reading practice to the historic case *The Queen v Dudley & Stephens*.[37] The accused were sailors who had been cast away at sea, with no water and barely any food. To save their own lives, they killed and ate the victim. The men were convicted of murder and sentenced to death. Capers argues that, at the time, there was widespread acceptance of cannibalism by mariners at risk of death from starvation.[38] This poses the question of why the Crown proceeded with the prosecution of Dudley and Stephens, if cannibalism was broadly condoned in situations of dire necessity. According to Capers, the answer lies in representations of Africans as cannibals in popular culture and, in particular, travel writing. Because cannibalism was associated with the savage Other, it could not be tolerated among Englishmen. To do so would threaten notions of racial supremacy, and hence, Dudley and Stephens could not avoid culpability for murder.[39]

The following section shows how *Henry v Thompson* can be read back, read Black by combining the judgments with socio-legal materials, such as historical accounts, newspaper articles, memoirs and the work of seminal inquiries, for example, the Royal Commission into Aboriginal Deaths in Custody.[40] Such engagement reveals which stories are privileged in judgments, those that are absent and how judgments buttress popular myths about Australian society. In *Henry v Thompson*, the diminution of the relevance of race in the judgments had the effect of affirming a narrative in which the plaintiff, Mr Henry, was the arbitrary victim of a few 'bad apples' in the Queensland

33 Edward Said, *Orientalism* (Vintage, 1979).
34 Capers (n 9) 11.
35 Capers (n 9) 12.
36 Capers (n 9) 11.
37 (1884) 14 QB 273.
38 Capers (n 9) 14.
39 Capers (n 9) 15–16.
40 *Royal Commission into Aboriginal Deaths in Custody* (Final Report, April 1991) <https://www.austlii.edu.au/au/other/IndigLRes/rciadic/national/vol1/>.

Police Service. At the same time, the judgments obscured a story that inheres within the experiential knowledge of Indigenous communities. According to this story, violence against Indigenous people at the hands of officers of the Queensland Police Service is not a rarity. It is habitual.

Part Two: *Henry v Thompson*[41]

The events that formed the backdrop to *Henry v Thompson* occurred in Normanton, in the Gulf Country in 1982. On 20 August, the plaintiff/respondent, Mr Henry, attended a dance with his partner. The trial judge found that Mr Henry was 'probably under the influence of liquor to some extent'[42] when he was arrested by officers Doolan and Thompson for the offence of using obscene language. On arrival at the Normanton Police Watchhouse, Mr Henry was pulled to the ground by Thompson and Doolan, who kicked him in the head and shoulders. When Mr Henry tried to escape, the Officer in Charge, Smith, pushed him back and held him against some wire mesh. While Mr Henry was lying on the floor, Thompson jumped up and down on his head. In a final act of humiliation, Doolan urinated on Mr Henry's stomach.

The elements of Mr Henry's cause of action were not discussed in the judgments of the Full Court of the Supreme Court. By that stage, the defendants/appellants had abandoned their appeal on the issue of liability.[43] However, the elements of battery had been clearly established. A battery consists of an intentional act by the defendant that directly causes contact with the plaintiff's body.[44] Each police officer committed acts that were intentional and directly caused contact with Mr Henry's body, whether by way of punching, kicking, pushing or urinating. As the elements of battery were laid out, the onus would have shifted to the defendants/appellants to show that their actions had a lawful justification,[45] an impossibility under the circumstances. The trial judge found that

> all three defendants were engaged that night in a joint enterprise which involved the affliction of pain and humiliation on the plaintiff. Needless to say the conduct which I have described is totally unacceptable in a member of the police force.[46]

41 *Henry v Thompson* [1989] 2 Qd R 412.
42 *Henry v Thompson* [1989] 2 Qd R 413.
43 *Henry v Thompson* [1989] 2 Qd R 412.
44 Pam Stewart and Anita Stuhmcke, *Australian Principles of Tort Law* (Federation Press, 5th ed, 2021) 57.
45 Pam Stewart and Anita Stuhmcke, *Australian Principles of Tort Law* (Federation Press, 5th ed, 2021) 148.
46 *Henry v Thompson* [1989] 2 Qd R 412, 414.

Mr Henry received wounds to his face and suffered intense pain from a serious injury to his right eye. He had some weeks away from work while he was recovering. The trial judge awarded compensatory damages in the sum of $5000, aggravated damages of $10,000 and exemplary damages in the figure of $10,000.[47] On appeal, the police officers argued that each damages award was excessive.

In the lead judgment, Williams J considered that it was a 'classic case for a high award of aggravated damages'.[48] The urination was intended to, and did, cause Mr Henry great hurt and humiliation. The award of compensatory damages was not manifestly excessive, given the serious injury to Mr Henry's eye. Finally, the award of exemplary damages was upheld. The reality that the appellants were

> at the time senior police officers and that they abused their position to commit this cowardly and unseemly attack on the respondent call[ed] for a severe penalty.[49]
>
> *Henry v Thompson* is often included in introductory Torts courses to enable students to understand when it is apposite for courts to award exemplary damages. Drawing upon my experiences of teaching Torts, it is fair to say that Mr Henry's Aboriginality is usually acknowledged in class discussions. But the decision is less commonly used to frame conversations about the significance of race in intentional torts cases. Therefore, what new layer of meaning would be gleaned if students were supported to develop a reading back, reading Black approach to the judgments?

First, students would be sensitive to the most glaring absence from the judgments, which was genuine engagement with Mr Henry's Aboriginality. Justice Williams briefly referred to the 'racial overtones'[50] of the case as one of the reasons that the award of aggravated damages was not excessive. Otherwise, race sits on the periphery of the text. This marginalisation of race supports a narrative in which Mr Henry's Aboriginality did not distinguish him from other citizens in any meaningful way. He was merely the random prey of three flawed police officers. However, Mr Henry's Aboriginality was a critical part of the story, affecting his status in Normanton and impacting the realisation of his right to equality before the law.

Home to the Gkuthaarn, Kukatj and Kurtijar Peoples,[51] Normanton is situated in the Gulf Savannah in north-west Queensland. The Native Police

47 *Henry v Thompson* [1989] 2 Qd R 412.
48 *Henry v Thompson* [1989] 2 Qd R 415.
49 *Henry v Thompson* [1989] 2 Qd R 417.
50 *Henry v Thompson* [1989] 2 Qd R 416.
51 Queensland Government, 'Normanton', *Communities N–P* (Web Page, 13 April 2015) <www.qld.gov.au/firstnations/cultural-awareness-heritage-arts/community-histories/community-histories-n-p/community-histories-normanton>.

became active in Normanton soon after it was proclaimed to be a town in 1868.[52] Aboriginal people were dispossessed and forced to live in fringe camps.[53] A century later, Aboriginal people were still subject to unofficial segregation. When the Bjelke-Petersen Government began construction on eight houses for Indigenous families in 1969, furious townsfolk wrote to the Premier, imploring him to spare them from having to live among 'ill-equipped, ignorant, unhygienic, bush natives'.[54] When Paul Richards began to represent Aboriginal clients in Normanton in the 1970s, Aboriginal people were still precluded from moving into the town.[55] Instead, they remained on the periphery in accommodation that Paul Richards likened to 'cattle sheds at an agricultural show pavilion'.[56]

In such circumstances, it is inconceivable that Mr Henry would not be accustomed to experiencing racial discrimination. As an Aboriginal man, his contact with the defendants was also attendant with risks that would not ordinarily be faced by the white townsfolk of Normanton. The first was vulnerability to arrest for a public order offence—a risk that did, in fact, materialise. Indigenous people have long been disproportionately affected by public order offences, such as the use of obscene language and public drunkenness. In its Regional Report of Inquiry in Queensland, the Royal Commission into Aboriginal Deaths in Custody observed that 'drunkenness, arrest and incarceration' was a common experience for Indigenous people in urban areas and 'almost inevitable' for those who resided in Aboriginal communities.[57]

The second risk faced by Mr Henry concerned the loss of the law's protection. Aboriginal people are no longer the prey of a paramilitary force that operates in the shadows. But the factual scenarios of some intentional torts cases can be described as metaphorical dispersals, during which the rule of law was paused so that Indigenous people could be subjected to extraordinary brutalities. It is difficult to imagine Mr Henry's terror as an adult jumped up and down on his head or the indignity of being used as a toilet receptacle. Such horrors do not characterise typical engagements between

52 Shaun Adams et al., 'Truth-Telling in the Wake of European Contact: Historical Investigation of Aboriginal Skeletal Remains from Normanton' (2018) 14(3) *Archaeologies: Journal of the World Archaeological Congress* 412, 417.

53 Shaun Adams et al., 'Truth-Telling in the Wake of European Contact: Historical Investigation of Aboriginal Skeletal Remains from Normanton' (2018) 14(3) *Archaeologies: Journal of the World Archaeological Congress* 418.

54 'Normanton Petitions Premier: Meeting Puts Plan for Aborigines', *The Canberra Times* (online, 26 May 1969) <https://trove.nla.gov.au/newspaper/article/131786352?searchTerm=Normanton%20and%20Aboriginal%20and%20housing%20and%20petition>.

55 Richards, *Adventures with Agitators* (n 21) 118.

56 Richards, *Adventures with Agitators* (n 21).

57 *Royal Commission into Aboriginal Deaths in Custody* (Regional Report of Inquiry in Queensland, March 1991) [2.1.4].

citizens and police officers. They are moments of time in which the suspension of the rule of law is uncontroversial.

Throughout the history of such violent entanglements, the perpetrators have usually avoided culpability for their actions. Despite the brutality of the Native Police, criminal prosecutions were rare. Officers whose imprudence in the killing of Aboriginal people attracted public attention were reprimanded, but the most onerous punishment appears to have been dismissal. In his history of the Native Police, *The Secret War*,[58] Jonathan Richards described the case of Acting Sub-Inspector Edward Seymour, who murdered an Aboriginal woman on the ground that 'she riled him'.[59] Seymour was merely discharged and paid three months' salary.[60]

This history of impunity on the part of the police found resonance in *Henry v Thompson*. The judgments suggest that the defendants/appellants suffered no adverse consequences to their careers. Between the date of the attack on Mr Henry and the trial, Smith was even promoted from Sergeant Second Class to Sergeant First Class.[61] As the Officer in Charge, Smith should have used his authority to bring Mr Henry's ordeal to an end. He failed to exercise that power, intervening only to foil Mr Henry's escape.

The appellants also appear to have avoided responsibility for paying the entirety of the damages awarded to Mr Henry. As a result of s 69B(1) of the then *Police Act 1937–1984* (Qld), the Crown was liable for torts committed by police officers in the execution of their duties. However, the Crown's liability did not extend to 'punitive damages'.[62] As a consequence, it is likely that the appellants only had to pay the exemplary damages.

When the judgments are read back, read Black, new questions emerge, such as whether judgments should acknowledge the history of Indigenous peoples' interactions with police. Students may also be prompted to step into the shoes of the plaintiff and consider whether justice is served when an important part of the plaintiff's story—namely, their Aboriginality—is largely overlooked. Finally, students may ponder whether damages alone are a sufficient remedy.

One of the glaring omissions from *Henry v Thompson* was the absence of recognition of the wrong by the police officers in the form of an apology. Some may argue that an apology would have been inappropriate in this case because, presumably, it would not have been genuine. However, this ignores the significance of apologies. In a persuasive piece on court-ordered apologies, Brent White argues that many plaintiffs prioritise an apology above

58 Richards, *The Secret War* (n 10).
59 Richards, *The Secret War* (n 10) 104.
60 Richards, *The Secret War* (n 10).
61 *Henry v Thompson* [1989] 2 Qd R 412, 413.
62 *Police Act 1937–1984* (Qld) s 69B(3).

other remedies, pursuing civil litigation only when this 'desire is thwarted'.[63] Apologies also send a message to the public at large about desired social norms.[64] Although a court-ordered apology would not have been adequate on its own, it may have provided public vindication of Mr Henry's right to equality before the law.

Part Three: *Bulsey v Queensland*[65]

In this case, the appellants, David Bulsey and Yvette Lenoy, were intimate partners who lived on Palm Island, which is located 65 kilometres north of Townsville in the Great Barrier Reef. Their home was raided by members of the Special Emergency Response Team and plain-clothed officers. The raid was part of a complex chain of events sparked by the death of Mulrunji Doomadgee in the Palm Island watchhouse on 19 November 2004.[66] A week after Mr Doomadgee's death, the first appellant, Mr Bulsey attended a public meeting at which strident criticisms were made of the police investigation. Civil unrest ensued, and later, one Detective Miles, who was on the mainland, compiled a list of people to be arrested. Although there was no evidence that Mr Bulsey had committed an offence, his name appeared on the list.

At six o'clock on the morning of 27 November 2004, the second appellant, Yvette Lenoy, was making a cup of tea. She heard a noise and peered outside to see men who were masked, dressed in black and armed. One shouted, 'Get away from the door'.[67] She replied that she would open the door,[68] but before she could do so, it was pushed open. Five of the men in black and two plain-clothed police officers walked inside. Understandably, Ms Lenoy was frightened and screaming. After telling her to 'shut up',[69] the men instructed Ms Lenoy to point out who was sleeping in the rooms in the house and identify what room Mr Bulsey was in. They then instructed her to lie down on the floor.[70] Ms Lenoy was unable to comply because she was heavily pregnant.

By this time, the children in the house were awake and screaming. Mr Bulsey was forced from his bed, handcuffed and compelled to lie on the floor.[71]

63 Brent T White, 'Say You're Sorry: Court-Ordered Apologies as a Civil Rights Remedy' (2006) 91(6) *Cornell Law Review* 1261, 1269.
64 Brent T White, 'Say You're Sorry: Court-Ordered Apologies as a Civil Rights Remedy' (2006) 91(6) *Cornell Law Review* 1279.
65 *Bulsey v Queensland* [2015] QCA 187.
66 *Bulsey v Queensland* [2015] QCA 187 [6].
67 *Bulsey v Queensland* [2015] QCA 187 [49].
68 *Bulsey v Queensland* [2015] QCA 187.
69 *Bulsey v Queensland* [2015] QCA 187.
70 *Bulsey v Queensland* [2015] QCA 187 [52].
71 *Bulsey v Queensland* [2015] QCA 187 [105].

He recalled guns being pointed at his head and back.[72] Although Mr Bulsey was partially undressed, the police dragged him out of the house. It was only when he was in the street that the police put trousers on him.[73] Mr Bulsey was taken to Townsville and spent two days in a watchhouse before being taken before a magistrate. He was charged with unlawful assembly and remanded in custody. At the committal proceedings, the Crown conceded that it had no case against Mr Bulsey, and he was discharged.[74] Mr Bulsey and Ms Lenoy sued the State of Queensland, as opposed to the police officers. The trial judge dismissed their claims,[75] but both appellants were ultimately successful in the Queensland Court of Appeal.

The first appellant, Mr Bulsey, sued the respondent in battery, assault and false imprisonment. Mr Bulsey's evidence, whose essence was captured earlier, was accepted by the trial judge, and Mr Bulsey therefore discharged the onus of proving all three torts. That is, he showed that the officers had engaged in intentional and positive acts that directly caused contact with his body (battery);[76] that the officers had carried out positive and intentional acts that directly created in his mind a reasonable apprehension of imminent contact (assault);[77] and that the officers had executed positive and intentional acts that directly caused the total deprivation of his liberty (false imprisonment).[78]

The onus then shifted to the respondent to prove that the conduct of the police officers was excused by law. The trial judge found that the arrest of Mr Bulsey was authorised by section 198(2) of the *Police Powers and Responsibilities Act 2000* (Qld), which made it lawful for a police officer to arrest a person without a warrant if the police officer reasonably suspected that the person had committed or was committing an indictable offence.[79] Even though he was not physically present, Detective Miles had a reasonable belief that Mr Bulsey had committed offences in connection with the civil unrest that broke out after the public meeting in which the police investigation into the death of Mr Doomadgee was condemned.[80] This finding was overturned by the Court of Appeal.

In the lead judgment, Fraser JA concluded that the arrest of Mr Bulsey was not permissible under section 198(2).[81] The respondent could not show that the police officer—presumably an unidentified member of the Special

72 *Bulsey v Queensland* [2015] QCA 187.
73 *Bulsey v Queensland* [2015] QCA 187.
74 *Bulsey v Queensland* [2015] QCA 187 [1].
75 *Bulsey v Queensland* [2015] QCA 187 [3].
76 Stewart and Stuhmcke (n 42) 57.
77 Stewart and Stuhmcke (n 42) 60.
78 Stewart and Stuhmcke (n 42) 68.
79 Stewart and Stuhmcke (n 42) [7].
80 Stewart and Stuhmcke (n 42) [6]–[7].
81 Stewart and Stuhmcke (n 42) [21].

Emergency Response Team—who arrested Mr Bulsey suspected that Mr Bulsey had committed an indictable offence.[82] Any such inkling possessed by Detective Miles was irrelevant because he did not carry out the arrest.[83] As there was no lawful excuse for the conduct of the police, the respondent was liable.

Fraser JA considered that a significant award of damages was necessary because of the harm caused to Mr Bulsey by the 'wrongful exercise of executive power'.[84] An appropriate award was $165,000, which consisted of damages (inclusive of aggravated damages) of $60,000 for the assault, battery and false imprisonment during the arrest of Mr Bulsey and $100,000 for the false imprisonment that occurred after he was taken to the mainland.[85] He was also awarded $5,000 for a chronic adjustment disorder that he developed because of his treatment by the police.[86]

The second appellant, Ms Lenoy, claimed that she had been assaulted by police officers. The assault was constituted by the officers 'pointing their guns at her in her own residence and ordering her to lie on the floor against her will'.[87] Ms Lenoy also sued the respondent for false imprisonment, arguing that when the police officers compelled her to 'go to different parts of the house against her will' she had been completely 'deprived of her liberty to refuse'.[88] Her claims were rejected by the trial judge, who found that Ms Lenoy was not a reliable witness. He explained this finding by reasons that included her pregnancy, ill health and the distressing circumstances of Mr Bulsey's arrest.[89]

These findings were set aside by the Court of Appeal. One of the 'striking feature[s]'[90] of the case was the consistency between Ms Lenoy's account of the events in question and the evidence of the police officers.[91] Some of the trial judge's reasoning for finding Ms Lenoy to be an unreliable witness, such as her pregnancy, was also not persuasive. In assessing damages, Fraser JA took account of the 'extraordinarily traumatic atmosphere'[92] and the indignity of Ms Lenoy being compelled to assist the police in finding her partner and then watching them drag him into the street while only partially dressed.[93] She was awarded $70,000 for the assault and false imprisonment.[94]

82 Stewart and Stuhmcke (n 42).
83 Stewart and Stuhmcke (n 42).
84 Stewart and Stuhmcke (n 42) [109].
85 Stewart and Stuhmcke (n 42) [110].
86 Stewart and Stuhmcke (n 42) [79].
87 Stewart and Stuhmcke (n 42) [54].
88 Stewart and Stuhmcke (n 42).
89 Stewart and Stuhmcke (n 42).
90 Stewart and Stuhmcke (n 42) [65].
91 Stewart and Stuhmcke (n 42) [69].
92 Stewart and Stuhmcke (n 42) [112].
93 Stewart and Stuhmcke (n 42).
94 Stewart and Stuhmcke (n 42) [113].

Reading Back, Reading Black

A reading back, reading Black approach requires the reader to be conscious of both the stated and the unstated. Beginning with the stated, all judgments were critical of the heavy-handedness of the police. This discomfort was echoed in McMeekin J's recognition that the 'quite startling feature'[95] of the case was the harsh treatment meted out to the appellants as though they were dangerous felons. But such treatment is only startling if the appellants' race and the history of Palm Island are both erased, which is what occurred.

Moving to what is unstated in the judgments, a reading back, reading Black approach would be conscious that none of the judgments contained a single reference to the Aboriginality of the appellants or the fact that Palm Island is a discrete Aboriginal community. This erasure supports a narrative in which the appellants were treated no differently by the police officers to other citizens by reason of their Aboriginality. Like Mr Henry, the appellants were the hapless casualties of behaviour that was regrettable but by no means reflective of a racist approach of the Queensland Police Service towards Aboriginal people. Such mythology flew in the face of the lived experience of the people of Palm Island for whom racial difference had been the justification for systematic repression for almost a century.

Palm Island is the home of the Manbarra and Bwgcolman Peoples.[96] From 1918 it operated as a prison camp for Aboriginal people throughout Queensland who defied the authorities.[97] According to historian Joanne Watson, the most tyrannical chapter in its history was the reign of Superintendent Roy Bartlam in the 1950s.[98] Bartlam was able to keep residents in fear by reliance upon a punitive local police force. The severity of this force was reflected in the ease with which Indigenous people were incarcerated. Men were jailed for simply being unkempt, and women could suffer similar consequences for wearing attire that exposed their knees.[99]

This history was a crucial part of the story in *Bulsey v Queensland* because it contextualised both the gratuitous violence associated with the arrest of Mr Bulsey and how such violence was experienced by Mr Bulsey and Ms Lenoy. Although this history was entirely overlooked by the Queensland Court of Appeal, its importance was recognised by Mortimer

95 Stewart and Stuhmcke (n 42) [125].

96 Queensland Government, 'Palm Island', *Communities N–P* (21 March 2018) <www.qld.gov.au/firstnations/cultural-awareness-heritage-arts/community-histories/community-histories-n-p/community-histories-palm-island>.

97 Joanne Watson, ' "We Couldn't Tolerate Anymore": The Palm Island Strike of 1957' (1995) 69 *Labour History* 149, 151.

98 Joanne Watson, '"We Couldn't Tolerate Anymore": The Palm Island Strike of 1957' (1995) 69 *Labour History* 153.

99 Joanne Watson, '"We Couldn't Tolerate Anymore": The Palm Island Strike of 1957' (1995) 69 *Labour History* 155.

J in *Wotton v State of Queensland (No 5)*.[100] This case concerned alleged breaches of section 9(1) of the *Racial Discrimination Act 1975* (Qld) arising from the investigation into the death of Mulrunji Doomadgee and the police response to the civil unrest on 26 November 2004. Although *Wotton v State of Queensland (No 5)* was not a torts case, it is relevant to this part because of the approach taken by Mortimer J to the Palm Islanders' lived experience of police officers being used as the conduits of racially discriminatory policies.

Justice Mortimer described the long story of domination as a 'living history':[101]

> Police were the ones who acted as guards, who placed locals in jail for minor infringements of rules applying only to Aboriginal people, who sought out those who fled the island and brought them back to be placed in jail. Control and subordination on a racial basis was central to the way this community has always been compelled to function. These matters were part of their lives, not simply entries in the history books and archives.[102]

Presumably this living history weighed heavily on Mr Bulsey and Ms Lenoy as the police forced their way through their front door and brandished guns as children and adults alike cried in fear. It also found resonance in the unnecessary arrest of Mr Doomadgee and the disproportionate response by police to the civil unrest a week later.

On the morning of 19 November 2004, Mr Doomadgee witnessed the arrest of another Aboriginal man, Roy Bramwell, by Senior Sergeant Chris Hurley, who was accompanied by Aboriginal Police Liaison Officer Lloyd Bengaroo. Mr Doomadgee said words to the effect that Bengaroo should not have been 'locking up' other Aboriginal people.[103] For this trivial insult, Mr Doomadgee was arrested for creating a public nuisance.[104] Mortimer J described what happened next:

> On the way into the police station, Mulrunji and SS [Senior Sergeant] Hurley fell through the rear door of the police station as they were entering it. There are various accounts of how this fall occurred and what it involved, including accounts by SS Hurley and by Mr Bramwell.
>
> Whatever occurred, Mulrunji ended up on the floor of the police station, in a corridor leading to the cells, with his head facing towards the

100 [2016] FCA 1457.
101 [2016] FCA 1457 [56].
102 [2016] FCA 1457.
103 *Wotton v State of Queensland (No 5)* [2016] FCA 1457, [860].
104 *Wotton v State of Queensland (No 5)* [2016] FCA 1457, [881].

> cells and his feet facing towards the door he and SS Hurley had entered through. The parties agree he was limp and unresponsive by this stage.
>
> While in that state, Mulrunji was dragged by Sergeant Leafe and SS Hurley into a watchhouse cell.[105]

Under an hour later, the police discovered that Mr Doomadgee was no longer breathing.[106]

Despite his close connection to the death of Mr Doomadgee, Hurley remained on active duty. He even met the investigating officers at the airport later that day and prepared a meal for them at his home.[107] Such actions were part of a pattern of behaviour that exhibited not only a disregard for the community's grief but also a belief that members of the Queensland Police Service could behave with impunity.[108] Community anger spilled over on 26 November, after a meeting in which the results of an autopsy were disclosed, revealing that Mr Doomadgee sustained injuries from an accidental fall.[109] In the melee that followed, the police station and Hurley's residence were set on fire.[110] The police responded with a declaration of a state of emergency and the involvement of the Special Emergency Response Team, a specialist unit that responds to terrorism.[111] In *Wotton v State of Queensland (No 5)*, Justice Mortimer found that such methods not only were disproportionate but also would not have been used in non-Indigenous communities.[112]

When the judgments in *Bulsey v Queensland* are read back, read Black, the argument that violence is intrinsic to interactions between Indigenous people and officers of the Queensland Police Service is persuasive. Such a reading of the judgments could also spark innovative questions for class discussions. For example, one of the themes that emerges from this story was the breadth of the harm caused by the wrongs, which was experienced by the entire community. In such circumstances, the intentional torts are inadequate because they are concerned only with the physical and psychological integrity of those most directly affected by the impugned conduct.

If Indigenous victims of police brutality are to receive a meaningful justice, then new responses are required. In this respect, students may turn to work published by American scholars. For example, John Felipe Acevedo argues that the impact of racist police misconduct should be understood as more

105 *Wotton v State of Queensland (No 5)* [2016] FCA 1457, [220]–[222].
106 *Wotton v State of Queensland (No 5)* [2016] FCA 1457, [223].
107 *Wotton v State of Queensland (No 5)* [2016] FCA 1457, [849].
108 *Wotton v State of Queensland (No 5)* [2016] FCA 1457, [890].
109 *Wotton v State of Queensland (No 5)* [2016] FCA 1457, [318].
110 *Wotton v State of Queensland (No 5)* [2016] FCA 1457, [321].
111 *Wotton v State of Queensland (No 5)* [2016] FCA 1457, [333].
112 *Wotton v State of Queensland (No 5)* [2016] FCA 1457, [1456].

than the hurt suffered by individual plaintiffs.[113] Although it encompasses such injuries, the harm extends to the taking of dignity from targeted communities. Appropriate responses are therefore those that aim to restore collective dignity, such as reparations.

Conclusion

One narrative that is often reinforced by the judgments in intentional torts cases is the myth that Indigenous people are treated no differently than other citizens by police on account of their race. This story is buttressed by the attenuation of the significance of the plaintiff's Aboriginality so that the tortious acts are understood as the random behaviour of imperfect individuals. However, such violence has its origins in a long tradition in which police have been used as instruments of colonisation. Today, this history continues to find resonance in interactions between Indigenous people and members of the Queensland Police Service.

Intentional torts represent an important opportunity to support students to develop a reading practice that enables them to engage with the social context of judgments. This does not suggest that legal doctrine is irrelevant. To the contrary, students should be familiar with the legal rules to be distilled from cases and appreciate how these rules are to be applied to relevant facts. But by developing a reading back, reading Black approach to intentional torts cases, students can unveil a new layer of meaning, one in which judgments play a role in fortifying popular 'truths' about race and racism.

113 John Felipe Acevedo, 'Restoring Community Dignity Following Police Misconduct' (2016) 59(3) *Howard Law Journal* 621.

13

REFLECTING ON THE 'GENERAL PART' WHEN THERE IS SYSTEMIC INJUSTICE

Do We Inadvertently Facilitate Overcriminalisation of First Peoples in Australia?

Mary Spiers Williams

Introduction: Can Criminal Law Doctrine Contribute to Systemic Bias against First Peoples?

The rules for Australian legal practitioner admission require all law courses to teach elemental proof—the theory and method of the 'general part' of the criminal law.[1] For this reason, criminal law courses and textbooks continue to emphasise the doctrinal account of the criminal law. Even in critically engaged contexts, such as a criminal law course where lecturers critique elemental analysis,[2] it is apparent to the students that mastering elemental

1 The topics of criminal law and procedure are set out in *Legal Profession Uniform Admission Rules 2015* (NSW), s3:

> Either the following topics: . . .
>
> (b) Elements of crime . . . [et cetera] or topics of such breadth and depth as to satisfy the following guidelines:
>
> The topics should provide knowledge of the general doctrines of the criminal law and, in particular, examination of both offences against the person and against property. Selective treatment should also be given to various defences and to elements of criminal procedure.
>
> As a legal practitioner, I would lug to court daily the loose-leaf service in which was set out the 'form of indictment' and commentary that deconstructed each offence into elements. This elemental deconstruction still appears in the annotated legislation available online; see, e.g., Rod Howie and Peter Johnson, *Annotated Criminal Legislation New South Wales 2019–2020 edition* (LexisNexis Butterworths, 2020).

2 See, e.g., David Brown et al., *Criminal Laws Materials and Commentaries on Criminal Law and Process in New South Wales* (Federation Press, 1st ed, 1990). Refer to the textbook, now in its 7th edition and the criminal law courses based on this. (Disclosure: I taught courses with its authors and others since while relying on this text). See, e.g., Brown et al.'s discussion of HM Hart's critique of the circularity of Glanville Williams' definition of crime: HM

DOI: 10.4324/9781003473404-16

analysis and proof is what matters. This is because we (teachers) continue to emphasise—in the final examination, in tutorials—problem questions that require application of the general part; mastery earns students a higher grade and—we are told—will earn them the job.

In this chapter, I explore how elemental proof—the theory and the method of the general part of the criminal law—contributes to systemic bias against First Peoples. Orthodox doctrines and definitions of crime and our training in the general part influence how we (lawyers) analyse complex social issues and perform our roles within a complex social system: the criminal justice system. Could this training impede a court's capacity to make sense of serious socially destructive and disruptive conduct? In what way might this create the potential for direct and indirect discrimination against First Peoples? The answers to these questions raise concerns about whether elemental proof gives effect to the rule of law, especially with respect to First Peoples.

This chapter has two parts. The first part critiques the continuing influence of the general part of the criminal law and how this may facilitate the perpetuation of systemic bias against First Peoples. The second part reflects on building our capacity as a profession to engage critically with criminal justice with a view to ameliorating systemic racism. These two parts are hinged with reflections on my experiences and perspectives of legal education and criminal law practice.[3]

Part 1: The Doctrinal Approach to Teaching Criminal Law: The Continuing Influence of the 'General Part'

In the mid-twentieth century, Glanville Williams purported to curate the common law of criminal law principles into what he called the 'general part' (or 'general principles') and the 'special part' of the criminal law.[4] In the 1950s and 1960s, law schools were yet to monopolise legal education; lawyers had only recently started to craft themselves as a profession.[5] The common law

---

Hart, 'The Aims of the Criminal Law' (1858) 23 *Law & Contemporary Problems* 404 cited at Brown et al. (*Criminal Laws Materials and Commentaries on Criminal Law and Process in New South Wales* (Federation Press, 6th ed, 2015) 59–60.

3 As will become obvious from my remarks and positioning throughout this chapter, my perspective is informed by my descendancy from the First Peoples of the sandstone Country (what is known as Sydney and stretches north of Dyarrabbin; my father is Darkeñung), my experiences as a criminal law practitioner, criminal law policy officer and desert peoples' law and justice projects officer (especially the Warlpiri), and my teaching and research in criminal law, criminology and critical Indigenous studies.

4 Glanville Llewelyn Williams, *Criminal Law: The General Part* (Stevens & Sons, 1961).

5 Michael Coper, 'Recent Developments in Australian Legal Education' (Research Paper No 10–85, ANU College of Law, 2010) <https://papers.ssrn.com/sol3/papers.cfm?abstract_id=1715262>; David Barker, *A History of Australian Legal Education* (PhD Thesis, Macquarie University, 2022) <https://figshare.mq.edu.au/articles/thesis/A_history_of_Australian_legal_education/19432868>.

(the courts) defined crime and standards of proof. Since then, legislatures have increasingly intervened in this space, and judiciaries have deferred to parliamentary sovereignty.[6]

Elements and Proof

Williams' curation continues to influence criminal law education and practice. Typically, the starting point in a criminal law course is an examination of the 'General Part' or 'General Principles' of the criminal law. These set out a legal definition of crime and a method for proving the guilt of a defendant.

Prosecutors are required to prove beyond reasonable doubt the 'elements' of an offence.[7] These elements, unique to each offence, can be imagined as a list of ingredients for a recipe that will fail if one is missing. The term 'element' associates the method with the scientific credibility of chemistry and the certainty of an element in the periodic table. The reality is that elemental proof is premised on a discredited yet resilient Cartesian concept about the self—the dualism of human mind and body.[8] The elements of an offence are broadly categorised into the *mens rea* (also referred to as 'internal' or 'mental' elements) and the *actus reus* ('external' or 'physical' elements). The method of elemental proof assumes that a crime is defined by the coincidence of an individual's action and thought.

Already, the requirement that a crime be composed of an *actus reus* and a *mens rea* narrows our thinking about what a 'crime' is: inherently, a crime is 'contained' within a human being and is knowable through an individual. The method allows us to imagine that only an individual can be responsible for a crime. Indeed, under the general part,[9] it is challenging to hold responsible more than one human unless all are directly involved in the event. This method of proof does not allow us to imagine, for example, that social structures, experiences and events could have contributed to the cause of the crime. The requirement that the elements must 'coincide' or be 'contemporaneous' can also result in such material being excluded from consideration.

6 For a discussion of this specifically with respect to the legislative reform of criminal law, see, e.g., John Pratt, *Penal Populism* (Routledge, 2007); Russell Hogg and David Brown, *Rethinking Law and Order* (Pluto Press, 1998).

7 *Woolmington v DPP* [1935] AC 462.

8 See, e.g., RA Duff, *Intention, Agency and Criminal Responsibility* (Wiley-Blackwell, 1990) 116 cited in Brown et al., *Criminal Laws* (Federation Press, 6th ed, 2015) 156; Ian Leader-Elliott, 'Benthamite Reflections on Codification of the General Principles of Criminal Liability: Towards the Panopticon' (2006) 9(2) *Buffalo Criminal Law Review* 391, 428–29; Dov Fox and Alex Stein, 'Dualism and Doctrine' in Dennis Patterson and Michael S Pardo (eds), *Philosophical Foundations of Law and Neuroscience, Philosophical Foundations of Law* (Oxford, 2016). Until now, the Cartesian conception of the dualism of the mind and body has strongly influenced western culture and ways of knowing.

9 Cf. the special part, which includes the extensions of criminal responsibility and exceptions to liability. I discuss the effects of appending the special part later.

Material outside the moment of the guilty act is not admissible evidence because it has been classified as irrelevant on the basis that it is outside the moment of an artificially isolated event.[10]

Another justification for exclusion of evidence deemed not relevant to the coincidence of the actus reus and mens rea is that it is 'relevant instead' to sentencing. This is not a reason for it to be irrelevant to proof; this justification is more accurately characterised as an uncritical commitment to components. The method of proof presumes that a crime has component parts, that these can be disassembled and that one can make sense of a crime by pulling such components apart. During proof, legal actors must disassemble the putative crime and then reassemble only some of its sundered parts, ensuring that there is a part that goes into each element 'box'. By this method, we are meant to reliably determine an individual's responsibility for the crime. We purport to make sense of a whole through dissection and disassembly, but, significantly, we do not reassemble *all* of the criminal conduct—the elements determine which parts we are permitted to reassemble.

Praxis reveals another weakness of a dualist deconstruction: some important concepts are simply not amenable to disassembly. 'Dishonesty' and 'possession', for example, are not meaningfully segmented into an act and a state of mind.[11] These concepts necessarily intertwine 'internal' elements (such as knowledge, awareness or intention) with the so-called 'external' element (typically, an act).

The general part of criminal law requires us to narrow the frame of our consideration to a moment and only to the evidence that is relevant to the elements of the offence. The legitimacy of this relies on the elements being a complete and accurate translation of what is 'criminal' into these components. The definition of an offence may be misleading and reductionist. This has the potential to impede our ability to make sense of a specific case and affects popular perception of what is an offence.

Such elemental reductionism also makes it easier for legislators to chip away at the normative coherence of the criminal law and the procedural protections that common lawyers have tried to ensure are constitutionally protected.[12] In the absence of constitutional enshrinement of the rule of law, a principle of antidiscrimination or some other civil right, there is nothing to inhibit legislatures from deracinating principle and removing nuance

10 The dicta on the principle of coincidence are more complex, but this is a basic rule.

11 See, e.g., discussion by English criminal law professor John Child, 'Teaching the Elements of Crimes' in Kris Gledhill and Ben Livings (eds), *The Teaching of Criminal Law: The Pedagogical Imperatives* (Taylor & Francis Group, 2016) 34, 35.

12 Andrew Ashworth, 'Is the Criminal Law a Lost Cause?' (2000) 116(2) *Law Quarterly Review* 225.

through which the common law may have imbibed an offence.[13] Australian citizens have almost no constitutional rights; nonetheless, many enjoy rights. I could say provocatively that we enjoy these rights by relying on the beneficence of the legislature and executive. For First Peoples, this beneficence manifests—at best—as paternalism. Settler colonisers gave themselves the power to determine without limit anything about our lives; they achieved this by constructing First Peoples as a 'race'.[14] For First Peoples, the politicisation of criminal law and its legitimisation of surveillance, intervention, control and violence by the state is felt as 'just' another aspect of the ongoing colonial project of dispossessing and rendering First Peoples outsiders in our home. The mechanistic conception of crime as elements and standards of proof is vulnerable to political whim that advances law and order agendas; First Peoples tend to experience the impact of these more than other populations.

Lawyers and law students are trained not only to focus on the elements but also to turn our attention away from, and discontinue inquiry about, any material deemed irrelevant. Indigenous defendants and their communities may consider such material relevant to the question of guilt, especially material concerning historical context, intergenerational trauma, contemporary discrimination, structural bias and other forms of injustice or material that gives insight into First Peoples' perspectives. A valued cultural practice can help to explain and de-stigmatise what might be viewed as criminal conduct—not merely to mitigate penalty but to acquit. Indigenous people have unique insight into the multiple ways of being caught in the state criminalisation system—the interventions for petty infractions, the persistent surveillance and intrusion that pre-empts reactions against over-selection and over-policing, the disrespectful way that some police treat Indigenous people. Rarely is such material permitted during the determination of the threshold question of guilt. Our scholarship regarding criminal proof does not inquire into how this could be relevant; such inquiry is inhibited by the elemental method of proof.

In my experience, when First Nations cultural material is raised at the guilt determination stage, it is diverted *quickly* to the sentencing hearing, where it cannot affect the threshold question of criminal responsibility—that is, of guilt. Those legally trained react swiftly to a proposal that such material be

13 See, e.g., observations of the Australian legal system as 'a pale and poorly version of itself, so it does not even recognise itself anymore' in a 'dilapidated condition': Anne Poelina et al., 'Reflecting on Australia's Current Legal System', in Anne Poelina et al. (eds), *Declaration of Peace for Indigenous Australians and Nature: A Legal Pluralist Approach to First Laws and Earth Laws* (Springer, 2024) 7; 'First Law and Songlines', *The Other Others* (Tyson Yunkaporta and Megan Kelleher, April 2021) <https://open.spotify.com/episode/3q0WY4VBhhs38iHTtTA3Nd>.

14 *Australian Constitution* s 51(xxvi).

included: 'But that's relevant to sentencing, not to proof.' That material is relevant to sentencing does not necessarily mean that it is irrelevant to proof. In itself, this is an insufficient justification for not taking it into account at the guilt determination stage and indicates that, to lawyers, it is the compartmentalisation (the delineation of relevance) that is important, not the substantive question of whether the material can relevantly help us to determine whether the state can punish a person. We can be too quick to determine helpful material irrelevant.

What impact might this training to divert such material have in practice? It may help to explain the preponderance of defendants who plead guilty. Despite the emphasis that we place on proof, the prosecution is rarely 'put to proof'. Less than 20 per cent of cases are tested in a defended hearing.[15] The overwhelming proportion of cases in the criminal courts proceed after a lawyer has advised the defendant, and the defendant has pleaded guilty. Such advice and instructions are privileged communications, rendering it impossible to research whether defendants have given instructions that potentially implicate settler social structures—the legal system, our shared histories, the effects of contemporary punishment practices—in criminal responsibility.

Are lawyers trained adequately to consider whether such evidence should be relevant to the threshold question of guilt? Or are we training lawyers to do something much simpler: divert such material away from being considered in guilt? If such material is available, then it is likely to be diverted because, historically, we (lawyers) have not been trained to understand how social systems can contribute to the cause of crime—because such material has not been classified *relevant*. More critically, we do not allow this to affect criminal law principles or practice. In essence, we are not developing our epistemology in line with other social science developments. Instead, elemental proof welds our analysis to only that of individual responsibility, diverting our attention from larger social forces at play.

The speedy diversion of this material on the basis of its relevance to sentencing is not only faux reasoning, it is misleading. In sentencing hearings, despite the promises of context being considered, legal practitioners struggle to have courts adequately consider material that a defendant—and their community—may consider relevant to criminality.[16] If a court *is* prepared to

15 For example, in the New South Wales District Court between 2011 and 2013, only 17 per cent of defendants pleaded not guilty: Clare Ringland and Lucy Snowball, 'Predictors of Guilty Pleas in the NSW District Court' (Issue paper No 96, NSW Bureau of Crime Statistics and Research, August 2014). See discussion of the preponderance of guilty pleas in Brown et al. (6th ed, n 2) 337–52.

16 I have argued this elsewhere in commentary on *Bugmy v The Queen* (2013) 302 ALR 192: Mary Spiers Williams, 'The Relevance of Colonialism and Structural Racism: "Turning the Gaze" in Bugmy' in Nicole Watson and Heather Douglas (eds), *Indigenous Legal Judgments: Bringing Indigenous Voices into Judicial Decision Making* (Routledge, 2021) 277.

consider such material, then legal practitioners find themselves constrained in the submissions that they can make about such material, *because* the threshold question of guilt has already been determined. We can only plead in mitigation and must tread carefully or risk the ire of the court. Judicial officers predisposed to engage critically with such material are similarly constrained, both in their interactions with barristers during submissions and in their remarks on sentences. This is because their findings and orders may be overturned on appeal.

The Special Part: The Arbitrary Inclusion of Other Material That Is Relevant to Proof

While the distinctive Indigenous culture and law and the unique experiences and perspectives of First Peoples tend to be excluded, settler cultural practices tend to be insulated from criminalisation. Protecting valued settler practices can excuse what would otherwise be a crime (for example, protection of one's property and the protection of private property generally). Settler cultural practices are normalised, centred and even looked to as the measure of constructive participation in society. Settler interests can even define what is a crime and influence the discretion of the settlers who work in the criminal justice system. The police discretion not to charge, a prosecutor's drafting of alleged facts, a defence lawyer's decision not to put before the court some of the client's instructions or a magistrate's decision to order 'no conviction be recorded' for the child of police officers—for all of these, there are always justifications that resonate with settler values. State criminalisation is structural, ideological and embedded in settler culture.

This is one way to make sense of the addition of the 'special part' to the doctrinal principles of the criminal law: the special part can be imagined as an 'addendum' to the 'general part'. The general part does not capture all instances of criminality, such as the wrongfulness of those not directly involved in committing the offence. It does not capture all of the justifications for what would be otherwise criminal. Rather than address the epistemological challenges of the insufficiency or incoherence of the principles of the general part, Williams grouped these exceptions, extensions and justifications by placing them into what he called the 'special part'. He avoided rather than solved the problems that the general part generates—and effectively diverted us from critiquing the criminal law epistemology. The epistemological justification for annexing the special part to the general part can seem like a loose appeal to a 'common sense'.

What implications might this have for contributing to First Peoples' overcriminalisation? Reliance on 'common sense' is a 'red flag' in my experience and is a useful indicator of potential prejudice, such as that inherent in whiteness and patriarchy. Where common sense is deployed, there are opportunities to ask questions—for example, is the status quo (or other asymmetry, such as systemic racial discrimination) reproduced here? Critical feminist and queer scholars, for example, have challenged the common sense of the construction of self-defence[17] and provocation,[18] specifically, the capacity of these 'defences' to exonerate or even legitimate male violence while excluding those who are 'othered' from accessing benefits of such justifications.[19]

Avoiding the problems that the general part creates by diverting students to the special part affects how law students think—and trains them—in other problematic respects.[20] The special part normalises exceptionalism and trains legal actors to respond to weaknesses in the theory by finding an exception or another rule that allows them to finalise a case. Some of these rules are so inconsistent with principle that we use them like bad playwrights use the 'deus ex machina': we lower them—like a god winched down onto a stage—to fix problems of narrative, structure or logic with a bald declaration.[21] Instead of solving the incoherence, lawyers learn and apply by rote a rule contrived to resolve a specific issue. This is not reasoning; it is more akin to dogma, demanding as it does faith and obedience. The epistemology of the general part is left uncritiqued by legal educators and scholars.

The normalisation of exceptionalism in a settler society has two effects: it advantages those who are privileged in a racialised hierarchy, and it normalises the suspension of reasoning, critique and principle with respect to First Peoples. Although exceptionalism indicates epistemological incoherence with the rule of law and civil rights, it is coherent with a legal ordering that is

17 For example, self-defence in the context of relationship entrapment: Heather Douglas, Stella Tarrant and Julia Tolmie, 'Social Entrapment Evidence: Understanding Its Role in Self-Defence Cases Involving Intimate Partner Violence' (2021) 44(1) *University of New South Wales Law Journal* 326.

18 For example, on the use of provocation in charge bargaining for men who kill women: Asher Flynn and Kate Fitz-Gibbon, 'Bargaining with Defensive Homicide: Examining Victoria's Secretive Plea Bargaining System Post-Law Reform'(2011) 35(3) *Melbourne University Law Review* 905; on the homosexual advance provocation defence: Kent Blore, 'The Homosexual Advance Defence and the Campaign to Abolish It in Queensland: The Activist's Dilemma and the Politician's Paradox' (2012) 12(2) *Queensland University of Technology Law and Justice Journal* 36.

19 There is an opportunity to critique the epistemological coherence of the general part and special part; praxis may be one way to resolve this. This, however, is beyond the scope of this chapter.

20 For example, in an instance of justifiable killing of another person, we separate the determination of guilt into two stages: first, prove all elements and determine guilt; second, undo this in the same hearing by relying on, for instance, self-defence. It is possible to cohere the assessment of guilt if one is not welded to elemental proof. However, elaboration of this is beyond the scope of this chapter.

21 Desmond Manderson references this in numerous publications: see, e.g., Desmond Manderson, *Kangaroo Courts and the Rule of Law: The Legacy of Modernism* (Routledge, 2012) 38.

racialised. 'Exceptional' treatment of First Peoples has been a feature of the settler legal system since colonisation commenced.[22] The Australian Constitution retrospectively recognised that former colonies had such power de facto when it made the race power de jure and divided the power to make laws for people who are racialised between the Commonwealth and the states. At the federation level, the power to make special laws about Indigenous peoples carried over to the states, and the Commonwealth then took over this power in 1967.[23] The tolerance of exceptionalism is one of the many ways that racism against First Peoples seeps into Australian law.

Engendering Obedience

The rules in the special part add to the volume of material that criminal law students and practitioners must study, and much of it is not coherent with general principles. The rules are voluminous and particular; this does not allow a student time for critical reflection and analysis. In Australian law schools, our examinations rest heavily, if not exclusively, on solving hypothetical cases—the answer to none of which requires critical engagement with the principles or the process on which students are examined. Obedience is inculcated in law students by overwhelming them with material on which they are examined. In the context of a settler culture that Kumbumerri philosopher Mary Graham calls 'survivalist',[24] law schools are competitive. That there are fewer legal practitioner vacancies than there are graduates exacerbates students' sense of precarity (a marker of these times).

Simultaneously, students are lured by privilege—the promise that high grades may win employment in a law firm. The privileges of a legal practitioner include financial stability and social status, which are also typical indicators of those who gain entry to a law school. Practitioners, their families and their communities are overwhelmingly settlers who also enjoy other advantages. If one has never experienced the negative effects of social systems and instead has benefitted from them (or rather, perceives this to be the case), then one may believe that one's survival and thriving is premised

22 Shelley Bielefeld, 'Compulsory Income Management and Indigenous Australians: Delivering Social Justice or Furthering Colonial Domination?' (2012) 35(2) *University of New South Wales Law Journal* 522, 539; Harry Blagg and Thalia Anthony, 'Disciplinary Power or Colonial Power?' in *Decolonising Criminology: Imagining Justice in a Postcolonial World* (Palgrave Macmillan, 2019); Aileen Moreton-Robinson, 'Imagining the Good Indigenous Citizen: Race War and the Pathology of Patriarchal White Sovereignty' (2009) 15(2) *Cultural Studies Review* 61. See also Desmond Manderson, 'Not Yet: Aboriginal People and the Deferral of the Rule of Law' (2008) 29/30 *Arena Journal* 219.

23 *Australian Constitution* s 51(xxvi).

24 Mary Graham, 'Indigenous International Relations: Old Peoples and New Pragmatism' (Lecture, Coral Bell School Inaugural Annual Lecture on Indigenous Diplomacy, Australian National University, 7 March 2023) <www.youtube.com/watch?v=p4yz9J31vtw>.

on the continuation of the status quo—even where the status quo involves the ongoing marginalisation of First Peoples and the reproduction of racial hierarchy. This is not only subordination to and reproduction of a legal hierarchy.[25] Such self-and group-interest facilitate the tolerance of and complacency towards others' suffering.

Making Better Sense of Crime

If a crime has been alleged, then a serious disruption to social order has occurred that requires the restoration of balance and wellbeing. If social systems are implicated, then these should be within the frame of legal analysis. If they are not within the frame, then they are not subject to critique, and the opportunity for the reform of any systemic issues is obviated. Conviction and punishment of an individual can give the false sense that the social harm has been resolved. Where social systems contribute to the cause of crime, such causes remain under-analysed and unaddressed, and the crime is more likely to be repeated.

Being There When They Teach the General Part (Some Reflections)

In a criminal law class, First Nations teachers and students sit in a room of overwhelmingly non-Indigenous people and study a system that affects our communities in ways that it does not affect settler middle and upper classes. Māori criminal lawyer Khylee Quince shared the following observation about being in a criminal law classroom:

> Like every Māori law student, I have had the experience of sitting in a criminal law classroom feeling the myriad of emotions that comes from knowing that we have a particular place in the justice system. . . . There is a sense of shame, embarrassment, anger, frustration, and indignation at opening a casebook to see row after row of case citations featuring our names. Whereas outsiders may have no connection or give no more than a passing thought, if any, to these names, these are our relatives—brothers, fathers, cousins, uncles, aunties. These are people convicted of significant harms, of damage to families, communities—mostly our own.[26]

Our experiences resonate with those of Aotearoa, but in our ngurra, now called Australia, a statement that the criminal justice system works primarily

25 Duncan Kennedy, 'Legal Education and the Reproduction of Hierarchy' (1982) 32(4) *Journal of Legal Education* 591.

26 Khylee Quince, 'Teaching Indigenous and Minority Students and Perspectives in Criminal Law' in Kris Gledhill and Ben Livings (eds), *The Teaching of Criminal Law: The Pedagogical Imperatives* (Taylor & Francis Group, 2016) 161, 163.

on Indigenous peoples is obviated. In most places in Australia, our names were colonised; we carry the names of cattle station owners and settler fathers. But this is not the only reason that it is not as obvious here that we also 'have a particular place in the justice system'—that we are the subjects of this system. In the judgments and legislation that we teach, there is no indication of the discomforting reality that the state's criminalisation system is racialised: the leading authorities rarely, if ever, involve Indigenous people and do not set out matters that we (Indigenous communities) consider justice issues. In Australia, this is one reason that it is easier for non-Indigenous lawyers to avoid thinking about whom the legal system affects most.

Meanwhile, Indigenous teachers, students and practitioners know that the criminalisation assembly line from police intervention to punishment is populated by Indigenous bodies as defendants and victims: rarely are we criminal justice system actors, and those who do work in it are assumed to be 'non-Indigenous'. The few of us who gain admittance to law school[27] and the even fewer of us who graduate[28] tend to be disinclined to practise in this system. For some of us, it is triggering to encounter our community members[29] and to see our concerns treated in this way. For some of us, despite this, criminal law remains a 'vocation' (as it is described in western cultures). Rather, it is the role that some of us are to play in the network of relationships in Country; it is our responsibility to fulfil this.

Many of us (and this is not a uniquely Indigenous perspective) find this system indifferent, ruthless and inherently traumatising. We struggle to reconcile our participation in it with our ideas about self. I wonder if law students who enter practice now are as slow to recognise the cognitive dissonance? Do they realise the dissonance between the claims of legal neutrality and the reality of the gross overrepresentation of one particular population—the population that happens to have a priori rights to be centred in this place? Do these early career lawyers still mistake the role of defence lawyers as outside the system, contesting it? Do they still believe that this system, for example, stops violence against women?

27 See, e.g., Torres Strait Islander legal academic Asmi Wood, 'Law Studies and Indigenous Students' Wellbeing: Closing the (Many) Gap(s)' (2011) 21 *Legal Education Review* 251. Harry Hobbs and George Williams disclose only that they are legal academics, that is, they 'whiten' their position; they completed a comprehensive statistical overview: Harry Hobbs and George Williams, 'The Participation of Indigenous Australians in Legal Education, 2001–18' (2019) 42(4) *UNSW Law Journal* 1294.

28 For example, only 63 per cent of the Aboriginal and Islander students enrolled in Australian universities in 2009 were still enrolled in 2010: Larissa Behrendt et al., *Review of Higher Education Access and Outcomes for Aboriginal and Torres Strait Islander People* (Final Report, July 2012) 8 <https://opus.lib.uts.edu.au/bitstream/10453/31122/1/2013003561OK.pdf>.

29 See, e.g., Mark Douglass, 'A Road Less Travelled: Footprints from Trauma' (2022) 34(6) *Judicial Officers' Bulletin* 62.

In the last decade, our students have been better educated about our shared histories and, more recently, have greater insight into how discrimination can be systematised. But to what end? These students, these legal practitioners, still do not have the means to resolve this dissonance. Being left only with awareness can engender distress. We are given tools (methods and concepts) inadequate to redress the system effects. These tools that we teach work only *within* the system, not *on* the system. If we continue to practise, then we become unwilling participants, doing our best to minimise the harsher impacts, kept busy using the system's ad hoc tools (such as defences, appeals or technicalities) or otherwise turning to the reform of law and process. Using these tools can be seen not as contesting the system but rather reinforcing its legitimacy.

In courtrooms and popular culture, the settler criminal legal system is represented as universal and monopolising. The authority of this myth is established in its doctrines and 'due process', which are represented as if they are coherent and complete. Where this representation cannot be sustained, the system is represented as self-correcting: checks and balances, distribution of roles and power, defences, exceptions and extensions of liability, appeals, and legislative reform.[30] However, the successful appeals and the legislative reforms have had no apparent effect on the trajectory of the overcriminalisation of First Peoples, which not only continues but worsens. These mechanisms have had little impact on the systemic bias against First Peoples in the criminal justice system or the other societal systems with which it is connected. The criminal justice system is resilient: its tools keep us busy and can seduce us; our engagement in the process innervates the system and reproduces myths about itself and about its justice. The reality is that legal practitioners are constrained in the interventions that we are allowed to make.

Even as this system purports to combat or ameliorate crime, Indigenous communities see the harm caused by the criminal justice system and recognise its criminogenic dynamics. Settler research has been late to confirm such impacts and recognise the connections between criminalisation and other settler systems that work against First Peoples. In the late 1980s to early 1990s, prominent inquiries conducted extensive research into the underlying causes of Aboriginal people dying in state custody[31] and the state removal of children from families.[32] The recommendations of the first major inquiries and

30 This begins before law school, in the social field, and continues after we are admitted to practice.

31 *Royal Commission into Aboriginal Deaths in Custody* (Final Report, April 1991) <https://www.austlii.edu.au/au/other/IndigLRes/rciadic/national/vol1/>.

32 National Inquiry into the Separation of Aboriginal and Torres Strait Islander Children from their Families, *Bringing Them Home* (Report, 1997) <https://humanrights.gov.au/our-work/projects/bringing-them-home-report-1997>.

subsequent inquiries[33] remain largely unimplemented.[34] Rates of deaths in state custody and child separations have worsened, so we must assume that the underlying causes have continued to be unaddressed and that the suffering of those who survive criminalisation or are not removed from their families is also increasing. These reports and subsequent research consistently identify that the systematisation of discrimination has been a driver of the state's overcriminalisation of First Peoples. Systems analysis has now become a critical tool for making sense of the experiences of First Peoples in Australia and other colonised places.

Part 2: Beyond Inclusion, Towards Structural Reform

Since the number of our bodies in law schools began increasing decades ago, there has been no substantive epistemological or methodological reform concerning the subject matter of the degree or the way that it is taught or practised. This is despite the innovation and tenacious advocacy of Indigenous legal scholars and others committed to decolonisation in law schools[35] and sociolegal critical justice perspectives.[36] What renders legal education relevant to us, to our values and our laws? Is it insider access to the settler

33 See, notably, *Royal Commission and Board of Inquiry into the Protection and Detention of Children in the Northern Territory* (Report, 2017). <https://childdetentionnt.royalcommission.gov.au/Pages/Report.aspx>.

34 See, e.g., Kirrily K Jordan et al., 'Joint Response to the Deloitte Review of the Implementation of the Recommendations of the Royal Commission into Aboriginal Deaths in Custody' (CAEPR Topical Issue No 4/2018, 2018) <https://openresearch-repository.anu.edu.au/bitstream/1885/154725/1/Topical_issue_4_2018_Jordan_et_al_final__KJ2.pdf>; Thalia Anthony et al., '30 Years On: Royal Commission into Aboriginal Deaths in Custody Recommendations Remain Unimplemented' (CAEPR Working Paper No 140/2021, 2021) <https://openresearch-repository.anu.edu.au/bitstream/1885/229826/2/WP_140_Anthony_et_al_2021.pdf>.

35 See generally the scholarship-advocacy of Gomeroi-Kamilaroi legal practitioner and academic Marcelle Burns, e.g., Marcelle Burns, Anita Lee Hong and Asmi Wood, *Indigenous Cultural Competency for Legal Academics Program* (Final Report, 2019) <https://openresearch-repository.anu.edu.au/bitstream/1885/311023/1/Indigenous%20Cultural%20Competency.pdf>. Scholarship/advocacy regarding legal curriculum decolonisation from allied scholars includes Heather Douglas, 'Indigenous Legal Education: Towards Indigenisation' (2005) 6(8) *Indigenous Law Bulletin* 12; Susan Bird (Larrakia Anmetjerre legal practitioner), John Trevor Rawnsley and Ciprian Radavoi, 'True Justice through Deep Listening on Country: Decolonising Legal Education in Australia' (2023) 19(4) *AlterNative: An International Journal of Indigenous Peoples* 892.

36 For example, at the University of New South Wales or Charles Sturt University law schools. See Melanie Schwartz, 'Retaining Our Best: Imposter Syndrome, Cultural Safety, Complex Lives and Indigenous Student Experiences of Law School' (2018) 28 *Legal Education Review* 1; Alison Gerard, Annette Gainsford and Kim Bailey, 'Embedding Indigenous Cultural Competence in a Bachelors of Laws at the Centre for Law and Justice, Charles Sturt University: A Case Study' (Conference Paper, Australasian Law Academics Association Annual Conference, 2019).

legal system? Are we being conditioned to leave behind our law and culture and to harden our hearts against the effects of the system on the people that it processes and their communities?

Risking failure can paralyse settler academics; some share that they are fearful of making mistakes, such as inadvertently reproducing racialised harms. Unfortunately, doing nothing is doing something: it maintains the status quo. Quince importunes teachers to be models for students. This asks us to change our attitude toward 'failure' and to reflect on what being an 'expert' means. We need to allow ourselves to be humbler and take students with us when initiating a process of change while assessing and ameliorating the risks involved but nonetheless, taking action. Change can occur if we put theories into practice and are ready to learn from this: this is praxis. We should not expect everything to work; this has never been tried before. It is an experiment with a lot at stake.

A known issue in settler institutions is placing the burden for reform on the few Indigenous academics who have managed to get in the door. When we are pressured to do this, we are taken away from our research agendas and, therefore, from career advancement, social impact, cultural responsibility and research passions. Many of us already feel pressures from our communities (imagined and otherwise) to make changes that we fear are not possible, at least in the timeframes that we hope. It can be difficult work reconciling one's cultural perspectives and life experiences with those of conservative, privileged, western-centric universities. To make these demands of us is to place on Indigenous people the burden that is settlers' responsibility for the colonial inheritance.

When we discuss inclusion, it is assumed that this means that the institution needs to assimilate Indigenous knowledges. At this point, Indigenous staff are called upon to be what Quince refers to as 'cultural sherpas'.[37] Our old people have consistently endeavoured to engage settlers in law and culture. I agree with this—it is lawful to share knowledge and to teach this through relationality—but with a key reservation: we should only share what can be heard and respected. Sharing our knowledges with settler educational institutions has been fraught and, unhappily, often marred by epistemic violence. For this reason, I argue that before one can share substantive matters, training in reflexivity skills and developing insight into one's own standpoint are necessary.

How to Begin? Always with Reflective Practice

To develop insight into another's perspective and understand their knowledge, one must first develop insights into one's own ways of knowing. The call to action is a humble one: develop insight into one's own standpoint

37 Quince (n 26) 164.

and recognise how this is affected by cultural context, history and social structures. For criminal lawyers, this means reflecting on one's role in and effect on the criminal justice system. In considering the overcriminalisation of First Peoples, the purpose of engaging in reflective practice is to realise how one 'knows' and reproduces knowledges as this reflective practice makes it possible to develop insight into Indigenous peoples' diverse perspectives and experiences of overcriminalisation. Such a practice can ameliorate (but not eliminate) the risk of misappropriation or misrepresentation of Indigenous knowledges and other forms of epistemic and ontological violence. Although we want others to have insight into our perspectives, insight is not possible without first disrupting the centredness of the western gaze. One needs to start with a critique of the discipline, its history and our role in it.

Let us think about what this could look like in a criminal law classroom.

Acknowledging Country

In the last decade, it has become conventional for university course conveners to open a course with an 'acknowledgement of Country'. Often, it is a formula of words prepared by an institution that is read verbatim. A land acknowledgement is an opportunity to demonstrate one's respect for First Peoples in a way that is particular to the course and to share one's standpoint as the teacher. Acknowledging Country does not mean acknowledging only First Peoples. Acknowledging Country means locating oneself within a place or perhaps demonstrating that one understands what Country is (it is not just 'land'). In an opening, there is an opportunity to acknowledge Country and signal its influence, then allow it to influence the pedagogy and content of the course. In acknowledging Country, one could ask, for example, 'What does it mean to teach and learn settler criminal law in Country?' One response could be the following:

> The First Peoples of this continent—like all societies—have had legal systems. These laws were part of the social structures that sustained the most successful and longest continuous cultures in human history. These nurtured the most ancient and fragile continent on the planet that flourished until the British commenced colonisation. These legal systems facilitated the interrelations of the diverse peoples across and beyond the continent and addressed social disruptions that inevitably arise in human societies. These legal systems—each distinctive but all sharing basic precepts—responded differently to what settler society calls criminal offending. First Laws emerged from philosophies about ways of being that understood human beings in relationship with other beings in Country, and that was highly responsive to praxis. These laws functioned and function differently to the transplanted and transformed legal system that the colonisers very recently imposed upon this place.

These basic observations of the fact of legal plural orders and their distinctiveness can help students situate and begin to make sense of settler criminal law in this place. They can prompt realisations about its brief history on this continent, its origin in and ongoing connection to English history and law and prompt reflection about the implications of this. For example,

> The criminal law has been applied unevenly and unjustly with respect to First Peoples. The rule of law has been promised but has rarely been used to curb the extraordinary violence that settlers wrought on First Peoples, and this failure to serve First Peoples facilitated colonisation and the usurpation of First Laws. Settler law has been the 'cutting edge of colonialism . . . central to the 'civilizing mission' of imperialism . . . [that] justified and legitimated conquest and control'.[38] If settler law is the 'cutting edge', then police wielded that blade: the police, originally a paramilitary force, played a critical role in 'settling' the frontier, in killing or removing people from their lands, especially separating children and women from families and clans. This history is neither ancient nor over. For these reasons and more, most First Peoples distrust the state's agents and the state's laws.

When opportunities are not taken to acknowledge First Peoples—to demonstrate insight into our diverse perspectives or the effects of settler criminal law and the criminal justice system on First Peoples—an acknowledgement is diminished to mere lip service. Acknowledging Country and its First Peoples should continue beyond the opening of the course or the opening minutes of a class.

Acknowledging First Peoples

What does it mean to acknowledge First Peoples in a criminal law course? Throughout Australian public life, there are nascent gestures of substantive inclusivity of First Peoples. When we discuss overcriminalisation, we necessarily are discussing negative matters; the challenge is to resist accounts that stereotype and racialize and to desist from deficit discourse about Indigenous people. I have observed gestures of inclusivity that involved presenting a quantitative account of First Peoples' overrepresentation. These statistics were taught in the first two-hour lecture and necessarily, given the time allowed, were taught with limited historical context and explanation about the continuities of colonialism. These statistics were accompanied by an image that drew the eye to a brown body rather than the carceral context.[39]

38 Sally Engle Merry, 'Law and Colonialism' (1991) 25(4) *Law & Society Review* 890.

39 Specifically, an unattributed image of deidentified and bodiless brown hands grasping prison bars (deidentified source) cf. Ricky Maynard's images—even where he includes First

The statistics of grossly disproportionate criminalisation and victimisation in every stage of the criminal justice system can elicit shock in some students—but to what end? With little or no explanation about structural discrimination and its impact on individuals, this shock is fetishisation, a buzz from an emotional reaction to something in which one has little at stake.

In 1991, when the findings of the Royal Commission into Aboriginal Deaths in Custody were published,[40] the scale of overrepresentation and its underlying causes shocked the public conscience. Decades later, *awareness* of the numbers of Indigenous people seems to have spurred no effective action; instead, the numbers are worse than ever.[41] Naïve students have been raised to trust the systems and their agents and to believe that those who are punished have brought it upon themselves. What conclusions do we expect that they will draw about First Peoples (as a cohort) when confronted with such overrepresentation without any skills or other information to make sense of them? Numbers without context repeat a story—perhaps the only one that many non-Indigenous Australians have heard—of deficit and disadvantage. Numbers about criminalisation are the most stigmatising of all. This effect is heightened where the statistics are expressed in the passive voice. 'Indigenous people are overcriminalised/overincarcerated/hyperincarcerated' is a normalised state of affairs—'the way that things are'. Those who are criminalised are identified; those who do the criminalising are not ('overincarcerated *by whom*?'). Have settlers become inured to the implications of the statistics? Meanwhile, First Nations people in the room may be triggered, feel stigmatised by a deficit account or wonder at the parochialism of such content.

Sharing statistical information about overrepresentation is not necessarily ontologically and epistemically violent. It can be effective if those who teach reflect upon its impact and then revise their concepts and practices—as one should in any experiment. To make sense of these statistics, we need to provide students with reliable and relevant information and train them how to make sense of it and how to continue to revise and critique such

---

Peoples, his images ask more questions about the incarcerating state and better questions about the people incarcerated. See 'Prison Series 20 No More Than What You See' (1993) <www.bettgallery.com.au/artists/90-ricky-maynard/works/17205-ricky-maynard-prison-series-20-no-more-than-what-1993–2023/>; 'Prison Series 29—No More Than What You See' (1993) <www.bettgallery.com.au/artists/90-ricky-maynard/works/17218-ricky-maynard-prison-series-29-no-more-than-what-1993–2023/>. I use this image when I discuss incarceration: 'THERE ARE THINGS IN THIS PICTURE YOU CANNOT SEE. "I enter here only with a pair of jocks. The walls are made of rubber and the blankets are made of canvas"' (1993) <https://searchthecollection.nga.gov.au/object/16523>.

40 *Royal Commission into Aboriginal Deaths in Custody* (n 31).

41 See, e.g., Law Council of Australia, 'Incarceration Rates of Aboriginal and Torres Strait Islander Peoples' (Discussion Paper 84, 6 October 2017) <https://lawcouncil.au/publicassets/eae6ee0a-23ae-e711-93fb-005056be13b5/3349%20-%20Incarceration%20Rates%20of%20Aboriginal%20and%20Torres%20Strait%20Islander%20Peoples%20(Discussion%20Paper%2084).pdf>.

methodologies. We also need to train them to recognise how this can affect their understanding and application of legal principles. Such training would at least involve developing insight into the effects that standpoint has on the production of knowledge.

Standpoint, Positioning and the Reification of Objectivity

To teach the law now, one needs to have reflected on standpoint. One can no longer assume that the 'othered' is outside the classroom. 'Talking about us without us'—and not *to us*—remains an issue, albeit one encountered less often and less blatantly. An aspect of this that troubles me is the faux corollary of inclusion: instead of positioning Indigenous students as 'other', we are positioned as the same.[42] This is assimilative. It primarily serves to make those who engage in whiteness comfortable—what Eve Tuck and K Wayne Yang might call 'white moves to innocence'.[43] Rarely does this appear to be done knowingly/consciously. Rather, it occurs through positioning.

Legal education and training prepare all students to be inured to the effects of the justice system on others. When law students learn about the criminal law, we are positioned as a gazer, experiencing the 'privilege' of not being gazed upon. The western value of impartiality is reinforced.[44] From a First Law jurisprudential perspective, such 'impartiality' is unlawful and unjust, as any determinations would be made based on incomplete knowledge of the context of the event, the community and those who are closest to the

42 Another aspect of deficit discourse that has become more apparent recently is a speaker expressing a racialised and deficit statement and then asking the Indigenous person (or, less often, people) in the room to address it, thereby positioning them either as an apologist for the statement, placing the responsibility on them to save the statement maker (fawn), make explicit the racism (fight) or remain speechless (freeze).

43 Tuck and Yang engage with Mawhinney's productive phrase 'moves to innocence': Janet Mawhinney, '"Giving Up the Ghost": Disrupting the (Re)production of White Privilege in Anti-racist Pedagogy and Organizational Change' (Master of Arts Thesis, University of Toronto, 1998) <www.collectionscanada.gc.ca/obj/s4/f2/dsk2/tape15/PQDD_0008/MQ33991.pdf> cited in Eve Tuck and K Wayne Yang, 'Decolonization Is Not a Metaphor' (2012) 1(1) *Decolonization: Indigeneity, Education & Society* 1. See also the work that informed Mawhinney: Law Council of Australia, 'Incarceration Rates of Aboriginal and Torres Strait Islander Peoples' (Discussion Paper 84, 6 October 2017), 6 at footnote 3.

44 Larissa Behrendt observes that

> The Western tradition assumes neutrality or objectivity by a scholar and a researcher. . . . It is suspicious of subjectivity. Indigenous approaches to knowledge are completely the opposite. They understand that where you are placed—your positioning or your standpoint—will fundamentally influence the way you see the world.

Larissa Behrendt, 'Indigenous Storytelling: Decolonizing Institutions and Assertive Self-Determination: Implications for Legal Practice' in Jo-Ann Archibald Q'um Q'um Xiiem, Jenny Bol Jun Lee-Morgan and Jason De Santolo (eds), *Decolonizing Research: Indigenous Storywork as Methodology* (Bloomsbury Publishing, 2019) 175, 176.

disruptive event. The superordination of 'neutrality'—rather than, for example, wisdom, insight and lived experience—is not only epistemically violent with respect to First Law concepts of justice but also ontologically violent, as it affects relationality, which is core to one's sense of self.

The representation of the law as neutral, objective and impartial (and, 'therefore', just), centres settler cultural practices. It also minimises its effects on those who are privileged by the system, and does this while managing to render invisible this privileging.[45] What are the implications of this centring/othering when we consider the education and practice of criminal law?

Realising the disproportionate impact that the criminal justice system has on First Peoples, this neutral, separate gaze uniquely affects Indigenous law students and lawyers. Being encouraged to gaze upon those to whom one is connected can feel like betrayal—distancing oneself from our kin and kith, straining the strings[46] that connect us and corroding our relationality. We are positioned as a lawyer only, our identity and connection to culture and other laws is obviated, whitewashed: more than 'white passed' (which happens more often than 'white pass*ing*'), we are 'lawyer passed'.[47] One may wonder about the cost of our participation as practitioners in and educators of the criminal justice system—must we suspend critique of its problematic aspects, and are we collaborating? For those of us who are also First Peoples, we might ask ourselves whether the price of participation is our ways of being and knowing.

Senior law men and women who I have worked with see what is not there: our laws and cultures are absent from the state's criminalisation processes, principles and purposes.[48] If our laws are considered in criminal processes, then they are misconceived and misrepresented. In the criminalisation of a defendant, the court may use the opportunity to denounce our laws, legal

45 This, by the way, is a feature of the reproduction of 'whiteness'.

46 See, e.g., discussion of Yolŋu 'strings' of relatedness in Bree Blakeman and Dhambiŋ Burarrwaŋa, '*Yolkala Gumurrlili*? with Whom Towards the Chest? A Relational Portrait of Yolŋu Social Organisation' (2023) 44(5) *Journal of Intercultural Studies* 678.

47 Several Indigenous academics have written powerfully about the ontological violence of legal education, for example, poignantly, Nicole Watson, 'Indigenous People in Legal Education: Staring into a Mirror without Reflection' (2004) 6(8) *Indigenous Law Bulletin* 4. Others recount legal education experiences akin to gaslighting—for example, Larissa Behrendt's account of being told the settler state story of terra nullius: Larissa Behrendt, 'Home: The Importance of Place to the Dispossessed' (2009) 108(1) *The South Atlantic Quarterly* 71, 74. See also Torres Strait Islander scholar Heron Loban, 'Decolonised Law Degrees: A Misnomer' (2022) 74(4) *Alternative Law Journal* 296; Marcelle Burns and Jennifer Nielsen, 'Dealing with the "Wicked" Problem of Race and the Law: A Critical Journey for Students (and Academics)' (2019) 28(2) *Legal Education Review* 1.

48 See, e.g., Mary Spiers Williams, 'Challenging Settler-State Legal Fantasies: Basic Precepts of First Laws' in Peter Cane, Lisa Ford and Mark McMillan (eds), *The Cambridge Legal History of Australia* (Cambridge University Press, 2022) 61, 61–62.

systems and even cultural practices.[49] When we observe settler law being represented as '*The* Law' (almost never qualified accurately as 'settler law' or 'state law'), we witness the ongoing discursive usurpation of our laws and legal systems. In learning doctrine premised on a settler legal monopoly, are we tacitly supporting this epistemic violence towards First Law,[50] our ways of being and other cultural values?[51]

Each of us identifies with our experiences, education, histories, ancestors and institutions. Reflexivity can disrupt the stories that we have been told and that we have told ourselves about these influences. Such disruption can manifest in emotional discomfort, in my experience, especially for settler students. For example, it can trigger intellectual resistance, a misplaced feeling of guilt or other emotional responses.[52] Such reactions differ markedly in nature and magnitude from the trauma and ontological violence that an Indigenous person may experience when we learn, are required to teach or are required to practise such principles, methods and related concepts.

Understanding Social Systems and Structural Injustice

A contemporary reflection of our commitment to uphold the rule of law requires education about what structural injustice is and how it can emerge. Iris Marion Young observes that structural injustice is produced when 'many people . . . interact in complex ways to produce the outcomes that many agree are unjust',[53] although such outcomes are unlikely to have been intended or foreseen by any of these actors.[54] The criminal justice system—like any human system—is susceptible to discrimination and injustice. The criminal justice system creates opportunities for discrimination through its assembly

49 See, e.g., *Police v Tommy Watson* (Alice Springs Court of Summary Jurisdiction, 1 December 2010, Magistrate Bamber), discussed in Mary Spiers Williams, 'The Impossibility of Community Justice Whilst There is Intervention' in Garry Coventry and Mandy Shircore (eds), *Proceedings of the 5th Annual Australian and New Zealand Critical Criminology Conference, 7–8 July 2011, Cairns, QLD, Australia* (James Cook University, 2012) <https://ssrn.com/abstract=2095839>.

50 Robert Cover would call this 'jurispathy': *Narrative, Violence, and the Law: The Essays of Robert Cover* (University of Michigan Press, 1992) 214; Robert M Cover, 'Violence and the Word' (1986) 95 *Yale Law Journal* 1601.

51 Irene Watson, 'Some Reflections on Teaching Law: Whose Law, Yours or Mine?' (2005) 6(8) *Indigenous Law Bulletin* 23.

52 Such emotions are unhelpful; guilt, for example, tends to trigger shame, avoidance and paralysis. See also Danielle Every, 'Critical Discursive Methods as a Resource in Education and Anti-Racism' in Rob Ranzijn, Keith McConnochie and Wendy Nolan (eds), *Psychology and Indigenous Australians: Effective Teaching and Practice* (Cambridge Scholars Publishing, 2008) 93, 97. A former student inspired by Ahmed called this 'white tears', indulging in emotions as if it were an antidote to complicity in racism; see Sarah Ahmed, *The Cultural Politics of Emotion* (Routledge, 2004).

53 Iris Marion Young, *Responsibility for Justice* (Oxford University Press, 2011) 107.

54 Iris Marion Young, *Responsibility for Justice* (Oxford University Press, 2011) 62–63.

line design. The segmentation of roles prevents legal actors from seeing or experiencing the effects of their decisions, thereby creating the conditions that foster in legal practitioners a sense of 'irresponsibility'[55] and a tolerance of what would otherwise be intolerable. The theory (or phenomenon) of structural discrimination can explain how discriminatory actions perpetuate injustice and how these actions concatenate into a system and accrete. Herbert Packer's generative (and resilient) model of the criminal justice system as an assembly line[56] remains helpful in understanding how injustice can become systematised and in developing insight into how racial discrimination against First Peoples is specifically reproduced.

Built into the criminal justice system are limits on each legal actor's discretion, a function of the doctrine prohibiting acting ultra vires, another systemic feature intended to curb excess of power (especially vis-à-vis an individual). Within these limits, a legal practitioner (and other criminal justice actors) can nonetheless make a decision that is discriminatory. This decision-maker may never realise the effect of their decision as the defendant moves through the assembly line—or legal actors may not realise their role and thus cannot feel 'responsibility'[57] for the larger effects to which their small part contributed, and they otherwise tolerate it. The assembly line may mask the origins of the discriminatory action and even be responsible for its effects: for the decision-maker, there are no consequences (except for the insightful one whose conscience may ache). This can result in a fatalistic attitude towards some of the discriminatory effects. This is one of the ways that discrimination can persist unchecked, be repeated and its effects become systematised.

Working with the Tools that We Have

Although our role in the assembly line is limited, there are opportunities within these limits. Imagine if we listened to Indigenous defendants, victims and communities more respectfully and did this in order to reflect more on the relevance of material about which they instruct us or inform us. We need to think more deeply and persistently about what is considered reliable and challenge the possibility of our own unconscious bias.

When assessing a case, legal practitioners routinely assess whether material would be admitted in a defended hearing—but have we applied a rule by rote or orthodoxy? Have we reviewed the material available, reflected on its reliability and reasoned it well? Is it possible to challenge an orthodox boundary that excludes matters that First Peoples nonetheless consider relevant? Are

55 In the sense meant by Veitch: Scott Veitch, *Law and Irresponsibility: On the Legitimation of Human Suffering* (Routledge, 2007).

56 Herbert L Packer, 'Two Models of the Criminal Process' (1964) 113(1) *University of Pennsylvania Law Review* 1. Packer was an American criminal law academic and criminologist.

57 Cf. 'irresponsibility' again in the sense meant by Veitch (n 55).

these boundaries legal, principled and reasonable or are they merely part of the customary practice of legal practitioners?

What I am proposing here—to master criminal law principles, practise advocacy and develop skills—is not a radical departure from principle. Rather, this is taking the common law's ideological claims seriously. Practitioners are officers of the court whose role is to support the judicial officer in not falling into error. We are trained to attend closely to the moment of the decision-making of legal actors and bring to the judicial officer's attention any weakness in inferential reasoning, assessments of reliability or sufficiency of evidence. However, with respect to material that is distinctive to First Peoples, we need to acknowledge that this can require tenacity, as structural discrimination affects the culture in a court, which can resist turning its gaze onto such material.

To Address Systemic Injustice, We Need New Tools

An individual can have little impact on a system as resilient and self-sustaining as the criminal justice system. A larger project of system transformation requires either collective action (coordination and tenacity over the long term) or a cataclysm. Both are outside the control of an individual in the short and medium terms.

The overrepresentation of a cohort of people indicates (if not conspiracy) systematic bias. This occurs within a system that is supposed to review for just such bias. That we do not have the theory, methods, competency or willingness to redress this means that structural injustice is ongoing.

We are trained in law school and practice to analyse a case in isolation and to determine that where there has been individualised justice there can be no miscarriage of justice. But such training does not, and perhaps cannot, address concerns about structural injustice. To understand structural injustice, we need different analytical tools to make sense of this accretion of unjust effects. To transform such structures, we need different methodologies and epistemologies. Unfortunately, it is difficult to see how it will be possible to develop new tools that are compatible with existing restraints of theory, methodology and customary practices of criminal law.

Conclusion: Fulfilling Our Responsibility

In this chapter, I have reflected on an aspect of the role that lawyers play in the criminal justice system. I have made some observations about the teaching of doctrinal criminal law theory and methods in relation to elemental proof and asked questions about whether this contributes—and, if so, how—to the systemic discrimination that the criminal justice system produces. Despite a key responsibility of legal practitioners being to uphold the rule of law, legal actors participate, albeit unwillingly, in the systematic injustice against First Peoples and their overcriminalisation. Although legal practitioners are constrained by system design, there are opportunities to ameliorate bias. I have reflected on the current practices in legal training in this respect and proposed some ways to support students and practitioners to be more reflexive, purposeful and constructive in our participation in the criminalisation process. As a starting point, I have proposed that we attend more closely to a critical moment in the criminalisation process: to the method of proof of guilt and the material that we routinely decide is irrelevant. This requires a determination to gaze critically—and to hold within this gaze legal doctrines, practices and culture.

Lawyers are only one part of a complex system of agents who create effects that would have been difficult, if not impossible, to plan. To disrupt this, we cannot rely on current theories and methods that individualise and isolate the defendant's crime. We do not currently have the tools to address systemic injustice. It may be that we cannot develop them within the current system. In every case, one can only reflect and develop theory, design a method to apply this theory and then learn through praxis. The least we can do is prepare this generation to do what we have not been able to do.

14

WHAT IS ARISTOTLE'S TOTEM ANYWAY? INDIGENOUS SYSTEMS OF LAW AND GOVERNANCE AND THE AUSTRALIAN PUBLIC LAW CURRICULUM

Aurora Milroy and Karinda Burns

Introduction

Everything we teach is a story, a narrative, a yarn—although some may hold onto the belief that teaching is the transfer of knowledge, of information, of fact. Every story is also located and told through someone's voice and from their place within it. The two following quotes both speak to systems of law and governance in this country; however, the stories that they tell are vastly different:

> In the 4th century BCE, the Greek philosopher Aristotle (384–22 BCE) described the organisation of humans by reference to a progression from the individual to the collective. The collective nature of our existence operates at a number of levels . . . [a]t each of these levels there are rules for how we interact with each other and with those who hold power.[1]
>
> [T]hat sense of belonging and that sense of place was ingrained into each and every person because they had a *boranga* [totem], they had a connect, they knew who they are and how they're connected. They also knew who was making decisions for them because they'd been through a process that gave them their cultural authority to speak about who they are.[2]

In the Juris Doctor at The University of Western Australia ('UWA'), law students are taught how 'Australia' came to be. They read about Aristotle's

1 Gabrielle Appleby, Alexander Reilly and Laura Grenfell, *Australian Public Law* (Oxford University Press, 3rd ed, 2019) 4.

2 Richard Walley, 'Australia's First Nations Show How to Make Democracy Better' (YouTube, 7 July 2021) 9, 35 <www.youtube.com/watch?v=htXuDhvzL3M>.

DOI: 10.4324/9781003473404-17

theories of organisation and how British laws were 'received' in this country. They learn about the importance of the Constitution as our founding document that is still the highest law in these lands. They become familiar with the institutions that govern us—the legislature, executive and judiciary—and come to understand how the principles of responsible and representative government keep the system accountable to us, the Australian people. The public law curriculum therefore presents the settler colonial narrative of the development of the Australian nation, albeit under the guise of a 'neutral' (if slightly celebratory) account of history.

There are always other versions of the story, other ways of seeing things. Aboriginal people[3] might raise an eyebrow when Aristotle is rolled out as the start of the story or when the Australian Constitution is described as the supreme law of these lands. These versions of Australia's public law history omit a more complete picture of Australia's legal origins and actively exclude Aboriginal and Torres Strait Islander history. Indigenous legal scholars have referred to this failure to engage with Indigenous knowledges and law as 'terra nullius-style thinking',[4] an extension of the colonial ideology and erasure that justified the doctrine of terra nullius.[5]

Indigenous systems of law and governance existed long before settlers came to Australia—from an Indigenous perspective, since time immemorial,[6] and from a western scientific perspective, somewhere between 62,000 and 75,000 years ago.[7] This is long before Aristotle (~2,400 years ago) and long before 'Australia' (~250 years ago). The sustained and ancient nature of Aboriginal society means that Indigenous systems will continue to exist alongside the imposed settler system and, as First Law[8] or Raw Law,[9] they will continue long after it is gone. Yet Aboriginal and Torres Strait Islander peoples and our knowledges are continually excluded from the origin story of Australia and from what we teach in the public law classroom.

3 In this chapter, we interchangeably use the terms 'Indigenous' and 'Aboriginal and Torres Strait Islander'. We sometimes just use 'Aboriginal' as we are based on Aboriginal land.

4 Ambelin Kwaymullina, 'Teaching for the 21st Century: Indigenising the Law Curriculum at UWA' (2020) 29(1) *Legal Education Review* 1, 7 ('Teaching for the 21st Century').

5 See especially Irene Watson, 'Re-Centring First Nations Knowledge and Places in a Terra Nullius Space' (2014) 10(5) *AlterNative: An International Journal of Indigenous Peoples* 508 ('Re-centring First Nations Knowledge').

6 Irene Watson, 'Re-Centring First Nations Knowledge and Places in a Terra Nullius Space' (2014) 10(5) *AlterNative: An International Journal of Indigenous Peoples* 517.

7 Morten Rasmussen et al., 'An Aboriginal Australian Genome Reveals Separate Human Dispersals into Asia' (2011) 334(6052) *Science* 94, 94–98. Note that we have referred to this source to highlight how western science understands the origins of Aboriginal peoples, but it is important to recognise that there is a different understanding in Aboriginal and Torres Strait Islander knowledge systems.

8 Martuwarra River of Life et al., 'Recognizing the Martuwarra's First Law Right to Life as a Living Ancestral Being' (2020) 9(3) *Transnational Environmental Law* 541.

9 Irene Watson, *Aboriginal Peoples, Colonialism and International Law: Raw Law* (Routledge, 2015) 11–13 ('*Raw Law*').

The aim of this chapter is to give voice to a different way of looking at Australian public law—to go beyond the colonial narrative and share some of the stories of this nation's ancient, living knowledge. We accomplish this by articulating the features of Aboriginal and Torres Strait Islander systems of law and governance and comparing them with the features of the Australian system taught in public law courses. We want not only to 'talk up to'[10] the assumptions and narratives embedded in the traditional public law curriculum but also to consider how we might bring Aboriginal and Torres Strait Islander knowledges, stories and voices into the curriculum.

There are many opportunities to bring Indigenous content into the public law curriculum through discussions of sovereignty, Indigenous activism, constitutional recognition, the 1967 and 2023 referenda, the race power and cases such as *Love v Cth*,[11] *Kartinyeri*,[12] *Mabo*[13] and *Koowarta*,[14] among others. We do not cover any of these topics in this chapter. Instead, our focus is on how curriculum can better engage with Aboriginal law and governance theories and how this engagement might also disrupt the starting point for Australian public law curriculum.

In writing this chapter, our perspectives on governance and public law have been shaped by our cultural, personal and professional experiences and training. We are Aboriginal women with lived experience of what governance practice looks like in our families and communities and in the Aboriginal organisations where we have worked. We are also legal educators trained in the western system of law and governance. Aurora Milroy is a Palyku woman who has worked in a number of policy roles in government and non-government settings, including in the Aboriginal community-controlled sector. Karinda Burns is a Wajarri Yamatji and Yued Noongar woman who has spent most of her career in the Indigenous tertiary and legal education sector. We are both academics at the Law School at the University of Western Australia, where we co-lead the Indigenisation of the Juris Doctor curriculum[15] by building on the work of Palyku scholar Ambelin Kwaymullina.[16] Aurora teaches in the core unit Foundations of Public Law, and we both teach aspects of public law in our Indigenous law elective units.

10 Aileen Moreton-Robinson, *Talkin' Up to the White Woman* (University of Queensland Press, 2000).

11 *Love v Commonwealth of Australia; Thoms v Commonwealth of Australia* (2020) 270 CR 152.

12 *Kartinyeri v the Commonwealth* (1998) 195 CLR 337.

13 *Mabo v Queensland [No 2]* (1992) 175 CLR 1.

14 *Koowarta v Bjelke-Petersen* (1982) 153 CLR 168.

15 'Indigenisation of the Juris Doctor', *UWA Law School* (Web Page, 11 December 2023) <www.uwa.edu.au/schools/law/indigenisation-of-the-juris-doctor>.

16 Kwaymullina, 'Teaching for the 21st Century' (n 4).

What Is Governance?

When we refer to 'governance' in this chapter, we are referring to the ways of ruling or stewarding a society or community. We recognise that languages are culturally derived and embody 'the way a society thinks',[17] which means that English will never be able to accurately capture the cultural worldview of Indigenous peoples and our systems.[18] Thus, our translation of the breadth, depth and diversity of Indigenous knowledges into the western concept of 'governance' is inherently limited. Still, a features-based analysis can help us flesh out what we mean by 'Indigenous governance' and 'Australian governance'.

Torres Strait Islander political scientist Josephine Bourne writes that governance includes 'power and who has it, decision-making and who can make particular decisions, how other stakeholders or interested parties are able to be heard and participate, and how financial accountability is managed'.[19] The Australian Indigenous Governance Institute states that

> [i]t's useful to think of governance as being about how people choose to organise themselves to: manage their own affairs; share power and responsibilities; decide for themselves what kind of society they want for their future; put those decisions into action.[20]

In our analysis, we examine the following governance features:

- Who has power and authority?
- What are the principles and values underpinning the system?
- How are decisions made?
- How do people participate in the system?
- How are conflicts resolved and rules enforced?

Our source base privileges Indigenous authors and draws on scholars from many disciplines including Indigenous studies, law, political science, philosophy and history. We also draw on the 'undisciplined'[21]—the

17 Leroy Little Bear, 'Jagged Worldviews Colliding' in Marie Battiste (ed), *Reclaiming Indigenous Voice and Vision* (UBC Press, 2000) 77, 78.

18 '#WeneedDiverseBooksAU: Interview with Ambelin Kwaymullina', *First Impressions* (Blog Post/Interview, 10 August 2015) <https://beckavanaghreads.wordpress.com/2015/08/10/weneeddiversebooksau-interview-with-ambelin-kwaymullina/>.

19 Josephine Bourne, 'National Indigenous Organisations in Australia: Why Governance Environments Matter' (2017) 20(1) *Journal of Australian Indigenous Issues* 71, 74.

20 'Defining Governance', *Australian Indigenous Governance Institute* (Web Page) <https://aigi.org.au/toolkit/defining-governance>.

21 Martin Nakata, *Disciplining the Savages: Savaging the Disciplines* (Aboriginal Studies Press, 2007) 182–92.

scholars and knowledge holders whose expertise is not confined by a specific area of western knowledge production. We avoid sources written by non-Indigenous scholars about Indigenous governance practice. In developing theories of Indigenous law and governance it can be particularly tempting to reach for anthropological sources that provide rich summaries of traditional practices. However, these sources are almost always written from the perspective of an outside observer, without the insight that comes from the located perspective of the actual knowledge holder.[22] It is also typically unclear, particularly with older sources, whether communities have consented to their knowledge being shared. Therefore, we privilege sources from a located or subjective Indigenous viewpoint as told through their own voice.[23]

Indigenous Systems of Law and Governance

The lands, waterways and skies that form the Australian nation are actually the unceded countries of distinct Aboriginal and Torres Strait Islander nations.[24] There are many Indigenous nations throughout Australia and the surrounding islands, which represent great diversity among Indigenous societies concerning the languages, cultural practices, legal systems, knowledge systems and governance structures. Within this diversity, however, there are commonalities in the fundamental philosophies that are consistent across Indigenous legal systems.[25]

The story of Indigenous law and governance begins in the time before time, or perhaps the space outside of time,[26] which is often referred to as the Dreaming. Tanganekald and Meintangk scholar Irene Watson describes the *Kaldowinyeri*, or Dreaming, as 'a time when song, stories and law were birthed, as were the ancestors—out of the land'.[27] The source of law in Indigenous systems is Country,[28] which was sung into being by our Ancestors

22 See Ambelin Kwaymullina and Blaze Kwaymullina, 'Learning to Read the Signs: Law in an Indigenous Reality' (2010) 34(2) *Journal of Australian Studies* 197; Aileen Moreton-Robinson, 'Whiteness, Epistemology and Indigenous Representation' in Aileen Moreton-Robinson (ed), *Whitening Race: Essays in Social and Cultural Criticism* (Aboriginal Studies Press, 2004) 75.

23 See Australian Institute of Aboriginal and Torres Strait Islander Studies ('AIATSIS'), *AIATSIS Code of Ethics for Aboriginal and Torres Strait Islander Research* (2020) 18–20, for information regarding the ethical engagement with Indigenous perspectives and knowledges.

24 Ambelin Kwaymullina, 'Aboriginal Nations, The Australian Nation-State and Indigenous International Legal Traditions' in Irene Watson (ed), *Indigenous Peoples as Subjects of International Law* (Routledge, 2017) 5.

25 Tjalaminu Mia, 'Kepwaamwinberkup (Nightwell)', in Sally Morgan, Tjalaminu Mia and Blaze Kwaymullina (eds), *Heartsick for Country: Stories of Love, Spirit and Creation* (Fremantle Press, 2008) 183, 186–87.

26 Kwaymullina and Kwaymullina (n 22) 198–200.

27 Watson, *Raw Law* (n 9) 11.

28 Note that 'Country' refers to the lands, waterways and skies to which Aboriginal people are spiritually connected. It is capitalised to reflect the animate nature of Country as a living being and ancestor, with its own agency.

at Dreaming.[29] In Indigenous systems, however, time is non-linear,[30] and, as such, our Dreaming continues as we perform, recreate and renew our laws.[31]

Country is the fundamental source of law and Indigenous legal systems, and Country is the source of all life. In Indigenous worldviews, all things have life.[32] As Aboriginal and Torres Strait Islander people, we are born from Country, and the centrality of our identity[33]—that is, our cultural positioning through which we are located—is derived from our 'embodiment based on bloodline to Country'[34] and our obligations to care for our Country.[35]

Central to the maintenance of law are our kinship networks or the 'web of relations',[36] which are also a source of law in their own right.[37] As Palyku scholars Ambelin Kwaymullina and Blaze Kwaymullina write, 'law cannot exist in isolation from the connections between all life. Law both sustains and reflects the nexus of relationships, the pattern of creation that is the world.'[38]

Everyone has a place within the web of relations, which brings with it responsibilities and obligations. It also lets you know who has responsibilities to you. This positioning of individuals within the web of relations adds another tier to the identity and located knowledge of each person. As Walley describes in the quote at the start of this chapter, everyone has a totem, such as a plant or animal within Country, and this totem tells you how you are connected and where you fit into the system.[39] Eualeyai and Gamillaroi scholar Larissa Behrendt reiterates this aspect of Indigenous governance:

> Aboriginal people in Australia when they meet you will ask you where you are from as a way of fitting you into our kinship network—which we do by family name, place, and nation group. There is power in asserting our place in the natural world and in our kinship network as we introduce each other. It is an assertion of our sovereignty.[40]

29 Watson, *Raw Law* (n 9) 12; Kwaymullina and Kwaymullina (n 22) 202; Larissa Behrendt, 'Indigenous Storytelling: Decolonizing Institutions and Assertive Self-Determination:

Implications for Legal Practice' in Jo-Ann Archibald Q'um Q'um Xiiem, Jenny Bol Jun Lee-Morgan and Jason De Santolo (eds), *Decolonizing Research: Indigenous Storywork as Methodology* (Bloomsbury Academic & Professional, 2019) 175, 177 ('Indigenous Storytelling').

30 Kwaymullina and Kwaymullina (n 22) 198–99.

31 Kwaymullina and Kwaymullina (n 22) 198–200; Watson, *Raw Law* (n 9) 12.

32 Kwaymullina and Kwaymullina (n 22) 196.

33 Watson, *Raw Law* (n 9) 69.

34 Aileen Moreton-Robinson, 'Towards an Australian Indigenous Women's Standpoint Theory: A Methodological Tool' (2013) 78(28) *Australian Feminist Studies* 331, 341.

35 Watson, *Raw Law* (n 9) 114.

36 Ambelin Kwaymullina, 'Seeing the Light: Aboriginal Law, Learning and Sustainable Living in Country' (2005) 6(11) *Indigenous Law Bulletin* 12 ('Seeing the Light').

37 Kwaymullina and Kwaymullina (n 22) 203; Leroy Little Bear (n 17) 77.

38 Kwaymullina and Kwaymullina (n 22) 198.

39 Walley (n 2) 9:35. See also Behrendt (n 29) 176.

40 Behrendt (n 29) 176.

Underpinning the network of relationships is the principle of relationality that guides how everyone interacts with one another. Goenpul and Quandamooka academic Aileen Moreton-Robinson writes that '[r]elationality is grounded in a holistic conception of the inter-connectedness and inter-substantiation between and among all living things and the earth, which is inhabited by a world of ancestors and creator beings'.[41] Relationality is more than just the existence of relationships, however; it is the practice of working in relation with others to maintain balance in the system as a whole.[42] Kombumerrri and Wakka Kimberli philosopher Mary Graham and non-Indigenous academic Morgan Brigg describe the relationalist ethos as 'abiding attentiveness and responsibility to the patterns, contingencies, and ethical obligations that arise with relations'.[43]

Power and authority are also revealed through the web of relations, since kinship and totem systems indicate who has the authority to make certain decisions.[44] If you want to use the *wonil*, or peppermint tree, then you must speak with the people who are related to the *wonil* and carry this knowledge.[45] Because everyone has responsibilities in the system, power and authority are more diffused across the network rather than concentrated in certain individuals who make decisions for everyone else.

Elders have a unique role in Aboriginal governance systems, reflecting the greater depth of responsibility and knowledge that they have acquired. Graham states, '[o]lder people are like a hierarchy but a soft hierarchy. It's a bit like a combination of gerontocracy and meritocracy. . . . But they can't tell you what to do like kings and queens.'[46] As Graham emphasises, the greater responsibility that elders have in decision-making does not equate with concepts of representative decision-making. No-one makes a decision *for* you or on your behalf. Instead, decision-making is generally a participatory process, wherein everyone in the group comes together to reach a conclusion in the best interests of the system as a whole.[47]

The participatory aspect of Indigenous governance means that law is enforced collectively through individual contributions of lawful conduct. This

41 Aileen Moreton-Robinson, 'Relationality: A Key Presupposition of an Indigenous Social Research Paradigm' in Chris Andersen and Jean M O'Brien (eds), *Sources and Methods in Indigenous Studies* (Routledge, 2017) 69, 71.

42 Kwaymullina and Kwaymullina (n 22) 203.

43 Morgan Brigg and Mary Graham, 'The Relevance of Aboriginal Political Concepts (8): The Relationalist Ethos for Managing Survivalism', *ABC* (online, 26 October 2021) <www.abc.net.au/religion/mary-graham-morgan-brigg-relationalist-ethos/13604298>.

44 Walley (n 2) 9:35.

45 The essence of this concept is taught to UWA law students by Whadjuk Noongar knowledge holders Richard Walley, Alton Walley and Rickeeta Walley in the Foundations of Law and Lawyering unit.

46 Mary Graham, 'Indigenous Conceptions of Governance' (online, 27 October 2017) 24, 55 <www.greeninstitute.org.au/indigenous-conceptions-governance/>.

47 Hannah McGlade, 'The McGlade Case: A Noongar History of Land, Social Justice and Activism' (2017) 43(2) *Australian Feminist Law Journal* 185, 209.

governance process flows naturally from the holistic character of Indigenous systems, where '[t]he whole is more than the sum of its parts, and the whole is in all its parts'.[48] Thus, everyone knows the law, and everyone works together to uphold the law, but everyone also embodies the law and carries it within them.[49]

Conflict resolution is, ultimately, another form of decision-making in Indigenous law and governance systems and is also undertaken in group settings. As Behrendt explains, 'our disputes were negotiated with that understanding that a broad range of people have an interest in the outcome. Everyone would get a chance to speak and to put their position forward.'[50] Conflict resolution, like decision-making, is done by consensus or general agreement of the group. The goal of both the decision-making and conflict resolution processes is restoring balance and sustaining the system of relationships[51] while also upholding individual and collective obligations and lawful conduct.[52]

The following table summarises some of the features of the Indigenous law and governance systems that we have discussed. We recognise that the table is reductive, over-simplified and unable to capture the complex, interconnected and holistic nature of Indigenous knowledge systems.[53] However, it does provide a useful snapshot that assists us in comparing the Indigenous and Australian systems later in this chapter.[54]

TABLE 14.1 *Features of Indigenous systems of law and governance*

Governance feature	*Indigenous systems of law and governance*
Power and authority	• Country, the Dreaming, the Ancestors and the web of relations are the source of law • The authority to speak is determined by the web of relations—it shows you who you are responsible to and who is responsible to you • Elders have a special place in the system with greater authority • No one purports to represent you or make decisions on your behalf • Everyone participates in the system, law is carried within everyone

(*Continued*)

48 Kwaymullina, 'Seeing the Light' (n 36) 13.
49 See also Little Bear (n 17) 84.
50 Behrendt (n 29) 177. See also Walley (n 2) 9, 48 for a specific example of Noongar dispute resolution.
51 Graham (n 46); Behrendt (n 29) 177–78.
52 Kwaymullina, 'Seeing the Light' (n 36) 13; Little Bear (n 17) 84.
53 Kwaymullina and Kwaymullina (n 22) 196–98.
54 Kwaymullina and Kwaymullina (n 22) 206.

TABLE 14.1 (Continued)

Governance feature	*Indigenous systems of law and governance*
Values and principles	• Relationality • Balance • Holism
Decision-making	• Collective and consensus-based • The aim is to maintain balance in the system and to sustain Country
Participation	• All living things actively participate in the system of law and governance
Conflict resolution and enforcement	• Collective and consensus-based • The aim is to maintain balance between relationships and balance in the system • It is enforced by the group, but all law is carried within the individual

Comparison with Australian Systems of Law and Governance

The features of Australian governance systems can be found in the introductory chapters of most Australian public law and constitutional law textbooks and in the introductory lectures for most public law courses. We have summarised them in the following table.

TABLE 14.2 *Features of the Australian system of law and governance*

Governance feature	*Australian system of law and governance*
Power and authority	• The sources of law are written and unwritten rules including the Constitution, legislation and case law • The Constitution sets out key aspects of Australia's system of governance • The three branches of government (legislature, executive and judiciary) have authority and power to make, execute and arbitrate laws and decisions • Power and authority are vested in the institutions of government and particular positions (such as the Prime Minister) • Power is exercised on a representative basis via these institutions of government • Many aspects of the system are hierarchical
Values and principles	• Separation of powers • Representative and responsible government • Federalism • Rule of law • Judicial review

(*Continued*)

TABLE 14.2 (Continued)

Governance feature	*Australian system of law and governance*
Decision-making	• Certain positions have power and authority to make decisions • Many decisions are made on a majority basis
Participation	• The people participate in the system via elections • The people participate in changing the system via referenda to change the Constitution
Conflict resolution and enforcement	• Conflicts are resolved through external arbiters—usually the courts • The judiciary maintains the process of judicial review • The legal system is adversarial; as such, conflict resolution is oppositional and combative • Laws are enforced by the executive branch

There are some similarities between the Indigenous and Australian governance systems, including that both models of governance are systems-based, both engage with relationships and both are linked to 'place'. However, these are relatively surface-level similarities underpinned by radically different worldviews. Consider the importance of 'place', for instance. In Australian systems of law and governance, 'place' relates to jurisdiction, authority and the federal balance. But it is conceived of in territorial terms, with boundaries derived from the way that colonisers (arbitrarily) carved up the landscape, ignoring existing Indigenous boundaries and songlines. There is also a relationship between place and authority in Indigenous systems, but it derives from an ontological connection to Country and recognises Country as a living being and a source of law.

Other differences also emerge when we compare Tables 14.1 and 14.2. Australian systems of law and governance are founded on a representative model, where certain people hold power and authority to make decisions on behalf of the group. This is particularly the case for the legislative branch, whose members are chosen to represent their electorates. Some may question the extent to which the legislature is truly representative or even 'directly chosen by the people',[55] given the role of preselection and party preferencing, among other features. Still, certain roles are given authority to represent the people and make decisions on their behalf. This is also true for the executive and judicial offices. They are not elected but have the authority to make decisions *for* you. As already discussed, Indigenous governance does not rely on representation; rather, everyone brings their located knowledge to actively participate in the system.

55 *Australian Constitution* ss 7, 24.

In Australian governance systems, power and authority are exercised not only through a representative model but also on a majority basis. This is evident across various aspects of the system, from elections (the majority of votes wins the seat, and the majority of seats forms the government), to the passing of laws (majorities in both houses of Parliament) and to High Court decisions (the majority of the bench decides the outcome). This contrasts with the collective, consensus-based decision making in Indigenous systems.

This analysis demonstrates that there are many differences in how governance is philosophised and practised in the Indigenous and Australian systems of law and governance. Ultimately, the greatest difference—and the most dangerous—is the way in which the Australian system of law and governance asserts supremacy and singularity, leaving no room for Indigenous systems.[56] By only teaching students about Australian systems of governance in the public law curriculum, law teachers not only misrepresent the origin story of this country but also contribute to ongoing attempts to erase and subjugate Indigenous knowledge systems. We think that it is time to subvert these dominant narratives and bring Aboriginal and Torres Strait Islander knowledges into the public law curriculum.

Indigenous Law and Governance in the Public Law Curriculum

Our approach to Indigenous curriculum development for the Juris Doctor at UWA is guided by the fifteen *Principles of Indigenisation*, which were developed by our reference group and outlined in Ambelin Kwaymullina's article about the project.[57] In this section, we examine how public law teachers might work through two of these principles to incorporate Indigenous law and governance theory into the curriculum.

Centring Indigenous Voices

Principle 7 states that curriculum should '[c]entre Indigenous voices as the primary sources of their own knowledges, cultures, laws, and experiences'.[58] One of the greatest challenges that teachers will face here is that Indigenous

56 Little Bear (n 17) 77, 82; Kwaymullina, 'Teaching for the 21st Century' (n 4) 177; Jill Milroy and Gladys Milroy, 'Different Ways of Knowing: Trees Are Our Families Too' in Sally Morgan, Tjalaminu Mia and Blaze Kwaymullina (eds), *Heartsick for Country: Stories of Love, Spirit and Creation* (Fremantle Press, 2008) 22, 23. See also the denial of Indigenous assertions of sovereignty in cases such as *Coe v Commonwealth of Australia and the Government of the United Kingdom of Great Britain and Northern Ireland* (1979) 24 ALR 118; *Mabo v Queensland [No 2]* (1992) 175 CLR 1; and *Walker v New South Wales* (1994) 126 ALR 321. Cf. some aspects of the system that enable pluralism, such as federalism.

57 Kwaymullina, 'Teaching for the 21st Century' (n 4) 6. For a list of the reference group members, see 'Indigenisation of the Juris Doctor', *UWA Law School* (Web Page, 11 December 2023) <www.uwa.edu.au/schools/law/indigenisation-of-the-juris-doctor>.

58 Kwaymullina, 'Teaching for the 21st Century' (n 4) 17.

voices are almost completely absent from classic public law texts, which instead centre western narratives and voices.

Australian public law textbooks all tend to tell a similar story of the origins of Australian public law.[59] When Aurora started teaching the Foundations of Public Law unit at UWA in 2022, the preferred textbook for the introductory content was Appleby's *Australian Public Law (3rd edition)*.[60] This edition begins with the quote at the start of this chapter, which effectively launches students' Australian public law education with Aristotle's theories of organisation. Aristotle was a white male philosopher writing centuries ago in Ancient Greece. He was a defender of slavery[61] and never set foot on the lands now known as Australia. It is difficult to understand how this could be the start of the story, particularly when the longest continuous cultures on Earth have been practising law and governance in these lands for millennia. However, the third edition of the Appleby textbook is not the only textbook to start the story with Aristotle[62] or to litter its opening chapters with references to HLA Hart, Dworkin, Derrida and other dead white male philosophers with no connection to these lands.[63] Aristotle never lived on Country, was never part of Aboriginal systems of governance and never had a totem. His ideas and those of the other cited philosophers are not connected to place and are therefore of limited relevance to an understanding of the governance and law of this *place*, from an Aboriginal point of view. This inspired our title, as we tried and failed to locate these revered scholars in our system by asking ourselves: *what is Aristotle's totem anyway?* This choice of starting point erases thousands of years of Indigenous law and governance systems. It is difficult to teach our stories when they are not reflected in the textbooks that we provide to students as the authoritative sources on Australian public law.

If teachers want to challenge the narratives in the textbooks, then they will need to critique them in the classroom or look for other readings and materials from Indigenous perspectives that can 'talk up to'[64] the textbook and provide different versions of the story. In this chapter, we cite a number of sources that teachers can draw on, including the works of legal scholars Irene Watson, Ambelin Kwaymullina and Larissa Behrendt and the works of other scholars and knowledge holders such as Mary Graham, Aileen Moreton-Robinson, Josephine Bourne and Richard Walley.

59 See Appleby et al. (n 1); Anthony Connolly, *The Foundations of Australian Public Law: State, Power, Accountability* (Cambridge University Press, 2017); David Clark, *Introduction to Australian Public Law* (LexisNexis Butterworths, 5th ed, 2016).
60 Appleby et al. (n 1).
61 Aristotle, *Politics*, tr Sir Ernest Barker (Oxford University Press, 1998).
62 Appleby et al. (n 1) 4; Connolly (n 59) 2. See also Clark (n 58) 55.
63 Appleby et al. (n 1) 4–36; Connolly (n 59) 1–36.
64 Moreton-Robinson (n 10).

Of course, the most relevant experts for curriculum on Indigenous law and governance systems are local Indigenous knowledge holders. However, drawing on this expertise requires long-term relationship building, ethical engagement and fair remuneration.[65] This helps to establish equitable engagement with Indigenous peoples and to avoid exploitative relationships whereby non-Indigenous people position themselves as knowledge holders who extract and represent 'knowledge' about Indigenous peoples.[66] Relationship building with local communities requires significant work, but it is essential—it is the most authentic and ethical approach to teaching Indigenous curriculum.

The difficulty of this relationship-building work poses a practical challenge, as we recognise that it is far easier for teachers to reach for a textbook called 'Australian Public Law' than undertake the far more labour-intensive task of working with the appropriate Indigenous knowledge holders. Because of these practical challenges, it is imperative that textbook writers work collaboratively with Aboriginal and Torres Strait Islander people to bring Indigenous perspectives into core texts. In fact, the Appleby textbook has changed considerably between its third and fourth editions with the input of two new contributors—Cobble Cobble constitutional law scholar Megan Davis and non-Indigenous constitutional law and colonialism scholar Dylan Lino. Their contributions include dropping Aristotle from the first paragraph, the addition of a new section on First Nations systems of law and government in the second chapter[67] and major revisions to the chapter 'Aboriginal and Torres Strait Islander Peoples and Australian Public Law'.[68] These changes are not necessarily revelatory, but they provide greater opportunities for law students to engage with Indigenous perspectives without having to search outside their textbook. This demonstrates the impact of having Indigenous people and culturally informed non-Indigenous people contributing to these texts.

Teacher Readiness

Principle 12 requires that we '[e]nsure all teachers are trained in inclusive teaching before delivering content'.[69] This is an important principle, and one that perhaps sets UWA's approach apart from Indigenous curriculum work in other Australian law schools. We are deeply committed to ensuring that our teachers have not only ongoing training to recognise their own biases and the role of privilege and whiteness in law and education but also sufficient knowledge of Aboriginal and Torres Strait Islander histories before they teach any Indigenous content. The training enables non-Indigenous teachers to provide more nuanced and informed discussions of Aboriginal and

65 AIATSIS (n 23).
66 AIATSIS (n 23); Kwaymullina, 'Teaching for the 21st Century' (n 4) 6–7.
67 Appleby et al. (n 1) 44–45.
68 Appleby et al. (n 1) xiii.
69 Kwaymullina, 'Teaching for the 21st Century' (n 4) 17.

Torres Strait Islander topics, with a greater awareness and responsiveness to bias, privilege and cultural sensitivities in the classroom. The training is not a cure-all, of course, since education and cultural development are lifelong processes, but it is an important foundation that allows us to have more sophisticated discussions with our colleagues about curriculum.

The inclusive training is an important threshold for non-Indigenous scholars to teach Indigenous content, but it does not give them the ability to teach *any* Indigenous content. In particular, it will never be appropriate for non-Indigenous people to frame themselves as experts on Indigenous knowledges. This knowledge is held by Indigenous people, and some things can be shared only by the custodians of this knowledge, while other things cannot be shared at all. This relates back to how Indigenous nations are governed and who has authority to speak. As Watson writes, '[i]n our way the story belongs to the storyteller and cannot be told by others without permission'.[70] In this sense, although some of the overarching concepts related to Indigenous law and governance theories from this article could be taught by law teachers (preferably Aboriginal and/or Torres Strait Islander teachers), specific aspects of an Aboriginal nation's law and governance system can be taught only by local knowledge holders with appropriate authority.

This brings us back to the importance of ethical relationship building at both the institutional and community levels. At UWA, the Indigenisation of the Juris Doctor project was established through a partnership between the Law School and the School of Indigenous Studies.[71] We also work closely with Uncle Richard Walley and his children Alton Walley and Rickeeta Walley, who teach law students about Whadjuk Noongar systems of law and later in the degree, about Noongar conflict resolution. Although neither of these topics are taught in the public law units, our broader engagement with the Walley family means that UWA students will be taught directly by knowledge holders about Aboriginal systems of law and governance throughout their degree. Working with Indigenous people to tell their own stories enriches the student experience and builds enduring relationships with the community. These types of partnerships also signal a commitment to epistemological equality[72] and can be a supporting factor in the attraction and retention of Indigenous law academics and students.

Ultimately, there are many challenges in teaching Indigenous systems of law and governance in the public law curriculum, but at least some of these can be addressed through a dedication to finding the right sources, training teachers and developing ethical relationships with local Indigenous knowledge holders.

70 Watson, *Raw Law* (n 9) 14.
71 Kwaymullina, 'Teaching for the 21st Century' (n 4) 6.
72 Kwaymullina, 'Teaching for the 21st Century' (n 4) 7–8.

Conclusion

At the Garma Festival in 2023, Djawa Yunupingu, a senior Gumatj man, spoke about his support for the proposed Voice to Parliament by saying 'you [settlers] are in our Constitution already'.[73] This statement speaks to the heart of Aboriginal and Torres Strait Islander systems of law and governance. Country is the fundamental source of law, where everyone has a place in the system, and everyone must *be* placed in the system. In this sense, settlers were incorporated into our systems as soon as they arrived on Country. They were placed in the web of relations and in our highest law, our 'Constitution', even though settlers do much to disturb the balance in the web of relations and little to sustain First Law. In stark contrast to Yunupingu's statement, the Australian people rejected the Voice to Parliament proposal in 2023, reiterating that there was no place for Aboriginal and Torres Strait Islander people in their system of law and governance. We were once again excluded from a story that looks longingly overseas for its origins rather than right here in Country that loves and sustains all life, including settlers.

Bringing Indigenous theories of law and governance into the public law curriculum offers opportunities for students to learn about one of the most sophisticated forms of governance in the world. It also generates opportunities for partnership and engagement with local Aboriginal and Torres Strait Islander people and nations. Perhaps, most of all, it provides an opportunity to reshape public law storytelling and create shared stories for the future.

73 Djawa Yunupingu, 'Australia Is Not Complete: Djawa Yunupingu Makes Powerful Case for the Voice' (YouTube, 5 April 2023) <www.youtube.com/watch?v=AgUiX2pFX-k>.

15

UNSETTLING AUSTRALIAN CLINICAL LEGAL EDUCATION

Amanda Porter and Eddie Cubillo

Introduction

'I can't breathe.' These were the final words spoken by 46-year-old father of one George Floyd, a Black man who died after a white Minneapolis police officer, Derek Chauvin, pressed his knee on Floyd's neck for eight minutes and 46 seconds. These were also the final words spoken by 26-year-old Dhunghutti man David Dungay Junior and countless other sovereign Aboriginal peoples in Australia. In April 2021, Derek Chauvin was found guilty of second-degree murder in relation to Floyd's death[1] and sentenced to 22.5 years in prison. At the time of writing, no Australian police officer has ever been convicted of criminal charges in relation to an Indigenous death in custody. Despite the hundreds of recommendations and the publication of many royal commissions and national inquiries since the late 1980s and early 1990s, the incarceration rates of Indigenous peoples have reached historic highs.[2]

The 15th of April 2021 marked the 30-year anniversary of the tabling of the *Royal Commission Into Aboriginal Deaths in Custody* ('RCIADIC') in the Australian parliament.[3] In capitals and townships around the nation,

1 Jordan Hayne, 'Why Derek Chauvin Was Found Guilty of Both Murder and Manslaughter Over George Floyd's Death', *ABC News* (online, 21 April 2021) <www.abc.net.au/news/2021-04-21/derek-chauvin-murder-manslaugher-george-floyd-sentence/100083494>.

2 Moana Jackson, *Maori and the Criminal Justice System: A New Perspective He Wahpaanga Hou* (Final Report, 1987); *Royal Commission into Aboriginal Deaths in Custody* (Final Report, 1991) ('RCIADIC') <https://www.austlii.edu.au/au/other/IndigLRes/rciadic/national/vol1/>; Georges Erasmus and Rene Dussault, *Canadian Royal Commission on Aboriginal Peoples* (Final Report, 1996).

3 RCIADIC (n 2).

DOI: 10.4324/9781003473404-18

thousands of protesters gathered in a series of coordinated actions to express their love and solidarity with the families of over 478 Aboriginal and Torres Strait Islander people who have died in police or prison custody in the three decades since the RCIADIC's publication. At a rally in Naarm/Melbourne, a crowd of protestors heard from bereaved family members who are leading campaigns to end white carceral violence. One of the speakers included Yorta Yorta, Wemba Wemba and Barapa Barapa woman Apryl Watson, who spoke of her family's successful campaign to decriminalise public drunkenness in the state of Victoria. Apryl's mother, Aunty Tanya Day, was a respected Yorta Yorta woman and advocate in the movement for Indigenous lives who died in police custody in December 2017. Tanya Day dedicated her life to the movement for Indigenous and Black lives from a young age, following the sudden death of her uncle, Harrison Day, in police custody.[4] In the inquest into the death of Harrison Day—one of the 99 individual death reports of the RCIADIC—Commissioner Wootten recommended the offence of public drunkenness be decriminalised 'as soon as possible'.[5]

The rallies built on the growing momentum of the previous year's Black Lives Matter ('#BLM') protests, which were held in solidarity between the families of bereaved sovereign Indigenous peoples here in Australia and the families of the late George Floyd, Breonna Taylor, Elijah McClain and countless others in the USA. The rallies also built on the growing momentum of Black deaths in custody and Invasion Day rallies, which have a much longer genealogy rooted in Indigenous refusal/resistance to the prison nation known as Australia going back to First Contact.[6]

Regrettably, though perhaps unsurprisingly, the occasion of the RCIADIC's 30-year anniversary passed with remarkable silence among Australian legal academics.[7] Neither the RCIADIC anniversary nor the global #BLM protests appear to have prompted much soul-searching or reflection within Australian legal studies. For example, the 30-year anniversary apparently did not warrant a special issue from any of the major Australasian law journals. The anniversary also did not seem to prompt action to correct the overwhelming whiteness of Australian law faculties, their journals and editorial boards, their peer-review processes and their governance structures.

4 Amy McQuire, 'There Cannot Be 432 Victims and No Perpetrators', *The Saturday Paper* (online, 6 June 2020) <www.thesaturdaypaper.com.au/news/law-crime/2020/06/06/there-cannot-be-432-victims-and-no-perpetrators/15913656009926>.

5 John Halden Wootten, *Royal Commission into Aboriginal Deaths in Custody* (Report into the Death of Harrison Day, 1990) [10].

6 Gary Foley and Crystal McKinnon, 'Civil Rights and Indigenous People' in Peter Kane, Lisa Ford and Mark McMillan (eds), *The Cambridge Legal History of Australia* (Cambridge University Press, 2021) 523.

7 An important exception to this has been the work produced by Aboriginal and Torres Strait Islander scholars. See, e.g., Eddie Cubillo, '30th Anniversary of the RCIADIC and the "White Noise" of the Justice System Is Loud and Clear' (2021) 46(3) *Alternative Law Journal* 185.

Australasian legal studies appear, on the whole, to be 'business as usual' across all indicators.

At present, there is minimal, if any, Indigenous representation on the editorial boards of the major Australian law journals: the *Sydney Law Review*, the *Melbourne University Law Review* or the *Australian Law Journal*. Although official statements of solidarity and support were issued by a range of academic departments, academic journals and professional societies and associations (for example, the British Medical Association,[8] the American National Association of Social Workers,[9] Harvard Law School[10] and the Harvard Journal of Law and Gender[11]), there was just one statement issued by Australasian legal academics (the Centre for Crime, Law and Justice, University of New South Wales[12]). In contrast, more than 1,200 epidemiologists, infectious disease doctors and other public health professionals and community stakeholders signed an open letter calling for an 'anti-racist public health response to demonstrations against systemic injustice occurring during the Covid-19 pandemic'.[13] A United Kingdom edition of *The Guardian* includes an editorial statement that mentions the death of David Dungay Junior in Australia and draws parallels with deaths in custody in the United Kingdom and globally.[14] The silence of Australasian legal studies is, at best, indifferent to or, at worst, complicit in the ongoing settler colonial project that sets itself the task of Indigenous erasure.[15]

Given these shortcomings, in this chapter, we probe the following questions: Why do law students not learn about Aboriginal and Torres Strait Islander histories of resistance in contemporary Australian legal education?

8 'We Stand in Solidarity—BMA Statement on Black Lives Matter', *British Medical Association* (Web Page, 5 June 2020) <www.bma.org.uk/news-and-opinion/we-stand-in-solidarity-bma-statement-on-black-lives-matter>.

9 'Anti-Racism Now and Forever', *National Association of Social Workers* (Web Page, 10 June 2020) <www.socialworkers.org/News/News-Releases/ID/2187/Anti-Racism-Now-and-Forever-More>.

10 'HLS Statement of Solidarity in Response to Recent Events', *Harvard Law School* (Web Page, 4 June 2020) <https://clinics.law.harvard.edu/advocates/2020/06/04/hls-advocates-statement-of-solidarity-in-response-to-recent-events/>.

11 'Statement of Solidarity', *Harvard Journal of Law and Gender* (Web Page, 6 June 2020) <https://harvardjlg.com/2020/07/statement-of-solidarity/>.

12 'Statement of Solidarity with the Aboriginal Lives Matter and Black Lives Matter Movements', *University of New South Wales* (Web Page, 1 July 2020) <www.unsw.edu.au/news/2020/07/statement-of-solidarity-with-the-aboriginal-lives-matter-and-black-lives-matter-movements>.

13 'Open Letter Advocating for an Anti-racist Public Health Response against Systemic Injustice Occurring During the COVID-19 Pandemic', *Forbes* (online, 19 June 2020) <https://drive.google.com/file/d/1Jyfn4Wd2i6bRi12ePghMHtX3ys1b7K1A/view>.

14 Editorial, 'The Guardian View on Black Lives Matter Worldwide: A Common Cause', *Guardian UK* (online, 8 June 2020) <www.theguardian.com/commentisfree/2020/jun/07/the-guardian-view-on-black-lives-matter-worldwide-a-common-cause>.

15 Patrick Wolfe, 'Settler Colonialism and the Elimination of the Native' (2006) 8(4) *Journal of Genocide Research* 387.

What are the strategies for embedding Indigenous knowledges in clinical legal education curricula? What are the pitfalls and potential of Australian clinical legal education? What are the limitations of liberal law reform? For all of the journals and departments of law in Australia, why is there silence on issues such as land theft, racism and settler colonialism in Australian legal education? We ask these questions to provoke a dialogue about racism and epistemic violence in law and in disciplinary knowledge production generally. Although we use a case study based on our experience teaching at an Australian law school, our focus lies squarely with law as a discipline and clinical legal education as a sub-discipline.

To examine these questions, we use a theoretical framework that foregrounds Aboriginal and Torres Strait Islander sovereignty[16] and centres Indigenous scholarship on legal storytelling, resistance and self-determination. Additionally, we draw on a range of Indigenous-authored works that theorise on recognition/refusal[17] and Indigenous legal storytelling[18] to deepen our analysis and to complicate the question of what it means to 'win' a case, run a 'successful' campaign or 'do social justice' lawyering in settler colonial societies such as Australia.

There is a rich history of Aboriginal and Torres Strait Islander resistance and justice movements in Australia. It is a history that continues into the present. From the Day of Mourning to the Invasion Day protests, from the 1988 Bicentenary protests to the 2020 BLM protests, from the Wave Hill

16 See, e.g., Kevin Gilbert, *Living Black* (Penguin, 1977); Kevin Gilbert, *Aboriginal Sovereignty: Justice, the Law and Land* (Burrambinga Books, 1988); Linda Tuhiwai Smith, *Decolonising Methodologies* (ZED Press, 1999); Larissa Behrendt, *Achieving Social Justice: Indigenous Rights and Australia's Future* (Federation Press, 2003); Hannah McGlade, *Our Greatest Challenge: Aboriginal Children and Human Rights* (Aboriginal Studies Press, 2012); Aileen Moreton-Robinson, *The White Possessive* (University of Minnesota Press, 2015); Larissa Behrendt et al., *Aboriginal and Torres Strait Islander Legal Issues* (Oxford University Press, 2nd ed, 2018); Alison Whittaker, *Blakwork* (Magabala Books, 2018); Amy McQuire, 'Black and White Witness' (2019) 79(2) *Meanjin*; Nicole Watson and Heather Douglas (eds), *Indigenous Legal Judgments: Bringing Indigenous Voices into Judicial Decision Making* (Routledge, 2021); Chelsea Watego, *Another Day in the Colony* (University of Queensland Press, 2021); Nicole Watson, *Aboriginal Women, Law and Critical Race Theory* (Palgrave, 2022); Larissa Behrendt, *Finding Eliza: Power and Colonial Storytelling* (University of Queensland Press, 2022); Megan Davis and George Williams, *Everything You Need to Know About the Voice* (University of New South Wales Press, 2023).

17 See, e.g., Audra Simpson, *Mohawk Interruptus: Political Life Across the Borders of Settler States* (Duke University Press, 2014); Audra Simpson, 'The Ruse of Consent and the Anatomy of "Refusal": Cases from Indigenous North America and Australia' (2017) 20(1) *Postcolonial Studies* 18; Crystal McKinnon, 'Enduring Indigeneity and Solidarity in Response to Australia's Carceral Colonialism' (2021) 43(4) *Biography* 691.

18 See, e.g., Larissa Behrendt, 'Indigenous Storytelling: Decolonizing Institutions and Assertive Self-Determination: Implications for Legal Practice' in Jo-ann Archibald Q'um Q'um Xiiem, Jenny Lee-Morgan and Jason De Santolo (eds), *Decolonizing Research: Indigenous Storywork as Methodology* (ZED Books, 2018) 175.

Walk-Off to the Palm Island class action, from the Aboriginal Tent Embassy to the decriminalisation of public drunkenness in the state of Victoria, from the creation of Aboriginal legal and medical services in the 1970s to the creation of the first Yoorrook Truth and Justice Commission in Victoria in 2020, Aboriginal justice movements have always played a pivotal role in Australian civic society and have a rightful place within Australian law school curricula.

Clinical legal education and social change lawyering present an opportunity to learn about Aboriginal and Torres Strait Islander history, self-determination, resistance and social justice movements. Too often, however, clinical legal education is plagued by the same problems that befall the Priestley 11 curricula: a failure to consider settler colonialism and its effects; a failure to consider racism and its effects; intellectual nullius; and psychological nullius. Perhaps because clinical legal education and social change lawyering are viewed as indelibly progressive and 'for the greater good', clinical legal education has long escaped the attention of sustained decolonial and anti-racist critique. This chapter seeks to rectify this by mapping some of the dimensions of epistemic violence in Australian clinical legal education. This chapter then provides a case study specifically focusing upon our own experiences teaching clinical legal education: the Indigenous Legal Advocacy Clinic.

What Is Clinical Legal Education?

Clinical legal education is a 'progressive educational ideology and pedagogy that is most often implemented through university programs'.[19] Clinical legal education is a legal practice-based method of legal education in which students assume the role of a lawyer and 'are required to take on responsibility, under supervision, for providing legal services to real clients'.[20] Clinics are interactive, hands-on classrooms that promote 'learning by doing'. Though not part of the Priestley 11, clinical legal education and experiential learning have come to form a staple part of Australian legal education, with many law graduates taking one or more clinical subjects as an integral part of their studies.

Clinical legal education typically involves an experiential component such as a placement at a host organisation: a law firm, community legal centre, public interest law clearing house or other private or public entity. It might involve legal policy or campaign work. Some law schools have

19 'About Clinical Legal Education', *Babseacle* (Blog Post, 2023) <www.babseacle.org/clinical-legal-education>.

20 Judith Dickson, '25 Years of Clinical Legal Education at La Trobe University' (2004) 29(1) *Alternative Law Journal* 41.

in-house clinics, such as at Bond University and Flinders University. The common components/characteristics are that the work is real and that the students (under supervision) 'assume professional responsibility for the work outcome'.[21] Government agencies, such as the public prosecutor's office, and community legal centres constitute the largest placements due to the resources of these entities and their consequent capacity to take on and supervise student interns. A scarcity of resources in public law organisations represents a major obstacle for social change lawyering in Australia generally speaking.[22]

The issue of scarcity of resources is compounded for Aboriginal Community Controlled Organisations ('ACCOs'), which face significant under-resourcing and under-funding vis-à-vis state entities and Non-Indigenous Non-Governmental Organisations ('NINGOs'). These structural inequalities in Australian society are mirrored by structural inequalities within Australian law schools: the under-representation of Aboriginal and Torres Strait Islander legal academics, the tendency of Australian clinical legal education to partner with state agencies and NINGOs over ACCOs, and the lack of institutional support for inclusive and culturally safe clinical legal education, including the lack of understanding and respect for the hidden work in delivering such clinics. For example, in our experience delivering Indigenous clinics, we were questioned by the Head of School for not meeting the allocated times needed for our teaching loads. These combined structural issues mean that Australian law students are more likely to experience a placement within government agencies or NINGOs than within an ACCO.

Critiques of Australian Clinical Legal Education and Liberal Social Change Lawyering

Australian legal education is, for the most part, inherently elitist, whitewashed and settler-centric. Critiques of the whitewashing of Black letter law abound.[23] These critiques tend to focus on Priestley 11 subjects such as

21 Judith Dickson, '25 Years of Clinical Legal Education at La Trobe University' (2004) 29(1) *Alternative Law Journal* 41.

22 Paula O'Brien, 'Changing Public Interest Law: Overcoming the Law's Barriers to Social Change Lawyering' (2011) 36(2) *Alternative Law Journal* 82.

23 Nicole Watson, 'Indigenous People in Legal Education: Staring into a Mirror without Reflection' (2005) 6(8) *Indigenous Law Bulletin* 4; Asmi Wood and Nicole Watson, 'Mirror, Mirror on the Wall, Who Is the Fairest of Them All?' (2018) 28(2) *Legal Education Review* 16; Marcelle Burns, Anita Lee Hong and Asmi Wood, *Indigenous Cultural Competency for Legal Academics Program* (Final Report, 2019); Eddie Cubillo, *Submission to the Yoorrook Truth and Justice Commission* (Submission, 2022).

corporations law[24] and equity[25] and extend to subjects such as intellectual property law[26] and international law.[27]

Clinical legal education has managed to avoid/escape sustained decolonial and anti-racist critiques, perhaps because clinical legal education does not form part of the core Priestley 11 subjects or perhaps because it is seen as an intrinsically 'good' and 'socially progressive' cause synonymous with social change and public interest lawyering. However, clinical legal education is a long way from 'woke', and the same problems that plague the Priestley 11 (failure to appreciate settler colonialism and its effects, failure to appreciate racism and its effects, intellectual nullius, a failure to include, let alone centre, Aboriginal sovereignty, etc.) are rife in Australian clinical legal education. In fact, it is potentially more problematic because it is masked by the veneer of being innately 'socially progressive' and concerned with liberal and nebulous causes such as 'public interest' and 'social justice' lawyering. But the decolonisation of clinical legal curricula raises some distinct and thorny questions, namely, what are the limitations and challenges of engaging in social justice lawyering in settler colonial societies such as Australia? What are the limitations of liberal notions such as 'access to justice' and 'the public interest' in settler colonial societies such as Australia? What does 'truth' and 'justice' look like in a post-Mabo and pre-treaty Australia?

The following section sets out four critiques of clinical legal education: its failure to consider settler colonialism and its effects; its failure to consider racism and its effects; intellectual nullius; and psychological nullius. Against these criticisms, we add that, more generally, Australian legal education and curriculum are also obsessed with a standards-based approach, which favours a particular type of learner. Standards-based curriculum policy does not promote the critical enquiry needed to make the necessary connections between local and global issues such as the food security, trade, poverty, police brutality and climate change movements.

Settler Colonialism

Clinical legal education and social change lawyering are often taught in Australian law schools without an appreciation of settler colonialism and its effects. The main concepts by which clinical legal education is introduced

24 Harris Bede, 'Embedding Indigenous Experiences in the Teaching of Corporations Law' (2012) 1(4) *Ngiya Talk the Law* 16.

25 Prue Vines, 'Putting Indigenous Issues into the Curriculum: Succession and Equity' (2012) 1(4) *Ngiya Talk the Law* 46.

26 Stephen Gray, 'Shaking the Skeleton of Principle: Teaching Indigenous Legal Issues in Intellectual Property Law' (2012) 1(4) *Ngiya Talk the Law* 5.

27 Ben Saul, 'Indigenous Peoples, Laws and Customs in the Teaching of Public and Private International Law' (2012) 1(4) *Ngiya Talk the Law* 63.

include 'social change lawyering', 'public interest lawyering' and 'access to justice'. A core component of clinical legal education is learning about public interest or social change lawyering. As defined by Simon Rice, social justice lawyers 'work to address social phenomena such as inequality, disadvantage, discrimination, marginalisation, oppression and abuse, addressing the immediate needs of a client, or the structural causes of those needs, or both'.[28] Definitions of social justice and public interest lawyering often hinge on the notion of 'access to justice'. For example, Paula O'Brien defines public interest lawyering as 'assisting disadvantaged individuals or groups to access the legal system, in order to solve some legal problem or secure a benefit for the wider group of a similarly-placed people or defend a progressive social value'.[29] However, as we argue in this chapter, access to justice is in many ways an unhelpful and unproductive framing of the nature of legal issues confronting Aboriginal and Torres Strait Islander peoples. 'Access to justice' is unhelpful or misleading in the sense that it mischaracterises the structural racism and discrimination experienced by Aboriginal and Torres Strait Islander peoples. It is unproductive in the sense that it mischaracterises the political disenfranchisement experienced by Aboriginal and Torres Strait Islander peoples and nations in a post-Mabo and pre-Treaty Australia.

Settler colonialism is a distinct process of invasion, settlement and nation-building that radically transformed the lives of the original peoples and tribal nations living in the occupied territories. It is a particular type of colonialism wherein the primary economic objective is securing permanent access to and control of land and resources. Historically, settler sovereignty was asserted on the basis of 'discovery', and it continues to be justified by the primitiveness of Indigenous peoples and their failure to 'productively' utilise the land.[30] As Patrick Wolfe argued, settler colonialism demands that Indigenous peoples must be either eliminated or contained and controlled to make land available as private property for settlers who had come to stay.[31]

Aboriginal and Torres Strait Islander nations and polities have existed on this continent for millennia. Aboriginal and Torres Strait Islander sovereignty pre-dates settler claims to sovereignty. In the case of *Mabo v the State of Queensland (No 2)*,[32] the High Court of Australia found that the doctrine by

28 Simon Rice, 'What Does a Social Justice Lawyer Need to Know?' (2021) 47(2) *Alternative Law Journal* 90.

29 O'Brien (n 22) 82.

30 Larissa Behrendt et al., *Discovering Indigenous Lands: The Doctrine of Discovery in the English Colonies* (Oxford University Press, 2018).

31 Patrick Wolfe, 'Settler Colonialism and the Elimination of the Native' (2006) 8(4) *Journal of Genocide Research* 387.

32 (1992) 175 CLR 1.

which the settler state claims its sovereignty—'terra nullius' or land belonging to no one—was a legal fiction. In the words of Mick Dodson,

> [w]hatever the High Court has left us with post-Mabo, as to what is now the foundations of sovereignty of the Australian nation state is a complete mystery to me. The sovereign pillars of the nation state are, arguably, at the very least, a little legally shaky.[33]

Settler colonialism and Aboriginal and Torres Strait Islander sovereignty should constitute a foundational cornerstone of clinical legal education and social justice lawyering. Experiential or place-based education holds much potential because the approach traditionally asks students to critically interact with social justice issues in their communities. When teaching Indigenous knowledges, however, the approach is limited. This is why Indigenous scholars are calling upon educators to apply land-based approaches.[34] The pedagogical practice of land-based education emphasises the importance of critiquing whose Indigenous lands we are currently on and how colonisation has obstructed society's understanding of land and custodianship, which illuminates how authority influences identities of place.[35]

(i) Psychological Nullius

Clinical legal education and social change lawyering are often taught in Australian law schools without an appreciation of the psychological nullius of the Australian legal system and its institutions. Megan Davis coined the phrase 'psychological nullius' to refer to Indigenous peoples' factual and ideological exclusion from Australian public institutions—parliament,

33 Mick Dodson, 'Our Nation Sits at a Crossroads: Enough with the Humbug', *Institute of Public Administration Australia* (Blog Post, 2019) <www.ipaa.org.au/professor-mick-dodson-our-nation-sits-at-a-crossroads-enough-with-the-humbug/>.

34 Leanne Betasamosake Simpson, 'Land as Pedagogy: Nishnaabeg Intelligence and Rebellious Transformation' (2014) 3(3) *Decolonization: Indigeneity, Education and Society* 1; Glen Coulthard and Leanne Betasmosake Simpson, 'Place-Based Solidarity' (2016) 68(2) *American Quarterly* 249.

35 David A Gruenewald, 'The Best of Both Worlds: A Critical Pedagogy of Place' (2003) 32(4) *Educational Research*; Geneva Gay, *Culturally Responsive Teaching: Theory, Research and Practice* (Teacher's College Press, 2010); Peter McInerney, John Smyth and Barry Down, 'Coming to a Place Near You? The Politics of Possibilities of a Critical Pedagogy and Place-Based Education' (2011) 39(1) *Asia-Pacific Journal of Teacher Education* 3; Gregory A Smith and David Sobel, *Place and Community-Based Education in Schools* (Routledge, 2014); Janice Woodhouse and Clifford Knapp, *Place-Based Curriculum and Instruction: Outdoor and Environmental Education Approaches, Clearinghouse on Rural Education and Small Schools* (Appalachia Educational Laboratory, 2000).

courts, police, state departments and other public entities.[36] Davis argues that the populist vision of the neutral and fair legal system ignores 'the gendered and racialised biases that exist on the bench'.[37] Although Davis frames her discussion in terms of the psychological nullius or exclusion of Aboriginal and Torres Strait Islander peoples from Australian public institutions, the argument applies with equal force to the Australian legal system, particularly judges, magistrates, coroners, barristers, King's Counsel, lawyers, partners of law firms, court officials, legal academics and ombudsman personnel.

Aboriginal and Torres Strait Islander peoples are under-represented across all sectors of the Australian legal system. At the time of writing, there has never been an Aboriginal or Torres Strait Islander justice of the High Court of Australia, and there has never been an Aboriginal or Torres Strait Islander coroner in any state or territory jurisdiction. Aboriginal and Torres Strait Islander peoples are significantly under-represented as barristers and solicitors in law firms, law societies, government, community legal centres, non-governmental organisations and all other stakeholders. The Law Society of New South Wales reports that Aboriginal and Torres Strait Islander peoples represented just 1.1 per cent of the number of solicitors holding New South Wales practising certificates in 2020, despite making up 2.8 per cent of the population.[38] A study conducted by the Australian National University found that job applicants with non-Anglo names had to submit more resumes to be offered an interview, with Aboriginal and Torres Strait Islander people having to submit them 34 times.[39] Similarly, a study involving American law firms suggests that there are substantial biases related to social class and gender that skew employment opportunities toward white men from privileged backgrounds.[40]

The psychological nullius of the Australian legal sector applies with equal force to the non-governmental organisation and community legal sector.

36 Megan Davis, 'Chained to the Past: The Psychological Terra Nullius of Australia's Public Institutions' in Jeffrey Goldsworthy, Tom Campbell and Adrienne Stone (eds), *Rights Without Bills of Rights* (Routledge, 2006) 1.

37 Megan Davis, 'Chained to the Past: The Psychological Terra Nullius of Australia's Public Institutions' in Jeffrey Goldsworthy, Tom Campbell and Adrienne Stone (eds), *Rights Without Bills of Rights* (Routledge, 2006) 1.

38 The Law Society of New South Wales, *Diversity and Inclusion in the Legal Profession: The Business Case* (2021) 4 <www.lawsociety.com.au/sites/default/files/2021-10/LS1856_PAP_DIV_CulturalDiversity_2021-10-14.pdf>.

39 'Minorities Find It Harder to Get Jobs—RSS Research Study', *Australian National University* (Web Page, 18 June 2009) <https://cass.anu.edu.au/news/minorities-find-it-harder-get-jobs-rsss-research-study>.

40 Lauren Rivera and András Tilcsik, 'Research: How Subtle Class Cues Can Backfire on Your Résumé', *Harvard Business Review* (online, 21 December 2016) <https://hbr.org/2016/12/research-how-subtle-class-cues-can-backfire-on-your-resume>.

Aboriginal and Torres Strait Islander peoples are under-represented in the community legal sector, including on the boards of many community legal centres. Aboriginal and Torres Strait Islander peoples and polities are also under-represented in social justice campaigns. A good example is drawn from our personal experience. In 2020, the Redfern Community Legal Centre ran a campaign, 'Safe and Sound', which sought to amplify the experiences of young people who had been strip searched by the New South Wales Police Force. Unfortunately, this campaign was run in a way that tended to centre whiteness and failed to accommodate the fact that young white people are not the only the victims of overzealous policing. This was especially disappointing given the historical context of Redfern/Waterloo[41] and the ways in which the overzealous policing of these areas continues to impact Aboriginal and Torres Strait Islander people, especially Indigenous young people.[42] We suggest that de-centring whiteness is a strategy that all lawyers and campaign-workers can implement in their advocacy work, and we address this issue in the following.

(ii) Intellectual Nullius

Clinical legal education and social change lawyering are often taught in Australian law schools in a way that is epistemically violent in the sense that it fails to engage with Aboriginal and Torres Strait Islander knowledges, including especially critical Indigenous and critical race theory. Lester Irrabinna Rigney coined the term 'intellectual nullius' to describe the phenomena of not engaging with Indigenous knowledges and source material,[43] although scholars have long observed, theorised and developed names to describe this pattern of neglect, exclusion and imperialism in knowledge production and pedagogy.[44]

41 Redfern was the site of many firsts in Aboriginal Community Controlled Organisations, a result of staunch and visionary activism in the 1960s and 1970s. See Gary Foley, 'Black Power in Redfern: 1968–1972', *The Koori History Website* (Web Page, 2001) <https://kooriweb.org/foley/resources/pdfs/228.pdf>.

42 Christopher Knaus, 'NSW Police Use Force Against Indigenous Australians at Drastically Disproportionate Levels, Data Shows', *The Guardian* (online, 31 July 2023) <www.theguardian.com/australia-news/2023/jul/31/nsw-police-use-force-against-indigenous-australians-at-drastically-disproportionate-levels-data-shows>.

43 Lester Rigney, 'A First Perspective of Indigenous Australian Participation in Science: Framing Indigenous Research Towards Indigenous Australian Intellectual Sovereignty' (2001) 7 *Kaurna Higher Education Journal* 1.

44 Aimee Césaire, *Discours Sur Le Colonialisme* (Presence Africaine, 1942); Frantz Fanon, *The Wretched of the Earth* (Grove Press, 1961); Richard Delgado, 'The Imperial Scholar' (1984) 132(3) *Pennsylvania Law Review* 561; Sarah Ahmed, 'Making Feminist Points', *feministkilljoys* (Blog Post, 11 September 2013) <https://feministkilljoys.com/2013/09/11/making-feminist-points/>; Boaventura De Sousa Santos, 'Epistemologies of the South and the Future of the University' (2023) 1 *From the European South* 17.

In a classic article on critical race theory, Richard Delgado documents the erasure of minority scholars from the civil rights literature. In his words,

> Courts rarely cite it [minority scholarship], and the legal scholars whose work really counts almost never do. The important work is published in eight or ten law reviews and is written by a small group of professors, who teach in the major law schools.[45]

Delgado continues as follows:

> My assistant and I prepared an informal sociogram, a pictorial representation of who-cites-whom in the civil rights literature. It is fascinating. Paul Brest cites Laurence Tribe. Laurence Tribe cites Paul Brest and Owen Fiss. Owen Fiss cites Bruce Ackerman, who cites Paul Brest and Frank Michelman, who cites Owen Fiss and Laurence Tribe and Kenneth Karst. *It does not matter where one enters this universe; one comes to the same result: an inner circle of about a dozen white, male writers who comment on, take polite issue with, extol, criticize, and expand on each other's ideas.* It is something like an elaborate minuet.[46]

Delgado coined the term 'politics of citation' to describe the exclusion of African-American, Hispanic and Native American scholars in civil rights scholarship, where a small group of white male professors dominate scholarly discourse and cite only among themselves. Elsewhere, Sarah Ahmed describes citation as a 'successful reproductive technology' that reinforces the intellectual influence of certain thinkers, typically white, male and heteronormative, over others who are often less represented.[47]

Clinical legal education and social change lawyering are often taught in Australian law schools in a way that erases Aboriginal and Torres Strait Islander knowledges, scholarship, theory and advocacy. Classic articles such as those by Paula O'Brien[48] and Simon Rice[49] are staple features in clinical law curricula across Australia. Less commonly featured are the writings of Aboriginal and Torres Strait Islander theorists, advocates, activist-scholars and knowledge holders. This is a shame for Australian legal education, as Aboriginal and Torres Strait Islander peoples and organisations are internationally renowned for ingenuity and leadership in advocacy, campaigns and social movements (discussed later). Similarly, less commonly featured are the films and new media of Aboriginal and Torres Islander documentary makers.

45 Delgado (n 44) 561.
46 Delgado (n 44) 561 (emphasis added).
47 Ahmed (n 44).
48 O'Brien (n 22).
49 Rice (n 28).

This is a missed opportunity for Australian legal education given the depth and breadth of documentary film and new media freely available in the public record that squarely relates to social justice campaigns and advocacy.[50] We return to this issue in the following.

We emphasise that the issues of intellectual nullius and imperial citation politics in Australian legal curricula are certainly not limited to clinical legal education; rather, they pervade citation practices in research and teaching across the legal discipline as a whole. In our experience, it is not uncommon for even seemingly progressive legal electives such as Race and the Law to operate without providing a single reading by an Aboriginal or Torres Strait Islander scholar. This is not due to a lack of extensive and substantive writings produced by Aboriginal and Torres Strait Islander scholars (whose work is cited extensively throughout this book, for example) but due to cognitive bias and prejudice on the part of settler legal academics. To this end, we introduce our students to the *Legal Guide to Indigenous Knowledges* as part of our teaching and recommend this as essential reading for all Australian legal academics.[51]

(iii) The Erasure of Aboriginal and Torres Strait Islander Sovereignty and Agency

Clinical legal education and social change lawyering are often taught in Australian law schools in a way that erases Aboriginal and Torres Strait Islander sovereignty and agency. Writing and teaching on clinical legal education tend to promote a two-dimensional understanding of activism and advocacy. For example, it is not uncommon in legal studies to read about or hear academics discuss how the RCIADIC was commissioned by the Federal Government in 1987. Such a reading of history, we suggest, tends to imply that royal commissions, state inquiries and social change are the product of a benevolent government. This reading, we suggest, robs Aboriginal and Torres Strait Islander families and activists of sovereignty, agency and a rightful place in the historical lead-up to the RCIADIC.

A more accurate reading of history would reflect the fact that the landmark inquiry was established in 1987 after a political campaign waged by Aboriginal and Torres Strait Islander families and organisations, including the

50 See, e.g., *After the Apology* (Lavarch Productions, 2017); *Innocence Betrayed* (Lavarch Productions, 2015); *Incarceration Nation* (Gibson, 2021); *Who Killed Malcolm Smith?* (Frankland, 1992); *We Can't Make the Same Mistake Twice* (ImagineNATIVE Film, 2016); *Australian Wars* (Blackfella Films, 2022).

51 Indigenous Archives Collective (Shannon Faulkhead, Kirsten Thorpe, Nathan Sentance, Lauren Booker and Rose Barrowcliffe), *Indigenous Referencing Guidance for Indigenous Knowledges* (Indigenous Archives Collective and the UTS Jumbunna Institute for Indigenous Education and Research, 2023).

families of John Pat and David Gundy among many others. In 1983, Ying-garda and Bibbulman woman Helen Corbett co-founded the Committee to Defend Black Rights ('CDBR') which was at the forefront of a national and international campaign to establish the RCIADIC. In 1986, Corbett and the CDBR took the issue of Indigenous deaths in custody to the United Nations in Geneva. Under mounting local and international pressure, including protests and advocacy, a royal commission was established to investigate 99 deaths of Indigenous peoples, almost two-thirds of whom had died in police custody.[52] In our following discussion, we draw out what Australian clinical legal education could look like when Aboriginal and Torres Strait Islander sovereignty and agency are centred.

Strategies for Unsettling Australian Clinical Legal Education

The Indigenous Law and Advocacy Clinic has been a subject at Melbourne Law School since February 2021. We have partnered with a range of ACCOs, including Change the Record, Australians for Native Title and Reconciliation, the Victorian Aboriginal Legal Service, Kinchela Boys Home Aboriginal Corporation and the National Aboriginal and Torres Strait Islander Legal Service. The purpose and rationale of the clinic was to carve out semester-length projects for the student interns to work on that were designed by and would directly benefit the partner organisations.

Over the course of the semester, the student interns progressed the case file, jointly supervised by an academic supervisor and clinical supervisor, with the aim of producing work that was of a publishable standard. The student interns produced work that was directly used and, in many cases, published by the partner organisations. Some examples of such published work include case notes and reports. Students were encouraged to produce work of a publishable standard and received a High Distinction if they obtained this standard. These students were assessed entirely on the quality of the finished work produced for their partner organisation. This was a mutually symbiotic arrangement that incentivised conscientious students to produce the best work of their ability with a view toward maximising the quality of the finished product for the partner organisation.

In addition to the case file component, the subject included a lecture series that complemented the clinical component, which provided theoretical and historical context and a series of workshops on practical skills such as the politics of citation and citation technique (citing with purpose and citing Indigenous knowledges), vicarious trauma and campaign messaging. The lecture series covered topics such as history, campaigns, strategic litigation, class actions, structural law reform, activism, abolition and creative expression.

52 RCIADIC (n 2).

The lecture series also incorporated several 'Question and Answer' guest lectures, with students having the opportunity to ask questions of leading advocates in the space. In 2021, the guest lecturers included Megan Davis (Cobble Cobble), Cindy Blackstock (Gixtan), Richard Frankland (Gunditjmara), Jonathan Hunyor, Anna Brown and Stewart Levitt. The reading guide included classic works from Gary Foley,[53] Cindy Blackstock,[54] Nicole Watson,[55] Larissa Behrendt,[56] Aileen Moreton-Robinson,[57] Alison Whittaker,[58] Hannah McGlade,[59] Linda Tuhiwai Smith[60] and Amy McQuire, among many others. The course also incorporated classic documentaries such as *Who Killed Malcolm Smith*,[61] *The Bowraville Murders*,[62] *Incarceration Nation*[63] and *After the Apology*,[64] as well as multimedia clips from YouTube and podcasts such as *Curtain: The Podcast* by Amy McQuire and Martin Hodgson. The following quote by Gary Foley highlights the values of humility and self-awareness that underscore the pedagogical philosophy of the unit:

> That's why I always [say] you've got to educate yourself, then educate the people around you. And the first process that needs to be gone through is the process of self-education and becoming fully aware of just how little you know. I mean some people will react to that sense of inadequacy by saying 'I can't handle this I'll go back to my safe little world'. Fine, do it. But for those people who are committed to bringing about some sort of meaningful change in society, not just for us, for everybody, then there's a much broader, bigger and more long-term path. And you've got to break through those barriers and really get down to the process of looking yourself in the mirror, realising the true nature of what we're up against. . . . Once you find that racist and realise the depth of the ignorance and the fear that is there, then you realise the real nature of just how enormous the task is that confronts us all. Because at the end of the day, it really is about these appalling attitudes that are out there. In the last week or so, the United Nations very belatedly, some 40 or 80 years later, after they first

53 Foley and McKinnon (n 6).
54 Cindy Blackstock, 'Social Movements and the Law: Addressing Engrained Government-Based Racial Discrimination Against Indigenous Children' (2016) 19(1) *Australian Indigenous Law Review* 6.
55 Watson, *Aboriginal Women, Law and Critical Race Theory* (n 16).
56 Behrendt, *Finding Eliza* (n 16).
57 Moreton-Robinson (n 15).
58 Whittaker (n 16).
59 McGlade (n 16).
60 Tuhiwai Smith (n 16).
61 *Who Killed Malcolm Smith?* (n 50).
62 *The Bowraville Murders* (n 50).
63 *Incarceration Nation (n 50).*
64 *After the Apology* (n 50).

> were told about it, now concedes that racism is embedded in Australian society, that the evidence is there in abundance. And people need to not only grapple with that, but also see how that relates to them personally. I mean, how many people here know who the Koori mob was who lived on the land where you live now? And it's not just a question of knowing who they were, say, the Wurundjeri, but knowing: *what happened to the people on whose land you live now*? And as you gain a sense of that, you gain a sense of just how enormous your own personal ignorance is.[65]

Conceptually and philosophically, the subject drew inspiration from Larissa Behrendt's three criteria for Indigenous legal storytelling and assertive self-determination. In her essay on advocating alongside the Bowraville families, Behrendt sets out the three cursory principles for engagement with Indigenous advocacy and campaign work, which are paraphrased as follows:

1. **Wait until asked or invited:** We did not get involved, even though we felt strongly about it, *until we were asked.*
2. **Self-determination in action:** Along the way, we gave suggestions about their options or how to achieve what they wanted but we never made decisions for them.
3. **De-centring one's self in campaign and advocacy:** We did not speak for them but found ways to have their voice elevated.[66]

The following section sets out two strategies for unsettling Australian clinical legal education. Each of these strategies is based on the key values and principles that guided the delivery and terms of engagement of the Indigenous Legal Advocacy Clinic.

(i) Partner with Aboriginal Organisations for the Benefit of Aboriginal Organisations

First, we partnered with a range of ACCOs, including those listed at the start of this section. Considerable lead-in time was provided to enable the partner organisations to design projects that would directly benefit the host organisation and assist with their workload. As course co-ordinators, our role was merely to provide guidance on expectations around a reasonable workload for student interns to ensure consistency and fairness in the workload of all student placements. Other than this, we provided minimal input on the

65 We apologise for the length of this quote, but it is an integral part of the values and ethos that guide the delivery of the Indigenous Legal Advocacy Clinic. Quote by Gary Foley in thejuicemedia, 'Educate Yourself, Then Educate the People' (Youtube, 2011) 5, 35 <www.youtube.com/watch?v=Iw8YVBbQgNg&ab_channel=thejuicemedia>.

66 Behrendt, 'Indigenous Storytelling' (n 18) 182.

design of the projects, with all projects being led, designed and constructed by the partner organisations. This was deliberate and an attempt to honour the first element of Behrendt's conditions of engagement: we waited '*until we were asked*'.[67] Additionally, this ethos underscored the importance of conducting research and advocacy that is for the benefit of Indigenous peoples.[68]

(ii) Centre Indigenous Sovereignty, Agency and Knowledges

A second strategy involves centring Aboriginal and Torres Strait Islander sovereignty, agency and knowledges. This includes the history of social justice campaigns and advocacy. The introduction to this chapter briefly summarises the rich literature on the #BLM rallies of 2020.[69] Some of this material may be found in alternative sources such as op-eds, blogs and social media posts. However, we submit that this recent history has a rightful place in law school research and teaching and so do so many campaigns for Aboriginal and Torres Strait Islander justice. For example, Latoya Rule's #BanSpitHoods campaign to ban spit hoods in all Australian states and territories,[70] Sisters Inside's #FreeHer campaign to release Aboriginal women imprisoned under the state of Western Australia's draconian Clamping Down on Fines policy[71] and Dr Raylene Nixon McKellar's #BanTheLVNR campaign to ban the lateral vascular neck restraint—which is associated with a high rate of fatalities in police custody—in the state of Queensland.[72] Many of these campaigns have received international press attention.[73]

Interestingly, similarly to the campaigns, it is not uncommon for Aboriginal and Torres Strait Islander academics and advocates to receive greater recognition internationally and prior to receiving similar recognition in Australia. High-profile examples include Aileen Moreton-Robinson, who was

67 Behrendt, 'Indigenous Storytelling' (n 18) 182.

68 Tuhiwai Smith (n 16).

69 Tarneen Onus-Williams, Crystal McKinnon and Meriki Onus, 'Why We Organised Melbourne's Black Lives Matter Rally', *Saturday Paper* (online, 13 June 2020) <www.thesaturdaypaper.com.au/opinion/topic/2020/06/13/why-we-organised-melbournes-black-lives-matter-rally/15919704009972#hrd>.

70 For more information on this campaign, see the Ban Spit Hoods Coalition: <https://banspithoods.com/>.

71 Maani Truu, 'Viral Campaign to Free Jailed Indigenous Women Reaches $230,000', *SBS News* (online, January 2019) <www.sbs.com.au/news/article/viral-campaign-to-free-jailed-indigenous-women-reaches-230-000/30xuooybd>. For more information on this campaign, see #FreeHer: <https://sistersinside.com.au/freeher-campaign/>.

72 For more information on this campaign, see Raylene Nixon-McKellar: <www.change.org/p/ban-use-of-neck-restraint-hold-by-queensland-police-service>.

73 'Australie: Une Cagnotte Pour Faire Libérer des Femmes Aborigènes', *RFI* (online, 10 January 2019) <www.rfi.fr/fr/asie-pacifique/20190110-australie-une-cagnotte-faire-liberer-femmes-aborigenes>; 'Thousands Raised to Free Aboriginal Women Jailed Over Debts', *BBC News* (online, 10 January 2019) <www.bbc.com/news/world-australia-46818447>.

recognised as a fellow of the American Academy of Social Sciences and Humanities decades prior to receiving the same honour by the Australian Academy of Social Sciences and Humanities, and Richard Frankland, whose work has received international awards such as at the Berlin Film Festival but has gone largely unnoticed by Australian audiences.

The final point that requires emphasising is that centring Aboriginal and Torres Strait Islander sovereignty, agency and knowledges is not about siloing Indigenous experiences. To the contrary, as Gary Foley's quote so eloquently illustrates, Aboriginal and Torres Strait Islanders' campaigns and advocacy benefit all Australians. An excellent example is the campaign to decriminalise public drunkenness, led by the family of the late Aunty Tanya Day. On 7 November 2023, Victoria became the first state or territory in Australia to decriminalise public drunkenness, without the creation of new police powers for protective custody. This development is a step towards decarceration and decriminalisation, which will benefit multiple socio-economically disadvantaged and minoritised populations who are unfairly targeted by the police.

Challenges and Opportunities

Along the way, we encountered challenges and opportunities for reflection and learning. At mid-semester, we delivered a questionnaire for students to complete as a way of providing feedback on the subject so far. Students asked for more training on vicarious trauma and the legal profession. We incorporated this feedback and provided a separate skillset seminar on vicarious trauma and the legal profession. This seminar included set readings by Nayuka Gorrie and Michael Kirby. The seminar was delivered with great success, with some students saying it was the highlight of the subject and others commenting on the need for vicarious trauma training as an essential part of Australian law school curricula. To this end, we recommend that legal academics teaching about ethics and the legal profession consider incorporating modules on vicarious trauma and the legal profession. This learning seems prudent not only for students going on to work in Indigenous legal advocacy but also for all lawyers working in the Australian legal profession.

Conclusion

This chapter examined some of the dimensions of epistemic violence in Australian clinical legal education. It provided a general overview of Indigenous exclusion due to the psychological and intellectual nullius of Australian legal education. Perhaps because clinical legal education and social change lawyering are viewed as indelibly progressive and 'in the public interest', clinical legal education has long escaped the attention of sustained decolonial and anti-racist critique. This chapter presented four critiques of clinical legal education: its failure to consider settler colonialism and its effects; its failure to consider racism and its effects; intellectual nullius; and psychological nullius. Against each of these criticisms, we considered the potential for clinical legal education when Aboriginal sovereignty and legal storywork are centred. This chapter equally discussed a case study specifically focusing upon our own experiences teaching clinical legal education in which we explain our pedagogical and philosophical approach.

Accordingly, we offer three brief suggestions for how this shift in ideas might start to happen. As a first step, lawyers who are currently involved in 'public interest' and social change lawyering are encouraged to consider Aboriginal and Torres Strait Islander sovereignty in their work and to individually and collectively ask the following questions: What are the limitations of liberal notions such as 'access to justice' and 'the public interest' in settler colonial societies such as Australia? What does 'truth' and 'justice' look like in a post-Mabo and pre-treaty Australia? How might we include—or better still, centre—Aboriginal and Torres Strait Islander sovereignty and agency in our advocacy, teaching and research? How would we start to incorporate such an approach into our practice? Second, Australian legal academics are to be encouraged to consider what they can do to unsettle clinical legal education. Legal academics tend not to teach Aboriginal and Torres Strait Islander content, theory and advocacy. Legal academics might reflect on the way in which the law school curriculum erases Aboriginal and Torres Strait Islander sovereignty, legal systems and laws. Third, Australian law schools are encouraged to prioritise placements and partnerships with ACCOs to equip students to engage in inclusive and meaningful social change lawyering that centres Indigenous sovereignty and self-determination.

16

NATIVE TITLE

Steps Toward a Decolonised Law Curriculum

Lee Godden[1]

Introduction: What Is It That We Teach and What Is It That We (Have Yet to) Learn?

Even before we investigate the pedagogy of native title in legal education, we must ask what is native title? The question and response simultaneously shape subsequent directions for legal pedagogy, frame curriculum objectives and set in play reverberations through socio-legal and political lenses that shake historical certainties but that to date have not erased entrenched positional views in settler societies. Moreover, we have not 'decolonised' law schools. There are efforts toward these goals, although a fractured understanding of what this might entail and resistance from a spectrum of standpoints are evident.

The multilayered way in which we may respond to 'What is native title?' frames this chapter's analysis or more accurately, my ruminations on having taught native title in various guises for over 30 years. This statement requires an admission. I am not an Aboriginal person or a Torres Strait Islander. As a person of settler background, I remain an outsider to a situated sense of connection to Country and the traditional responsibilities that this confers.[2] Instead, as a legal educator, researcher of native title law and project

1 The author wishes to thank Madhushika Jayachandra who provided valuable research assistance in checking references and assisting with reviewing and proofing the chapter. The author acknowledges the support provided by the Australian Research Council Discovery Project DP190101373—Property as habitat: Reintegrating place, people and law.

2 There is significant scholarship by Aboriginal Peoples and Torres Strait Islanders on native title and the nature of such obligations. Increasing familiarity with Indigenous scholarship is central to any change in legal education. This chapter has benefited from collaborative

DOI: 10.4324/9781003473404-19

collaborator with Indigenous communities in several jurisdictions, the obligation on me is ethical. It is an obligation of respectful interaction. The challenge is in acknowledging a different legal relationship to that from which 'settler' legal responsibilities emanate, without seeking to subsume such relationships within another order of being.

This challenge animates the aspiration for a decolonised law school. It also points to a dilemma facing legal education in that, given a legacy of colonisation, it may not be able to fully respond to an aspiration of untrammeled acceptance of another law. Alternatively, caution may be needed in how we 'open up' First Nations' laws to the institutions of legal education and law schools.[3] Given the persistence of embedded western-centric institutions in 'post'-colonial nations, such states constitute hybrid legal entities.[4] Australia thus remains an ambivalent postcolonial nation, and native title is resonant of such ambivalence.

The very nomenclature of 'Native title' should alert us to its colonial past and its current hybridity as a recognition doctrine. Native title is deeply instantiated in a colonial past; it emanates from an imperial and colonial history that shaped and continues to shape the institutions of legal education and law schools in Australia. Even so, while recognising this past, the historical entanglement of native title and the deeply hybrid character of its legal form, it is also a platform to progressively sharpen the focus on prefigurative pathways toward a more authentic form of recognition when we teach native title.

Recognition and Native Title

The framing of recognition as the discursive introduction has salience in another way. In Australia, native title is given legal existence pursuant to a common law recognition doctrine, as exemplified in *Mabo v Queensland [No 2]* ('*Mabo [No 2]*'),[5] and by its adoption in the *Native Title Act 1993* (Cth) ('*Native Title Act*').[6] Accordingly, this chapter concentrates on native title in the Australian law curriculum; however, given a shared derivation for native title, there is comparative reference to settler common law jurisdictions.

---

scholarship. I would like to particularly acknowledge Marcia Langton and all researchers who were part of the Agreements, Treaties and Negotiated Settlements project (see <www.atns.net.au/>).

3 Irene Watson, 'Re-Centring First Nations Knowledge and Places in a Terra Nullius Space' (2014) 10(5) *AlterNative: An International Journal of Indigenous Peoples* 508, 509.

4 Irene Watson, 'Assimilation Agendas of the State: What Space Remains for Aboriginal Law and Culture?' in Priti Singh (ed), *Indigenous Identity and Activism* (Shipra Publications, 2009) 124.

5 *Mabo v Queensland [No 2]* (1992) 175 CLR 1.

6 *Native Title Act 1993* (Cth) s 3(c).

Australian native title law has developed well beyond common law doctrinal recognition per se to include legislative, procedural and evidential requirements, shifting policy positions and court-mandated practices and litigation and dispute resolution. Each sphere of legal and political authority that adheres to native title law requires Aboriginal Peoples and Torres Strait Islanders to engage with the postcolonial institutions of the nation state—typically over long periods—to claim native title.

Indeed, the claimant application process typifies the prescriptive manner in which Aboriginal Peoples and Torres Strait Islanders must navigate such institutional forms.[7] Even before traditional owners are designated as 'claimants' under the *Native Title Act*, they must satisfy exhaustive evidential thresholds of state recognition by demonstrating links to a designated ancestral descent line.[8] The determination of 'belonging' is ostensibly predicated on Indigenous kin relationships. Yet the manner of their investigation prioritises western-centric methodologies.[9] Anthropological framings of Indigenous belonging interlink to onerous evidentiary requirements to prove the continuity of traditional practice of law and custom as the prerequisite for settler law recognising the rights and interests that comprise native title.

Recognition of native title sits in the shadow of sovereign powers of extinguishment. These powers are given extensive manifestation and procedural complexity in the *Native Title Act*.[10] The statute sets the 'consequences' of extinguishment, which can include not only the suspension of native title rights and interests but also their elimination. The Act allows for compensation for extinguishment or impacts on native title in prescribed circumstances, as aligned to the *Racial Discrimination Act 1975* (Cth).[11] The Preamble of the *Native Title Act* references human rights and reconciliation.[12] A central objective of the Act is 'recognition and protection of native title',[13] notwithstanding substantive provisions that undercut this function. Somewhat incongruously, these can be contrasted with the 'hope' of common law redress, which 'will, by the ordinary processes of law and equity, give remedies in support of the relevant rights and interests to those who hold them'.[14]

7 See, e.g., Lee Godden, 'Legal Geography—Place, Time, Law and Method: Time and the Archival in "Connection to Country"' in Tayanah O'Donnell, Daniel F Robinson and Josephine Gillespie (eds), *Legal Geography: Perspectives and Methods* (Routledge, 2020) 130. There is substantial literature on such topics.

8 *Native Title Act 1993* (Cth) ss 61, 223, 225. Cf. *Traditional Owner Settlement Act 2010* (Vic).

9 Godden (n 7) 142.

10 *Native Title Act 1993* (Cth) ss 11, 23B–23I.

11 *Racial Discrimination Act 1975* (Cth). See also *Mabo v Queensland [No 1]* (1988) 166 CLR 186.

12 *Native Title Act 1993* (Cth) Preamble and s 3.

13 *Native Title Act* 1993 (Cth) Preamble and s 3(a).

14 *Commonwealth v Yarmirr* (2001) 208 CLR 1 [42].

The wider institutional sphere of native title also must be understood in the context of agreement-making under the Act.[15] Such provisions interact through agreement-making among native title holders, government and industry (and subsequent benefit-sharing arrangements), with a plethora of intersecting national and state government legislation. Agreement-making pertains to various socioeconomic activities, including mineral and energy resource extraction, pastoral activities, fisheries, forestry, tourism and infrastructure and development that take place on Crown lands.[16]

The extensive legal and institutional spheres that shadow 'native title' are not normally the focus of native title in legal education, unless in specialist native title courses. Such aspects are highlighted here to reveal the expansive interactions demanded of Aboriginal Peoples and Torres Strait Islanders in their contact with the native title system. In contrast, the pedagogical focus of native title teaching continues to be the case law and common law method.

The Jurisprudential Construct of Native Title

Turning to how native title is construed by the courts, it is worth simply restating that in *Mabo [No 2]* the High Court found that pre-existing rights and interests in land held by Aboriginal and Torres Strait Islander peoples survived the assertion of sovereignty by the Crown.[17] The *Native Title Act* reflects Brennan J's judgment in *Mabo [No 2]*.[18] Section 223(1) provides that

> (1) The expression ***native title*** or ***native title rights and interests*** means the communal, group or individual rights and interests of Aboriginal peoples or Torres Strait Islanders in relation to land or waters, where:
>
> (a) the rights and interests are possessed under the traditional laws acknowledged, and the traditional customs observed, by the Aboriginal peoples or Torres Strait Islanders; and
> (b) the Aboriginal peoples or Torres Strait Islanders, by those laws and customs, have a connection with the land or waters; and
> (c) the rights and interests are recognised by the common law of Australia.

15 *Native Title Act 1993* (Cth) ss 24BA—24DM; see also Kirsty Howey, 'The Ranger Uranium Mine Revisited: Space-Times of Indigenous Agreement-Making in Australia' (2020) 33 *Transformations* 96.

16 Lee Godden and Lily O'Neill, 'Agreements with Indigenous Communities: The Native Title Act in Australia' in Lila Barrera-Hernandez et al. (eds), *Sharing the Costs and Benefits of Energy and Resource Activity: Legal Change and Impact on Communities* (Oxford University Press, 2016) 135.

17 *Mabo v Queensland [No 2]* (n 4) 57 (Brennan J, Mason CJ, McHugh J agreeing at 69, Deane and Gaudron JJ agreeing at 100–01, Toohey J agreeing at 184).

18 *Mabo v Queensland [No 2]* (n 4) 70.

Claimants bear the onus or burden of proving each of the elements of section 223(1). A determination of native title is a determination of 'whether or not native title exists' in accordance with section 225 of the Act. A determination can occur by consent of the parties.[19] The interpretation of each element of section 223 has been subjected to extensive judicial exegesis. Beyond *Mabo [No 2]* in 1992 and *Wik Peoples v Queensland* in 1996,[20] myriad judicial formulations of native title exist. In *Yanner v Eaton*, the majority stated that

> Native title rights and interests must be understood as what has been called 'a perception of socially constituted fact' as well as 'comprising various assortments of artificially defined jural right'. . . . And an important aspect of the socially constituted fact of native title rights and interests that is recognized by the common law is the spiritual, cultural and social connection with the land.[21]

Although defining native title as socially constituted fact, the court in *Yanner v Eaton* still engaged in ascertaining the degree to which native title rights and interests might evolve but still be 'traditional'.

Given its conferral of native title jurisdiction, the Federal Court has provided diverse interpretations of section 223 and the meaning of recognition. In 2005, the court articulated native title as

> [t]he metaphorical result of applying rules whereby rights and interests are defined at common law as having vested, at the time of annexation, in the members of an Aboriginal society by reason of its traditional laws and customs and the way in which they define its relationship to land and waters. It is not a 'mere' metaphor. Its choice reflects a desire to give effect legally to the human reality involved in the ordinary meaning of 'recognition'.[22]

The judicial construct of native title has been interpreted by superior courts in a manner that narrowed its reconciliatory potential[23] and tightly constrained 'the human reality' involved in the ordinary meaning of recognition.[24]

19 *Native Title Act 1993* (Cth) s 39(4).
20 *Wik Peoples v Queensland* (1996) 187 CLR 1.
21 *Yanner v Eaton* (1999) 201 CLR 351, [38].
22 *Sampi v Western Australia* [2005] FCA 777, [948].
23 Noel Pearson, 'Land Is Susceptible of Ownership' in Marcia Langton et al. (eds), *Honour Among Nations? Treaties and Agreements with Indigenous People* (Melbourne University Press, 2004) 83. See also Crispin Hull, *The High Court of Australia: Celebrating the Centenary 1903–2003* (Lawbook, 2003) 3.
24 *Members of the Yorta Yorta Aboriginal Community v Victoria* (2002) 214 CLR 422, [37] ('*Yorta Yorta*'). For a rewriting of this judgment through an Indigenous lens, see Marcelle

Australian jurisprudence has grappled, at times expressly[25] and at other times implicitly,[26] with the 'ordinary meaning' of recognition as an intersection point between two legal systems. In *Members of the Yorta Yorta Aboriginal Community v Victoria* ('*Yorta Yorta*'), the High Court noted as follows:

> The native title rights and interests which are the subject of the Act are those which existed at sovereignty, survived that fundamental change in legal regime, and now, by resort to the processes of the new legal order, can be enforced and protected. It is those rights and interests which are 'recognised' in the common law.[27]

The constituent colonial hybridity of native title and its vulnerability resonates in the re-emphasis in this definition that it is through the processes of the new legal order that it is enforced and protected.

What, then, is native title—poised in a new legal order but referencing an 'other'? Sketchy Venn diagrams depicting the common law on one side and Aboriginal and Torres Strait Islander law/lore on the other side, with a cross-hatched overlap labelled 'native title', are an enduring memory of my efforts in the mid-1990s to teach first-year law students this complex entity.[28] The contribution of Aboriginal lawyers such as Noel Pearson in problematising the relationship of native title to the common law and in probing the relationship between two systems is acknowledged.[29] Whether Indigenous law and custom are to be acknowledged as law remains an enduring and unresolved legal, constitutional and political tension that must be addressed at the outset in any respectful teaching of native title.[30]

Burns, '*Members of the Yorta Yorta Aboriginal Community v Victoria* (2002) 214 CLR 422' in Nicole Watson and Heather Douglas (eds), *Indigenous Legal Judgments: Bringing Indigenous Voices into Judicial Decision Making* (Routledge, 2021) 92.

25 Maureen Tehan, 'A Hope Disillusioned, an Opportunity Lost? Reflections on Common Law Native Title and Ten Years of the Native Title Act' (2003) 27(2) *Melbourne University Law Review* 523.

26 *Yorta Yorta* (n 24).

27 *Yorta Yorta* (n 24) [77]. See also *Akiba v Commonwealth* (2013) 250 CLR 209, [9]. For a rewriting of this judgment through an Indigenous lens, see Virginia Marshall, 'Akiba on Behalf of the Torres Strait Regional Sea Claims Group v Commonwealth [2013] HCA 33' in Nicole Watson and Heather Douglas (eds), *Indigenous Legal Judgments: Bringing Indigenous Voices into Judicial Decision Making* (Routledge, 2021) 116.

28 Lisa Strelein, 'Conceptualising Native Title' (2001) 23(1) *Sydney Law Review* 95, 104–06.

29 Noel Pearson, 'The High Court's Abandonment of "the Time-Honoured Methodology of the Common Law" in Its Interpretation of Native Title in Mirriuwung Gajerrong and Yorta Yorta' (2003) 7(1) *The Newcastle Law Review* 1.

30 See, e.g., Lisa Strelein, *Compromised Jurisprudence: Native Title Cases since Mabo* (Aboriginal Studies Press, 2009) 10–17.

To teach native title necessarily raises the matter of what we understand to be law.

Over time, the 'Law' has provided a spectrum of designations for how it views the other 'half' of that Venn diagram. Across centuries, the legal designations that reference Indigenous law in Australia have ranged from a status of non-recognition (terra nullius, settled colonies and discovery doctrines at international law) to rights and interests under law and custom, to a form of normative ordering that is not law, and more recently, to 'self-determination' at international law.[31] Each iteration reveals native title as being 'subjected to' recognition by another legal system. The fluctuating formulation of common law designations is not confined to Australian jurisprudence. In comparative jurisdictions, Indigenous law is clothed in common law descriptors such as trusts or corporations,[32] as subject to fiduciary obligations,[33] and historically crystallising as 'domestic dependent nations'.[34] From the early 2000s, however, there was a distinct turn in Australian jurisprudence whereby native title was drawn out from the common law and held to be a creature of statute, despite its common law derivation.[35] The High Court emphasised the *Native Title Act* as the starting point for understanding native title.[36]

More recently, commentary on the relationship between native title and settler law refers to legal pluralism and constitutional bilateralism.[37] A groundswell of Indigenous scholarship has brought the objectives of decolonisation to bear on the nature of the relationship between settler and Indigenous legal 'systems'.[38] The question 'What is native title?', now outlined against an uneasy tranche of recognition, is an important conceptual frame in teaching native title. It points to reflection on the human reality involved in the ordinary meaning of recognition and the interrelationships between laws and peoples, alongside the technical proclivities of categorisation in native title law.

31 United Nations Declaration on the Rights of Indigenous Peoples, opened for signature 13 September 2007, GA Res 61/295 (entered into force 13 September 2007).

32 *Guerin v The Queen* (1984) 2 SCR 335. As incorporated entities and trusts, see, e.g., Te Arawhiti, *Te Kāhui Whakatau (Treaty Settlements)* (online, 24 May 2024).

33 *Delgamuukw v British Columbia* (1997) 3 SCR 1010.

34 *Johnson v McIntosh*, 21 US 543 (1823).

35 See generally Kent McNeil, *Common Law Aboriginal Title* (Clarendon Press, 1989).

36 *Commonwealth v Yarmirr* (2001) 208 CLR 1, [7]; *Western Australia v Ward* (2002) 213 CLR 1 [16], [25]; *Yorta Yorta* (n 24) [32], [70], [75].

37 See, e.g., Shane Chalmers, 'Terra Nullius? Temporal Legal Pluralism in an Australian Colony' (2019) 29(4) *Social & Legal Studies* 463, 483–85; John Borrows, *Freedom and Indigenous Constitutionalism* (University of Toronto Press, 2016).

38 Christos Mantziaris and David Martin, *Native Title Corporations: A Legal and Anthropological Analysis* (Federation Press, 2000) 10.

What Is Native Title: Explanatory Strategies

When introducing the law as a teacher, reversion to how native title was understood in *Mabo [No 2]* may assist in raising wider themes that situate native title in a socio-legal and historical context, particularly given the significant jurisprudence defining native title and the voluminous commentary.[39] Such issues can focus on the requirement that the satisfaction of section 223(1)(a) is a question of fact,[40] namely, as to whether 'traditional connection with the land has been substantially maintained'.[41] Where 'any real acknowledgement of traditional law and any real observance of traditional customs' has ceased, 'the foundation of native title has disappeared'.[42] In this potent euphemism, the judgment sets an onerous evidential threshold for Aboriginal Peoples and Torres Strait Islanders to 'prove' native title. What claimants must establish to demonstrate 'continuity' and the extent of the adaptation of laws and customs to modern conditions have been considered at length in determinations of native title.[43] Investigation of 'real acknowledgement' has contributed to significant delays for claimants and the need to amass voluminous evidence. The process of proving native title has reinforced inequities in the availability of redress under the Act. Where the impacts of colonisation are most profound—that is, where the 'foundation disappeared'—native title claims are difficult to sustain.[44]

When teaching, this central paradox at the heart of native title law might be highlighted. Indigenous law and custom must factually 'exist', but a much narrower constellation of rights and interests passes the legal filter of recognition. A fact/law distinction still casts a shadow over native title law.

This shadow has been cast for a long time in Australian native title jurisprudence, including in the Gove Land Rights case.[45] It is, in essence, the recognition doctrine at international law. Eurocentric doctrines in early international law prescribed that where a land was discovered (i.e., found by the European power to be terra nullius), then this gave that sovereign a right to occupy that land. Where it was held to have either no inhabitants, or where

39 Australian Law Reform Commission, *Connection to Country: Review of the Native Title Act 1993 (Cth)* (Report No 126, 2015) chapter 4 <www.alrc.gov.au/publications/alrc126>.

40 *Western Australia v Ward* (2002) 213 CLR 1, [18] (Gleeson CJ, Gaudron, Gummow and Hayne JJ); *De Rose v South Australia (No 1)* (2003) 133 FCR 325, [161].

41 *Mabo v Queensland [No 2]* (n 4) 60.

42 *Mabo v Queensland [No 2]* (n 4) 60.

43 *Yorta Yorta* (n 24) [37]–[45].

44 Simon Young, 'The Trouble with "Tradition": Native Title and the Yorta Yorta Decision' (2001) 30(1) *The University of Western Australia Law Review* 28.

45 *Milirrpum v Nabalco Pty Ltd and the Commonwealth of Australia* (1970) 17 FLR 141 (Blackburn J). For a critical review of this judgment, see Osca Monaghan, 'Milirrpum v Nabalco Pty Ltd (1971) 17 FLR 141' in Nicole Watson and Heather Douglas (eds), *Indigenous Legal Judgments: Bringing Indigenous Voices into Judicial Decision Making* (Routledge, 2021) 25.

there were inhabitants deemed so low on the scale of civilisation as to have no law, then there was no necessity for the recognition of property rights.[46] The unilateralism of the power relationship has been extensively critiqued. As is well known, *Mabo [No 2]* rejected the view that Australia was terra nullius at the point of acquisition of British sovereignty. Under an 'act of state doctrine' the judgments did not impugn the acquisition of sovereignty, however; they only examined its domestic legal consequences.[47] Terra nullius became the signifier of obsolete law based on a false historical perception, but designation of Australia as a settled colony remained.[48] Gerry Simpson suggests this anomalous position can be explained in that Brennan's judgment was 'a courageous attempt to satisfy a number of fairly compelling and often competing versions of law, history and politics. That he failed to provide a wholly coherent reconciliation is unsurprising.'[49]

Despite its inconsistencies, *Mabo [No 2]* was the catalyst for a revision of laws relating to Aboriginal Peoples and Torres Strait Islanders, although the process is incomplete and often contested. It focused efforts on reconsidering the relationship between Indigenous Peoples and the Australian state. It contributed to building momentum for change—such as proposals for constitutional recognition for First Nations, the Uluru Statement from the Heart[50] and the Voice to Parliament referendum. Moreover, most pertinently here, it required a more critical lens on legal history and the origins of law in the Australian nation state, building momentum for change in legal education.

Alongside legal and socio-political changes, efforts to decolonise knowledge systems gave a vantage point from which to examine law's pedagogy as fixed on the common law method and its implicit assumption of western knowledge. Scholarship in other disciplines has challenged the primacy of Eurocentric knowledge traditions, methodologies and pedagogy.[51] In describing the influence of colonialism in developing a set of ideas, practices and representations about Indigenous Peoples, Linda Tuhiwai Smith notes,

> [w]ithin each set of ideas are systems of classification and representation—epistemological, ontological, juridical, anthropological and ethical—which are coded in such ways as to 'recognize' each other and either mesh

46 Gerry Simpson, 'Mabo, International Law, Terra Nullius and the Stories of Settlement: An Unresolved Jurisprudence' (1993) 19(1) *Melbourne University Law Review* 195, 198.

47 *Mabo [No 2]* (n 5) 32 (Brennan J).

48 Simpson (n 46) 204.

49 Simpson (n 46) 206.

50 Referendum Council, *Uluru Statement from the Heart: Final Report* (Report, 30 June 2017) <www.referendumcouncil.org.au/final-report.html>.

51 Linda Tuhiwai Smith, *Decolonizing Methodologies: Research and Indigenous Peoples* (Zed Books, 2013) 100.

together, or create a cultural 'force field' that can screen out competing and oppositional discourses.[52]

The challenge for native title teaching is to hold together oppositional discourses and to examine how systems of discriminatory classification and representation are implicit to the legal ordering in which native title is positioned. As native title interfaces Eurocentric and traditional law, the epistemological question of how we teach assumes importance alongside the ontological dimensions of what we teach. Integration of Indigenous knowledge, methods and content have filtered into the teaching and curriculum design in multidisciplinary courses. Increasingly, these can be found in the law curriculum. Currently, law subjects not only integrate native title case law and statute but also bring to the fore issues of the inclusion of Indigenous peoples' knowledges into legal method as a matter of pedagogy.

The support for the integration of Aboriginal Peoples and Torres Strait Islander law and values into legal education[53] finds parallels in Aotearoa New Zealand and in Canada.[54] Typically, law curricula have professional accreditation standards that prescribe the teaching of designated legal content in accredited subjects. Aotearoa New Zealand has prescribed the integration of Tikanga Māori into the law curriculum commencing in 2025 under a model developed by an expert panel of Māori moderators. From 2025, Tikanga Māori teaching across the 'core courses' will be required, including a Te Reo (language and culture) course.

Native Title in the Australian Law Curriculum

Although a stronger integration of Indigenous peoples' knowledges, methodologies and pedagogies is evolving in the Australian law curriculum, the history and hybrid form of native title, together with seemingly intractable cultural framings of native title in a socio-political sense, requires specific

52 Lauren Tynan, 'What Is Relationality? Indigenous Knowledges, Practices and Responsibilities with Kin' (2021) 28(4) *Cultural Geographies* 597.

53 See Council of Australian Law Deans, 'CALD Statement on Racism and Law Schools 2024' (online, 31 January 2024) <https://cald.asn.au/first-nations-peoples/>: 'CALD affirms the positive contribution Australian law schools can, should and will make, in full partnership with First Nations peoples, in exposing, critiquing and remedying all forms of institutionalised injustice.'

54 New Zealand Council of Legal Education, Professional Examinations in Law (Tikanga Māori Requirements) Amendment Regulations made by the New Zealand Council of Legal Education under section 278 of the Lawyers and Conveyancers Act 2006. The Canadian Council of Law Deans released reports in 2018 and 2021 identifying steps that law schools have instituted to respond to recommendations arising from the Truth and Reconciliation Commission Report 2015; see, e.g., <https://ccld-cdfdc.ca/wp-content/uploads/2021/07/2021-TRC-Positions-of-Canadian-Universities-June-2021-Copy.pdf>.

attention to how native title might be better aligned to law curriculum change. Options for a more culturally appropriate integration of native title, led by and in continuing consultation with First Nations, could include progressive revision of native title content and 'method' and reforms to 'graduate attributes' for law students.[55] Reflections on teaching 'native title' with respect to three areas may act as prefigurative pathways.

- **Native title in property law and/or land law**

Law schools may differ in the scope of law covered in such subjects. Many property law courses may cover native title law in some manner. Property law may include native title references in teaching property concepts, the nature of a proprietary interest, the doctrines of estates and tenure, the transactional elements of property law, Torrens Title and the legal and equitable measures that regulate the alienability of property interests.

- **Introductory law subjects**

These may include teaching *Mabo [No 2]* and native title as an introduction to the Australian legal system, legal history and the reception of the common law. Native title may be included when teaching common law reasoning and the judicial method or subjects covering the institutions of the legal system, including constitutional structures.

- **Native title law as an elective subject or component of another subject**

Common subjects in the latter category may include environmental law, resources and energy law, human rights law, negotiation and dispute resolution, climate change law and family law. Native title law is less often taught as a standalone subject, although comparative 'native title' or Indigenous law subjects may explore the laws in several jurisdictions.

Teaching a Critical Account of Native Title

Although teachers and law schools are best placed to develop context-specific approaches, the following offers preliminary thoughts on a critical account of native title pedagogy in the three identified representative areas. The analysis of native title in earlier sections may contribute to this perspective. Such pedagogy can draw on a wide range of pertinent scholarship.[56] Rather than

55 Regarding graduate attributes, a preferable characterisation is an ethical position or value set.
56 Compilations of case law and commentary can be found in Richard Bartlett, *Native Title in Australia* (LexisNexis, 5th ed, 2023); Melissa Perry and Stephen Lloyd, *Australian Native*

set detailed subject content, the intention is to raise three to four 'starting points' for a revision of native title pedagogy.

(i) Property Law and Native Title

In re-evaluating law curriculum design from a decolonising standpoint, it may be helpful to start by considering how native title is situated within (or as a counterpoint to) the framework for teaching property law. The rationale stems from '[p]roperty law [being] both an expression of sociopolitical values and a legal institution'.[57] Thus, exploring the relationship between property and native title can surface a set of contrasting sociocultural discourses.[58] First is the predominance of private property in western legal systems, whereas native title is a communal interest for Indigenous peoples. Second, strategies of change that critically evaluate the interaction between native title and property law invoke fundamental questions about legal hybridity. Third, property law comprehends a spectrum of significant legal relationships, but typically, the model of property that is taught is emblematic of individual autonomy and the right of exclusion of others (Blackstone's sole, despotic dominion). A reassessment of such models that inform legal practice is important,[59] and a growing body of scholarship on relational theories of property law may assist such reassessment. Andre Van der Walt suggests that property law is about 'those who do not own property and whose lives are shaped and affected by the property holdings of others'.[60] Finally, changing the model of property as the yardstick against which native title is framed, as a bundle of rights, may enhance a more perceptive understanding of the culturally-embedded proprietary interests of Aboriginal Peoples and Torres Strait Islanders and precipitate a realignment of how property law itself is taught. Aboriginal proprietary interests are 'a spiritual bequest' and 'subservient to the fundamental social relationships with the sacred ancestral past from which the legacy is derived'.[61] The bequest bestows not just rights but 'a social world, and

Title Law (Lawbook Co, 2018); Lauren Butterly, *Reconciling Sovereignties Over Sea Country in the Northern Territory* (Federation Press, 2024).

57 Margaret Davies, Lee Godden and Nicole Graham, 'Situating Property within Habitat: Reintegrating Place' (2021) 6 *Journal of Law, Property and Society* 1, 7.

58 Margaret Davies, Lee Godden and Nicole Graham, 'Situating Property within Habitat: Reintegrating Place' (2021) 6 *Journal of Law, Property and Society*, 7.

59 For example, the *Native Title Act* test for exclusive possession native title is predicated on control over access.

60 Andre Van der Walt, 'Property and Marginality' in Gregory Alexander and Eduardo Penalver (eds), *Property and Community* (Oxford University Press, 2010) 90.

61 Marcia Langton, 'The Estate as Duration: "Being in Place" and Aboriginal Property Relations in Areas of Cape York Peninsula in North Australia' in Lee Godden and Maureen Tehan (eds), *Comparative Perspectives on Communal Lands and Individual Ownership Sustainable Futures* (Routledge, 2010) 75–98, 76.

for particular people, arduous duties and responsibilities that are transmissible across generations'.[62] In turn, this approach may allow for learning (and working with First Nations in co-constructing) a more culturally sensitive way of teaching property law in its relationship with native title.

(ii) Mabo [No 2] as a Common Law Narrative for Australian Law

The second pathway for re-evaluating native title in the law curriculum is to critically review how *Mabo [No 2]* and native title law are positioned in narratives about the common law. Many narratives that now 'explain' the origins of law in Australia were incorporated into law teaching and textbooks after 1992. Such narratives remain significant in highlighting the fundamental issue that until 1992, Australian law *had not* legally recognised Aboriginal Peoples and Torres Strait Islanders as 'present' in Australia prior to British Sovereignty.[63] Nonetheless, *Mabo [No 2]* is often 'situated', not as a break with British Imperial law, but as an affirmation of the common law. At times, the decision is framed as an imperial counterpoint without a 'hard look' at other 'imperial' aspects of the judgments such as the sovereign extinguishment test. To adjust this focus, teaching a wider selection across the judgments and helping law students navigate the complex legal language within them are suggested.

The decision is also celebrated as reflecting human rights standards in international law and at common law, in terms of the appeal to social justice and civic values.[64] However, the Mabo judgments are woven between extremes:

> On the one hand, the implications of sovereignty and the demand for a coherent skeleton of principle in the law prevented a wholesale reappraisal of Australian land law. On the other hand, the demands of justice prevented a simple confirmation of the extinguishment of all Indigenous rights to land.[65]

After 30 years, it is difficult to envisage the initial legal rupture ushered in by the recognition of native title. Over time this impact has lessened. When

62 Marcia Langton, 'The Estate as Duration: "Being in Place" and Aboriginal Property Relations in Areas of Cape York Peninsula in North Australia' in Lee Godden and Maureen Tehan (eds), *Comparative Perspectives on Communal Lands and Individual Ownership Sustainable Futures* (Routledge, 2010) 75–98, 76.

63 'Surviving annexation' is problematic as an accurate narrative of the colonisation of Australia.

64 'Whatever the justification advanced in earlier days for refusing to recognize the rights and interests in land of the indigenous inhabitants of settled colonies, an unjust and discriminatory doctrine of that kind can no longer be accepted': *Mabo [No 2]* (n 4) [42] (Brennan J).

65 Alex Reilly, 'From a Jurisprudence of Regret to a Regrettable Jurisprudence: Shaping Native Title from Mabo to Ward' (2002) 9 *E Law Journal: Murdoch University* [21].

Mabo [No 2] is framed now primarily as exemplifying common law evolution, this can gloss the violence of the colonial dispossession of Aboriginal Peoples and Torres Strait Islanders. The bringing of law to Australia is normalised and neutralised through such legal narratives. The inclusion of Indigenous peoples' voices in these narratives is vital to redress past injustice. The Yoorrook Justice Commission, with its function of truth telling, is a valuable model for opening windows into native title and colonisation.[66] Finally, *Mabo [No 2]* is often conceived as the culmination of the native title narrative. This chapter expressly extends the narrative to the *Native Title Act* and explores the 'apparatus of the state' to which Aboriginal Peoples and Torres Strait Islanders are subjected in their engagement with native title. It is important to provide students with an understanding of the 'long view' of native title law in Australia and that the process of decolonisation is ongoing.

(iii) Native Title in 'Elective' Subjects

Over time, the teaching of native title law has merged with a wide range of elective subjects in the law curriculum. It is valuable to have native title as a component of specialist subjects given the previous marginalisation of Indigenous peoples' interests. Typically, however, only selected aspects of native title, such as agreement-making, cultural protections and/or high-profile disputes and litigation are featured. Alternatively, there may be a focus on the 'rights' aspects of native title, including free, prior and informed consent in project/development settings. A rounded view of native title built on close engagement with Aboriginal and Torres Strait Islander representatives, as in all subjects, is helpful in teaching these 'native title' components, bearing in mind the 'consultation fatigue' experienced by many Traditional Owners.

Environmental law teaching has long referenced Indigenous peoples' management of lands and waters. Initially a 'frozen in time' view of this management reinforced stereotypes about Indigenous knowledges.[67] More recent engagement with First Nations in numerous environmental settings has enhanced appreciation of the depth of the Indigenous environmental governance that, in part, finds expression in native title concepts.[68] Traditional ownership and governance of Country, however, may not necessarily 'match' the objectives and methods on which environmental law is predicated.

66 'About Yoorrook', *Yoorrook Justice Commission* (online) <https://yoorrookjusticecommission.org.au/about/>.

67 Lee Godden and Stuart Cowell, 'Conservation Planning and Indigenous Governance in Australia's Indigenous Protected Areas' (2016) 24 (5) *Restoration Ecology* 692–97.

68 Jacinta Ruru, 'Decolonising Property Law: Realising the Sense of Indigenous Laws in Aotearoa New Zealand' in Nicole Graham et al. (eds), *Routledge Handbook of Law, Property and Society* (Routledge, 2022) 229.

Thus, direct synergies between Indigenous peoples' relationship with traditional Country and the aims of western-centric law should not be assumed. Indigenous peoples' views may vary, for example, with respect to culturally appropriate economic development.[69] Blending the teaching of Indigenous ontologies with settler philosophies such as in 'rights for nature' should carefully acknowledge Indigenous peoples' struggles to have their native title rights and interests respected by courts and in legislation.[70] Nonetheless, environmental law teaching offers a rich context for advancing a decolonisation of native title law.

The sheer scope and complexity of native title law requires a depth of knowledge when teaching native title as a specialist subject. A teaching team that includes Traditional Owners is ideal, but the many demands experienced by Traditional Owners are noted. When teaching native title as a specialist subject, contrasting Australian native title jurisprudence with development in the settler nations of Canada, Aotearoa New Zealand and the USA can highlight differences.[71] In Aotearoa New Zealand, for example, tikanga has been 'judicially described as the first law of Aotearoa New Zealand'.[72] Native title law in Australia is rather insular in its reference to comparative jurisprudence. The presence of treaties in other jurisdictions, however, adds a layer of difference to the historically shared concept of native title. Even so, comparative analysis can enhance critical thinking about native title in Australia and advance decolonisation in the teaching of native title law.

The pathways discussed offer points of reflection on native title teaching and curriculum development, and these starting points are not suggested as being prescriptive. Where these reflection points are embedded in a pedagogy that allows insights into how native title functions as a hybrid legal institution, they may further loosen the ties to the colonial past. Accordingly, the chapter turns to consider one of many possible future directions for decolonising native title.

Native Title and First Nations Language

In decolonising native title in legal education, support for Aboriginal and Torres Strait Islander languages is still nascent. Prior to colonisation, over 350 First Nations languages were spoken, and multilingualism was the norm.[73] There has been significant Indigenous language loss since colonisation. In

69 Australian Law Reform Commission (n 39) 43.

70 Ruru (n 68) 231–34.

71 See, e.g., Australian Law Reform Commission (n 39) ch 9.

72 Te Aka Matua o te Ture: New Zealand Law Reform Commission, 'The Study Paper He Poutama' (NZLC SP24, 2023) 8 <www.lawcom.govt.nz/assets/Publications/Study>.

73 Felicity Meakins, 'The Land Still Speaks: Supporting First Nations Languages in Australia' in Kevin McConkey and Chris Hatherly (eds), *The Social Future of Australia: The 50th*

acknowledgement of the linkages among language, law, custom and culture, First Nations communities have 'been galvanizing over the past two decades to reclaim and renew their languages'.[74]

Native title law navigates many aspects of Indigenous languages. The retention of traditional language (given the centrality of oral traditions to Indigenous societies) is vital for 'proving' native title. Perversely, native title claimants' recovery of language may be regarded as a break in continuity of connection or an evolution of 'traditional' culture.[75] In the past, native title case law reinforced a narrow test of continuity that discouraged what settler law deemed an inauthentic revitalisation of culture.[76]

At the heart of native title law is the test for connection to Country—this test has been deployed to displace an Aboriginal oral tradition by settler preference for the written word.[77] Slowly, native title law and practice have shifted to acknowledge the value of an Indigenous oral tradition and the 'lifeworlds' entailed in connection to Country. More substantial change is needed, as languages are vital to the survival of these cultures given the devastating effects of colonialism.[78] Indigenous languages 'encode the social dynamics of groups over time and transmit cultural practices'.[79] A decolonised native title in the law curriculum, with a reformulated connection concept for cultural transmission, can build resilience and assist in the continuity of First Nations' languages.

Conclusion

This chapter began by emphasising that native title, in its configured hybridity, was not to be confused with the laws and customs of Aboriginal Peoples and Torres Strait Islanders. 'Native title is not a common law title, but a title recognised by the common law.'[80] In Australian jurisprudence, this recognition of another 'title', while potentially transformative, became preoccupied with articulating through a settler law lens a narrow set of rights. Such perspective limited the law's cognisance of the sociolegal and cultural relationships that animate Indigenous Peoples' rights and responsibilities that are inadequately captured by the designation native title. A decolonised 'native

---

Anniversary Symposium of the Academy of the Social Sciences in Australia (Academy of the Social Sciences in Australia, 2023) 29.

74 Felicity Meakins, 'The Land Still Speaks: Supporting First Nations Languages in Australia' in Kevin McConkey and Chris Hatherly (eds), *The Social Future of Australia: The 50th Anniversary Symposium of the Academy of the Social Sciences in Australia* (Academy of the Social Sciences in Australia, 2023) 29.

75 *Bennell v State of Western Australia* (2006) 230 ALR 603.

76 *Bennell v State of Western Australia* (2006) 230 ALR 603.

77 *Yorta Yorta* (n 24).

78 Meakins (n 73) 29–32.

79 Meakins (n 73) 29–32.

80 Pearson, 'Land Is Susceptible of Ownership' (n 23).

title' requires careful reconstruction to animate its latent potential to reconstitute the relationship between settler law and the law of Aboriginal Peoples and Torres Strait Islanders.

Native title law currently still relies on an authoritative narrative of past law to endow dominant claims of entitlement and distributions of legal advantage and property with legitimacy. However, the recognition of native title has shifted the legal imagination to explore possibilities of plural legal orders.[81] Where once native title signified frozen rights caught in the warp of pre-historic time, there are now references to songlines on Country that performatively illuminate the myriad dimensions of Indigenous peoples' relationships to traditional lands and waters.[82] Decolonisation of native title recognition is not just relevant to an artificial legal moment of sovereign acquisition but requires cognisance of an ongoing, open and grounded reconciliation and redress. Reflections on how we teach native title in the law curriculum and in acknowledging what we have yet to learn can position legal education as a critical agent of change and potentially, ultimately contribute to reforming the institution of native title. Native title teaching can firmly be aligned to efforts to decolonise law schools.

81 Butterly (n 56).
82 Christine Black, *The Land Is the Source of the Law: A Dialogic Encounter with Indigenous Jurisprudence* (Routledge, 2010).

SUGGESTED RESOURCES FOR LAW TEACHERS

The following resources are suggested for legal educators who aim to bring Indigenous voices and experiential knowledge into their classrooms. As a starting point, we refer readers to the 'Indigenous Law Resources' page of the Council of Australian Law Deans website (*https://cald.asn.au/first-nations-peoples/*), which contains links to works written by scholars who work in the space of Indigenous people and the law and other useful material.

The following resources are organised to align with the Legal Admissions Consultative Committee's *Prescribed Academic Areas of Knowledge* (known as the 'Priestley 11' because of the 1992 committee chaired by Lancelot Priestly), which lists the areas of law that Australian law degrees must include for accreditation. This is by no means an exhaustive list, and it is hoped that the list will inspire educators to draw further connections to embed First Nations' experiences, laws and pedagogies in the prescribed curriculum.

As highlighted by many authors in this collection, teaching materials related to Aboriginal and Torres Strait Islander peoples should be thoughtfully identified, delivered in a culturally safe way and by academics who have been trained to appropriately engage with such content in the classroom. Where a judgment is included, the social context and stories of Indigenous parties should frame the discussion. As much as possible, academics should defer to First Nations authors who speak to topics that affect their communities.

Administrative Law

- *R v Toohey (Aboriginal Land Commissioner); Ex parte Northern Land Council* (1981) 151 CLR 170, [1981] HCA 74 <https://www.austlii.edu.au/cgi-bin/viewdoc/au/cases/cth/HCA/1981/74.html>.

- *Minister for Aboriginal Affairs v Peko-Wallsend Ltd* (1986) 162 CLR 24, [1986] HCA 40 <https://www.austlii.edu.au/cgi-bin/viewdoc/au/cases/cth/HCA/1986/40.html>.
- *Tickner v Chapman* (1995) 57 FCR 451.
- *Onus v Alcoa of Australia* (1981) 149 CLR 27, [1981] HCA 50 <https://www.austlii.edu.au/cgi-bin/viewdoc/au/cases/cth/HCA/1981/50.html>.
- Inquest into the Passing of Veronica Nelson (Coroners Court of Victoria, Coroner Simon McGregor, 30 January 2023).
- Narelle Bedford and Peter Billings, 'Tickner v Chapman (1995) 57 FCR 451' in Nicole Watson and Heather Douglas (eds), *Indigenous Legal Judgments: Bringing Indigenous Voices into Judicial Decision Making* (Routledge, 2021) 73 <www.routledge.com/Indigenous-Legal-Judgments-Bringing-Indigenous-Voices-into-Judicial-Decision-Making/Watson-Douglas/p/book/9780367467456>.
- Alexander Reilly, 'Finding an Indigenous Perspective in Administrative Law' (2009) 19(2) *Legal Education Review* 271.

Civil Procedure

- Kate Ogg, 'Decolonising Civil Procedure: Court Process as Continuing Colonisation and Tool for Indigenous Justice' in Foluke I Adebisi, Suhraiya Jivraj and Ntina Tzouvala (eds), *Decolonisation, Anti-Racism, and Legal Pedagogy: Strategies, Successes, and Challenges* (Routledge, 2023) 164.
- Melanie Schwartz, Fiona Allison and Chris Cunneen, *The Civil and Family Law Needs of Indigenous People in Victoria* (Report, Australian Indigenous Legal Needs Project, 2013) <www.jcu.edu.au/__data/assets/pdf_file/0011/121889/jcu_131180.pdf>.
- Sarah Ciftci and Deirdre Howard-Wagner, 'Integrating Indigenous Justice into Alternative Dispute Resolution Practices: A Case Study of the Aboriginal Care Circle Pilot Program in Nowra' (2012) 16(2) *Australian Indigenous Law Review* 81 <https://www8.austlii.edu.au/cgi-bin/viewdoc/au/journals/AILRev/2012/14.html>.
- Larissa Behrendt and Loretta Kelly, *Resolving Indigenous Disputes: Land Conflict and Beyond* (The Federation Press, 2008).

Company Law

- Heron Loban, 'Embedding Indigenous Perspectives in Business Law' (2011) 5(2) *eJournal of Business Education and Scholarship of Teaching* 11 <https://go.gale.com/ps/i.do?id=GALE%7CA281564749&sid=googleScholar&v=2.1&it=r&linkaccess=abs&issn=18359132&p=AONE&sw=w&userGroupName=loyoland_main&aty=ip>.

- Aboriginal and Torres Strait Islander Social Justice Commissioner, *Native Title Report 2007* (Report No. 2, 2008) chapter 6 <https://humanrights.gov.au/sites/default/files/content/social_justice/nt_report/ntreport07/pdf/ntr2007.pdf>.
- Marina Nehme, 'Aboriginal and Torres Strait Islander Corporations: Time for a Rethink?' (2023) 48(2) *Alternative Law Journal* 127 <https://journals.sagepub.com/doi/10.1177/1037969X231163602?icid=int.sj-abstract.similar-articles.8>.
- Bede Harris, 'Embedding Indigenous Experiences in the Teaching of Corporations Law' (2012) 4 *Ngiya—Talk the Law* 16 <https://www8.austlii.edu.au/au/journals/NgiyaTLaw/2002/10.pdf>.
- *Shaw v Minister for Families, Housing, Community Services and Indigenous Affairs* [2009] FCA 1397 <www.austlii.edu.au/cgi-bin/viewdoc/au/cases/cth/FCA/2009/1397.html>.

Constitutional Law (Federal and State)

- *Love v Commonwealth; Thoms v Commonwealth* [2020] HCA 3 <https://www.austlii.edu.au/cgi-bin/viewdoc/au/cases/cth/HCA/2020/3.html>.
- *Kartinyeri v Commonwealth* (1998) 195 CLR 337, [1998] HCA 52 <https://www.austlii.edu.au/cgi-bin/viewdoc/au/cases/cth/HCA/1998/52.html>.
- *Uluru Statement from the Heart* (National Constitutional Convention, May 2017) <https://ulurustatemdev.wpengine.com/wp-content/uploads/2022/01/UluruStatementfromtheHeartPLAINTEXT.pdf>.
- Marcia Langton, 'The Hindmarsh Island Bridge Affair: How Aboriginal Women's Religion Became an Administerable Affair' (1996) 11(24) *Australian Feminist Studies* 211.
- Larissa Behrendt and Taryn Lee, '*Kartinyeri v Commonwealth* [1998] HCA 22' in Nicole Watson and Heather Douglas (eds), *Indigenous Legal Judgments: Bringing Indigenous Voices into Judicial Decision Making* (Routledge, 2021) 131 <www.routledge.com/Indigenous-Legal-Judgments-Bringing-Indigenous-Voices-into-Judicial-Decision-Making/Watson-Douglas/p/book/9780367467456>.
- Dani Larkin et al., 'Aboriginal and Torres Strait Islander Peoples, Law Reform and the Return of the States' (2022) 41(1) *University of Queensland Law Journal* 35 <https://journal.law.uq.edu.au/index.php/uqlj/article/view/6353>.
- Wayne Martin, 'Passing the Buck: Has the Diffusion of Responsibility for Aboriginal People in Our Federation impeded Closing the Gap?' (2017) 44(9) *Brief* 28 <https://classic.austlii.edu.au/au/journals/SGSocUphAUCon/2017/13.pdf>.

- Marcia Langton and Aaron Corn, *Law: The Way of the Ancestors* (Margo Neal ed, Thames & Hudson Australia, 2023).
- Aurora Milroy and Karinda Burns, 'What's Aristotle's Totem Anyway? Indigenous Systems of Law and Governance and the Australian Public Law Curriculum' in Nicole Watson and Heather Douglas (eds), *Legal Education through an Indigenous Lens: Decolonising the Law School* (Routledge, 2025).

Contracts

- *Australian Competition and Consumer Commission v Keshow (No. 2)* [2005] FCA 989 <www.austlii.edu.au/cgi-bin/viewdoc/au/cases/cth/FCA/2005/989.html>.
- Heron Loban, 'Australian Competition and Consumer Commission v Ramon Lal Keshow' in Heather Douglas et al. (eds), *Australian Feminist Judgments: Righting and Rewriting Law* (Bloomsbury, 2015) 180.
- Bronwyn Naylor, 'Unconscionability, Education and Indigenous Women: *ACCC v Keshow*' in Heather Douglas et al. (eds), *Australian Feminist Judgments: Righting and Rewriting Law* (Bloomsbury, 2015) 175.
- *Australian Securities and Investments Commission v Kobelt* [2019] HCA 18 <www.austlii.edu.au/cgi-bin/viewdoc/au/cases/cth/HCA/2019/18.html>.
- Heron Loban, 'Aboriginal and Torres Strait Islander People and Consumer law' (PhD Thesis, James Cook University, 2018) 236–255 <https://researchonline.jcu.edu.au/56957/>.
- Rachel Yates and Sharmin Tania, 'The Place of Cultural Values, Norms and Practices: Assessing Unconscionability in Commercial Practices' (2019) 45(1) *Monash Law Review* 232.

Criminal Law and Procedure

- Tanya Mitchell and Amanda Porter, '*Walker v New South Wales* [1994] HCA 64' in Nicole Watson and Heather Douglas (eds), *Indigenous Legal Judgments: Bringing Indigenous Voices into Judicial Decision Making* (Routledge, 2021) 54 <www.routledge.com/Indigenous-Legal-Judgments-Bringing-Indigenous-Voices-into-Judicial-Decision-Making/Watson-Douglas/p/book/9780367467456>.
- Mary Spiers Williams, 'Bugmy v The Queen (2013) 302 ALR 192' in Nicole Watson and Heather Douglas (eds), *Indigenous Legal Judgments: Bringing Indigenous Voices into Judicial Decision Making* (Routledge, 2021) 277 <www.routledge.com/Indigenous-Legal-Judgments-Bringing-Indigenous-Voices-into-Judicial-Decision-Making/Watson-Douglas/p/book/9780367467456>.

- Amanda Porter and Chris Cunneen, ‘Policing Settler Colonial Societies’ in Philip Birch, Michael Kennedy and Erin Kruger (eds), *Australian Policing: Critical Issues in 21st Century Police Practice* (Routledge, 2020).
- Dean Gibson (Director), *Incarceration Nation* (Bacon Factory Films, 2021) <https://incarcerationnation.com.au/>.
- Australian Law Reform Commission, *Pathways to Justice—An Inquiry into the Incarceration Rate of Aboriginal and Torres Strait Islander Peoples* (Report No 133, December 2017) chapters 5, 6, 14 and 16 <www.alrc.gov.au/publication/pathways-to-justice-inquiry-into-the-incarceration-rate-of-aboriginal-and-torres-strait-islander-peoples-alrc-report-133/>.
- Chris Cunneen, ‘Part II: Equal before the Law: Criminalisation’, in Larissa Behrendt et al. (eds), *Aboriginal and Torres Strait Islander Legal Relations* (Oxford University Press, 2nd ed, 2019).

Equity (Including Trusts)

- *John Bulun Bulun & Anor v R & T Textiles Pty Ltd* [1998] FCA 1082 <www.austlii.edu.au/cgi-bin/viewdoc/au/cases/cth/FCA/1998/1082.html>.
- *Pearson v State of Queensland (No 2)* [2020] FCA 619 <www.austlii.edu.au/cgi-bin/viewdoc/au/cases/cth/FCA/2020/619.html>.
- Martin Hardie, ‘The Bulun Bulun Case: John Bulun Bulun & Anor v R & T Textiles Pty Ltd’ (1998) 4(16) *Indigenous Law Bulletin* 24 <https://classic.austlii.edu.au/au/journals/IndigLawB/1998/87.html>.
- Stephen Gray, ‘Holding the Government to Account: The ‘Stolen Wages’ Issue, Fiduciary Duty and Trust Law’ (2008) 32(1) *Melbourne University Law Review* 115 <https://law.unimelb.edu.au/__data/assets/pdf_file/0004/1705765/32_1_4.pd>.
- Greg McIntyre, ‘Indigenous Equality: The Long Road’ (2020) 8(2) *Griffith Journal of Law and Human Dignity* <https://griffithlawjournal.org/index.php/gjlhd/article/view/1207>.
- ‘Stolen Wages and Generations of Disadvantage: Is This Australia’s Version of Slave Labour?’ *SBS the Feed* (Video, 11 September 2019) <www.youtube.com/watch?v=iELQR74RI54>.

Ethics and Professional Responsibility

- Eddie Cubillo, ‘30th Anniversary of the RCIADIC and the ‘White Noise’ of the Justice System Is Loud and Clear’ (2021) 46(3) *Alternative Law Journal* 185 <https://journals.sagepub.com/eprint/YJS3TH7HTRRQVWFP8CGQ/full>.
- John Rawnsley et al., ‘Cultural Competency in a Legal Service and Justice Agency for Aboriginal Peoples’ (2018) 28(2) *Legal Education*

Review 1 <https://ler.scholasticahq.com/article/7613-cultural-competency-in-a-legal-service-and-justice-agency-for-aboriginal-peoples>.

- Ambelin Kwaymullina, 'Research, Ethics and Indigenous Peoples: An Australian Indigenous Perspective on Three Threshold Considerations for Respectful Engagement' (2016) 12(4) *AlterNative: An International Journal of Indigenous People* 437.
- *Bugmy Bar Book* (Webpage) <https://bugmybarbook.org.au/chapters/>.
- See state-based resources for lawyers working with Indigenous clients, e.g., *Indigenous Protocols for Lawyers* (Law Society Northern Territory, 2nd ed, 2015) <www.lawsociety.com.au/sites/default/files/2018-03/indigenous_protocols_for_lawyers_0.pdf>.

Evidence

- Lorena Allam, 'Kumanjayi Walker Inquest: 'Racist' Text Messages from Police Officer's Phone Allowed as Evidence' *The Guardian* (online, 13 September 2022) <www.theguardian.com/australia-news/2022/sep/13/kumanjayi-walker-inquest-racist-text-messages-from-police-officers-phone-allowed-as-evidence>.
- Kent Roach, 'The Wrongful Conviction of Indigenous People in Australia and Canada' (2015) 17 *Flinders Law Journal* 203 <https://classic.austlii.edu.au/au/journals/FlinLawJl/2015/7.pdf>.
- Australian Law Reform Commission, *Recognition of Aboriginal Customary Laws* (Report No 31, June 1986) <www.alrc.gov.au/publication/recognition-of-aboriginal-customary-laws-alrc-report-31/>.

Property

- *Milirrpum v Nabalco Pty Ltd* (1971) 17 FLR 141 ('Gove Land Rights Case').
- *Mabo v Queensland [No 2]* (1992) 175 CLR 1; [1992] HCA 23 <www.austlii.edu.au/cgi-bin/viewdoc/au/cases/cth/HCA/1992/23.html>.
- *Yanner v Eaton* (1999) 201 CLR 351; [1999] HCA 53 <www.austlii.edu.au/cgi-bin/viewdoc/au/cases/cth/HCA/1999/53.html>.
- *Western Australia v Ward* (2002) 213 CLR 1; [2002] HCA 28 <www.austlii.edu.au/cgi-bin/viewdoc/au/cases/cth/HCA/2002/28.html>.
- *Members of the Yorta Yorta Aboriginal Community v Victoria* (2002) 214 CLR 422; [2002] HCA 58 <www.austlii.edu.au/cgi-bin/viewdoc/au/cases/cth/HCA/2002/58.html?context=1;query=yorta;mask_path=au/cases/cth/HCA>.
- *Akiba on Behalf of the Torres Strait Regional Seas Claims Group v Commonwealth* [2013] HCA 33 <www.austlii.edu.au/cgibin/viewdoc/au/cases/cth/HCA/2013/33.html>.

- Simon Young and Marcelle Burns, '*Members of the Yorta Aboriginal Community v Victoria* (2002) 214 CLR 422' in Nicole Watson and Heather Douglas (eds), *Indigenous Legal Judgments: Bringing Indigenous Voices into Judicial Decision Making* (Routledge, 2021) 92 <www.routledge.com/Indigenous-Legal-Judgments-Bringing-Indigenous-Voices-into-Judicial-Decision-Making/Watson-Douglas/p/book/9780367467456>.
- Alison Whittaker and Virginia Marshall, '*Akiba on Behalf of the Torres Strait Regional Seas Claims Group v Commonwealth* [2013] HCA 33' in Nicole Watson and Heather Douglas (eds), *Indigenous Legal Judgments: Bringing Indigenous Voices into Judicial Decision Making* (Routledge, 2021) 112 <www.routledge.com/Indigenous-Legal-Judgments-Bringing-Indigenous-Voices-into-Judicial-Decision-Making/Watson-Douglas/p/book/9780367467456>.
- Nicole Watson, Asmi Wood and Robynne Quiggin, 'Part III: Law, Land and Culture' in Larissa Behrendt et al. (eds), *Aboriginal and Torres Strait Islander Legal Relations* (Oxford University Press, 2nd ed, 2019).
- Aileen Moreton-Robinson, 'The High Court and the *Yorta Yorta* Decision' in *The White Possessive: Property, Power, and Indigenous Sovereignty* (University of Minnesota Press, 2015) 79.
- Nicole Ma (Director), *Putuparri and the Rainmakers* (Sensible Films, 2015).

Torts

- *Henry v Thompson* [1989] 2 Qd R 412 <www.sclqld.org.au/caselaw/11595>.
- Kirsten Gray, '*South Australia v Lampard-Tevorrow* [2010] SASC 56' in Nicole Watson and Heather Douglas (eds), *Indigenous Legal Judgments: Bringing Indigenous Voices into Judicial Decision-Making* (Routledge, 2021) 214 <www.routledge.com/Indigenous-Legal-Judgments-Bringing-Indigenous-Voices-into-Judicial-Decision-Making/Watson-Douglas/p/book/9780367467456>.
- Julie Cassidy, 'The Best Interests of the Child? The Stolen Generations in Canada and Australia' (2006) 15(1) *Griffith Law Review* 111 <https://www6.austlii.edu.au/au/journals/GriffLawRw/2006/5.pdf>.
- 'Pabai Pabai v Commonwealth of Australia', *Federal Court of Australia* (Online File) <www.fedcourt.gov.au/services/access-to-files-and-transcripts/online-files/pabai-v-australia>.
- Kathleen Mahoney, 'The Untold Story: How Indigenous Legal Principles Informed the Largest Settlement in Canadian Legal History' (2018) 69 *University of New Brunswick Law Journal* 198 <https://kathleenmahoney.wordpress.com/wp-content/uploads/2018/05/kathleenmahoneytheuntolds.pdf>.

- Toni Buti, 'The Stolen Generations and Litigation Revisited' (2008) 32(2) *Melbourne University Law Review* 382.
- *Cruse v State of Victoria* [2019] 59 VR 241 <https://victorianreports.com.au/judgment/view/59-VR-241>.
- Nicole Watson, 'Teaching Students about the Significance of the Plaintiff's Aboriginality in Intentional Torts Cases' in Nicole Watson and Heather Douglas (eds), *Legal Education Through an Indigenous Lens: Decolonising the Law School* (Routledge, 2025).

INDEX

For Product Safety Concerns and Information please contact our EU representative GPSR@taylorandfrancis.com Taylor & Francis Verlag GmbH, Kaufingerstraße 24, 80331 München, Germany